"*Aggiornamento* is back! Paul Turner has updated the first volume of Adrien Nocent's *The Liturgical Year* in a discrete, respectful, and informed manner, enabling the author's reflections on the feasts and seasons as well as on the Lectionary to connect effectively with the concerns and interests of present-day readers. I look forward to the next two volumes."

Patrick Regan, OSB
Author of *Advent to Pentecost*

"Though originating in the postconciliar period, Adrien Nocent's volumes remain one of the church's finest commentaries on the Lectionary and contain remarkable up-to-date insights for our times. Thanks to the emendations and annotations of Paul Turner, one of today's finest liturgical scholars, these volumes will enrich the thoughts of parish liturgists, presiders, homilists, musicians, lectors, theology students, and participants in the church's liturgy."

Stephen J. Binz
Author of *Conversing with God in Advent and Christmas*

"Adrien Nocent was truly a remarkable scholar, well ahead of his time! . . . He weaves the paschal mystery, eschatology, and living liturgy daily into a core tool for interpreting Advent, Christmas, and Epiphany in a fresh way. In this reissue, Fr. Paul Turner sensitively respects Nocent's own voice as he bridges the time after the Council to the present age. . . . This work needs to be on every priest's, liturgist's, musician's, and assembly member's 'go to' shelf."

Joyce Ann Zimmerman, CPPS
Institute for Liturgical Ministry, Dayton, Ohio

"In 1977 when Adrien Nocent's book appeared in English translation, I was studying the liturgical year with him at Sant'Anselmo. I remember how moved I was to read his deep reflections after having experienced the new lectionary with its three-year cycle of readings at that point only a couple of times. Now, having experienced the three-year cycle more than a dozen times, I am still moved by his writings. I am delighted that his book has been updated by Paul Turner and is coming into print again."

Michael S. Driscoll
University of Notre Dame

The Liturgical Year

Volume Three

SUNDAYS TWO TO THIRTY-FOUR IN
ORDINARY TIME

by
Adrien Nocent, OSB

Translated by
Matthew J. O'Connell

Introduced, Emended, and Annotated by
Paul Turner

LITURGICAL PRESS
Collegeville, Minnesota

www.litpress.org

Nihil Obstat: Reverend Robert Harren, *Censor deputatus.*
Imprimatur: ✠ Most Reverend John F. Kinney, J.C.D., D.D., Bishop of Saint Cloud, Minnesota, August 29, 2013.

Cover design by Ann Blattner. Illustration by Frank Kacmarcik, OblSB. Saint John's Abbey, Collegeville, Minnesota. Used with permission.

Available in three volumes, *The Liturgical Year* is the authorized English version of *Célébrer Jésus-Christ, L'année Liturgique,* published by Jean-Pierre Delarge, 10, rue Mayet, 75006 Paris, France. The English translation of *The Liturgical Year* was first published by Liturgical Press in four volumes in 1977.

Volume 3: ISBN 978-0-8146-3571-1   ISBN 978-0-8146-3596-4 (e-book)

1	2	3	4	5	6	7	8	9

Library of Congress Cataloging-in-Publication Data

Nocent, Adrien.
    [Célébrer Jésus-Christ. English]
    The liturgical year : Advent, Christmas, Epiphany / by Adrien Nocent, OSB ; Translated by Matthew J. O'Connell ; Introduced, Emended, and Annotated by Paul Turner.
      volumes   cm
    Includes bibliographical references.
    ISBN 978-0-8146-3569-8 (v. 1 : pbk. : alk. paper) —
    ISBN 978-0-8146-3594-0 (v. 1 : e-book)
     1. Church year.   I. Title.

  BV30.N6213   2013
  263'.9—dc23

                                2013011152

Contents

Sundays Two to Thirty-Four in Ordinary Time

Year B

Year C

Abbreviations

CL   *Constitution on the Sacred Liturgy*

CSEL *Corpus Scriptorum Ecclesiasticorum Latinorum*. Vienna, 1866–

PG   *Patrologia Graeca*, ed. J. P. Migne. Paris, 1857–66

PL   *Patrologia Latina*, ed. J. P. Migne. Paris, 1844–64

SC   *Sources Chretiennes*. Paris, 1942–

Series Introduction

When the postconciliar lectionary first fell into the hands of priests, musicians, and parish liturgists in 1970, few could fully grasp the significance of the event. The vast selection of readings, the nimble choice of responsorial psalms, and the blossoming of the liturgical year would become clearer only in time.

One of the first companions to the revised lectionary was composed by Adrien Nocent, a Belgian monk who became a consultor for the Sacred Congregation for Divine Worship in 1969. In 1964 he had served as a consultor for the Consilium for the Implementation of the Constitution on the Sacred Liturgy of the Second Vatican Council. He was the secretary for the Consilium's Study Group 17, which worked on the revision of Holy Week, and, among other responsibilities, was part of Study Group 11, which revised the Lectionary for Mass. He drew up the preliminary schemas for Advent, the Sundays after Epiphany, and the Sundays following Pentecost.

For Nocent, a commentary on the lectionary could not be a mere commentary on a book but an exploration of the dialogue between the Word of God and humanity in every culture and time. The Church had been through only one complete three-year cycle of the lectionary when Nocent was writing this book. He shared his vision of this project for eager readers, students, and worshipers.

On the occasion of the fiftieth anniversary of the Constitution on the Sacred Liturgy, Liturgical Press is proud to reissue Nocent's work. I was deeply honored at the invitation to contribute annotations— honored because when I was in the seminary, *The Liturgical Year* was the main resource I consulted to prayerfully approach my participation in the Sunday Mass; honored because as a young priest, I used *The Liturgical Year* to help prepare my homilies; honored because as a liturgical catechist, my brain had been hardwired to Nocent's approach to the lectionary: Start with the gospel, then look at the first reading, then the psalm, and be ready to discard the second reading from your treatment of the Sunday lectionary.

Readers today may criticize Nocent's approach as too "thematic" in content. He presumes that each Sunday carries a theme and that he knows what it is. In reality, there is no single theme, and the second reading deserves its place in the sun. Still, in practice, Nocent's ability to explain the layout of the lectionary is still vital. Although a specialist in liturgy, he reveals himself as a most capable biblical exegete; although a man of philosophical depth, he constantly returns to the question of relevance: What does this passage have to say to us today? I have added a few annotations where I thought the reader needed a bridge between Nocent's day and our own, but I have kept these at a minimum to let the author's voice speak.

I have also refrained from changing too much of Matthew J. O'Connell's fine original translation. He wrote before issues of gender-inclusive language became important, however, and I felt that the book could not be reissued without attention to this detail. The greatest number of changes I introduced to the translation have to do with this concern. I have also emended O'Connell's work where I thought it needed greater clarity due to the length of sentences, obscure vocabulary, or theological imprecisions. Otherwise, again, I wanted his voice to win.

Nocent's seven-volume work in French, which had been rearranged into four volumes in English, is now redistributed again into three. All the material is here, along with Nocent's desire to share his profound faith and scholarship. I am confident that you, the reader, will meet a friend, a spiritual father, and a compelling mentor in Adrien Nocent.

Paul Turner

1. The Organization of Ordinary Time

The final volume in this series of commentaries on the liturgical year will be different in format from the first two. This is because the material to be handled is quite different. Each of the special seasons—Advent, Christmas–Epiphany, Lent, and Easter—has its characteristic theology, but the "Sundays after Pentecost" have no special coloring of their own. These Sundays simply celebrate the paschal mystery as it is being fulfilled in the Church and the world. Consequently, except for the theology of Sunday, there is no question of elaborating a special theology for Ordinary Time. Nor is there any point in drawing up tables that would show how the Sundays of Ordinary Time were organized at other periods of history or in other Churches. Since Ordinary Time follows no special line, the choice of readings and prayers has varied without following any pattern.

This volume, then, will be very simple in format and will limit itself almost entirely to commentary. Doubtless such comment could have been organized in various ways. May the one we have chosen serve its purpose to the reader's satisfaction.

1. Work of the Commission for Reform of the Missal

If readers are to understand what we have attempted to do in this book, they must first be made aware of how the commission for the reform of the Missal understood its role and how it went about achieving the goal it set for itself. The work of the commission is doubtless not beyond criticism, and some of the norms it followed are questionable, but the commission certainly took great pains in its work.

Enrichment of the Lectionary

The first task of the commission was to greatly expand the lectionary. We need only run our eye over the list of readings in the older lectionary to see that it was quite impoverished. The Second Vatican

Council, therefore, was very insistent in the Constitution on the Sacred Liturgy that a richer fare be provided (51). In responding to this strongly worded desire, however, the commission found itself faced with a complicated and ticklish situation. We shall point out some of the complexities so that readers may understand that no completely satisfactory solution was possible.

A Central Theme for Each Sunday?

The celebrations of the major liturgical seasons have always been so constructed, even in the early Church, as to illustrate a broadly conceived theme. This is evident when we examine, for example, the liturgies for the Sundays of Lent. In the judgment of many, such celebrations organized around a theme are pastorally successful, since the attention of the faithful is not easily dispersed in several different directions. From Advent to Pentecost the congregation is therefore accustomed to hearing readings on a particular mystery, while the chants and prayers likewise call attention to a limited range of ideas. Would there not be an advantage, then, in following a similar pattern for each Sunday of Ordinary Time?

Obviously, the commission asked itself that question. The exegetes, however, did not care for the idea. There is always a danger of telling the texts what they must say and of using them in a subjectivist manner to make them fit into a predefined framework; it cannot be said that the liturgy has always resisted such a temptation. The exegetes' warning was well-grounded, and it would have been imprudent to neglect it. In this day and age, we cannot ignore the scholarly study of Scripture, which has made such great advances. We must indeed respect the special nature of liturgical proclamation, but we must also respect the objective meaning of the texts and not force them into an alien mold.

The members of the commission were in agreement, then, that the Sunday celebrations could have themes only if these were loosely and flexibly conceived. It was possible, for example, during some weeks and on some Sundays, to bring together texts among which there was an objective correspondence; it would be almost impossible, however, to do this for a very large number of celebrations. Experience with "Masses on a theme" had shown that the biblical texts ended up being distorted in the effort to pursue a narrowly conceived theme. The commission therefore rejected outright any effort to implement themes that would have to run through all the texts; they allowed, however, for the possibility of themes conceived more in the Semitic manner and not requiring a material parallelism between the texts.

How Organize the Readings?

Once this decision had been made, the commission faced another complicated problem: What type of readings was to be offered on these Sundays? The question gave rise to endless discussions and a large variety of views. The end sought was to foster contact with Scripture as proclaimed by and in the Church. Was this goal always pursued in a measured way? We shall see. At this point, however, we may say that perhaps the commission was excessively conditioned by its desire to achieve that goal and that the abundance, indeed the superabundance, of the texts proclaimed did not always yield the expected result. We may even say that the goal of proclaiming a great number of texts may have caused distortions in the individual celebrations.

A Single-Year Cycle

We shall advert briefly to a few of the tendencies at work in the reform commission. Some members wanted a single-year cycle of readings. They argued that the faithful cannot easily digest a large number of varied passages from the Bible and that the repetition of the same passages year after year was therefore not a bad thing in itself. If the commission chose to have a single-year cycle, however, it would not be meeting the wishes of Vatican II. The material of Scripture was so vast that a single set of selections for about thirty Sundays would be entirely inadequate, even if further readings were introduced for each weekday. Once this was realized, the only question to be answered was this: How many years in the cycle would be needed for a "more abundant" reading of Scripture? The number of years did not have to be the same for Sundays and for weekdays.

The Gospel

Since the gospel is the climactic stage in the proclamation of the word, the distribution of the gospel texts was the necessary starting point for the commission's work. How many years would be needed—two, three, or even four—for an adequate distribution with ever-new texts?

Some of the experts felt that the Sunday proclamation of the gospel should be limited solely to the logia or *ipsissima verba* of Christ, that is, to what contemporary critical exegesis regards as the words of Jesus himself; the whole framework added by the evangelists should be dropped. The pericopes would then admittedly be very short, but they would have the striking force of a slogan and would thus prove a valuable pastoral tool. Others, however, were of the opinion that short sentences cannot be thrust upon the faithful without any context and that when thus read in isolation, the sentences do not stick in the mind. Moreover, from the ceremonial viewpoint, how could the solemn ceremonial surrounding the reading of the gospel be maintained if the text proclaimed were, for example, only a single sentence or even less than that?

There was an even more important objection to the idea, for what the idea represents may at times be only an exegetical hypothesis, not something certain, and it is difficult to involve oneself deeply in a liturgy that rests on such a fluid base. In addition, there is a material stumbling block: the limited number of such pericopes would have made it impossible to proclaim the Old Testament, the text of which is far more extensive than the New, even when the latter is taken in its totality. Other members of the commission, therefore, asked whether, instead of getting involved in exegetical hypotheses, it would not be far better to proclaim almost the entire text of each gospel. That was the choice the commission finally made.

A Three-Year Cycle: The Synoptic Gospels

The decision required new choices. Ancient tradition has the Church read the Gospel of John during Lent and Easter Time. It would therefore not be appropriate to begin the reading of John all over again later in the year. Once it was decided to have three cycles, it was also decided to exclude the Gospel of John, inasmuch as it is proclaimed yearly at certain times. To fill out the Gospel of Mark, however, which is shorter than the other two Synoptics, certain passages of John would be introduced into the Sundays of Ordinary Time. Thus, for practical purposes, one of the three Synoptics would be read in each year of the three-year cycle. For weekdays, a two-year cycle proclamation of the gospel was envisaged.

There was no thought of attempting a continuous reading of the Old Testament, for it is simply too long. A number of the experts, however, did want all the other books of the New Testament to be read in the course of the year; the second reading on the Sundays of Ordinary Time was to help in achieving this goal.

The Second Reading

The decision gave rise to difficulties, however, as we have by now come to experience. The chief difficulty is the following: Since there is no continuous reading of the Old Testament on these Sundays, the reading for each Sunday is chosen with an intelligent eye on the gospel reading for that day. But the second reading consists of a quasi-continuous reading of the letters; thus, an element that usually has no relation to the other two readings is introduced into each Sunday's liturgy. When such a relation does exist, it does so only by accident.

Here we have a new situation. During Easter Time, for example, the readings may not fit perfectly together, but at least they are all concerned with the mystery of the resurrection, and this gives unity to them. In the case of the Sundays in Ordinary Time, however, the second reading introduces a new factor, being unconnected to the other two readings (unless, of course, one attempts to establish artificial and arbitrary links with them).

The Homily

The lack of unity between the second reading, on the one hand, and the first and third, on the other, creates a real and insoluble problem when it comes to the homily. One must either concentrate on the second reading and say nothing about the Old Testament reading and the gospel, or else say little or nothing about the second reading and concentrate on the Old Testament and the gospel. Where approved by the conference of bishops, it is permissible indeed to have only two readings;* then the first of these, for obvious reasons, must always be from the Old Testament and the second from the gospel.

---

* In the third edition of the Missal, this permission was removed from what is now GIRM 357, and in its place is found this comment about the three Sunday Scriptures: "These readings should be followed strictly."

Some celebrants have found a solution that makes it possible to retain the three readings and to comment on them all: Before the beginning of the penitential act, the second reading is proclaimed, and the penitential act then is structured around the theme of that reading. Then, at the proper time, the Liturgy of the Word is celebrated, using only the Old Testament reading and the gospel. In some ways this is a fairly good solution, provided we do not anticipate the Liturgy of the Word by assigning the same solemnity to the proclamation of the second reading.[†]

The Other Texts

There is this further difficulty: Except for the responsorial psalm after the Old Testament reading and for the Alleluia that introduces the reading of the gospel, the chants, like the prayers, are the same in all three years of the cycle. This means further new elements that, like the second reading, often have no connection with the gospel.

These difficulties are fully real. We had to mention them at the beginning in order to explain why the final volume of this series of commentaries must follow a different format from the first two.

2. The Commentary

Readings

In light of the problems mentioned, how is this commentary to be arranged? The theme of the second reading, as we said, rarely fits in with the broad theme of the given Sunday. In both the second and the third readings we are admittedly dealing with a continuous reading of the text, but the two cases are nonetheless different. Even though the reading of the gospel is continuous or quasi-continuous, we cannot be satisfied with a commentary that is exclusively exegetical. This is because the gospel pericope is related to the first reading, the one from the Old Testament, and this latter reading tells us the point of view from which the gospel should be read and commented on.

The second reading, on the other hand, is self-contained and unrelated to the other two readings. The solution here is to give a com-

---

[†] There is no provision for this solution in the rubrics.

mentary that is pretty much a straight exegesis of it and to add a spiritual commentary; the fact that the passage is proclaimed in a liturgy will not cause us to read it from some special viewpoint. All this being so, we think it enough to devote a few lines to each of these second readings, offering some reflections that will serve as a guide to readers and referring them for further developments to some works of exegesis or spiritual commentary on Scripture. As in previous volumes, a heavy line separates the second reading from what precedes in the many instances in which the second reading is not related to the theme of the day's celebration. And in the outline charts preceding the commentary, an asterisk is used to identify such selections.

Prayers

The prayers and chants are the same in all three years, except for the responsorial psalm and the chant that introduces the gospel. There is, therefore, no advantage to be gained by joining the commentary on them to the commentary on the readings for each Sunday. As a matter of fact, the entrance and communion antiphons of Ordinary Time, together with the prayers for these Sundays, form a separate whole that has no necessary relation to the readings. On the one hand, then, the proclamation of the word, the responsorial psalms, and the chants that introduce the gospel form one whole; on the other, the various prayers and the other chants form a second whole. Each of these wholes is independent of the other.

In view of all of this, we judge it better to offer a short general commentary, at least on the prayers, which we shall examine and try to treat synthetically; at the same time, however, we shall be on the watch for the possibility of seeing a given prayer as an integral part of the Sunday to which it is assigned. As for the chants, there would have been little value in attempting a synthesis of them.

There could be no question, of course, of commenting on the liturgy for each weekday of Ordinary Time. To do so would have required several more volumes. Finally, we could, in the course of the commentary, have cited numerous works on the theology of Sunday and especially on the Scriptures. That would only have made the volume unwieldy and would have added little of value, given the nature of the volume.

2. The Lord's Day: A Theology of Sunday

We would manifest an odd view of things if we were to maintain that the period between Pentecost and Advent is the time of real spiritual growth, as though the special seasons of Advent, Lent, and Eastertide were not climactic moments in our supernatural odyssey. What we now call "Ordinary Time," because in it we do not celebrate some special mystery of Christ, is not inferior to the other seasons; on the other hand, neither is it superior to them, as though it were the time of fulfillment while the celebrations in the other seasons would be more theological and contemplative. In point of fact, the whole liturgical year is centered on a single mystery: the mystery of Christ's death and resurrection, and we live that mystery, and live by it, at all times. Ordinary Time, like the special seasons of the liturgical year, is simply a continuation of that basic mystery. The mystery, moreover, is celebrated in a special way on every Sunday of the year. It is rather important, then, that we possess a life-supporting theology of Sunday.

Sunday

For most persons, Sunday means rest and the obligation of attending the eucharistic celebration. The obligation is too often thought of in disciplinary terms; people do not grasp the real reason for it. Yet, if the Church intended to enrich the Sunday celebration by means of the new lectionary, she did so because she wanted people to understand once again the true meaning of Sunday. We will not be able to grasp that meaning unless we recall briefly the situation in which the newborn Church found itself; the Acts of the Apostles gives us a picture of that Church and its experiences.

The Jewish Week

The Jewish week, as known to the apostles and lived by Judeo-Christians until their conversion, begins with the Sabbath and leads back to the Sabbath. The Jewish theology of the Sabbath is based on the account of creation in Genesis, in which we are told that God rested after finishing his work.

It would, however, be simplistic to see in the Jewish Sabbath nothing but a pious imitation of God's rest. No, the Sabbath is above all a day of thanksgiving and prayer. The legalist approach contributed to distorting the real meaning of the Sabbath, making people forget that it is meant to be a day of special communion with the Lord of creation. The Sabbath rest certainly has beneficial social repercussions, but when it is imposed in an excessively rigid manner, it can obscure the other possible dimensions of the Sabbath.

The Sabbath was of such central importance for the Jews that the other days of the week are not even named but only numbered. Only the eve of the Sabbath has a special name: *parasceve*, or "preparation" day, that is, the day when all that is needed for the Sabbath must be prepared, since on the Sabbath itself nothing can be bought or prepared. The Jewish week, then, consists of: the first day (our Sunday), the second day (Monday), the third day (Tuesday), the fourth day (Wednesday), the fifth day (Thursday), the sixth day (Friday), and the Sabbath (our Saturday). The Latin liturgy has retained this manner of designating the days of the week: *feria secunda* (Monday), *feria tertia* (Tuesday), etc.

The Planetary Week

In antiquity, the Hellenistic contemporaries of the Jews were familiar with a week in which the days were named after the planets. Mars, Mercury, Jupiter, Venus, and Saturn lent their names to the days from Tuesday to Saturday. The sun and moon gave their names to the days that the Germanic world would later call Sunday and Monday, while the Latin world would speak of the "Lord's (day)" for Sunday and of "the day of *luna*" (Latin for "moon").

The planetary week had no official standing, but it became increasingly popular. People believed that the planet after which a day was named influenced the action of human beings. Christian evangelization did not everywhere succeed in imposing even the new name, "the Lord's day," for the first day of the week (Latin: *dies dominicalis*; Italian: *domenica*; Portuguese: *domingo*; Spanish: *domingo*; French: *dimanche*). The Germanic languages continued to speak of the "sun's day" (German: *Sonntag*; Dutch: *Zondag*). The Hellenistic world accused the Jews of really being followers of Saturn, since they celebrated Saturday, while it accused Christians of being worshipers of the sun, because they celebrated Sunday. Meanwhile, within the Christian community the leaders had to be on guard against the superstitions of the faithful who were at times inclined to overestimate the influence of the stars on their behavior.

Christians chose the name "Lord's day" instead of "Sunday" in order to show that this was a memorial of the Lord's resurrection. Christian symbolism was also to speak of this day as "the eighth day," that is, a day entirely outside of the traditional week, in order to emphasize the fact that a new era had begun with the resurrection of Christ. The name "eighth day" was never officially adopted by the Church, despite the wealth of meaning it conveyed, but the fathers of the Church did make use of it in their catechetical instructions.

The Lord's Day

For Christians, one day of the week had incomparable importance: the first day, immediately after the Sabbath. That is the day on which the evangelists locate the Lord's resurrection (Matt 28:1; Mark 16:2; Luke 24:1; John 20:1, 19). Christians considered this day to play an unconditionally definitive role in the history of the world, and so they wanted to celebrate it in a special way. As Judeo-Christians, they continued to attend the synagogue on the Sabbath, but they also wanted to celebrate the first day of the week, which the evangelists had said was the day of the resurrection. This day they called "the Lord's day"; the name itself occurs for the first time in the book of Revelation (1:10). There was no possibility of confusing this "day of the Lord" with the "day of the Lord" when he returns at the end of time; the latter was called, in Greek, *hēmera Kyriou*, while Sunday was called *kyriakē hēmera* or simply *kyriakē*. It is the word *kyriakē* that enters the Romance languages by way of Latin (*dominicalis* or *dominica*) and provides the modern Romance word for Sunday: *domenica, domingo, dimanche*.

Meaning and Importance of Sunday

Is Sunday a day just like other days? Is there any point in celebrating the Eucharist on Sunday rather than on some other day of the week? Would it not be possible for each individual to pick any day of the week instead of Sunday and celebrate a weekly liturgy on that day? Isn't the important thing, after all, that the Church should not let too long a time pass without celebrating the Eucharist in memory of Christ's death and resurrection?

We must reflect at least briefly on the answers to these questions. These days we tend to dislike fixed times for doing things; we regard them, perhaps a little too quickly, as artificial. As a matter of fact, in many cases they have been. The question is this: Is the choice of Sunday for the Eucharist something artificial, and can we shift to some other practice without loss?

To get an answer we must first of all look to the past. The ways of those who have gone before us, especially the apostles and the early Church, cannot be a matter of indifference to us, especially if we can determine why they acted as they did. We cannot solve our Christian problems by looking solely to what we call, in a somewhat vague and indefinite way, "modern humanity" and "contemporary anthropology."

Practice of the Early Church

A first and striking fact is that Scripture and the early ecclesiastical writings do not focus attention on a celebration of the annual Pasch; they speak first and foremost of celebrating Sunday as a special day, the day of days for the Christian assembly (1 Cor 16:2). This is the more remarkable in that, down to the Peace of Constantine, only Saturday was a holiday; Christians had to work on Sunday. That is something we tend to forget. Nowhere do we read that Christians rebelled or suffered martyrdom because they wanted to have Sunday free. This means that the idea of Sunday as a day of rest was not very important and certainly not decisive.

Despite this fact, the Church regarded it as extremely important that the Eucharist should be celebrated on Sunday, the first day of the week. The Acts of the Apostles mentions the Sunday gathering (20:7). At a period when people had to work on Sunday, the idea of Sunday rest was not characteristic of the day. The focus of attention was on celebrating the act of worship that commemorated the resurrection of Christ, an event that occurred on the first day of the week, according to the evangelists.

A Creation of the Christian Community

The facts show that the early Church was firmly bent on celebrating the first day of the week in a special way, even though in order to do so it had to overcome many obstacles. What we seem to have here is a creation of the early Christian community. Some interpreters have seen in this act a deliberate contrast to Judaism, with the cultic celebration of the first day as a conscious rejection of the Jewish Sabbath. The opposition was intended, in this view, to call attention to the new situation in which Christians found themselves in relation to Judaism.

Other scholars see in the Sunday celebration an extension of a Jewish harvest feast that was celebrated on the first day of the week, although only once a year. Still others have suggested the influence of the planetary cults; the difficulty with this explanation is that nowhere do we find the worship of the sun (to take the most obvious example) being assigned to the first day of the week. The most we can say is that the passages of Scripture relating to Sunday inform us about the customs of Christian communities whose members were converts from Gentile religions (1 Cor 16:2; Acts 20:7; Rev 1:10) and that these communities made the first day, rather than the Sabbath, the most important day of the week.

It seems, however, that we must see in the celebration of Sunday a Christian creation that is neither continuous with nor set in conscious opposition to any other celebration, including the Jewish celebration of the Sabbath. For one thing, the content of the Christian celebration of Sunday is completely unrelated to the content of the Jewish Sabbath. In Judeo-Christian communities we find the two observances existing side by side, with Christians observing the Sabbath and even attending the synagogue but also observing Sunday. There is no indication that these Christians saw any continuity between the two observances.

Sabbath and Sunday

The Jewish Sabbath was marked by abstention from all work, whereas Sunday was simply a day of worship in commemoration of the risen Christ. Sunday was not a prolongation, transposition, or revision of the Sabbath. When, finally, Christians no longer observed the Sabbath, Sunday was not taken as a kind of shifting of the Sabbath to another day. Rather, the Sabbath was taken as a "figure," and Sunday as its perfect fulfillment. We pass from the cultic observance and imitation of what had taken place at the first creation to a paschal celebration that renews the creation of humanity and the world.

Rest and Worship

The history of the Christian Sunday thus bids us distinguish carefully between Sunday as a day of worship and Sunday as a day of rest. From the very beginning, Sunday was a day of worship, whereas the idea of rest became the subject of a "precept" only around the sixth century. Even then, we may note, the "rest" meant a more complete focusing of the mind and heart on God rather than a prohibition against all work.

The Constitution on the Sacred Liturgy speaks of Sunday in two articles:

> Holy Mother Church believes that it is for her to celebrate the saving work of her divine Spouse in a sacred commemoration on certain days throughout the course of the year. Once each week, on the day which she has called the Lord's Day, she keeps the memory of the Lord's resurrection. She also celebrates it once every year, together with his blessed passion, at Easter, that most solemn of all feasts.[1]

> By a tradition handed down from the apostles, which took its origin from the very day of Christ's resurrection, the Church celebrates the paschal mystery every eighth day, which day is appropriately called the Lord's Day or Sunday.[2]

Gospel Inspiration for Sunday

The paschal mystery and the resurrection are the events that determined the choice of the first day of the week for the Christian assembly and eucharistic celebration. Indeed, the gospels made the Church's choice of Sunday inevitable. According to the evangelists, the risen Christ first showed himself on the morning of the first day. By so doing, he already made the day a specially holy one; at this point, however, there was nothing to suggest a weekly return of this day of glory. Then, on the following Sunday the risen Lord appeared again to his disciples (John 20:26). Once the apparitions and manifestations of the risen Christ were thus attached to Sunday, there was an evident basis for choosing this day as the day for the Christian assembly; to the Church of the first years the choice must have seemed inevitable.

Chapter 20 of the Acts of the Apostles shows that the celebration of Sunday was already an institution: "On the first day of the week when we gathered to break bread, Paul spoke to them" (20:7). When Paul writes to the Corinthians urging them to take up collections, he refers to Sunday as the day for doing this (1 Cor 16:2). When St. John at a much later date is recounting his visions, he designates "the Lord's day" as the day when he received his revelations (Rev 1:10).

Sunday: A Permanent Institution

We must bear in mind the fact that Christians in the early days still had to work on Sundays; it was on the Sabbath that they rested. This is to say that the choice of the first day of the week was not dictated by convenience and did not fit nicely into the life pattern of the day. The choice of Sunday was thus not an accident or something secondary. Sunday has a quasi-sacramental character about it, so much so that it is hard to imagine the Church leaving open the day on which communities or individuals may celebrate the Lord's resurrection and not continuing to celebrate it on a fixed day that is in no sense artificial but was chosen by Christ himself for his resurrection and his appearances to his Church. It is important, moreover, that the entire Church should, together and on the same day, celebrate with joyous worship the event of the resurrection, the event that is the ultimate ground of her birth in the Spirit.

Clearly, then, the Church cannot make optional the choice of the day for celebrating the resurrection of Christ. This does not mean that Christians who are legitimately prevented from joining the celebration on that day may not feel it their duty to celebrate this central event on another day. If they do so, however, that other day does not become the real equivalent of Sunday.

It must be acknowledged that the frequent celebration of the Eucharist during the week has obscured the significance of Sunday as a special day, particularly since every Eucharist commemorates and proclaims the death and resurrection of Christ. Objectively, however, each celebration of the Eucharist has its own proper character; the Sunday Eucharist is not the same as the Easter Eucharist, nor is a weekday Eucharist the same as the Sunday Eucharist or the Easter Eucharist.

Memorial of the Resurrection

When the Christian community assembles on Sunday, it does so in order to celebrate the resurrection of Christ, its Lord. His resurrection is the essential object of Christian faith and the basis of Christians' assurance that they too will pass from death to life. On Sunday the community also celebrates the day when the new and eternal covenant was brought to fulfillment; that covenant is the sign of a new world and a new creation and thus is the source of the joy that marks the celebration. The Church recalls this world that the Lord created anew by his cross and his victory over death. The fathers of the Church compare this new creation, effected in the paschal mystery, with the first creation and relate them as figure and fulfillment. Every Sunday celebration thus brings joy because of Christ's triumph and present glory as well as because humanity has been clothed in Christ and transformed into a new creation.

Presence of Christ

Every celebration of the Church means the presence of the past. Sunday brings Christians together around the victorious Christ, for if the Church is the Body of Christ, that Christ must be the risen Christ. In his defense of the Christians to Emperor Antoninus Pius, St. Justin Martyr describes a Christian assembly of about the year 150 and tells how the Christians of Rome came together joyously to praise their Lord, hear his word, and celebrate his Eucharist. Justin thus shows us how the local Church of Rome considered it extremely important to celebrate the Eucharist, the sacrifice of praise, as the crown of the Sunday liturgy of the word.

The risen Christ is present in his word; he is also present in his Eucharist. When the Church celebrates the resurrection of the Christ who is present in her midst, she also celebrates her own resurrection. She knows that her Lord communicates himself to her, that the risen Lord who is present in his word and present, Body and Blood, in the eucharistic bread and wine gives her an ever new life that will make her perpetually youthful through the centuries. It is on Sunday above all that the Church approaches the Father through Jesus in the Spirit and thanks him for the creation of the world, for redemption, and for the whole plan of salvation that has been carried out and is now bearing its fruit.

Sign of the World That Is Coming

If every celebration in the Church makes the past present, it also actualizes the future, that is, gives it a presence here and now. The Church now awaits the risen Lord whom she celebrates each Sunday; she proclaims him until he comes. Sunday is thus linked to the future, the end of time. On Sunday we utter our *Marana tha*, "Our Lord, come!" It is thus a day on which we have a foretaste of the kingdom that will not pass away and of our future rest in the Lord.

This explains why Christian symbolism has thought of Sunday as the "eighth day." The First Letter of St. Peter speaks of it, while the Second Letter presents Noah as the eighth one saved (2 Pet 2:5). In the fourth century, the number eight symbolized the resurrection itself, because the resurrection occurred on a Sunday, and Sunday is the eighth day. If the risen Christ lives in the unending eighth day, the baptized too live in the same eighth day because they are already risen with Christ.

The concept of obligation can evidently not do justice to the Christian reality of Sunday and its celebration. We can understand, then, the attitude of some of the fathers of Vatican II who wished to remove Sunday from the realm of juridical obligation. They were doubtless being very idealistic, and yet we can certainly deplore the lack of enthusiasm Christians have for Sunday and the fact that they attach so little importance to its celebration. Perhaps the fault is to be found in an excessively juridical training and the lack of an authentic catechesis in regard to Sunday.

3. Let Us Give Thanks to the Father on the Lord's Day

Sunday is marked chiefly by the celebration of the Eucharist. We think it very important, therefore, to dwell on the theology contained in the eucharistic prayers that are now used in the Western Church and to see how they are to affect our lives. Catholics who realize what they have become through baptism should study these prayers so that they may make more profitable use of them, draw sustenance from them, and make them the basis of their habitual personal prayer.

1. The Prefaces

The first part of the eucharistic prayer is chiefly exclamatory in tone; it reminds us of our duty to praise the Lord for what he has done. In the Eastern liturgy this first part of the eucharistic prayer has always been unvarying and closely connected with the body of the anaphora.[1] The Roman liturgy, on the other hand, has shown great creativity in this first part of the eucharistic prayer, and the old liturgical books, such as the Gelasian Sacramentary (the manuscript dates from about 750, but the texts are often at least a century older), provide quite a large number of prefaces. For several reasons, however—the variety itself; the singing of the *Sanctus*, which at times became quite ornate; the solemn singing of the preface as contrasted with the silence of the Canon—the participants in the liturgy could be led to think that the preface, with its more exclamatory style, was not part of the eucharistic prayer, whereas, in fact, it is the opening part of that prayer.

The illuminated manuscripts, later imitated by the printed books, contributed to foster the same misunderstanding. The Roman Canon begins with the Latin words *Te igitur*; the letter *T* was embellished by artists to form a cross, and the illustration became so important that it was blown up to full-page size, thus separating the preface from the body of the eucharistic prayer or Canon (this last word then being written at the top of the next page in large capitals).

In the reformed liturgy we have recovered a sense of the unity of the eucharistic prayer—this, despite an increased number of prefaces, since these, though quite varied, are always in evident continuity with the eucharistic prayer, of which they are a part.

Our reason for these initial remarks about the preface will become clearer as we go through the texts of the eucharistic prayers.

Theology of the Prefaces

It is our intention here to give a short synthesis of the content of the prefaces in order to show the wealth they contain. Eight prefaces are provided for Ordinary Time. They remind us of the story of creation (Preface V) and the history of salvation (Preface IV). We are urged to meditate on the mystery of salvation within which we live our lives (Preface II). Moving more deeply into the theology of this mystery of salvation, we see how humanity was saved out of the mortality of Christ (Preface III) or, more accurately, through the obedience of the incarnate Son (Preface VII), who, by accomplishing his paschal mystery, gives birth to the new people of God (Preface I). We live now as members of the one Church, the Body of Christ, and as sharers in the life of the Blessed Trinity (Preface VIII). Every celebration of the Eucharist, which is the Pasch of Christ and his Church, gives us a more secure possession of the firstfruits produced by the new Passover (Preface VI).

Creation (Preface V)

We noted earlier that Sunday represents to some degree a break with the Sabbath. The reason for this is that the central factor in the Christian Sunday is the celebration of Christ's resurrection, whereby he creates a new people and brings a new creation into existence. At the same time, however, the biblical components of the Jewish Sabbath are to be retained, although within a Christian perspective. In fact, it is especially necessary that Christians of our time learn to contemplate the God of whom the preface says: "you laid the foundations of the world and have arranged the changing of times and seasons." Otherwise they may well succumb to the pervasive pride that marks the mind of the day. Our age is very much under the impression that it has replaced the Creator, that it is lord of time and history, and that it is at the root of reality. There is danger that this outlook may find its way even into the liturgy, as though humanity is to be the norm, whereas everything, in fact, originates in God and leads back to him.

OUR FORGETFULNESS OF GOD

The mentality to which we refer is doubtless to some extent a reaction against a contempt for the real and even sacred values of the world, against the tendency to curse the world and forget that it too had come from the creative hand of God. These attitudes, however, have in large measure changed; Vatican II's Pastoral Constitution on the Church in the Modern World faced up to that kind of pessimism and general distrust of earthly values.

But this justifiable reaction has gotten out of hand. As a result, we who work for the advancement of the world, whether in the technological or in the social spheres, are forgetful of him who created all things, the world and all that is in it; we forget that all we can do is transform the elements God himself has prepared for us. In our anxious concern for the ongoing evolution of the world, we forget that in the last analysis God alone is Lord of time and history and that we indulge in naive and dangerous presumption when we imagine that we can infallibly influence the course of history.

THE CHRISTIAN ATTITUDE

Preface V defines the Christian attitude by telling us that the Lord has entrusted his creation to us. But he has not done so in order that we might simply restore it to him exactly as it was, thus imitating the steward whose master gave him a sum of money to invest and who returned the exact amount he had originally received. On the other hand, the created world has not been entrusted to us so that we might pursue our selfish goals and seek a well-being that puts paradise to shame. No, if God entrusted the created world to us, it was in order that we might "for ever praise you in your mighty works." To forget this aspect of things is to betray the trust God has placed in us; it is to use his blessings for limited purposes while forgetting the will and intentions of him who created what he entrusted to us. The Christian attitude toward creation, then, should be one of wonder and thanksgiving; such is the Christian meaning of all work and the Christian way of using created things.

This preface shows us where every work for the advancement of humanity and the world should start. It tells Christians what their basic attitude should be to the real values God has created and incorporated in their world.

The History of Salvation (Preface IV)

If the creation of the world and its component elements should constantly inspire us to thanksgiving, the Church should also ceaselessly proclaim the history of salvation.

The history of the world has been and continues to be conditioned by the passion and resurrection of Christ, by his ascension, and by his sending of the Spirit. In the Christian view, the whole history of the world, and not merely the history recorded in the Old Testament, must be read in the light of those decisive events, as well as of the events we experience in our own time and those yet to come. We are really not sufficiently aware of the revolutionary force that Christ introduced into the world through his paschal mystery. He brought a new people into existence: the baptized, who are in the world without being of it and who already belong to the world of God even while being constantly filled with concern for the fears and anxieties of our age. The paschal mystery created not only a new people but a new world, one that is slowly being renewed until it attains the better state that it had at its first creation.

The history of salvation is our personal history; it is the history we should be living and helping others to live. That means that our value judgments should constantly be undergoing revision, until what is foolishness in others' eyes becomes for us the way to God.

The Mystery of Salvation (Preface II)

As we continue to contemplate and live the history of salvation, we see this mystery reaching its climax in Christ, who "out of compassion for the waywardness that is ours . . . humbled himself and was born of the Virgin." That is the root and foundation of everything. (The birth of Christ raised problems for the Church from the very beginning, and especially from the fourth century on. The reality of human nature likewise raised serious problems, as did the unity of this complete human nature [which is composed of a soul as well as of a body] with the divine nature; these problems the councils tackled and solved. This is not the place for discussing these various issues.)

We should ask ourselves whether we keep the incarnation of the Word of God constantly in mind and whether we see in it an event that has reshaped the whole course of history. St. Leo the Great, with his usual clarity, points out to the Christians of Rome the conclusions to be drawn from the great event of Christ's birth:

> Thus, by being born a real human while never ceasing to be true God as well, our Lord Jesus Christ became the beginning of the new creature. By the manner of his birth he established a spiritual origin for the human race so that the contamination attached to carnal generation might be eliminated and that those to be reborn might have an origin unconnected with the seed that transmits original sin. Of the men and women thus reborn Scripture says: "They are born not of blood nor the desire of the flesh nor human desire, but of God." What human mind can grasp this mystery, what tongue tell of this gift? Guilt reverts to innocence, the old becomes new; strangers become adopted children, and outsiders enter into the inheritance. The wicked become just, the avaricious generous, the lecherous chaste, and the earthbound heavenly.[2]

The saint is not exaggerating. We have all frequently observed how the history of the world and of humanity can take a new direction. We have been made aware (too rarely, indeed) of how people's lives are transformed; I refer not only to the transformations recorded for our edification in the lives of the saints but also the transformations that sometimes occur without publicity, in silence and hiddenness. The sight of the evils that afflict the present world should not make us forget that things can always change, and indeed that all is already changed in principle once a person adverts to the incarnation of God.

Mortals Saved by Mortality (Preface III)

"[Y]ou came to the aid of mortal beings with your divinity and even fashioned for us a remedy out of mortality itself."

Everyone says that humanity is sick and in need of healing, and, beyond a doubt, humanity is indeed sick—physically, psychologically, spiritually, and politically. In principle we are already freed in all of these areas, even though, as we are well aware, there is so much still to be done to make freedom reign.

We are freed because one of our number had the power to free us, and he had the power because he came from God and was God. By his own dying he overcame death and thus freed us. Do we believe that? Our liberation will not, of course, take place without our own efforts—not in the sense that we are able to save ourselves, but in the sense that our liberation cannot be effectively implemented unless we cooperate with the human Jesus and with the God whom Jesus is. The liberation of humanity is the joint work of God and humans, although God always has the initiative in it and can alone make our cooperation effective.

The Spirit who dwells in the Church continues the work of redemption and calls us to collaborate with him. It is accurate to say that mortals have been saved by the mortality of Christ, but we must add that, on the basis of what Jesus did and under the powerful influence of the Spirit, humanity saves itself and works for its own liberation until Christ comes again. The astounding, magnificent fact that we can thus collaborate with Christ, the incarnate God, no longer moves us to wonder, and that is too bad. We really need to recover a sense of wonder in the face of this absolutely fundamental divine work that is our liberation.

We have forgotten, for example, how sublime is the attitude of the sick who are apparently useless but offer their lives and suffering to God, thereby helping to liberate the world, in union with Christ, their fellow in the flesh. We no longer understand the life of those who withdraw into solitude and by their very existence give striking proof that Christ can enable a human being to live in utter independence, with God alone for company. We take a purely political view of those who seek to better the lot of their companions, and yet there are people who work with Christ to save humanity. We judge specialists only in terms of the success of their inventions, and we forget that they too are working, with the Word-made-flesh, for the liberation of humanity.

We could easily go on listing the people all around us who can, if they wish, transform their own lives by helping in the liberation of humanity. Because Christ has become incarnate, there is not a single human being that cannot play a useful role in the vast workshop where the world is being rebuilt. Perhaps if people realized this, they would find life a time of joy: the joy of being liberated themselves and of joining Christ in the liberation of others.

We are, then, not freed from outside ourselves; rather, we free ourselves, and humanity in its entirety is called to achieve this kind of self-liberation. Christ came among us as a human in order to teach us to free ourselves, and he gives us all the tools we need for effecting this liberation. Moreover, in thinking of this liberation, we must not limit our sights to only one aspect, namely, the restoration of humanity's state before the first sin. There are two other aspects of it that we must bear in mind: the continuation of the work of creation and divinization.

The discoveries made by science have perhaps made us more aware than our forebears were that the process of creation is continuing and that the created world is constantly being made more perfect. People used to think of creation as having been perfect at the beginning and as having then gradually been spoiled. We, however, are in a position to observe that the created world is becoming better. This aspect of liberation fits in with what St. John writes: "My Father is at work until now, so I am at work" (5:17). The created world is still the work of God and Christ. The Word Incarnate, acting in our midst and with us, continues the work of creation, and one of the ways he does so is to send his Spirit and make us more conscious of God's plan for the world and each of us and of our duty to cooperate with him.

The Obedience of the Son (Preface VII)

All that we have been saying would be inexplicable if we were not living under the new covenant that was sealed by the blood of Christ. "[By the obedience of your Son,] we have been restored to those gifts of yours that, by sinning, we had lost in disobedience." To accept humiliation and be "like us in all things but sin" was the attitude of the obedient Christ, and his obedience in turn is the basis for our liberation and our ability to cooperate in our own redemption. If we are saved and can work for our own liberation, it is because God chose to "love in us what you loved in your Son." In the Son, the Father found a world that subjected itself to him through the sacrifice of the Son's life.

The Paschal Mystery and the People of God (Preface I)

"For through his Paschal Mystery, he accomplished the marvelous deed, by which he has freed us from the yoke of sin and death, summoning us to the glory of being now called a chosen race, a royal priesthood, a holy nation, a people for your own possession."

Jesus willed to unite into a single people those whom he had liberated. Yet the Church is not a world within the world; it continues to be part of humanity and is to be thought of rather as the leaven in the mass. The Church does not always clearly act as such, and we for our part are more sensitive to the scandals that can be attributed to her than we are to the power given her by the continued presence of Christ her Head and by the action in her of the Holy Spirit. Yet this presence and activity are fully real and cause the Church to be not isolated but constantly growing. The Church, then, is truly human and as such is a community of sinners who are only more or less faithful and who share the weakness and corruption of the rest of the human race. At the same time, however, the Spirit of God is constantly at work in the Church and proceeding with his constructive work. The Church is scandalous at times because she is human, but she is also divine and clad with majesty and power.

We are a new people and must make ourselves conscious of that fact. But then it should not surprise us that we cannot always go along with the principles the world accepts. We sometimes feel inferior because we are afraid of appearing reactionary; we are not always at ease in the new world of those who have been redeemed by the mystery of Christ. The Sundays of Ordinary Time will provide material for meditating on our state as Christians. It is a glorious thing, but also a burden and a duty, to be "a chosen race, a royal priesthood, a holy nation, a people for [God's] own possession."

The One Church and the Blessed Trinity (Preface VIII)

The Church is a holy people because the Blessed Trinity wills her to be such and is constantly making her such.

> For, when your children were scattered afar by sin,
> through the Blood of your Son and the power of the Spirit,
> you gathered them again to yourself,
> that a people, formed as one by the unity of the Trinity,

made the body of Christ and the temple of the Holy Spirit,
might, to the praise of your manifold wisdom,
be manifest as the Church.

If we form a united body, it is because the Blessed Trinity dwells in each of us; it is because we are the object of the Trinity's activity and enter into the very sphere of that activity. The Father has eternally loved us to the point of sending his Son. The Son has given his life for us, has risen from the dead, and has sent us his Holy Spirit, who creates in us the image of the Son. As a result, every time the Father gazes upon us, he now sees in us the image of his own Son. By the power of the Spirit, then, we have become a single being in Christ, to the glory of the Father. The liturgical assembly, and especially the liturgical assembly on Sunday, is the image of this Body of Christ that the Spirit has brought together under the benevolent eye of the Father of all things.

Pledge of Eternal Life (Preface VI)

The life of the Church, the people of God, seems to pass as all lives do: in an everyday greyness and dullness. Even the series of Sundays may strike the Christian as simply another set of joyless or even sad and gloomy days. And yet, "we not only experience the daily effects of your care, but even now possess the pledge of life eternal." We need faith, however, if we are to be convinced of what the words are saying; if we look only at the earthly dimension of things, there is nothing to show us what lies deeper. There is no proof that eternal life is there and that we already lay hold of it. Only faith can make that a vital conviction for us.

Such a conviction is, however, essential for the life of God's people, the holy nation, because on it depend the Church's energy and her criteria for judging and acting.

Eternal life has already begun. The "proof": we have "the first fruits of the Spirit, through whom you raised up Jesus from the dead." It is a proof, however, only for those who believe in the testimony of Scripture as proclaimed in the Church and by the Church. The gift of the Spirit and its charisms make us live in hope that the paschal mystery will be fulfilled in us. The definitive and irreversible passage to eternal life still lies before us; at that moment all mere signs will be done away with because we will be in direct contact with the divine realities and will contemplate and touch them through love. There will be no more reason for faith and hope.

Such is the teaching contained in the prefaces for the Sundays of Ordinary Time. They are short poems that seek to capture the reality of our daily lives, a reality we seek to make new again for us each Sunday as we exercise our faith and strive to recognize the signs of God's infinite wisdom at work in our history. The prefaces thus sum up the whole meaning of our Christian life. They make us mindful again of true reality and introduce us to the great Eucharist in which we sing the Father's glory through Christ in the Spirit.

2. The Eucharistic Prayers

The Structure of the Eucharistic Prayer

When commenting on Holy Thursday, we recalled the Jewish framework within which the Last Supper must be set if it is to be entirely comprehensible. We refer the reader to the description there given.[3]

By way of further background, we must turn here to the structure of the eucharistic prayer in the early Church. The structure was, in fact, very simple. The prayer began with an exclamation of wonder at what the Lord had done: "It is truly right and just that we should praise you. . . ." In this, Christians were making their own the manner in which Jewish prayer had begun.

The second component is closely linked to the first and consists of an enumeration of the reasons for the praise and thanksgiving. This part will later on be given the technical name of "anamnesis," or "remembrance": "We give you thanks because you have. . . ." As we noted elsewhere, many of the Old Testament prayers follow this pattern, as do the New Testament canticles in the infancy narrative: "Blessed be the Lord, the God of Israel, for he has visited and brought redemption to his people" (Luke 1:68); "My soul proclaims the greatness of the Lord . . . For he has looked upon his handmaid's lowliness" (Luke 1:46, 48). This second part may be quite lengthy; some of the psalms, for example, recall the whole history of salvation in outline.

The recall or anamnesis leads psychologically to a further development, which is the third component in the structure. The remembrance of what God has done contains an implicit praise of his power, and the person praying instinctively turns to this new aspect: "You have done thus and so in the past; grant us now this new favor." In other words, the grateful remembrance of God's past favors leads to petitions, or intercessions as they are technically called. The realization of the power that God exercises in all he does rouses confidence that he will meet our further needs. We can see from this that the distinction between prayer of praise and prayer of petition is rather artificial, since in asking we acknowledge the Lord's power and, at least implicitly, give him praise.

The fourth and final section of the prayer is a return to the element of praise. He has done the wonderful things we have recalled, and we confidently await new deeds from him: "To him be glory forever!"

These four parts, which are closely linked and correspond so well to humanity's instinctive way of praying, are to be found in all the eucharistic prayers. They may be differently arranged or there may be repetitions, but the four parts are always evidently present. It was a prayer of this kind that Christ himself used when celebrating the Last Supper with his disciples. Christians should be encouraged to make this simple prayer formula their own in personal prayer; it will familiarize them with liturgical prayer and make it easier to pass from personal (private) prayer to liturgical prayer.

The Plurality of Eucharistic Prayers

The Jewish elements present in Christ's prayer at the Last Supper have remained through the centuries. The first disciples, after all, continued to attend the temple, as the Acts of the Apostles reminds us (2:46). We are told, by way of summary, that the first Christians "devoted themselves to the teaching of the apostles and to the communal life, to the breaking of the bread and to the prayers" (Acts 2:42). As a result, the early Christians probably accepted as obligatory and even inevitable the prayer structure we have just analyzed.

The first known text of a eucharistic prayer comes to us from Rome and is contained in the book *Apostolic Tradition*, which St. Hippolytus wrote around 217.[‡] In context, the prayer is suggested for the use of

‡ It is doubtful that this is the earliest example, that it came from Rome, and that Hippolytus is the author. See comments in vol. 1, p. 218.

a bishop who has just been consecrated and is presiding for the first time, as bishop, at the Eucharist of his community. The prayer follows the pattern we have indicated; we shall give the text of it a little further on because Eucharistic Prayer II in use today is based on it.

Beginning in the fourth century, a variety of eucharistic prayers came into existence, and the Eastern liturgies would end up with a large number of them. They can be reduced to two main types, according to their structure. Liturgies of the Antiochene type have eucharistic prayers organized as follows: exclamation; account of the history of salvation (anamnesis); consecration; continuation of the anamnesis and act of offering; prayers of petition (intercessions), among them a petition for the sending of the Spirit (epiclesis); final doxology. This is the more simple structure and is closer to the Jewish prayer of blessing. The Byzantine liturgy, which is the Eastern liturgy most familiar to us, usually uses a eucharistic prayer of this type.

Liturgies of the Alexandrian type have eucharistic prayers that follow a somewhat different structure: exclamation; intercessions and first epiclesis; consecration; anamnesis; second epiclesis and second group of intercessions; final doxology. The distinguishing mark of this group is that they introduce intercessions and an epiclesis before the consecration and then have a second epiclesis and a second group of intercessions after the consecration. The first of our present-day eucharistic prayers, that is, the old Roman Canon, is of this type.

The Eucharistic Prayers in Use Today

The single eucharistic prayer that was used for centuries down to our own time and is still used as Eucharistic Prayer I was already known, in a primitive form, to St. Ambrose, who records it in his little book *De sacramentis*. We cannot, of course, claim that such a prayer was used at Rome around 378 (the date of composition for the *De sacramentis*), but the fragmentary prayer there is very close.[§]

Why has the Church not continued to use only this single eucharistic prayer, which is, after all, quite beautiful? The answer is somewhat complex. From a catechetical viewpoint, the Roman Canon is

---

[§] Some commentators hesitate to claim that the text in Ambrose was actually in use because it appears to be an abbreviated form of the Roman Canon. Such concerns take an anachronistic view of the prayer.

not a whole whose internal structure can be readily grasped. It stands, as we indicated, in the Alexandrian line of eucharistic prayers, which have two epicleses and two groups of intercessions. The Antiochene pattern, on the contrary, is very simple and corresponds to an almost instinctive way of praying. Moreover, it is closer to the Jewish prayer of blessing and thus closer to the prayer Christ himself would have used. Thus, the adoption of other eucharistic prayers would be useful from both the historical and the catechetical points of view.

Furthermore, though the Roman Canon is a very beautiful composition, it does not bring out the action of the Holy Spirit in the eucharistic celebration. The Canon could have been "corrected," of course, but that would have marred an ancient composition that has its own values.

The choice was made, therefore, to introduce three new eucharistic prayers.** What is now our second eucharistic prayer is largely inspired by the prayer the *Apostolic Tradition* suggests for a newly consecrated bishop; we shall give the two texts side by side below. The third eucharistic prayer is a new composition, inspired by the Eastern anaphoras, as is the fourth, which contains a lengthy anamnesis.

The Pattern of the New Eucharistic Prayers

What scheme was adopted for the new eucharistic prayers? Well, to begin with, the theologians and liturgists faced a problem: the epiclesis. We must say a few words about this.

The epiclesis (Greek: *epikalein*, "to appeal to for help; invoke upon") is a prayer asking the Father to send the Holy Spirit. In itself, the term might be applied to any such prayer; in practice, the name is usually reserved for the prayer asking the Father to send the Holy Spirit upon the gifts that the Church is offering.††

Our Roman Canon seems never to have known an epiclesis. St. Ambrose, in his *De sacramentis*, lays a great deal of emphasis on the

---

** Nocent is referring to Eucharistic Prayers II, III, and IV. The ones for Masses of Reconciliation, Masses with Children, and Masses for Various Needs and Occasions were added later.

†† The nuptial blessings of the Roman Rite now include a prayer for the coming of the Holy Spirit upon the couple, which is commonly called an epiclesis. See, for example, the United States Conference of Catholic Bishops' Committee on Divine Worship's *Newsletter* 48 (July 2012): 32.

dynamic power of the word, and the "words of institution," of course, form the center of the eucharistic prayer. According to the traditional faith of the Church, it is these words that effect the change of the bread and wine into the Body and Blood of Christ.[4]

On the other hand, the eucharistic prayer of the *Apostolic Tradition* and the various Eastern eucharistic prayers all contain one or two epicleses. This epiclesis, however, raises a problem, though this is less true of the *Apostolic Tradition's* prayer than of the others. The epiclesis is a prayer that the Holy Spirit transform the bread and wine into the Body and Blood of Christ. But is that not accomplished by the words of institution? When the epiclesis comes before the consecration, it can be taken as a petition that the Spirit would come and act through the words the priest utters and thereby change the bread and wine into Christ's Body and Blood. But when the epiclesis comes after the con- secration, as it does in some liturgies, does it not implicitly deny the power of the words of institution? Such seemed to be the problem.

As a matter of fact, this statement of the problem reflects a typically Western outlook. Once the schism occurred between the Eastern and Western Churches, the problem thus posed became increasingly im- portant, and we find both sides marshaling even the most recondite and least probative arguments in order to brand the other side he- retical. And yet Eastern Catholics use the Eastern eucharistic prayers, for example, those of St. John Chrysostom and St. Basil, in which there is only one epiclesis, and it comes after the consecration—but they have never felt the slightest theological scruple!

If we look at the problem a little more carefully, we find that it is not as important as the theologians like to think. The theologians are the ones who have gotten themselves into difficulty by the way they carve up reality; the Christian people see no problem, because they hardly raise questions of this kind. Nonetheless, the Church has thought it wise not to cause possible disturbance to Western Christians and has therefore introduced two epicleses into each of the new eucharistic prayers: the first comes before the consecration and relates to it (a con- secratory epiclesis); the second comes after the consecration and relates chiefly to the union to be effected among those who will participate in the sacrifice by receiving Communion (a communion epiclesis).[‡‡]

---

‡‡ The second is never called an epiclesis in the *General Instruction on the Roman Missal*.

The new eucharistic prayers are thus of the Alexandrian type as far as the epiclesis is concerned, because there are two epicleses. They are, however, of the Antiochene type as far as the other intercessions are concerned, because they appear only at the end of the eucharistic prayer. The eucharistic prayers of the Alexandrian type, as we saw, have intercessions both before and after the consecration.

Before proceeding to a short analysis of the texts of the new eucharistic prayers, we should recall that the word *anaphora*, which Eastern Christians use, designates the eucharistic prayer as an "offering" of the sacrifice of Christ, whereas the Latin word *canon* designates the manner (*canon* = norm) in which the sacrifice of Christ is to be offered. "Anaphora" refers to the content of the prayer, while "canon" refers to the rule the prayer must follow in its construction.

A. EUCHARISTIC PRAYER II

The Anaphora of the Apostolic Tradition, the Source of Eucharistic Prayer II

The best and simplest way to approach Eucharistic Prayer II is to compare it with its source, the anaphora of the *Apostolic Tradition*, which we mentioned above. Here, then, is a literal translation of its text set side by side with the official English translation of the new Eucharistic Prayer II.[5]

Anaphora of the *Apostolic Tradition*	Eucharistic Prayer II
The Lord [be] with you . . .	℣. The Lord be with you.
And with your spirit.	℟. And with your spirit.
Up [with your] hearts.	℣. Lift up your hearts.
We have [them] to the Lord.	℟. We lift them up to the Lord.
Let us give thanks to the Lord.	℣. Let us give thanks to the Lord our God.
It is worthy and just . . .	℟. It is right and just.

Anaphora of the *Apostolic Tradition*	Eucharistic Prayer II
We render thanks to you, God,	It is truly right and just, our duty and our salvation, always and everywhere to give you thanks, Father most holy,
through your beloved Child Jesus Christ,	through your beloved Son, Jesus Christ,
whom in the last times you sent to us as savior and redeemer and angel of your will, who is your inseparable word, through whom you made all things and it was well pleasing to you,	your Word through whom you made all things, whom you sent as our Savior and Redeemer,
you sent from heaven into the virgin's womb, and who conceived in the womb was incarnate and manifested as your Son, born from the Holy Spirit and the virgin;	incarnate by the Holy Spirit and born of the Virgin.
who fulfilling your will and gaining for you a holy people stretched out [his] hands when he was suffering, that he might release from suffering those who believed in you;	Fulfilling your will and gaining for you a holy people, he stretched out his hands as he endured his Passion,
who when he was being handed over to voluntary suffering, that he might destroy death and break the bonds of the devil, and tread down hell and illuminate the righteous, and fix a limit and manifest the resurrection,	so as to break the bonds of death and manifest the resurrection.
	And so, with the Angels and all the Saints we declare your glory, as with one voice we acclaim: Holy, Holy, Holy Lord God of hosts. Heaven and earth are full of your glory. Hosanna in the highest. Blessed is he who comes in the name of the Lord. Hosanna in the highest.
	You are indeed Holy, O Lord, the fount of all holiness. Make holy, therefore, these gifts, we pray,

	by sending down your Spirit upon them like the dewfall, so that they may become for us the Body and + Blood of our Lord Jesus Christ.
taking bread [and] giving thanks to you, he said: "Take, eat, this is my body that will be broken for you." Likewise also the cup, saying: "This is my blood that is shed for you. When you do this, you do my remembrance."	At the time he was betrayed and entered willingly into his Passion, he took bread and, giving thanks, broke it, and gave it to his disciples, saying: TAKE THIS, ALL OF YOU, AND EAT OF IT, FOR THIS IS MY BODY, WHICH WILL BE GIVEN UP FOR YOU. In a similar way, when supper was ended,
	he took the chalice and, once more giving thanks, he gave it to his disciples, saying: TAKE THIS, ALL OF YOU, AND DRINK FROM IT, FOR THIS IS THE CHALICE OF MY BLOOD, THE BLOOD OF THE NEW AND ETERNAL COVENANT, WHICH WILL BE POURED OUT FOR YOU AND FOR MANY FOR THE FORGIVENESS OF SINS. DO THIS IN MEMORY OF ME.
	The mystery of faith. We proclaim your Death, O Lord, and profess your Resurrection until you come again. Or:
	When we eat this Bread and drink this Cup, we proclaim your Death, O Lord, until you come again. Or: Save us, Savior of the world, for by your Cross and Resurrection you have set us free.
Remembering therefore his death and resurrection, we offer to you the bread and cup, giving thanks to you because you have held us worthy to stand before you and minister to you.	Therefore, as we celebrate the memorial of his Death and Resurrection, we offer you, Lord, the Bread of life and the Chalice of salvation,

	giving thanks that you have held us worthy to be in your presence and minister to you.
And we ask that you would send your Holy Spirit in the oblation of [your] holy church, [that] gathering [them] into one you will give to all who partake of the holy things [to partake] in the fullness of the Holy Spirit, for the strengthening of faith in truth,	Humbly we pray that, partaking of the Body and Blood of Christ, we may be gathered into one by the Holy Spirit. Remember, Lord, your Church, spread throughout the world, and bring her to the fullness of charity, together with N. our Pope and N. our Bishop and all the clergy. Remember also our brothers and sisters who have fallen asleep in the hope of the resurrection, and all who have died in your mercy: welcome them into the light of your face. Have mercy on us all, we pray, that with the Blessed Virgin Mary, Mother of God, with the blessed Apostles, and all the Saints who have pleased you throughout the ages, we may merit to be coheirs to eternal life, and may praise and glorify you through your Son, Jesus Christ.
that we may praise and glorify you through your Child Jesus Christ, through whom [be] glory and honor to you, Father and Son with the Holy Spirit, in your holy church, both now and to the ages of ages. Amen.[§§]	Through him, and with him, and in him, O God, almighty Father, in the unity of the Holy Spirit, all honor and glory is yours, for ever and ever. Amen.

Even a cursory reading of the two texts shows that there are likenesses, but also rather profound differences, between them. We shall first offer some general reflections on them and then go on to particular points.

[§§] Paul Bradshaw, Maxwell E. Johnson, and L. Edward Phillips, *The* Apostolic Tradition: *A Commentary*, ed. Harold W. Attridge, Hermeneia (Minneapolis: Augsburg Fortress, 2002), 38–40.

Why Revise the Apostolic Tradition's *Text?*

Just as we would have found it regrettable had the ancient Roman Canon been revised, so we find it regrettable that the *Apostolic Tradition*'s text has been altered in the process of turning it into our present Eucharistic Prayer II. Why did this happen? We can see two motives operating: one was the desire to have its language resemble that of the other new eucharistic prayers; the other was the fear lest certain expressions or prayers undermine the orthodox faith.

The desire for *likeness* or parallelism is what led to the modification of the words of institution as found in the *Apostolic Tradition* as well as to the modification of the very beautiful, original, and theologically rich final doxology. *Fears* with regard to orthodoxy, on the other hand, led to the alteration of some expressions, to the introduction of an epiclesis before the consecration, and to the almost complete revision of the epiclesis after the consecration.

Likeness

In dealing with the first point, that is, the likeness between the eucharistic prayers, we shall enlarge the scope of the problem a bit by looking more closely at several expressions.

The anaphora of the *Apostolic Tradition* is addressed simply to "God" and not explicitly to the Father: "We render thanks to you, God. . . ." Yet clearly enough the Father is meant, since we thank God "through your beloved Child Jesus Christ." The words "your beloved Child" have, however, a fullness of meaning that is not quite captured by the English "your beloved Son." The Greek word for "child" also means "servant" and thus is linked up with the terminology of Isaiah and with his poem about the servant who gives his life for the multitude. When the first part of the anaphora was turned into a "preface," the experts preferred to make the text resemble other prefaces in style and language.

The eucharistic prayer of the *Apostolic Tradition* contains no *Sanctus*. It was decided to introduce one; this, in turn, made it necessary to introduce the words that traditionally lead into the *Sanctus*.

In addition, it was quite to be expected that some expressions that are vague and difficult to understand should be eliminated, for example, "fix a limit." On the other hand, there was perhaps an excessive fear of such expressions as "break the bonds of the devil" and "tread down hell." After all, it would have been easy for anyone who understood the text to read it with the eyes of those who lived at the time of its composition and to draw profit from these vivid, visual expressions.

The modification of the doxology was probably due to the desire to be able to sing it according to the familiar melody. Yet it would not have been difficult to compose another doxology for use in singing while preserving the original doxology for use when the prayer was to be spoken rather than sung. The reason for thus preserving it would be that it contains a theology that is of some interest. It expresses very well the meaning of the eucharistic offering: the praise and glory of the Father, which, however, we cannot give without faith and the interior action of the Holy Spirit. Then too the expression "with the Holy Spirit, in your holy church" (a favorite found elsewhere in the *Apostolic Tradition*) offers a perspective with which Western Christians are unfamiliar. It emphasizes the importance of the Holy Spirit's action in everything the Church does.

Fears

Some corrections were motivated by fear of doctrinal confusion. Thus, early in the anaphora the *Apostolic Tradition* speaks in a way that might have caused the modern Christian to raise an eyebrow: "conceived in the womb was incarnate and manifested as your Son." On first hearing this, we might suppose the prayer to be saying that the Son became the Son through the incarnation, whereas, in fact, the Son, like the Father, is from all eternity.

That is not what the *Apostolic Tradition* means. Rather, its theology is very close to that of St. John. In St. John's view, that which characterizes the Son and gives the very name "Son" its full depth of meaning is Christ's will to be obedient and to serve. He came on earth to do the Father's will, and that meant becoming incarnate; it was this act of obedience that elicited the Father's words at the transfiguration: "This is my beloved Son" (Matt 17:5). Thus, the incarnation earned the name of "Son" for Jesus even more than before; that is to say, he shows himself to be truly the Son by becoming incarnate out of obedience. He is certainly the Son from all eternity, but the incarnation, like the paschal mystery, reveals him more than ever to be the Son who makes his own the Father's eternal plan and carries out the

Father's redemptive will. The *Apostolic Tradition* expresses the same idea in the next sentence when it speaks of Christ as "fulfilling your will and gaining for you a holy people."

The most important changes introduced into the text relate to the epicleses. We mentioned the problem of the epiclesis earlier; let us dwell on it here again for a moment.

It is not exceptional to find a single anaphora containing two prayers asking the Father to send the Spirit; the various anaphoras of the Alexandrian type have two epicleses. The *Apostolic Tradition*'s prayer, however, has only one and thus resembles anaphoras of the Antiochene type.

The old Roman Canon has no epiclesis before the consecration, but it does have a prayer asking for the consecration. In order to make the new Eucharistic Prayer II resemble the Roman Canon more closely, it was decided to introduce into it a pre-consecration epiclesis. (The prayer in the Roman Canon reads: "Be pleased, O God, we pray, to bless, acknowledge, and approve this offering in every respect, make it spiritual and acceptable, so that it may become for us the Body and Blood of your most beloved Son, our Lord Jesus Christ.")

The chief purpose in thus making the two eucharistic prayers parallel was to highlight the full consecratory power of the words of institution. It is a matter of faith that the words of Christ are what effects the consecration of the bread and wine. The power of the word is much stressed by the fathers, and especially by St. Ambrose, whose treatise *De sacramentis* quotes the central section of the Roman Canon,*** as we shall see. In this treatise the saint coins a phrase that expresses the power of the words used in the sacraments: *operatorius sermo*, "effective words."[6] In the context, he is speaking of baptism and of Christ's words at the end of St. Matthew's gospel, but he makes the same claim with regard to the Eucharist:

> By what words is the consecration effected, and whose words are they? The words of the Lord Jesus. . . . It is the words of Christ that produce the sacrament.
> What is the nature of this word of Christ? It is the word by which all things were made. . . . He spoke and it [the body of Christ] was made;

*** Nocent presumes that Ambrose knew a longer prayer and quoted part of it, but it is more likely that Ambrose recorded all that he knew and that the Roman Canon grew in length afterward.

he issued the order and it was created. . . . Understand, then, that the word of Christ is accustomed to transforming every creature and that it changes the very laws of nature when he so wills.[7]

In another little work, the *De mysteriis*, we find the same emphasis on the power of Christ's words:

If a blessing bestowed by a human [Elisha] was powerful enough to change nature, what are we to say of a consecration that God himself effects, that is, a consecration in which the words of the Lord and Savior himself are the active force at work? For the sacrament you receive is produced by the words of Christ. . . . If the word of Christ could make out of nothing that which previously did not exist, can it not change what exists into what previously did not exist?[8]

It was this power of the word that the liturgical experts and theologians wished to emphasize, and they were afraid that if the eucharistic prayer had only an epiclesis after the consecration, this epiclesis would lessen the importance of the consecration itself in the minds of those listening to the prayer. A pre-consecration epiclesis, on the other hand, directs attention ahead to the consecration that will take place through the intervention of the Spirit, as the Spirit gives power once again to the words that Christ once spoke and that he now speaks again.

As for the post-consecration epiclesis common to all the Eastern anaphoras, it was decided not to eliminate it. The text has, however, been much altered.

The *Apostolic Tradition* asks simply that God would send his Holy Spirit upon the Church's offering. It is not explicitly asking for the Spirit to effect the change of the elements, though many have so interpreted it. In what, then, does the activity of the Spirit consist? The prayer seems to tell us in the next sentence: The Spirit's activity consists in uniting the faithful who participate in the mysteries. The Spirit is to act within them and strengthen their faith in the truth.

We should note the connection the *Apostolic Tradition* establishes between participation in the Eucharist (the point at which the Spirit intervenes), the unification of the faithful, and the strengthening of their faith. In Eucharistic Prayer II the connection is weakened because the components of the original epiclesis are separated and distributed in two epicleses: the pre-consecration epiclesis asks that the Spirit be sent for the consecration, while the post-consecration epiclesis asks that, having shared in the Body and Blood of Christ, we may be gathered by the Spirit into a single body. It is not quite clear that the reason why we are gathered into a single body is because we share in the Body and Blood of Christ in which the Spirit works upon us.

A final point to be made is that the intercessions of Eucharistic Prayer II are not to be found in the *Apostolic Tradition*'s anaphora.

In summary, the eucharistic prayer of the *Apostolic Tradition* is of the Antiochene type, while the new Eucharistic Prayer II is of a mixed type: it is Alexandrian in that it contains two epicleses and Antiochene in that it contains intercessions only after the consecration.

One last note: The anaphora of the *Apostolic Tradition* contains a number of expressions that match typical expressions of St. Irenaeus that are found nowhere else. As such, this venerable prayer is a real jewel. We should learn to love it, use it, and meditate on it. We shall have an even better understanding of it after we have studied the other eucharistic prayers now in use.

B. EUCHARISTIC PRAYER III

This eucharistic prayer, like the fourth, is a recent composition inspired by the Eastern anaphoras.

Its Structure

The preface of this eucharistic prayer can vary according to the celebration; the body of the prayer is linked to what precedes the *Sanctus*, by means of the words: "You are indeed Holy, O Lord."

The structure of the prayer is quite simple. It begins with an exclamation of praise: "You are indeed Holy, O Lord, and all you have created rightly gives you praise." This is followed by the motives for the exclamation: the gift of life, the sanctification of all things, the gathering of a people that is capable of offering the Father a pure sacrifice. These motives form the anamnesis, or "remembering," which actualizes the mysteries now past.

The intervention of the Spirit is required if the Church is to be able to offer this pure sacrifice. Therefore, there is a first epiclesis, which asks for the consecration that will immediately follow. We bring the gifts, but it is God who must consecrate them by sending his Spirit upon them.

After the consecration, there is a continuation of the anamnesis, with reference now to the mysteries of Christ: his passion, resurrection, and ascension. This is followed by the climactic act of offering: Together with Christ and his Church, we offer the holy and living sacrifice that is now present on the altar, thanks to the intervention of the Holy Spirit. We make this offering as a people that awaits Christ's return at his second coming. Each Eucharist advances us on the road toward the last day.

There is now a second epiclesis, which asks that the Holy Spirit fill us at our reception of the Body and Blood of Christ and unite us all into a single body.[†††]

The second epiclesis is followed by intercessions. We should note the emphasis on reconciliation with God, on salvation that is meant to reach the entire world, and on the strengthening of faith and love. As for the commendations of human beings to God, there could have been a different order in the listing. As it stands, the list begins with the pope and ends with "the entire people you have gained for your own." Vatican II's Dogmatic Constitution on the Church gives first place to the people of God; perhaps the list should have been modified slightly to begin with the people of God and then move on to its head, the pope, and the local bishop, priests, and deacons.

At the end of the intercession for the living, there is a happy repetition of the prayer for unity: "in your compassion, O merciful Father, gather to yourself all your children scattered throughout the world." The phrasing of the intercession for the dead is excellent: "To our departed brothers and sisters and to all who were pleasing to you at their passing from this life, give kind admittance to your kingdom." The eucharistic prayer ends with the doxology.

The structure, then, is the same as in Eucharistic Prayer II, but it is filled out somewhat more. This is a prayer all of us should love and use in our personal prayer.

[†††] To be precise, the prayer is only for unity. It presumes that those who are nourished with the Body and Blood of Christ will be filled with the Holy Spirit. The missal never refers to this as an epiclesis.

C. EUCHARISTIC PRAYER IV

Its Structure

Although broken up to a certain extent by the *Sanctus*, this prayer is nicely unified. It is the prayer closest to the Jewish blessing that we mentioned earlier. Unfortunately, it is used too infrequently, and this for a paltry reason: "It's too long!" Its structure, again, is simple, but its content is rich.

Following the normal structure of an anaphora, the prayer begins with an exclamation of praise—in this instance, praise of God for creation. The Father is the source of life and has created the world so that he might heap his blessings upon his creatures. This first part of the anamnesis leads us into the *Sanctus*, after which the anamnesis resumes. The focus shifts now to the creation of humanity in God's image and to the history of salvation: sin, repeated covenants, and finally the sending of the Son and the mystery of our redemption.

The Holy Spirit brings Christ's work in the world to completion; it is appropriate at this point, therefore, to ask the Father to let the Spirit sanctify the gifts so that they may become the Body and Blood of the Son (first epiclesis). After the words of institution, the anamnesis resumes once again and terminates in the offering of the Son's Body and Blood to the Father. It is followed in turn by the second epiclesis, which asks that the Holy Spirit make one body of all who participate in Christ's Body and Blood so that the participants may themselves become, in Christ, a living sacrifice to the praise of God's glory.

At this point the intercessions begin. Here again (as in Eucharistic Prayer III), the list of those commended to God could have begun with the holy people of God and then gone on to the visible head (the pope), the local bishop, all the bishops, etc. Note the fine prayer for all who seek God with a sincere heart. The prayer ends with the classical doxology.

Value of the New Eucharistic Prayers

It must be acknowledged that the new eucharistic prayers form an attractive initiation to prayer. If trouble were taken to teach people the very simple scheme followed in these prayers, the scheme that is almost instinctive when one enters into conversation with God, the results would be most advantageous for the prayer life of the Church. The divorce too often found between personal prayer and liturgical prayer would be ended, since the style of prayer would be the same in both cases. If we ignore the technical aspect of the eucharistic prayers and focus our attention on their basic form, must we not judge them capable of leading many to a kind of prayer that they have hitherto thought beyond them? How readily the Christian might learn to respond almost instinctively to any event of the week with a prayer along the lines of these anaphoras! The habit of quick and spontaneous dialogue with God would soon develop.

D. Eucharistic Prayer I and the Roman Canon

Why do we consider last the Roman Canon, which is the first of our present-day eucharistic prayers? We do so because we think the Roman Canon becomes more accessible once we have examined the other three prayers, which in their structure are more like the original source, namely, the Jewish blessing. The problem with the Roman Canon, which is an anaphora of the Alexandrian type in that it has intercessions both before and after the consecration, is that it does not strike us as a unified whole; it gives the false impression of being a composite of elements juxtaposed and artificially united. This impression used to be intensified by the fad that Amens had been introduced into the body of the text as acclamations that rendered possible a certain amount of active participation by the faithful.‡‡‡

We will gain a better understanding of the Roman Canon if we look at its sources and evolution. It is clearly impossible, of course, to do a complete study that would begin with St. Ambrose's *De sacramentis* and follow the development of the text through the intermediate forms to the time of St. Gregory the Great, when the text achieved a form almost identical with the one we now have. We must be satisfied to give the text as found in St. Ambrose, then the text used in the old Spanish liturgy, and finally the Canon as we have known it in modern times.

---

‡‡‡ The practice was indeed a "fad" never officially promoted in the Church. Even when the Amens first appeared in the Roman Canon, the prayer was being recited entirely by the priest in a low voice.

Here is what St. Ambrose says about the part of the Canon that precedes the consecration:

> By what words is the consecration effected, and whose words are they? The words of the Lord Jesus. *Everything that is said up to this point is said by the priest: praise is given to God, prayer is offered to him, intercessions are made for the people, the rulers, and everyone else.* But when the moment comes to produce the august Sacrament, the priest no longer uses his own words but the words of Christ.[9]

That is a description of how the eucharistic prayer began in the time of St. Ambrose. As we can see, there was an exclamation of praise, along with intercessions whose objects are named.

We can turn now to the heart of the Canon. We shall place in parallel columns the text given by St. Ambrose, the text found in the old Spanish liturgy, and the text of the Roman Canon of St. Gregory the Great (which we shall here translate in a literal manner, for the sake of the parallelism):

St. Ambrose	Old Spanish Liturgy	Gregorian Sacramentary
Acknowledge this oblation for us, make it spiritual and acceptable, for it is a figure of the body and blood of our Lord Jesus Christ.	Be pleased, O God, to bless their offering, make it spiritual and acceptable. It is the image and likeness of the body and blood of Jesus Christ your Son and our Redeemer.[11]	Be pleased, O God, we pray, to bless, acknowledge, and approve this offering in every respect; make it spiritual and acceptable, so that it may become for us the Body and Blood of your most beloved Son, our Lord God Jesus Christ.
On the day before he was to suffer, he took bread in his holy hands, looked to heaven, to you, holy Father, almighty, eternal God, giving thanks, he said the blessing, broke, and passed it broken to the apostles and his disciples, saying, "Take this, all of you, and consume of it, for this is my body, which will be broken for many."[10]		On the day before he was to suffer, he took bread in his holy and venerable hands, with eyes raised to heaven to you, O God, his almighty Father, giving you thanks, he said the blessing, broke the bread, gave it to his disciples, saying: "Take this, all of you, and eat of it, for this is my body."[12]

St. Ambrose	Old Spanish Liturgy	Gregorian Sacramentary
Take note. Similarly also, on the day before he was to suffer, when supper was ended, he took the chalice, looked to heaven, to you, holy Father, almighty, eternal God, giving thanks, he said the blessing, and passed it to the apostles and his disciples, saying, "Take this, all of you, and drink from it, for this is my blood." . . .		In a similar way, when supper was ended, he took this precious chalice in his holy and venerable hands, and once more giving you thanks, he said the blessing, gave the chalice to his disciples, saying: Take this, all of you, and drink from it, for this is the chalice of my blood, the blood of the new and eternal covenant, the mystery of faith, which will be poured out for you and for many for the forgiveness of sins. Whenever you will have done these things, you will do them in memory of me.
Therefore, as we celebrate the memorial of his most glorious passion and resurrection from the dead and ascension into heaven, we offer you this spotless victim, a spiritual sacrifice, an unbloody victim, this holy bread and the chalice of eternal life.	Therefore, eternal and almighty God, as we celebrate the memorial of the most glorious Passion of your Son, our Lord Jesus Christ, and of his resurrection and his ascension. . . .	Therefore, O Lord, as we celebrate the memorial of the blessed Passion, the Resurrection from the dead, and the glorious Ascension into heaven of Christ, your Son, our Lord God, we who are your servants and your holy people, offer to your glorious majesty from the gifts that you have given us, this pure victim, this holy victim, this spotless victim, the holy Bread of eternal life and the Chalice of everlasting salvation.
A upon your altar on high through the hands of your angels,	**B** We implore that as you have accepted this offering, you will also bless those humbly praying, as you accepted the gifts of your servant Abel the just, the sacrifice of Abraham our Father Patriarch in faith, and the offerings of your high priest Melchizedek.	**B** Be pleased to look upon these offerings with a serene and kindly countenance, and to accept them, as once you were pleased to accept the gifts of your servant Abel the just, the sacrifice of Abraham, our father in faith, and the offering of your high priest Melchizedek, a holy sacrifice, a spotless victim.

St. Ambrose	Old Spanish Liturgy	Gregorian Sacramentary
	Let your blessing descend here invisibly, I pray you, as once it descended visibly on the sacrifices of our fathers.	
B just as you were pleased to receive the gifts of your servant Abel the just, the sacrifice of Abraham, our father in faith, and the offering of the high priest Melchizedek.[13]	**A** May an aroma of sweetness ascend by the hands of your Angel from this your high altar in the sight of your divine majesty.[14]	**A** In humble prayer we ask you, almighty God: command that these gifts be borne by the hands of your Angel to your altar on high in the sight of your divine majesty, so that all of us, who through this participation at the altar receive the most holy Body and Blood of your Son, may be filled with every grace and heavenly blessing. Through Christ our Lord.

Likeness of the Three Prayers

Let us stop here after this first half of the Canon. The likeness of each of the three prayers to the others is striking. The most important thing to be noted, however, is the eucharistic theology that finds expression in the three prayers.

The Gregorian Sacramentary has omitted the words "figure," "image," and "likeness." On the other hand, it connects the acceptance of the offering by God with the fact that the offering becomes the Body and Blood of Christ.

For St. Ambrose, the Father accepts the sacrifice because it is "a figure" of the Body and Blood of our Lord Jesus Christ. In the Spanish prayer, he accepts it because it is "the image and likeness" of the Body and Blood of Jesus Christ. The Gregorian Sacramentary does not contain this idea, though it is an important one, for it expresses a sacramental theology we cannot afford to neglect.

The *Euchologion* (prayer book) of Bishop Serapion of Thmuis contains an anaphora of the Alexandrian type in which the term "likeness" occurs with relation to the Body and Blood of Christ:

> We offer you this bread, the likeness of the body of the Only-Begotten.
> This bread is the likeness of the holy body. For the Lord Jesus Christ,
> on the night he was handed over, took bread and broke it and gave it
> to his disciples, saying: "Take and eat, this is my body which is broken
> for you for the forgiveness of sins." Therefore, celebrating the likeness
> of his death, we have offered the bread, and we pray: Through this
> sacrifice be reconciled with all of us and have mercy, God of truth.[15]

The same expressions are then repeated in regard to the cup.

There is thus only one sacrifice, that of the cross, but it is actualized,
that is, made present and operative here and now. This element of
actualization is proper to Catholic worship. We do not celebrate just
any sacrifice; we offer the sacrifice, namely, the sacrifice of Christ
himself. "Likeness" does not mean something that resembles that
sacrifice, just as "image" does not mean a simple analogue, or "figure," an object that is somehow like another. Each of these terms, on
the contrary, signifies the reality itself as present in a different mode.
They all mean, concretely, what we in the West speak of as "the unbloody manner" in which the historical sacrifice of Christ is present.

The key idea, then, is that our offering is accepted precisely because
it contains the very reality of the one sacrifice of Christ. St. Ambrose
and the Gregorian Sacramentary emphasize this when they speak of
the offering as "spiritual." It is accepted because it is spiritual; the
Lord has no need of material offerings.

Differences

The Spanish liturgy and the Gregorian Sacramentary contain some
important modifications in comparison with the text of St. Ambrose.
In St. Ambrose the sections we have marked A and B form a single
whole. The prayer begins by asking that God would have his angels
bring the offering to the heavenly altar and that he would accept it.
It then goes on to give examples of such acceptance by God in the
pre-Christian period: Let God accept the offering as he accepted those
of Abel, Abraham, and Melchizedek.

In the Spanish liturgy and the Gregorian Sacramentary, A and B
are reversed. That is to say, the prayer begins with the plea for acceptance and the giving of the motivating parallels from the Old Testament. In the Gregorian Sacramentary, this first part, or B, is an
independent entity. In the Spanish liturgy, the examples are given in

the very first place and are followed by the prayer that God would accept the present sacrifice in the same way; this prayer is expanded, however, and runs over into A, that is, the prayer that God would let the sacrifice ascend into his glorious presence.

In the Gregorian Sacramentary, B, as we said, is an independent entity, clearly distinct and separate from what follows. A is introduced, in fact, by a formula frequently used at the beginning of presidential prayers: "In humble prayer we ask you, almighty God." It would seem that the introduction of this formula took place at a relatively late date and had the effect of separating A from B. The Gregorian Sacramentary asks not only that an angel carry the sacrifice into God's presence but also that God would bestow his heavenly blessings on all who receive the Body and Blood of Christ; thus, the latter becomes an epiclesis in the broad sense (the Spirit is not explicitly mentioned), comparable to the post-consecration epiclesis in the *Apostolic Tradition*.

We may note also that the Spanish prayer does not ask that the offering be taken to the heavenly altar, as the Gregorian Sacramentary does, but rather that it be taken from the earthly altar of the Lord into his heavenly presence. Ambrose's prayer asks that the offering be taken in the hands of *angels*, while the Spanish prayer and the Gregorian Sacramentary speak of it being carried by an *angel*. Consequently, there is no reason to see in the angel of the Roman Canon a reference to Christ or the Holy Spirit or some other nonangelic personage.

It is easy, in the light of our analysis, to discern the Alexandrian structure of the Roman Canon: exclamation, beginning of an anamnesis, intercessions, prayer for the consecration, consecration, anamnesis, offering and petition for acceptance of the sacrifice, intercessions, and doxology.

This eucharistic prayer has certain deficiencies, such as the lack of an explicit prayer for the intervention of the Holy Spirit. It has the great merit, however, of strongly emphasizing the sacrificial aspect of the Mass. It also makes it clear that the one sacrifice of Christ, which is actualized in the Mass, is present and manifested through an unbloody rite. This is a theology we find in both Serapion and Ambrose and later in the teaching of the Council of Trent.

4. Liturgical Theology of the Presidential Prayers: God's Love for Humanity, Humanity's Love for God

The various presidential prayers of the Sundays of Ordinary Time were not chosen with the readings or chants in mind; they are, in fact, used in all three years of the cycle. Consequently, it is neither necessary nor useful to comment on them when dealing with the readings for each Sunday.

On the other hand, these prayers should not simply be overlooked, and we have therefore decided to offer a synthetic presentation of them. They contain a theology we should not neglect; in fact, when we bring together those that follow the same general line of thought, we find a theology that is quite rich. We shall, of course, make no effort to exhaust the content of these prayers; this essay should rather be thought of as a first approach to the prayers. Since our interest here is pastoral, we shall not indicate the ancient sources of the prayers or, alternatively, the fact that they are modern compositions; that kind of information can easily be found elsewhere. The reader can consult the articles published by the experts who worked on the revision of the Roman Missal.[1] (In the following pages, the bracketed numbers indicate the Sunday in Ordinary Time to which the prayer in question belongs.)

1. The Collects

These prayers are called "collects," that is, prayers in which the celebrant gathers together and summarizes in a general statement the intentions of all.

A simple survey of these prayers will bring to light the broad range of themes that find expression in them. The prayers have to do with the history of creation, with the guidance of providence, and above all with the love of God, with his grace that anticipates and accompanies our actions, and with the response we should make to God's concern for us. We must eliminate evil from our lives and keep ever before our minds the blessings to come. Such are the main thoughts to be found in these prayers.

Creation, Providence, Today's World

The Lord is Creator and ruler of all things [24]; he is the God of the universe who governs heaven and earth [2]; he is also the King of the universe (feast of Christ the King) and guides the world with a providence that never fails in its design [9].

When we contemplate the whole work of creation and the whole divine plan of salvation, we glory that God is our Creator and guide [18]. The proof of God's power is given to us not only by his creative action and his providential guidance of all things but also by his unwearying pardon and mercy [26].

Creation was ruined by sin, and the sins of humanity continue to deface it. We ask the Lord to restore his creation [18] and to free it from its enslavement (feast of Christ the King). He alone can establish in the world the peace that we need [8] and that our age seeks [2]. Amid a world that is constantly changing, we ask him to establish us where true gladness is found [21].

God's Love for Us

God's kindness is limitless [27]. He loves us like a father [23], and his kindness to us, like his love, is inexhaustible [18].

This love is manifested in the blessings that God constantly bestows so lavishly on us. The first and greatest blessing is his very own Son, whom he sent so that we might become adoptive sons and daughters [23]. His grace has made us children of light and will keep us ever within the bright light of truth [13]. We are capable of manifesting the light because God himself shows us that light and points out the right path to us [15]. It is from him that every good gift comes [22]; he is the source of all good things [10].

God's basic action on the world's behalf is his will to raise it up through the abasement of his own Son [14]. God's love for humanity is so great that he desires to dwell in just and true hearts and to make of us his dwelling place [6].

His love is constantly being manifested by the way he keeps safe his family, the Church [5].

The Response to Love

The aim of every Christian must be to revere and love God's holy name, set firm on the foundation of God's love [12] that allows us to call God our Father [19].

The proper response to love consists in following God's commands and in devoting ourselves, in resolve and deeds, to what the love of God requires of us [11]. Our weakness, however, does not allow us to live in so perfect a way, and God himself therefore must give us the power to love what he commands [30]. He must instill a filial spirit in us and make it grow to perfection [19]; he must pour into our hearts a warm love for him [20]; he must put love for his name into our hearts [22] and direct our actions according to his good pleasure [3]. In this way we shall gradually come to love God in all things and above all things [20], for it will be God himself who makes us love what he commands [30] and confirm our wills to his [29].

The love of God and the unconditional worship he requires necessarily imply a love for others that springs from truth of heart [4]. The law requires that we love not only God but our neighbor too [25].

If the faithful who have been rescued from slavery thus conform themselves to God's will in both word and deed [7], they will live with holy joy [14] and will feel the working of God's mercy [24]. They will rejoice as people who serve the Lord in peace [8] because they serve him with all their heart [24]. This people will know the full and lasting happiness that springs from service [33] rendered to the majesty of the Lord [29]; their happiness will be all the greater because they know that the Lord himself must give his grace if people are to be able to offer right and praiseworthy service [31].

God, the Servant of Humanity

God is truly at the service of humanity when it comes to going before people and following after them in all they do [28]. God constantly guides people [12], inspires them to discern what is right, and guides them in the doing [10]. He fills them with his kindness far beyond their merits and even their desires [27]; he will even bestow on them what they do not dare to ask for [27]. He increases his gifts of grace [16], which alone gives people hope [5], and without which they can do nothing [11] and nothing is holy or has a firm foundation [17].

We look to the gracious God to increase our faith, hope, and love [30]. Only if he grants us true freedom [23] and enables us to unite our hearts in a single purpose [21] will we be so fashioned by his grace [6] that God, ever at our service, constantly wishes to give us.

Called in Christ's Name

Because of God's gifts to us, we can live in Christ's name, rejecting what is contrary to that name and striving after all that does it honor [15]. Such a rejection and pursuit presuppose that we are free enough to pursue the things that are God's [32] with constant gladness [33] and a peaceful conscience [27]. No one is perfect, however; each in the course of life experiences the unwearying pardon and mercy of God [26].

We cannot successfully make good use of things that pass and hold fast to those that endure [17] unless the Lord gives us power to carry out good works [28] and fosters what is good in us, by watching over us and keeping safe what he has nurtured [22]. Consequently, if we abound in good works in Christ's name, that too is already God's gift to us [3].

The Vision of the World to Come

In accord with our baptismal promises, we are to live a life of love by keeping God's precepts to attain eternal life [25]. But we must even look to God to desire what God promises [21]. God must enable the faithful to hasten without stumbling [31; 26] toward the promised blessings. It is the Lord himself who must give them eternal gladness [14] and the unseen blessings prepared for them [20]. The Christian therefore has but one desire: to merit what God promises [30]; to enter into the promised inheritance, which surpasses all human desire [19; 20]; and to reach the treasures of heaven [26]. Such a concentration on the world to come, while we are still residents of this world, would be impossible if God himself were not the strength of those who hope in him [11].

The collects thus contain a rich teaching about the encounter between God and humanity, between God's generous, indeed limitless, initiative and humanity's need. These prayers were certainly not selected in order to present a carefully elaborated systematic theology, but nonetheless, Sunday after Sunday, they do help deepen our appreciation of the divine realities that are the basis of our life, though only too often we do not reflect upon them.

2. The Prayers over the Offerings

The collects were fairly general in their statements. The prayers over the offerings will now offer us an experiential theology of the life of worship. In these prayers the worshipers are seen offering with Christ and the Church the sacrifice that establishes the world in unity and leads it toward its final salvation. The prayers contain a profound theology of the Eucharist and of the meaning of the sacrifice; they also bring to light the various effects of the spiritual sacrifice that is offered in the celebration, especially the effects of pardon and purification, which are an aspect of the eucharistic celebration that is too often neglected.

We Offer What the Lord Has Given to Us

Four of the prayers over the offerings emphasize the fact that it is God himself who has given us what we are now offering to him. (This idea found expression long ago in the Roman Canon, which is now our first eucharistic prayer.) The Lord provides us what we are then to offer to his name [8]; the gifts we give we have because of his abundant generosity to us [17]. It is in an act of mercy that he has given them to us so that we may offer them back to him [19]. One of the four prayers gives a more theological expression to the deeper meaning of our offering: The offering of the eucharistic gifts is part of a marvelous exchange in which we offer God what he has first given us, and then he in turn gives us his very self [20]. This last happens because when we offer the gifts we have received, they are transformed into the Body and Blood of the Lord.

A Spiritual Sacrifice

Our offering is first and foremost an act of love, the desire being signified by what we offer [8]. We must be careful to understand what is meant by our placing our offerings on the altar [4] and the Lord's receiving them from the faithful [16]. There is, in fact, a single sacrificial offering: it was made by the one Priest, Christ, as a spiritual sacrifice [18]. We, however, participate in the offering of that sacrifice [2] and thereby enter into the mystery of Christ's passion [32].

The gifts we bring signify our interior disposition; they will be sanctified [3] and become for us the sacrament of a new life and a food to nourish us [11].

The Lord can make of our offering the mystery of our salvation [19]; the bread and wine God originally gave us for our earthly nourishment become here the sacrament of eternal life [5]. The eucharistic celebration actualizes the paschal mystery (i.e., makes it present and effective here and now), for every time this memorial sacrifice is celebrated, the work of our redemption is accomplished [2]. The power of the Lord himself accomplishes what we celebrate in mystery [22], that is, in the commemoration of the perfect sacrifice of the cross, which itself brought to completion the sacrifices of the old law [16].

The eucharistic celebration thereby gives glory to the Father for what he has done: we pray that the celebration may give homage to God's glory and majesty [23; 30]. In fact, since the offerings represent us, we can ask the Lord to turn us, and not only our gifts, into an eternal offering to God [18].

God's Adopted Children, United in Mind and Heart

The sacrifice of the cross was a covenant sacrifice that reestablished the world in unity. Through the one sacrifice of the cross, the Lord acquired a people by adoption [21]. Participation in the Eucharist is meant to strengthen the bonds of unity in mind and heart [23]: our offering will obtain growth in charity [10]. In the eucharistic celebration the Lord bestows on his Church the gifts of unity and peace [21], so that the gifts offered by each one may benefit the salvation of all [16].

We Are Purified and Renewed

The effect of purification and forgiveness, which in the past was frequently mentioned in the postcommunion prayers as a reminder to those who had shared in the Body and Blood of Christ, is now more frequently to be found in the prayers over the offerings.

The Eucharist cleanses and renews us [6]; we are cleansed by the mysteries we serve [9]. The sacrifice we offer is one of conciliation and praise [12], and the Lord looks upon it with favor [32]. The Eucharist is a holy outpouring of God's mercy to us [31], and we are purified by the very mystery we serve [14; 29].

Our bodies and our spirits both profit by the sacramental sustenance given us for our new life [11]; the Eucharist sanctifies those whom the Father has redeemed through his Son [27]. The faithful who receive these gifts advance toward greater holiness [15], for in these mysteries divine grace is powerfully at work [17] to sanctify us in our present way of life [17].

Salvation and the Blessings to Come

One of the most common themes is the effectiveness of the Eucharist in leading us to salvation; we pray that the offerings may become the sacrament of our salvation [3; 4; 7; 22]. The eucharistic celebration wins for the faithful those blessings they profess with devotion and faith [25]. Faith and hope, though, are not enough; the Christian must also do the Father's will, for it is to those who do God's will that the Eucharist is the source of eternal reward [6]. If we have faith and hope and if we do God's will, the mysteries will lead us to eternal gladness [17; 33]. The gifts we offer will then help us attain their reward [8]. The eucharistic sacrifice leads us day by day to the life of heaven [14], and the liturgy, when celebrated with love, will help us pass over to the glory of heaven [28].

3. The Prayers after Communion

As we would expect, these prayers likewise provide a rich experiential theology of the eucharistic celebration. Our effort here, once again, will simply be to outline the content of the prayers with a minimum of interpretive commentary.

Become What We Have Received

Our deeply intimate union with the Christ we have received is one of the favorite themes of these prayers after Communion. The idea that we will be transformed into what we have consumed [27] best sums up the hope of the believer who participates in the Body and Blood of Christ. Communion with the holy mysteries foreshadows the union of the faithful with Christ [11] and makes us coheirs with him [20]. Partaking of the Eucharist conforms us to the image of Christ while we are on earth [20] and also makes us sharers of his divine nature [28].

The prayers are thus emphasizing the profound renewal and transformation that takes place. The Eucharist is meant to heal and perfect us [21]. It frees us from doing evil and leads us to what is right [10], giving us new help for the purpose [29]. Participation in the Eucharist affects minds and bodies [24], restoring them both [26]. This idea of the restoration of humanity is a frequent theme: we are renewed by heavenly gifts [18], by the Body and Blood of Christ [12]; we receive the grace of a new life [3], into which our Communion makes us pass [16].

The sacraments thus perfect in us what lies within them [30]. The eucharistic celebration is a perpetual memorial of the passion of Christ [17], and from it we are to gain the prize of our salvation [14]. Bound now to Christ by a love that will never pass away, we are to bear fruit that will likewise last forever [13], while the manner of our life strengthens us to do so [25].

The Eucharist is in all truth the sacrament of our eternal salvation [4]; it confirms us [19] and intensifies the effects of salvation [15]. It makes us advance in the light of the truth [19]. The influence of eucharistic grace prevails over our own desires [24], to the point that our words and speech become a witness to the Lord [9].

The action of the Holy Spirit is perhaps too infrequently mentioned in these prayers, but it is extremely important. Now that God has fed us with his Son's Body and Blood, may he also govern us by his Spirit [9]; now that we have received power from on high, may the Spirit keep us in the grace of integrity [32].

The Sacrament of Unity

We have been fed with the one bread; may we now be one in mind and heart [2]. Such unity demands that we serve one another; the

Eucharist intensifies our love and rouses us to serve our neighbor [22]. Being the actualization of the paschal mystery, the Eucharist unites the Church, and our Communion contributes to this unity [11].

The Eucharist has effects beyond the Church, however, for it transforms the world as a whole, inasmuch as we who eat the one bread and drink the one cup must be so one with Christ in our lives that we will be able to bear fruit for the salvation of the world [5].

The Sacrament of the Kingdom

What do we do in the Eucharist if not praise the Father for all he has accomplished through the paschal mystery of his Son? We therefore ask that we may be fully redeemed and share in what we celebrate in each Eucharist [12]. We are destined one day to enter into the full, unveiled possession of the realities we celebrate now in signs [30]. Communion imbues us with heavenly mysteries [16] and enables us to enter the kingdom of heaven [9]. It gives us participation in heavenly things [29] by giving us a taste of heavenly delights and a longing for the food by which we truly live [6].

The Eucharist is wholly focused on eternity. We pray, in the prayers after Communion, that the sacrament that feeds us in this present age may also make us partakers of life eternal [8] and may make us sharers in the life of the Son [23] and coheirs with him in heaven [20]. The Eucharist is the pledge of the effects of salvation [7]; it makes us worthy of eternal redemption [18] and helps profit us for salvation [17]. It makes us coheirs in glory with Christ [26] and prepares us to receive what the sacrament promises [31].

Sundays Two to Thirty-Four in Ordinary Time

Year A

TABLE OF SUNDAY READINGS

In the following table, the general theme of each celebration and the particular theme of each reading are indicated. If the second reading is connected with the general theme of the day, it will be commented on together with the first reading and the gospel. These second readings are marked by an asterisk in the following list.

More often the second reading does not fit in with the theme proposed for the first and third readings. In such instances a heavy line separates the second reading from what precedes in the commentary below. This line of demarcation is to remind the reader to avoid looking for connections between the semi-continuous reading of Paul's letters and the readings from the Old Testament and the gospel, since such connections are usually nonexistent. The commentary itself will be brief. We are dealing in the second reading with a semi-continuous sequence in which the liturgical context plays no part; no proper liturgical commentary, therefore, is required. There are many exegetical commentaries on the Pauline letters to which the reader can easily refer. We shall limit ourselves to some basic observations that may help the readers' personal reflections and introduce them to the more extended commentaries.

Year A		
Sunday 2	God's Choice	
	John 1:29-34	The Son of God is here
	Isa 49:3, 5-6	Choice of the servant
	*1 Cor 1:1-3	The apostle is called; so are we
Sunday 3	The Good News: A Great Light Has Shone	
	Matt 4:12-23	Galilee of the Gentiles
	Isa 8:23–9:3	A great light has shone
	1 Cor 1:10-13, 17	No divisions among us

Sunday 4	*God Chooses the Poor*	
	Matt 5:1-12a	Blessed are the poor in spirit
	Zeph 2:3; 3:12-13	A people humble and lowly
	*1 Cor 1:26-31	God has chosen the weak
Sunday 5	*Salt of the Earth and Light of the World*	
	Matt 5:13-16	Light of the world
	Isa 58:7-10	Your light shall rise in the darkness
	*1 Cor 2:1-5	Proclaim a crucified Messiah
Sunday 6	*A New Law in Continuity with the Old*	
	Matt 5:17-37	You have heard . . . but I say
	Sir 15:15-20	Condemned to freedom
	*1 Cor 2:6-10	Wisdom is revealed to us for our glorification
Sunday 7	*The Love of Others*	
	Matt 5:38-48	Love your enemies
	Lev 19:1-2, 17-18	Love your neighbor
	1 Cor 3:16-23	Boast not of human beings but of God
Sunday 8	*Seek First the Kingdom*	
	Matt 6:24-34	The duty of improvidence
	Isa 49:14-15	God does not forget us
	1 Cor 4:1-5	God will disclose the purposes of the heart
Sunday 9	*The Obedience of the Heart*	
	Matt 7:21-27	Do the Father's will
	Deut 11:18, 26-28, 32	Lay up the commandments in your heart
	*Rom 3:21-25a, 28	Justified by faith
Sunday 10	*Love, Not Ritualism*	
	Matt 9:9-13	Yes to mercy, no to ritualism
	Hos 6:3-6	Yes to love, no to holocausts
	Rom 4:18-25	Faith made Abraham strong

Sunday 11	Chosen by God	
	Matt 9:36–10:8	Chosen and sent to the lost sheep
	Exod 19:2-6a	A kingdom of priests
	Rom 5:6-11	Saved by the death of Christ
Sunday 12	Proclaim the Will of God	
	Matt 10:26-33	Do not fear people
	Jer 20:10-13	The persecutors will fall
	Rom 5:12-15	Where sin was, grace now abounds
Sunday 13	Receive the Lord	
	Matt 10:37-42	Whoever receives you receives me
	2 Kgs 4:8-11, 14-16a	Receive the holy one of God
	Rom 6:3-4, 8-11	We died with Christ and now live with him
Sunday 14	The Lord Is Humble	
	Matt 11:25-30	Gentle and lowly in heart
	Zech 9:9-10	A humble king
	Rom 8:9, 11-13	To live, put to death the disorders of the sinful
Sunday 15	The Efficacious Word	
	Matt 13:1-23	Receive the word
	Isa 55:10-11	The word of God
	Rom 8:18-23	Creation longs to see God's children revealed
Sunday 16	The Patient Justice of God	
	Matt 13:24-43	The justice that saves
	Wis 12:13, 16-19	You judge with clemency
	Rom 8:26-27	The Holy Spirit prays in us
Sunday 17	Choose the Real Treasure	
	Matt 13:44-52	Sell all for the real treasure
	1 Kgs 3:5, 7-12	Ask for the real treasure
	Rom 8:28-30	Become the image of God's Son

Sunday 18	*A God Who Feeds People*	
	Matt 14:13-21	They ate their fill
	Isa 55:1-3	Be filled
	Rom 8:35, 37-39	Who can separate us from the love of Christ?
Sunday 19	*Face the Obstacles and Advance toward the Lord*	
	Matt 14:22-33	Bid me come to you
	1 Kgs 19:9a, 11-13a	Stand before the Lord as he passes
	Rom 9:1-5	I could wish even to be accursed for the sake of my kin, the Jews
Sunday 20	*A House for All Peoples*	
	Matt 15:21-28	Israel, but all believers as well
	Isa 56:1, 6-7	A house of prayer for all peoples
	*Rom 11:13-15, 29-32	All peoples can obtain mercy
Sunday 21	*Firm Ground*	
	Matt 16:13-20	On this rock I will build my church
	Isa 22:19-23	A peg in a sure place
	Rom 11:33-36	From him and through him and for him are all things
Sunday 22	*The Suffering Required of the Disciple*	
	Matt 16:21-27	Renounce self and follow the Lord
	Jer 20:7-9	I am insulted and mocked
	*Rom 12:1-2	Offer one's person and life in sacrifice
Sunday 23	*Correcting Others*	
	Matt 18:15-20	Win your brother over
	Ezek 33:7-9	Warn the wicked
	*Rom 13:8-10	Love fulfills the law

Sunday 24	*Forgiveness*	
	Matt 18:21-35	Forgive seventy times seven times
	Sir 27:30–28:7	Forgiveness of neighbor and forgiveness of sins
	*Rom 14:7-9	We live and die for the Lord. Why judge?
Sunday 25	*God's Thoughts and Value Judgments*	
	Matt 20:1-16	Do you begrudge my generosity?
	Isa 55:6-9	My thoughts are not your thoughts
	Phil 1:20c-24, 27a	For me to live is Christ
Sunday 26	*Repent and Live*	
	Matt 21:28-32	Sinners are saved by faith and repentance
	Ezek 18:25-28	Turn from your sins and be saved
	Phil 2:1-11	Have the mind of Christ
Sunday 27	*The Fruitless Vineyard*	
	Matt 21:33-43	He will lease his vineyard to others
	Isa 5:1-7	The Lord's vineyard is the house of Israel
	Phil 4:6-9	The God of peace will be with you
Sunday 28	*The Banquet of the Lord*	
	Matt 22:1-14	Those invited to the wedding feast
	Isa 25:6-10a	The banquet of the saved
	Phil 4:12-14, 19-20	Bear with everything by the power of Christ
Sunday 29	*The Primacy of God's Service*	
	Matt 22:15-21	Give to Caesar what is Caesar's
	Isa 45:1, 4-6	I am the Lord and there is no other
	1 Thess 1:1-5b	A life of faith, love, and hope

Sunday 30	Love of Neighbor	
	Matt 22:34-40	Love your neighbor as yourself
	Exod 22:20-26	Love the orphan, the widow, the foreigner, and the poor
	1 Thess 1:5c-10	Turn from idols and serve God
Sunday 31	The Law and Obedience to It	
	Matt 23:1-12	They speak but do not act
	Mal 1:14b–2:2b, 8-10	Watering down the law
	*1 Thess 2:7-9, 13	Sharing the Gospel and our very selves
Sunday 32	Watch and Wait	
	Matt 25:1-13	Stay awake, for you know neither the day nor the hour
	Wis 6:12-16	Watch, and find wisdom
	1 Thess 4:13-18	God will bring forth those who have fallen asleep in Jesus
Sunday 33	Fidelity to Duty and Work	
	Matt 25:14-30	You have been faithful in small things: enter into the joy of your Lord
	Prov 31:10-13, 19-20, 30-31	A worthy wife is a precious jewel
	1 Thess 5:1-6	If we are watchful and sober, we will not be taken by surprise
Our Lord Jesus Christ, King of the Universe	Christ, King of the Universe	
	Matt 25:31-46	The Son of Man, the shepherd who will separate the sheep from the goats
	Ezek 34:11-12, 15-17	The Lord will judge between one sheep and another
	*1 Cor 15:20-26, 28	The final reign of the glorious Christ

Second Sunday: God's Choice

He Is the Son of God (John 1:29-34)

The continuous or semi-continuous reading of St. Matthew's gospel does not begin until the Third Sunday. During Ordinary Time passages from St. John's gospel (which traditionally is read during Lent and the Easter Season) are read on some Sundays. The Second Sunday (all three years of the cycle) is one of these.

The present reading from the Fourth Gospel is linked to the celebration of the Lord's baptism (First Sunday of Ordinary Time; Sunday after Epiphany) and continues the evangelist's meditation on John the Baptist. What is especially striking in John the Baptist's words is the designation of Christ and his role by the Spirit who descends from heaven and remains on him. This is traditional language for describing God's choice of a prophet. "But a shoot shall sprout from the stump of Jesse, / and from his roots a bud shall blossom. / The spirit of the LORD shall rest upon him" (Isa 11:1-2). The rest of this chapter of Isaiah should be read here, for it shows the qualities and function of a person who is thus singled out by the Spirit.

Later on, Isaiah says: "Here is my servant, whom I uphold, / my chosen one with whom I am pleased. / Upon him I have put my spirit" (42:1). The Spirit here is the prophetic Spirit of chapter 11. His outpouring is the great sign of the messianic age: "It shall come to pass / I will pour out my spirit upon all flesh. . . . / I will set signs in the heavens" (Joel 3:1, 3).

St. Luke describes for us the scene in which Jesus enters the synagogue at Nazareth and, when the moment comes for the reading from the prophets, takes the scroll and reads: "The Spirit of the Lord is upon me, / because he has anointed me / to bring glad tidings to the poor. / He has sent me to proclaim liberty to captives / and recovery of sight to the blind, / to let the oppressed go free, / and to proclaim a year acceptable to the Lord" (Luke 4:18-19; Isa 61:1-2). Jesus then comments on the passage by applying it to himself.

For John the Baptist, who would have been quite familiar with these various texts from the prophets, they must have taken on a vivid meaning, for he saw them fulfilled in a very concrete way at the baptism of Jesus. John was blessed by being able to identify Jesus as the person whom God had chosen and pointed out to his people: "the one who sent me to baptize with water told me, 'On whomever you see the Spirit come down and remain, he is the one who will baptize with the holy Spirit.' Now I have seen and testified that he is the Son of God" (John 1:33-34).

John fully understood Jesus and his mission. He bears witness to him by attributing to him all the qualities of God's Son. First, he asserts the eternity of the Son: "A man is coming after me who ranks ahead of me because he existed before me" (1:30). A true Son, however, is one who does his Father's will, and so John points to Jesus with the words: "Behold, the Lamb of God, who takes away the sin of the world" (1:29).

The expressions "Lamb" and "takes away the sin of the world" bring us back to Isaiah, but they also acquaint us straight off with the style and special concerns of St. John the Evangelist. The phrase "Lamb of God" immediately calls up the idea of sacrifice (cf. Exod 13:13; 29:38; 34:25; Lev 3:7; Num 28:9; Isa 7:9; Sir 46:19; Isa 53:7; Jer 11:19), especially the sacrifice of the Passover lamb (Exod 12:3; 2 Chr 35:7, 11). Both Isaiah and Jeremiah, though with different references, speak of a lamb being sacrificed: "Like a lamb led to slaughter / or a sheep silent before shearers, / he did not open his mouth" (Isa 53:7); "Yet I was like a trusting lamb led to slaughter, not knowing that they were hatching plots against me" (Jer 11:19).

When Isaiah speaks of the Servant of Yahweh as a lamb, he anticipates John the Baptist's words, "Behold, the Lamb of God." Jesus is the Son, but he is also the Lamb, the Servant who takes away the world's sins. In the prophets, the word "lamb" emphasizes the innocence of the person who is about to be sacrificed. "Taking away sins" is the Servant's function, for "the LORD laid upon him / the guilt of us all" (Isa 53:6); "Yet it was our pain that he bore, / our sufferings he endured" (Isa 53:4); "[He] bore the sins of many" (53:12). Jesus is truly the Lamb, the Servant, the beloved Son, because he does the Father's will. With the words "Behold, the Lamb of God," John says in his own way what the Father says of Jesus at the latter's baptism and transfiguration.

The Father, then, has chosen his only Son as Lamb and Servant to take away the world's sins. The Spirit has remained on him and chosen him for his task. The incarnation of the Word is for a service that brings him to death so that the world may be redeemed and so that all who receive him in his coming may become children of God.

Choice of the Servant (Isa 49:3, 5-6)

The reading from Isaiah takes us back to one of the great figures who typify Jesus and proclaim him in advance across the centuries. There are four "Servant Songs" in the book of Isaiah (42:1-7; 49:1-9; 50:4-9; 52:13–53:12). There is fairly general agreement among exegetes that these songs were added later to the work of the original Isaiah and are, in fact, compositions of a later writer, whom they speak of as "Second Isaiah." The verses chosen for the present reading are those that speak of the choice of the servant (Isa 49:3, 5-6).

"The LORD said to me: You are my servant, / Israel, through whom I show my glory" (v. 3). The choice of him by the Lord confers an important mission on the servant: that of gathering Israel and of being a light for the nations so that salvation may reach the ends of the earth (Isa 49:6).

Psalm 40, which serves as the responsorial psalm after the first reading, has a refrain that emphasizes the special characteristic of the servant and the Lamb: "Here am I, Lord; I come to do your will." The servant offers himself as a victim, but what the Lord really wants is that the servant do his, the Lord's, will: "In the scroll of the book it stands written of me: / 'I delight to do your will, O my God" (Ps 40:8b-9).

The Apostle Is Called; so Are We (1 Cor 1:1-3)

The second reading for this Sunday happens to fit in with the theme of the first reading and the gospel: the theme of choice for a mission. In the opening words of his First Letter to the Corinthians, St. Paul speaks of himself as called by God's will to be an apostle of Jesus Christ. As John the Baptist was called to bear witness to Jesus, Paul has now been chosen to proclaim the Good News of Christ. But the faithful too are the object of a divine choice; because of that call, they form a holy people and call on the name of the Lord Jesus Christ. In other words, they too have been chosen by the Lord and set apart to be witnesses to Christ.

If Paul has been chosen for the apostolate, the body of Christians has been chosen for holiness. The holiness is lived within the communion of the Church that calls upon the name of its Messiah and has for its principal function the offering of praise and adoration; these will in turn be the basis of the Church's witness and apostolate.

God's Choice Today

All that we have been reading and saying does not refer solely to the past. On the contrary, it applies very much to the here and now and provides an occasion for us to try to understand better the teaching and spirituality of the liturgy generally. The liturgy is interested not in concepts but in concrete Christian life; it shows what it means to be chosen by God and what mission the choice involves. Nor is the liturgy interested in any abstract theology of God's choice; it intends, rather, to show us the God who chooses.

All this is relevant to us. We do not need theories about God's choice. We know for a fact that through our baptism we were chosen by God. Indeed, the name given in antiquity to those preparing for baptism was "the elect, the chosen." What they were elected to and chosen for was to share in God's life and to accept the consequences of that sharing. We must accept those consequences in our own lives.

Third Sunday: The Good News: A Great Light Has Shone

Galilee of the Gentiles (Matt 4:12-23)

The semi-continuous reading of the Gospel of St. Matthew begins today in Year A. The choice of reading is very good, because it recalls the beginning of Jesus' preaching in Galilee, where there were many Gentiles. Matthew shows us Christ in his work of preaching the Good News and sees it as a fulfillment of the Isaian prophecy found in the first reading for this day. One theme of Matthew's gospel is to show that Jesus is the true Messiah, whom the Gentiles accept and the Jews reject.

John the Baptist had pointed him out. Now Jesus leaves the region where John is working and comes to Galilee. This is the first of his various shifts of locale, and it is important that the first such shift should be to Galilee, where many Gentiles lived. John the Baptist was not the only one to proclaim Jesus; Isaiah had done so before him.

Having been thus doubly proclaimed, Jesus begins his ministry. His message is simple but staggering: "Repent, for the kingdom of heaven is at hand" (Matt 4:17). Jesus goes about Galilee always preaching the same message: The kingdom is at hand; he backs up his words, "curing every disease and illness among the people" (Matt 4:23). We note on several occasions throughout this series of commentaries that such cures were the sign of the kingdom's presence.

Jesus shows the presence of the Messiah and the kingdom by another very special action: He begins to establish his Church and to prepare for the building of it by gradually shaping the columns that must support it. He looks around among his companions for those who will work with him in helping the world achieve its freedom from Satan and sin; those whom he chooses will be fishers of people. Simon, renamed Peter, Andrew, James, and John are called.

In this passage Matthew twice stresses the fact that those called immediately leave nets and boat and father to follow Jesus. There can be no doubt that Matthew deliberately emphasizes this "immediately." The light of Christ shines out so strongly in this land of the Gentiles that nothing can resist it. The first disciples do not sit down and discuss the matter; they recognize Christ and immediately follow him. It is then that Jesus begins to teach in the synagogues.

A Great Light Has Shone (Isa 8:23–9:3)

Matthew has chosen to hark back to Isaiah and see the latter's prophecies fulfilled in the first events of Jesus' public life. The passage from Isaiah relates to events connected with the invasion by the Assyrians of Northern Palestine—the land of Zebulun and the land of Naphtali—in 732 BC. Many Galileans were deported. Isaiah sought to restore the people's confidence: "The people who walked in darkness / have seen a great light" (9:1).

It is clear how this applies to the Messiah and the Good News. The people living in ignorance of God and enslaved by darkness now see the Messiah coming and his light shining upon them. On those dwelling in a land of deep darkness a light has shone; the yoke that weighed them down is broken. The words of the prophet sum up the whole mission of Christ, and St. Matthew quotes them to serve that purpose.

The light and the Good News are always being offered to us, for the work of evangelization goes on. But we are not simply to observe the work or to be the recipient of it; we are to share in it. The prophecy read today and the gospel pericope are addressed to us in order to stir us to action. In fact, Christ stirs us to action at two levels. First, there is the inner spiritual movement incumbent upon us: the kingdom is at hand, proclaimed to us by the light we received at our baptism, and we must therefore unwearyingly carry on the work of our own conversion. But we must also leave all things and follow Christ in order to share with him the task of preaching the Gospel.

The Gospel is demanding, for we must take steps that are costly to our weak nature if we are to see the light and accept it. And yet the extension of the kingdom depends in part on us. The Church is already established, of course, and its supporting pillars are the apostles. But each of us is called to work for the expansion of the Church and the spreading of the Good News. The sacrifices required of us in the pursuit of this goal may be hard ones. The apostles, the first ones whom Christ called, responded without hesitation; not everyone else would do so, and the rich young man, though he had observed all the commandments, gave up when it came to following Jesus.

In the sometimes difficult following of Christ, the responsorial psalm, Psalm 27, can give us courage: "The LORD is my light and my salvation; whom shall I fear?" (v. 1). There is, however, a condition for acquiring this courage: we must have our hearts set on a single goal, namely, to "live in the house of the LORD" (v. 4). If we follow the guidance of the Lord and look actively for his coming, we will receive the courage and strength to follow in his steps: "I believe I shall see the LORD's goodness / in the land of the living" (v. 13).

No Divisions among Us (1 Cor 1:10-13, 17)

After only a very short time, divisions cropped up in the life of the early Church. If, in this Letter to the Corinthians, St. Paul adopts a serious, almost dramatic tone, it is because divisions are, in his eyes, a basic contradiction to a properly Gospel outlook and a negation of the very being of the Church. The men and women of this quite young community were filled with enthusiasm; unfortunately, the enthusiasm was directed to the special themes of each evangelist, to his person and his manner of teaching, rather than to basic content and, more important, the person of the Lord, who is Teacher of all Christians and in whom all have been baptized.

The divisions in the Church of Corinth were due to their proponents having failed to understand either Christ crucified or what it is that forms men and women into the people of God. The unanimity at which they should have been aiming was a single faith and a common effort to create unity because all had been reborn by the same sacrament of baptism and all had been saved by the same Christ crucified.

How relevant such a passage is to us today! Despite our contemporary concern with action, even excessive action, people love to listen to speeches and are on the watch for new and original presentations of their faith. They are often more concerned with the manner of presentation than with the content, and their attachment to the "star" can even lead them to form autonomous cells within the Church. Is this a manifestation of the quest for God? It may well be regarded rather as a lack of genuine faith and of an understanding of what it means to belong to the Body of Christ, in which there should be, not uniformity on accidentals, but unity in faith for the good of the whole.

Fourth Sunday: God Chooses the Poor

Blessed Are the Poor in Spirit (Matt 5:1-12a)

The gospel preaches a world turned inside out. This is not to say it claims poverty to be something good or that God's blessing cannot be manifested in the gifts of material things. The gospel does, however, foresee that it is difficult to keep our hearts free in the midst of earthly possessions. That is the point of the beatitudes, which we read today in St. Matthew's version of them. (St. Luke's will be read on the Sixth Sunday, Year C.)

The beatitudes in St. Matthew form a paragraph of rhythmic prose. A comparison with the beatitudes of Luke shows that the two authors surely drew inspiration from a common source, but this is of little concern to us here. The power of the beatitudes over us becomes all the greater if we really believe that God is addressing his words to us here and now in the liturgical celebration.

Within the total context provided by the readings of this Sunday, the thematic beatitudes are poverty of spirit, meekness, mourning, hunger and thirst, and persecution—in short, everything that represents weakness, everything the world looks down its nose at and has trouble taking seriously. By contrast, if we think of the first beatitude ("Blessed are the poor"), the second ("Blessed are they who mourn"), the fourth ("Blessed are they who hunger and thirst"), and the eighth ("Blessed are they who are persecuted"), we have the essence of the beatitudes in relation to the coming kingdom. In his Sermon on the Mount, Jesus comes forward as preacher of the Good News of the kingdom. Persecution, we may note, is mentioned both as a present and as a future reality and is accompanied by a special exhortation to those who must experience it. The exhortation is in the form of a call to rejoice because the reward in heaven will be great.

The gospel passage urges us to examine our life and especially our value judgments in the light of the new values with which Christ presents us and which are disconcerting to those who do not believe in the kingdom. Christianity will show the world people who suffer and yet rejoice, Christians who are persecuted and yet are filled with the joy of witnessing, families that lack the necessities of life and yet are marked, not by bitterness, but by youthfulness of spirit. Above all, Christianity will show the world people who may be materially rich but whose hearts are open, receptive, humble; people who are not puffed up by their wealth and who know that they have much to receive from others who are better than they in other than material ways.

We can never meditate seriously enough on this great charter of the Christian life or ever be done with the attempt to implement it fully. It can always be read with a still greater faith and a still deeper sense of God.

A People Humble and Lowly (Zeph 2:3; 3:12-13)

If material poverty is not a good in itself, it does nonetheless help us toward the freedom that in turn enables us to search more effectively for God. This freedom is really what Zephaniah is talking about when he bids us seek righteousness, humility, and the will of God. These are the goals the humble and lowly set their hearts on. Such people will be protected against God's wrath on the last day, because it is to the last day and the Lord's coming that they have been looking forward all along.

Against this background, we can see why the prophet speaks of Israel as a "nation without shame" (2:1). We may think of our own world, in which the rich and their children cannot dissipate their boredom and disgust with everything, a world that sets its heart on perishable material goods and yet is filled with an indefinable anxiety because there is nothing of the permanent and the absolute in their lives.

It is to be observed, however, that the prophet Zephaniah is not thinking simply of the material state of the humble and lowly. If God will preserve only those who are humble and lowly, it is because the latter will not sin or play false. In short, the ultimate concern is with a lowliness and a poverty that are above all spiritual, with what St. Matthew will call poverty "of spirit." The people who will survive will be no more than a remnant of Israel; this presupposes a major purge, indeed a catastrophe. The time will come when the only refuge is in the name of the Lord.

God Has Chosen the Weak (1 Cor 1:26-31)

The second reading on this day fits in very well with the theme of the other two readings. St. Paul fully grasped the inversion of values that the coming of Christ caused. From now on, God chooses what is weak in the world's eyes. No one can boast of oneself before God.

It seems clear that Paul is here referring to a contemporary philosophical snobbery. He does not want Christians to be led astray by that kind of thinking, and so he calls their attention to some basic facts. He contrasts, for example, the wisdom of the world and the wisdom of God and tells us that God alone is to be our wisdom and justice.

The church of Corinth had recruited its members from among the lowborn and despised: few were rich and influential; few were wise as people account wisdom. But God is not bound to the value judgments of humans; he chooses precisely those for whom the world has little esteem, but it is he, after all, who knows how to judge properly! God chose "those who count for nothing, to reduce to nothing those who are something" (v. 28). He did this in order that "no human being might boast before God" (v. 29). The only pride a Christian can rightly cultivate is a pride in the Lord, from whom all that is worthwhile comes. Apart from Christ, nothing human is of value.

The readings for this Sunday really put everything in its proper place and are an invitation to Christians to review their value judgments on persons and things. We ourselves have worth only in relation to God.

The responsorial psalm, from Psalm 146, is full of meaning for us, and can be taken as a summary of the whole thought of the day. The response is from the gospel: "Blessed are the poor in spirit; the kingdom of heaven is theirs!" The verses chosen from the psalm are these:

The LORD . . .
does justice to those who are oppressed.

It is he who gives bread to the hungry,
the LORD who sets prisoners free,
the LORD who opens the eyes of the blind,
the LORD who raises up those who are bowed down.

It is the LORD who loves the just,
the LORD who protects the stranger
and upholds the orphan and the widow,
but thwarts the path of the wicked.

The lesson taught on this Sunday is truly fundamental for the Catholic of our day. God does not choose those who have sophisticated concepts of religion and the quest for God; he chooses, above all, the humble who have no theories about God and about how to follow him but are open to the Lord and his demands. The lesson is undoubtedly a hard one for our contemporaries, who like to build conceptual systems and gnostic approaches to the search for God. All of that is irrelevant to God's choice; he has no interest in the little groups that spend hours developing methods of seeking God and deciding on the best way to follow him. God does not need that kind of workshop. He acts in ways that are usually quite unexpected, and chooses the weak things of the world.

Fifth Sunday: Salt of the Earth and Light at the World

Light of the World (Matt 5:13-16)

In the gospel, this passage follows immediately upon the beatitudes. Christians know, in a general way, how they must conduct themselves; they know that they must follow Christ and what this means. Now, employing rather strong images, Matthew wants to make his readers more fully aware of what they really are: the salt of the earth and the light of the world.

"Salt of the earth" is not a commonly used expression. It can be taken in a realistic sense as a salt that serves as fertilizer; of this St. Luke says that if it loses its strength, "It is fit neither for the soil nor for the manure pile" (Luke 14:35). In the present passage, however, we have the impression that "earth" is rather a way of saying "world"; the meaning is that the disciples of Jesus are a force that makes the world bloom. Every

Christian possesses an inner power that should be active in the world. If Christians were to lose their "taste," they would also lose their meaning and would have to be "thrown out." These last words are strong ones, and we meet them elsewhere as indicating eternal damnation. St. Matthew uses the words on several occasions with reference to those who do not act as their vocation in Christ requires (7:19; 13:48, 50; 18:8, 9; 22:13). Jesus was probably using proverbial phraseology. There is no point in puzzling here over the riddle of a salt that loses its taste. We are dealing with a proverb, and everyone knows quite well what the words mean as applied to human beings who should be living up to their responsibilities. The problem is one we all face. We have become the salt of the earth by reason of our baptism; we must continue to be salt for the world and develop the power given us and the dynamic, outgoing energy that in principle is at our disposal.

Christ still stands before us with the example of his life, and we are forced to ask ourselves to what extent each Christian in the Church is truly "salt" for the world. Do Christians simply "practice," or are they really "salt"? If they are no longer "salt," what significance do they still have? That is the problem, but only God can give the answer. We have no right to judge others, but we do have an obligation to examine ourselves and decide what we must do.

We are also "the light of the world." In thus designating his disciples, Christ enjoins on them the attitude that befits people in such a luminous state. The words in St. Matthew seem to imply a contrast and might be translated: "It is you who are the light of the world." The point would be that this function has now passed from the Jews, who formerly possessed it (Isa 42:6; 49:6; 60:3), to Christ's disciples and his new people.

Christians must proclaim the Messiah who has come and saved the world. It is by doing so that they will be a light in the darkness. Their situation as Christians imposes certain duties on them that they cannot simply shrug off: they must not let their salt lose its taste or put their light under a basket. At the same time, however, they must remember that while they may be legitimately proud of sharing in Christ's work and his Spirit-inspired activity in the world, they must communicate not their own light but that of Christ, who has come to enlighten every person.

The Christian's activity should lead all people to praise the Father for what he has done. The basis for praising God is the marvelous deeds he has done, and the Christian should be one of these deeds that leads to wonder and praise of the Lord. Glorifying God is a sign of conversion. Thus, the Christian is really called to shed a light that will lead to the salvation of the world.

Your Light Shall Rise in the Darkness (Isa 58:7-10)

In this passage from the prophet, the shedding of light is connected with charity to others. If people want to be truly a light, they must shelter the homeless, clothe the naked, and not hide themselves from their own flesh. If they do these things, their light will break forth like the dawn, and their own wounds will be quickly healed. If people open their hearts to the hungry and satisfy the desire of the afflicted, their light will rise in the darkness, their gloom will become like noonday.

Thus, the light that the Christian is called to be cannot be translated into terms solely of faith and knowledge but is intimately linked with love and concern for the neighbor. The verses of chapter 58 that precede those read today all move in the same direction. The point being made is that the prophet sent to Israel is an authentic prophet when he is open to the needs of others; similarly, we today are authentic Christians and authentic prophets when we too open our hearts to others. The aim is not merely to eliminate injustice; it is to build a just world. If we are this kind of Christian, the Lord is near at hand to us; we need only call and he will answer, "Here I am!" The "light," then, is in reality orthodox charity concretely shown to our neighbor.

Proclaim a Crucified Messiah (1 Cor 2:1-5)

The Corinthians seem to have been ever ready to divide into opposing groups according to the preacher they favored at the moment. St. Paul here reminds them that the effective preacher is not the one who is a master of language or a master of human wisdom. The preacher who is effective in God's eyes is the one who preaches Christ crucified and whose preaching manifests the power of the Spirit.

We may, without forcing things, link this second reading with the other two in terms of "light." We are meant to be the light of the world (the gospel); we will, in fact, be a light to others only if we are inspired by charity and do the concrete works of charity (first reading). In addition, however, the light we are to bring is light concerning the central object of our faith, namely, Christ crucified. It is for this that the Spirit fills us with his power. To bring light to others, then, means to enable them to meet Christ, the crucified Messiah who is now the risen Lord of glory.

True faith is not grounded in human wisdom but in the power of God. The gift of faith, the "light," is to encounter the mystery of Christ or Christ himself in his paschal mystery. The true Catholic preacher—and this applies to every Catholic—is the one who enables others to encounter the Light, the Word-made-flesh, who was crucified and then rose from the dead. It is the Spirit who really makes the mystery known and gives the strength to embrace it.

Sixth Sunday: A New Law in Continuity with the Old

You Have Heard . . . but I Say (Matt 5:17-37)

At first glance today's gospel shows Jesus issuing a revolutionary challenge: "You have heard that it was said. . . . But I say to you." And yet the impression soon proves ungrounded, for we are told at the very beginning of the passage, "Do not think that I have come to abolish the law or the prophets. I have come not to abolish but to fulfill" (v. 17). In what does this fulfillment consist by which the law is not abolished but perfected to the fullest degree? An easy answer would be: the fulfillment consists in love. Doesn't St. Paul tell us so in his letter to the Romans that "love is the fulfillment of the law" (13:10)?

If we stop here, we may remain rather vague—understanding without really understanding and content with only a kind of superficial insight into this "fulfillment." The fulfillment is, in fact, the fulfillment of the law, but it is also the fulfillment of those who obey it, for the fulfillment of the law now consists in being able to become like God. As St. Matthew tells us later in this same chapter, "So be perfect, just as your heavenly Father is perfect" (5:48). When did Jesus enable us to become as perfect as his heavenly Father? When did Jesus bring to fulfillment the purpose of the law and the prophets? *In and through his Passover mystery.* The Law and the Prophets were preliminary stages or pedagogical preparation unto the attainment of Christian intimacy with God. In his Pasch Jesus achieved ontologically and to the fullest perfection the preliminary steps taken by the law and the prophets. Because of the passion, death, and resurrection of Jesus it has become possible, and necessary, for us to become perfect as our heavenly Father is perfect.

It is in this perspective that Christ does issue a revolutionary challenge: "You have heard that it was said. . . . But I say to you." He lists a whole series of areas with which the law dealt but with regard to which the new covenant is much more demanding. A person must not only not kill another but also not even say an insulting word toward another (Matt 21:22). There is no point in bringing a ritual offering to the altar without first giving sincere signs of love and union with others (vv. 23-26). Not only must a man not commit adultery, but he is already guilty of adultery in his heart if he looks on a woman lustfully (vv. 27-30). It used to be that a man could dismiss his wife; henceforth marriage is indissoluble (vv. 31-32). Do not take oaths (vv. 33-36), but let your answers be simply yes or no (v. 37).

This is not the place to study minutely each of Christ's statements, as, for example, the very important one about marriage being indissoluble. The focus of the liturgical proclamation is not on the details, for the point of reading this passage is to emphasize the fact that observance of the law has now entered the time of paschal fulfillment. Details become unimportant in view of the evident motive for the choice of the first reading.

Condemned to Freedom (Sir 15:15-20)

The phrase "condemned to freedom" aptly sums up humanity's condition from the moment of creation.[1] Ben Sirach puts it in his own way: "God in the beginning created human beings, / and made them subject to their own free choice" (v. 14). This verse has unfortunately not been included in today's reading, but it lies behind the verses that follow, for the latter presuppose the full freedom of God's creature, humanity. In speaking of the commandments, it is important that we stress the fact that their fulfillment is within human power and that one is, on the other hand, not forced to obedience (Sir 15:15).

One even has the privilege of choosing life or death; people need only to stretch out their hand for whichever they wish (vv. 16-17). These words must, however, be properly understood. It is true enough that even life and death are not forced on a person, and that the choice people make is theirs. At the same time, it is clear that those who obey

God's commandments will receive life and blessing (Deut 11:26-28); life is to be found by following the path of justice (Prov 12:28).

People are free indeed, but they must bear in mind that God possesses wisdom, that he knows all of a person's actions, and that his goodwill rests on those who fear him (Sir 15:18-19). God offers us either life and blessing or death and wretchedness, but the one who obeys the Lord's commandments will live (Deut 30:15-20). Wisdom, then, bids a person freely choose the ways of God and accept the wisdom of the Lord himself. This divine wisdom invites people to a life in which they observe the law and avoid sin. Ben Sirach puts the point negatively: "No one does he command to act unjustly, / to none does he give license to sin" (Sir 15:20).

The responsorial psalm for this first reading is taken from Psalm 119, which sings of the happiness of those who walk according to the word of God. You know, we can cultivate a certain oversimplification with regard to the Old Testament. We may think that the law of the Old Testament had nothing to do with love and that only Christ in the New Testament revealed the true way by teaching people to live in the spirit of love. Such an opposition is unfounded; we have failed to read the texts carefully enough. Both creation and God's gift of the law to his people were acts of love on his part, while the people's free observance of God's commandments was first and foremost an act of love on their part.

It is true enough, however, that Christ came to fulfill the purpose of the law, not to abolish it; moreover, the New Testament is clearly characterized by the supremacy it gives to love, even in the observance of the commandments, which one obeys freely but with love as well. This is not to say that a person may not be weak and unfaithful or that one may not suffer interior conflicts. For all of their freedom, people are also frail. St. Paul certainly makes no bones about this fact; he is not afraid to voice his own confusion at being unable to do what he wishes to do, while doing the opposite of what he wants (Rom 7:14-20). The real point is that all Christians, like St. Paul before them, know that their strength is from the Lord (Phil 4:13).

Wisdom Is Revealed to Us for Our Glorification (1 Cor 2:6-10)

We would be exaggerating if we claimed that the second reading is fully integrated with the other two. But we can, without straining, find aspects that objectively link this reading to the other two and may therefore help enrich the theme of the law as being fulfilled perfectly in Christ's paschal mystery and of its consequences for us.

The purpose of the law, reconciliation and union with God, was achieved objectively by Jesus as he accomplished God's way of redemption. But we are able freely to choose or reject God's way. If we do choose it, then no sooner have we bowed to God's will than we find wisdom. It is a wisdom revealed to us by the Spirit, who enables us to understand what God has prepared for those who love him; the Spirit reveals to us what no one has ever seen or heard, what no one has ever been able even to imagine (1 Cor 2:6-10). As soon as Christians set out on the way of the Gospel, their eyes are opened; the Spirit urges them on toward evangelical perfection and encourages them to be perfect as our heavenly Father is perfect (Matt 5:48).

This perfection and wisdom cannot be grasped by the worldly mind, for they are on a different level than the things of this world. The "wisdom" that God gives relates, in fact, to the entire plan of salvation that God has prepared for us from the beginning of time. This wisdom comes to us through Christ, for by his paschal activity he is its revealer; the wisdom hidden in God through the ages is now revealed in Jesus.

Hidden wisdom is revealed to us by Jesus. This amounts to saying that St. Paul's use of the word "mystery" does not mean something we cannot understand. On the contrary, the "mystery" is that which was formerly hidden in God but is now revealed to us. In the last analysis, the mystery is Christ himself, and in Christ we see the divine plan that he is carrying out. If we adhere to Christ and the saving plan he reveals, we become, by the power of the Spirit, perfect human beings, and we advance toward the glory whose firstfruits we have possessed ever since we were baptized.

Yet this divine wisdom is foolishness to the wise and the rulers of this world (1 Cor 2:6). Only those who are mature in faith can draw near to the mystery and enter upon the path of wisdom; only they can become perfect by living according to this wisdom. They obey the law, and, paradoxically, they become freer, for they are filled with the wisdom that the Holy Spirit of Jesus has revealed to them.

In the Office of Readings, the second reading is from St. Ephrem. In it he says: "The word of God is a tree of life that offers us blessed fruit from each of its branches. It is like that rock which was struck open in the wilderness, from which all were offered spiritual drink. As the Apostle says: *They ate spiritual food and they drank spiritual drink.*"² The book of Proverbs describes the quite different situation of those who refused to follow true wisdom through free obedience:

> Because they hated knowledge,
>   and the fear of the LORD they did not choose.
> They ignored my counsel,
>   they spurned all my reproof;
> Well, then, they shall eat the fruit of their own way,
>   and with their own devices be glutted. (Prov 1:29-31)

Seventh Sunday: The Love of Others

Love Your Enemies (Matt 5:38-48)

"You have heard that it was said. . . . But I say to you. . . ." Twice in today's passage we hear this solemn contrast voiced. In chapter 5 of Matthew's gospel, it is repeated six times; today's passage contains the final two, both dealing with one's neighbor. And yet the contrast does not mean that Jesus has come to negate the law's purpose; rather, as he himself explicitly says, he has come to fulfill it.

The code of the (old) covenant says: "But if injury ensues [from a fight], you shall give life for life, eye for eye, tooth for tooth, hand for hand, foot for foot, burn for burn, wound for wound, stripe for stripe" (Exod 21:23-25). This is the "law of talion" (retaliation), but since there exists no evidence that it was ever actually implemented in the literal sense, we must understand it as the equivalent of the principle of just or legal compensation for injury done—a sanction imposed. What specifically the compensation would consist in would be determined by a court of law. Jesus' law of love called for complete forgiveness, with no compensation for the injury inflicted.

Later on in this same Gospel of Matthew, Jesus will say that we must forgive seventy times seven times; in so saying, he deliberately juxtaposes his spirit against that of Lamech who said that if Cain was avenged sevenfold, he, Lamech, will be avenged seventy-sevenfold for any injury done him (Gen 4:24). In our present passage Christ also bids us turn the other cheek. If someone wants to sue us and take our coat, we should give him our cloak as well; if he forces us to go one mile with him, then go two miles; we should not refuse anyone who wishes to borrow from us.

Then Jesus issues a still more paradoxical order: Love your enemies! That is, we are not only to refrain from vengeance but also to love the person who injures us! We must even pray for that person! Perhaps St. Matthew was thinking of the difficulties the Church found herself in at the time when he was writing. In any case, the theme of persecution is repeated on three different occasions (5:10-11; 10:23; 23:33).

To act as Christ counsels us is to live as a child of the heavenly Father. Anyone who obeys this commandment becomes like God, who makes his sun rise on the just and the unjust alike. The thing that marks Christians and distinguishes them from tax collector and Gentile is their attitude of forgiveness and love of neighbor.

Those who make this manner of life their own become perfect as the heavenly Father himself is perfect.

Love Your Neighbor (Lev 19:1-2, 17-18)

"Be holy, for I, the LORD, your God, am holy" (Lev. 19:2). The gospel bids us be perfect as the heavenly Father is perfect. Yet Israel too was already holy, for it had been set apart (which is the basic meaning of "holy").

But Israel had also been always obliged to advance in the holiness bestowed upon her. Thus it is that the command of the Lord in the present text (vv. 17-18) contradicted existing custom: "You shall not bear hatred for your brother or sister in your heart . . . . Take no revenge." This does not mean, of course, that we are simply to accept everything others do. We must not hesitate to reprimand others, so that we may not share in their sin.

The text thus tries to strike a balance: on the one hand, no hesitation in reproaching; on the other, no hatred and no vengeance. We must hate the sin but love the sinner. In this passage from the book of Leviticus, an attempt is probably being made to establish proper social relations between members of the same clan. Similar counsels given by Jesus are on a quite different level of application and prepare the way for the new law.

When all is said and done, we are to love our neighbor as we love ourselves. The point of this saying is not that we are to cultivate similar emotions but that we are to acknowledge our neighbor's rights just as we want others to acknowledge ours, to respect others as we want others to respect us. Those who wish to obey the Lord must be involved with their neighbor and must recognize the bonds that unite them to others.

The responsorial psalm tells us how the Lord acts toward us: "He does not treat us according to our sins, / nor repay us according to our faults" (Ps 103:10). When Christians pardon, they rise to the level of God himself. Vengeance is beneath a human being; it cannot be an acceptable attitude in a child of God. If we want to be perfect as the Lord is perfect, we must love our neighbor. According to the gospel, we must even love our enemy.

Love of neighbor will always be the distinguishing mark of the Christian. Christians are in danger of succumbing to a more or less deliberately cultivated illusion: they can trust in outward observances as their way to God, to the point of forgetting the obligation to love their neighbor. Readings like those of this Sunday should stir the hearers to a critical evaluation of their Christian life today. Are there still Christians around who yield to the delusion that they can live a Christian life without having a real love of others, even of their enemies?

Boast Not of Human Beings but of God (1 Cor 3:16-23)

The Seventh and Eighth Sundays of Ordinary Time contain the final readings from the First Letter to the Corinthians. There can be no doubt that Paul found the community at Corinth trying at times; it seems to have been constantly in a state of high tension and always threatened by divisions. For all its attractiveness, the community seems to have been rather superficial in its approach to things and to have had its share of partisans who were more interested in individual preachers and their ways of teaching than in promoting unity and orthodox faith.

In their propensities the Corinthians seem to have been driven by a false notion of what the preaching of the Gospel was all about. Paul is therefore careful to point out that he is presenting Christ to them without relying on a particular philosophy. His role is simply to provoke contact with Christ, to become all things to all people so that he may help all to salvation. All who share the work of evangelization are working for the same goal, varied though the gifts of each may be. All Christians toil in the field that belongs to God; all share in the erection of a building that belongs to God, not to them.

In this penultimate reading from First Corinthians in Year A, Paul speaks of building the temple of God. The Christian community is precisely a temple of God. The community is not just any group; Paul has compared it to a body and to a building, and now he sees it as a holy temple, God's temple. What we have here is not really an image but the reality that expresses what the community really is. Christ, risen from the dead, is a temple that far transcends all temples built with hands, and Christians form the Body of that risen Christ. Woe to those who profane this temple! That, however, is what people do when they prefer the wisdom of this world, the reasonings that are simply wind.

St. Paul returns in this passage to his main concern: Christians must not find their pride in celebrities. He then repeats also the theme of liberty, which has found expression on other Sundays. Christians already live and work in a temple that will last forever; they must rise above what is secondary, for they belong to Christ, and Christ belongs to God. St. Paul's words are an invitation to us all to discern in the community a dynamic presence that is greater than all else there, and that requires us to rise in faith above worldly wisdom, so that we may live as free men and women in Christ and in God our Father.

Eighth Sunday: Seek First the Kingdom

The Duty of Improvidence (Matt 6:24-34)

A book written back in the 1930s bore the intriguing title *The Duty of Improvidence*.[3] The title captures the theme of today's passage from the gospel. The gospel is not telling the Christian to be neglectful of, or indifferent to, success in business or the security of one's family. It is making a quite different point and inculcating a quite different attitude.

This different attitude may, however, involve such confidence in God that in certain situations we may abandon our habitual human prudence. Pope St. Gregory the Great, in his *Dialogues*, tells the story of a cellarer in St. Benedict's monastery who refused to give a poor man the only bit of oil left for the community's needs. St. Benedict was filled with a holy anger at the refusal, took the flask of oil, and threw it out the window. Then, however, all the receptacles for oil in the monastery were found to be filled to overflowing!

Whether or not the story is true, its aim is to teach a certain kind of improvidence. It is emphasizing, like the gospel itself, the one thing necessary, namely, to give absolute priority to the service of God, whether directly in himself or indirectly through the neighbor. The evangelical ideal of St. Francis of Assisi, which is shared by many groups today, even outside the religious orders, is the pursuit of detachment so as to be totally at the service of God and his kingdom.

Rarely does a passage of the gospel address itself so clearly and, we might almost say, "brutally" to the contemporary world and the contemporary Christian. Do not serve two masters, for you will only end in a compromise that will not fool God! God's jealousy is a favorite theme in the Old Testament. At the time of the Exodus, it is applied to the Lord, who speaks of himself to Moses as "a jealous God" (Exod 20:5). The same point is made in the Decalogue: "You shall not bow down to any other god, for the LORD—'Jealous' his name—is a jealous God" (Exod 34:14). The book of Deuteronomy applies the same adjective three times to God (Deut 4:24; 5:9; 6:15). The proverb that Jesus cites in today's gospel—no one can serve two masters—is related to the same theme of God's jealousy, especially when it comes to worshiping other gods. Deuteronomy, for example, shows the people rousing God's jealousy by adoring alien gods (32:16).

In the gospel, the opposition is put in down-to-earth terms, with money (mammon) being treated as a god that is opposed to the true God. In the last analysis, however, the opposition is between what is definitive and eternal and what is weak, transient, of passing value, and perishable. The Christian is warned that there is an utter incompatibility between anxious worry about the morrow and the quest for the kingdom. It is on this kingdom that Jesus insists in the second part of today's passage.

Once again he speaks of the detachment that must be the mark of the Christian. His words remind us of the beatitudes, especially of the happiness promised to the poor. A person has to be truly free to enter the kingdom; that is why it is easier for a camel to pass through the eye of a needle than for the rich to enter the kingdom (Matt 19:23). The Scripture returns frequently to the subject of wealth and the rich—and justly so, for wealth is a real problem in this world, whether past or present.

The Bible stresses the uselessness of wealth as far as people's attainment of their ultimate end is concerned. The expressions it uses with regard to the rich are quite strong: "The riches he swallowed he shall vomit up" (Job 20:15); "In his riches, man does not endure; / he is like the beasts that are destroyed" (Ps 49:13); "People's riches serve as ransom for their lives" (Prov 13:8); "Neither their silver nor their gold / will be able to save them / [o]n the day of the LORD's wrath" (Zeph 1:18).

But in contrast to this wealth that is useless for salvation, or even harmful, since it prevents hearing God's word (Mark 4:18-19; Luke 8:14), there is a genuine wealth: "The LORD himself is his portion" (Deut 10:9); "[Y]ou will have treasure in heaven" (Mark 10:21); the role of the apostle is to tell the Gentiles of "the inscrutable riches of Christ" (Eph 3:8).

The kind of detachment needed cannot be reached without a deep faith in a provident God and a clear understanding of our own destiny. When St. Paul tells the Philippians, "The Lord is near. Have no anxiety at all" (Phil 4:5-6), he is making his appeal to a lively faith in Christ and in the coming kingdom. We must set aside all anxiety about temporal things so that we may believe in providence and spend our energies seeking the kingdom.

The second reading in the Office of Readings for this eighth Sunday is from St. Gregory the Great's commentary on the book of Job:

> Whoever seeks our eternal country surely lives a blameless and upright life. He is blameless in his deeds, upright in his faith; blameless in the good actions he performs here on earth, upright in the lofty ideals he perceives deep within himself. Now there are some who are not simple in this good action, for they seek not an inner reward, but outward approval. Thus the wise man rightly said: *Woe to the sinner who walks the earth along two paths.* The sinner indeed walks the face of the earth in two directions: externally, his actions seem to be holy, but inwardly his thoughts are worldly.[4]

God Does Not Forget Us (Isa 49:14-15)

Isaiah here uses a powerful image to bring out God's continual concern for us: "Can a mother forget her infant, be without tenderness for the child of her womb? Even should she forget, I will never forget you." We do not have room here even to list all the passages in which

Scripture speaks of God as a Father. The New Testament will emphasize this theme even more than the Old by developing the idea of our
adoption.

Psalm 62, from which the responsorial psalm is drawn, sings of
our self-surrender to the Lord, who is our only refuge: "Trust him at
all times, O people. / Pour out your hearts before him, / for God is
our refuge" (Ps 62:9).

As we celebrate the Eucharist, we cannot but think of today's gospel, in which the Lord tells us not to worry about material food. He
will feed us, as he did at the multiplication of the loaves, but the food
he gives is his own body and blood. We know that those who eat his
flesh and drink his blood abide in God and God in them (John 6:56).

The preceding reflections may well appear to be nothing but pious
babbling to many Christians of our day. And they would be right if
we failed to make, not a compromise, but a realistic synthesis of the
demands of the gospel and the demands of everyday life. What, then,
can and should "the duty of improvidence" mean to a Christian of
our day?

The improvidence of which the gospel speaks certainly does not
mean a lack of concern for the advancement of the world and for the
welfare of society. Quite the contrary, for it is precisely in this context
that Jesus' words take on their real meaning. When God, beginning
in the book of Genesis, made humans his collaborators in the work
of creation ("Be fertile and multiply"; Gen 1:28), he evidently intended that they should be very much concerned with the world.
Christians, therefore, cannot excuse themselves from an active concern for progress, be it of the technical order or, above all, of the social
order. People would have utterly failed to understand today's gospel
if they were to be unconcerned about technical and social advancement on the pretext that Jesus bids us seek the kingdom and be unconcerned about the passing things of time.

Christians are serving God, not mammon, when they cooperate
with efforts to secure progress and when they dedicate their human
potentialities to the service of all—that is, to the service of their own
family first of all, but as part of the larger world, not reserving their
talents and efforts exclusively to the advantage of their immediate
family, but being open to the needs of all humankind. When Christians who are working for technical, social, and political progress do
not seek personal honor and wealth or the exaltation and increased

prestige of their group, but look above all for the kind of human advancement God wants, then they are perfectly in accord with the divine will. They are not divided.

Such a Christian outlook is admittedly difficult; it requires constant self-examination. A choice of this kind, which is required of every Christian, supposes true humility of soul and an unremitting readiness to abandon ways that may seem normal to others but are, in fact, unconscious deviations from the Christian view of human activity. Here we see the importance of a true Christian community to which each individual can submit problems and receive a Christian evaluation that is not inspired by passion or politics but is reached in the light of the kingdom, the ultimate point of reference in Christianity.

God Will Disclose the Purposes of the Heart (1 Cor 4:1-5)

Once again Paul must issue a warning to the community at Corinth, which is so prone to divisions. He has already reproached them for being overly attached to the manner displayed by one or another preacher, that is, for not looking beyond the person and the manner to the message. They are also too attached to a philosophy and tend to be proud of their attachment.

St. Paul now tells his readers what an apostle should be: a servant of Christ and a steward of the mysteries of God. These titles say everything, and there is no point in looking for some further characteristic that will mark out the apostle. The only judgment we have a right to pass on Paul concerns his fidelity to his mission. Everything else is secondary, and he is not to be judged thereby.

Paul feels himself responsible before God for the way he acts. He does not, however, wholly trust his own conscience in this matter but looks to the judgment of God. He asks the Corinthians to do the same: to reserve their judgment and wait for the Lord to reveal what is in people, for he alone knows the secrets of the human heart. He alone will manifest a person's hidden intentions, and it is certainly he who will give individuals the praise they deserve.

The lesson is clear and is taught without any effort to be diplomatic. It is also an important lesson, one that still holds for us today. It is a serious matter to pass judgment on the Church, especially if we focus our attention on what is really peripheral. God alone knows a person's real intentions, and we must leave justice to him.

Ninth Sunday: The Obedience of the Heart

Do the Father's Will (Matt 7:21-27)

Neither petitions to the Lord nor outward marks of honor given to him are enough; such is the clear point made in today's text. Nor does the text mean only that liturgical prayer is not enough; the same must be said even of activities that themselves depend on God and seem at first sight to be surely inspired by a desire to serve him, such as prophesying, expelling demons, and performing miracles. The mere cry of faith, the mere calling on God's name—these are not enough. What more is required? The doing of the will of the heavenly Father. Those who do not do it will find God treating them as a stranger and an evildoer.

Jesus' words are important and always relevant. Those who do as Christ teaches here, that is, who seek to do the Father's will, build their house on solid rock, so that nothing can shake it. Those who do not do as Christ instructs them here build on sand, and their house will collapse.

The example is simple and illuminating and should make us stop and reflect. Faith alone or devotion or even confidence in the Lord is not enough. In fact, we must go even further: pious practices, attendance at the liturgy, and the reception of the sacraments can delude us about the real quality of our Christian lives. And yet there is a way of preventing self-deception and judging our situation accurately by asking ourselves, "Do we do the Father's will?" We may act in the name of Jesus, we may even act as his ministers and representatives, but none of that is relevant on the last day if we have not done the Father's will.

The gospel pericope thus urges Christians to test their conduct. No practice, even sacramental, and no devotion to the "cause" of God is of any value if there has not been the practical will to do what God wants us to do.

These words of Jesus exclude any possible hypocrisy and tell us clearly what awaits us at the end. God will not acknowledge us because of our prayer or Christian practices if these are simply formalities or actions that spring from our own liking. No, we must submit to God's will and seek to know what he wants of us. There is no secret about what he wants; it is expressed in the commandments and especially in the commandment of love for God and neighbor. Faith, prayer, and devotion acquire value only if they are built upon the doing of God's will.

Does this mean that the gospel is here preaching a more external conformity? Not at all, since in doing the Father's will we are not simply being automatons but are forming our very selves according to revelation and right reason. The parable of the house built on rock or on sand shows that this is the case. To do God's will is to form ourselves in harmony with divine wisdom for life on earth and for eternal life. The solidly built person, who will enter the kingdom as "justified" and "built" in God, is the one who does the Father's will.

Lay up the Commandments in Your Hearts (Deut 11:18, 26-28, 32)

Had St. Matthew wished to give scriptural backing to Jesus' words about the disciple who does God's will, he could have simply cited the book of Deuteronomy. The passage used in today's liturgy helps us grasp the constructive aspect of obedience to God's will.

In the first part of the book of Deuteronomy, Moses explains at length the meaning and importance of the law. It was first and foremost a love-inspired gift of God, who wanted to form his people. The law was a seal upon the covenant, guaranteeing its permanence and solidity, while at the same time constantly reminding the people of the duty of fidelity. By obeying the law, the people of God would gradually form themselves and build themselves up; they were responsible, therefore, for what they were and would be. That is why the passage we read in today's liturgy uses so many images in its exhortation: "Take these words of mine into your heart and soul. Bind them at your wrist as a sign, and let them be a pendant on your forehead" (v. 18).

This people whom God loved was thus obliged constantly to choose, and it would be blessed or cursed by God, depending on the choice it made. The central choice demanded was, of course, fidelity to the one God and rejection of every other god. In a second stage, the choice was to follow the way of the Lord (an expression used with great frequency in the Old Testament, especially in the psalms).

To do as the Lord commanded was to keep the covenant and to walk in his ways. Doing God's will was thus something very positive, not merely a passive acceptance of obligation. In the same way, when Christians of today do the Father's will, they are cooperating with the Lord in the formation and building up of God's people.

People are not entirely wrong in seeing Catholicism at times as a religion of devotion and sacramental practice; they are simply judging Catholicism by Catholics. And yet the Lord spoke clearly enough; we need only read his words to realize that neither faith nor sacraments are enough to guarantee true Christianity and to build the kingdom. The true builder is God himself. He is the Lord of the covenant, and the covenant will be fruitful and turn into a genuine dialogue between God and humanity only when humanity is willing to choose and do God's will.

Justified by Faith (Rom 3:21-25a, 28)

This short passage from St. Paul's Letter to the Romans gives us an opportunity to state in a more nuanced way the teaching given in the passages from the book of Deuteronomy and the Gospel of St. Matthew.

On the surface, St. Paul is contradicting the teaching of Christ. A superficial reading of the passage might suggest that far from realizing the importance of practical obedience, the Apostle is making faith the essential thing: "we consider that a person is justified by faith apart from works of the law" (v. 28). We seem to be faced with a dilemma, for Jesus says in St. Matthew that neither faith nor prayers nor devotions are enough to save a person, while St. Paul says that faith justifies independently of actions or works. Which of the two are we to choose?

The Church, as we know, does not accept the Protestant position that faith "alone" saves. Is the Church departing from the teaching of St. Paul, or has Protestantism somehow exaggerated what St. Paul is saying? We cannot enter here into all the theological discussions, and yet at the same time we cannot simply pass the problem by, especially since the principle of continuous reading has accidentally led to this passage of St. Paul being set side by side with the passages from St. Matthew and the book of Deuteronomy. Paul either contradicts the other two, or he sheds a further indispensable light on the subject.

A first point to be made is one that Paul himself makes in this passage: All people are under the domination of sin. People must therefore inevitably despair if God does not intervene with his mercy. That is precisely what God has done: He has shown mercy and of his own accord justified people. But there is a condition that must be met if God's mercy is to be effective in us, and that condition is faith in Jesus Christ. The one who decided on this new order of things is God himself, and his decision was that salvation through Jesus Christ should be independent of the old law. Yet the decision does not come suddenly, for Scripture had predicted this new way of salvation, and the law and the prophets have their fulfillment in Christ.

Since we are all sinners and since we cannot by our own efforts free ourselves from this situation, God freely saves us by giving us his grace in virtue of the redemption wrought by Jesus. Our part is to accept the gift by believing in him who wins it for us through his death. "God set [Christ Jesus] forth as an expiation, through faith, by his blood" (Rom 3:25). Jesus has become for us wisdom, righteousness, sanctification, and redemption (1 Cor 1:30). In his blood the new covenant has been sealed (1 Cor 11:25). Though Jesus was without sin, God made him to be sin for our sake, so that we might become the righteousness of God (2 Cor 5:21). To be saved, therefore, we must through faith accept God's love for us and the gift of salvation he offers us in Jesus Christ. In this passage, then, what St. Paul is emphasizing is the gift-character of salvation and, on our part, the fact that faith is an indispensable condition for our receiving the gift.

At this point, however, we must be careful in interpreting St. Paul's thought. If we put the thought of the present passage into the context formed by his other letters, we see that he is much concerned with those who imagine that they can find salvation by their own efforts. Consequently, he lays a great deal of stress on the fact that salvation is God's gift to us. At the same time, however, the one who is to receive the gift must believe. Faith, in turn, does not relieve people of any further efforts. In the Letter to the Galatians, Paul reminds his readers that a Christian must be active and that good deeds are needed if one is to be saved. He tells his readers that they must produce in themselves the fruits of the Spirit who dwells and acts in them, and he lists the vices that exclude a person from the kingdom; he bids his readers crucify their flesh with its passions and lusts (Gal 5:16-25).

What does all this mean? It means that while Christians are no longer subject to the old law, they are certainly subject to the law of Christ, which they fulfill by "[bearing] one another's burdens" (Gal 6:2). Paul writes: "the one who sows for the spirit will reap eternal life from the spirit. . . . [L]et us do good to all" (Gal 6:8, 10). He bids

his Roman readers renounce sin (Rom 6:2, 6, 12-14); he tells the Philippians that they must work out their salvation with fear and trem-
bling (Phil 2:12). Elsewhere he depicts the preacher as one who
exhorts his hearers to an obedient faith (Rom 1:5), and later in the
same letter, in a fine passage on the righteousness of God foretold by
Moses, he speaks of obedience to the Good News (Rom 10:16). At the
end of the letter he refers again to obedient faith, this time with regard
to the Gentiles (Rom 16:26).

Evidently, then, while faith in Christ is the only way to attain to
salvation, this faith supposes and indeed consists in obedience to the
Gospel. Faith requires the involvement of the person's entire existence, for while faith alone can save (since Christ alone can give us
salvation), it presupposes a response to Christ, an adherence to his
person and his Good News. Christians thus see themselves obliged
to a choice that frees them and makes them responsible for their own
formation and the building of the kingdom.

Tenth Sunday: Love, Not Ritualism

Yes to Mercy, No to Ritualism (Matt 9:9-13)

St. Matthew records his own calling in a simple, straightforward
way. The story is marked, in fact, by the moving simplicity of all the
vocation narratives in the New Testament: Christ chooses and calls;
the person chosen and called immediately leaves everything and
follows Jesus. In its very simplicity, the calling is so wonderful that
it defies commentary. In this instance, however, the choice is quite
unusual, and St. Matthew deliberately emphasizes this aspect of it
by describing the sequel. Jesus comes to dine with Matthew and the
other disciples in Matthew's house at Capernaum; they are joined at
table by many tax collectors and sinners, to whose ranks Matthew
has belonged until now.

It is easy to see the point Matthew wants to make, namely, that
Jesus has come into the world to save not only Jews but others as
well, including sinners. When Jesus is challenged for eating with
sinners, we observe that he does not justify himself but simply speaks
of himself as "a physician." A physician does not have to justify his
presence among the sick; neither does Jesus. Matthew is thus once
again offering us a theology of the Christ. Jesus is characterized by

mercy, because his Father is mercy itself and he, Jesus, has been sent in order to communicate God's mercy.

Those who listened to Jesus must have had at least a rudimentary understanding of what "mercy" meant when applied to God. The Old Testament was filled with passages on divine mercy. The Old Testament expression "God of mercy" or "merciful God" was the concise statement of a whole theology. For the book of Deuteronomy, God is the "merciful God" (Deut 4:31), as he is for the book of Wisdom (Wis 9:1) and the book of Psalms (Ps 86:15).

It would be impossible, of course, to list here all the Old Testament passages that speak of God's mercy, since mercy is one of his constant attributes. Here are a few texts: "The LORD is compassionate and gracious, / slow to anger and rich in mercy" (Ps 103:8); "The LORD is gracious and merciful" (Ps 111:4). How often had the people of Israel not experienced that mercy! "I, the LORD, your God, am a jealous God . . . but showing love down to the thousandth generation" (Exod 20:5-6); "showing love down to the thousandth generation" (Deut 5:10); "You are righteous, Lord, / and all your deeds are just; / All your ways are mercy and fidelity" (Tob 3:2).

The psalms especially are full of references to God's mercy: "I trust in your merciful love" (Ps 13:6); "Remember your compassion, O LORD, / and your merciful love, / for they are from of old" (Ps 25:6); "All the LORD's paths are mercy and faithfulness" (Ps 25:10); "Your merciful love, O God, / we ponder in your temple" (Ps 48:10); "to proclaim your loving mercy in the morning" (Ps 92:3). This mercy is immense and limitless: "your mercy reaches to the heavens" (Ps 57:11); "his merciful love has prevailed over us" (Ps 117:2). This mercy is also eternal (Pss 100:5; 103:17; 107:1; 118:1, 29; 136:1). The psalms are often an appeal for God's mercy: "Display your merciful love" (Ps 17:7); "Hear, O LORD, and have mercy on me" (Ps 30:11); "May your merciful love be upon us" (Ps 33:22). God's mercy is identical with his loving concern for humanity, which he wants to save.

Jesus' hearers, then, must have understood quite well what he meant. Being God's Son, Jesus must himself be merciful as God is merciful. He came on a mission of mercy, and to him mercy shown to others was far more important than ritual observances. Christianity is a religion of love, not of ritual.

At the same time, however, the catechist must be careful in explaining this passage. Elsewhere, in explaining the gospel in which Jesus

pardons the adulterous woman because she loved much, an unde-
manding catechesis might justify a facile forgiveness of all the sins
of the flesh. So here a simplistic and opportunistic catechesis might
be built on the fact that Jesus ate with tax collectors and sinners, that
he chose an apostle from among them, and that he says his chief
desire is for mercy. But the fact that Jesus ate with sinners and tax
collectors is not a legitimate basis for propaganda in favor of a party
and of overturning the existing social structure. Jesus is not talking
politics in this passage. His teaching aims not at creating new human
and social situations but at establishing justice and bestowing on all
humanity a salvation that is to be enjoyed in the world to come.

The emphasis here must be on the fact that Jesus, in working for
the conversion and salvation of the world, brings together all sorts
of people into the group of disciples, people who will form the Church
without regard to their race or social class or previous moral status.
He does the choosing, and he makes it possible for individuals so
different in cultural background, social status, and moral quality to
live together and cooperate in spreading the kingdom. He came to
call sinners, not to confuse sinners with a particular social class, as
though sinners were not to be found in every social class. It may be
necessary to overhaul certain attitudes cultivated in the past and to
overcome a certain fear of sinners that sometimes affects present-day
apostles. This is a far cry from saying that the Church of today must
side with every claim against society or be concerned only with sinners and rebels. Every age must examine its conscience, but it must
do so honestly and within an understanding of the kingdom for
which the Church toils.

It is true enough, however, that the Church and the faithful cannot
withdraw into the celebration of the liturgy, prayer, and the sacraments while paying no heed to the needs of contemporary humanity
and forming a kind of elitist Church that is concerned only for the
pious. If the Church or Christians were to take such an attitude, they
would soon learn from today's gospel that they were traveling a
different road than Christ.

Yes to Love, No to Holocausts (Hos 6:3-6)

Love, not holocausts: God makes this statement in connection with
a penitential liturgy being celebrated by the people. We cannot assert,

however, that the liturgy was hypocritical and an example of the kind of thing often attacked by the prophets when they saw people seeking pardon out of simple fear and without any desire for real conversion. This passage from Hosea does not support such an interpretation. What God complains of is something different, though quite serious: The love of his people for him is as fleeting as the morning dew. The people are inconstant in their fidelity, and the text hints at a kind of infinite sadness in the heart of God.

Jesus cites this passage in the gospel pericope we have just been reading: "I desire mercy, not sacrifice" (Hos 6:6; Matt 9:13). The prophet adds: "knowledge of God rather than holocausts." What the Lord wants is that people should be united to him in intimate, faithful love.

Here again a crucial problem is raised for our meditation. Are not today's Christians, like the believers of the Old Testament, tempted to opt for an easy sacramental ritualism that would dispense them from the hard task of loving? Do they look for sacramental forgiveness rather than to be truly converted and become more loving? Do they not tend to take refuge in ritual and forget about forgiveness and love of others? Each of us must face the question and try to answer it without self-indulgence.

Faith Made Abraham Strong (Rom 4:18-25)

Paul has launched into his dissertation on "justification." He tells us that it is through faith in Christ that God "justifies," that is, saves, humanity. In simplest terms: Faith in Christ saves.

The present pericope has two themes: the faith of Abraham as a model of saving faith and the Christian's saving faith. Abraham's faith justified him. He believed against all hope; he believed in the promise God had made; because of that faith, God declared him just. Paul had explained a bit further back (see last Sunday) that Abraham was justified, not by any merit attached to his works, but by God's free gift, given on account of Abraham's faith in God's promise and without any dependence on the observance of the law. Neither the law nor works justified Abraham; he was justified on account of his faith and by a free gift.

Because of his faith, Abraham became the father of many peoples. Paul tells us that Abraham's faith never wavered. In all simplicity he believed God's promise, despite all the human circumstances that seemed to say the promise would not be kept. Faith made Abraham strong; he glorified God and remained convinced that God would do as he had promised.

It was this faith that justified Abraham. His faith was, in fact, a certainty that God is Lord of everything; it was based on God's power, whereby he can do what he chooses to do. This attitude of Abraham pleased God, who justified him for his abandonment to the divine will and his utter reliance on the divine power. Abraham did not merit justification as a reward but received it as a gift from God. God made justification dependent on a person loving him and accepting whatever he sent.

St. Paul, who bases his teaching on Scripture, notes that the latter speaks not only of Abraham but of all Christians as well; it speaks of us all. If we have faith, we are the heirs of Abraham; we inherit justification if we believe as he did. We receive this justification, not because of our merits, but as a free gift given to us by God at the moment we abandon ourselves into his hands. We Christians, however, believe in a God who raised Jesus from the dead, for our justification, after he had handed himself over on account of our sins. What was still lacking in Abraham's faith was belief in the merciful power of God as manifested in the sending of the Son and raising him from the dead.

Eleventh Sunday: Chosen by God

Chosen and Sent to the Lost Sheep (Matt 9:36–10:8)

This passage is basic for an understanding of what the Church is meant to be through the centuries that will pass before Christ's return. It sketches for us, in broad strokes, the missions of the apostles and the Church.

The pericope begins with the mention of Jesus' compassion for the crowds. This is not the only time an important passage begins with this mention; we find a similar remark in the second gospel in the account of the multiplication of the loaves (Mark 6:34). The Lord sees the needs of the crowd, and he is moved by them. In our present passage, the crowd is in need of someone to lead it. It is like fruitful seed that could produce a great yield, but there are few laborers to work in these fields. Christ urges prayer to the owner of the harvest that he would send workers out to gather it.

This is the moment Jesus chooses for selecting a group of men who will be the first workers to go into the field. Thus it is the boundless compassion of Jesus for the crowd that leads to the selection of the apostles, their mission, and the mission of the future Church.

Jesus sees the crowd prostrate, exhausted, shepherdless. The shepherd who leads his flock is an image that frequently recurs in the Old Testament, which so often records the experience of a people in distress. The book of Numbers, for example, shows Moses fearful for a prostrate and leaderless people; he begs God to send a guide who will go before them (Num 27:17). The prophet Zechariah describes the people as wandering like sheep, afflicted for want of a shepherd (10:2). Jesus, the great Shepherd, is likewise deeply moved and longs for the coming of leaders for the flock and workers for the harvest. The workers are few, and this should move the apostles to pray that God might send workers to offer their services.

The image of the harvest too is not rare in the Old Testament, although there it signifies chiefly the judgment on the last day (see Jer 51:33; Joel 4:13). In the New Testament, the image is associated with the work that makes the grain grow and the dividing of the good grain from the bad, with the Lord who himself sows the good seed and hopes that it will fall on good soil, and finally with the last day and the final judgment (Matt 13:30, 39). Yet people must pray that the harvest be gathered; they must pray because it is the Lord, not humanity, who is lord of the harvest.

Christ chooses the first harvesters; he calls the Twelve and bestows powers on them. These powers, which are carefully spelled out in the text, may surprise us: the power to expel evil spirits, the power to heal every illness and infirmity. Such powers seem strange to us at first sight, and yet if we look back, we see that they were the powers that Christ exercised in his own missionary activity: "He went around all of Galilee, teaching in their synagogues, proclaiming the gospel of the kingdom, and curing every disease and illness among the people" (Matt 4:23); "Jesus went around to all the towns and villages, teaching in their synagogues, proclaiming the gospel of the kingdom, and curing every disease and illness" (Matt 9:35). Thus, if the Twelve are given these powers, it is because their mission is the same as Christ's.

We are also invited, however, to look beyond purely physical sufferings. According to St. Matthew, the disciples are called to do what Christ did. The latter, however, fulfilled the Isaian prophecy that St. Matthew himself quotes (8:17): he bore our griefs and carried our sorrows (Isa 53:4). As servant of God, the missionary must carry the burdens of others and, as proclaimer of the coming kingdom, expel demons and heal the sick.

St. Matthew then gives the list of the apostles chosen by Jesus. Finally, he reports the careful instructions that Jesus gives the Twelve: They are not to approach the Gentiles or the Samaritans but are to concentrate on the lost sheep of the house of Israel. We must bear in mind that we are seeing here the very beginning of the apostles' mission, at a time before Jesus has carried out his own mission fully through his paschal mystery. That is why he limits the field of their work to Israel; after Easter, missionaries will be sent to "make disciples of all nations" (Matt 28:19).

The activity of the apostles is chiefly to proclaim the kingdom. That is why, as we have seen, they heal the sick, raise the dead, cleanse lepers, and expel demons, for all these are signs of the kingdom. They have been called by Christ without any merit on their own part, and therefore they must give freely and without requiring recompense.

A Kingdom of Priests (Exod 19:2-6a)

What the Lord Jesus here does for his apostles, the God of Israel had done, in a measure, for his whole people. His entire people was to be a missionary people, proclaiming to the nations that their God was one and that he had entered into a covenant with them. The people of Israel were not allowed to be a people closed in on themselves. If they were privileged and were bound to make their privileged status manifest, this was for the sake of the Gentiles who would come to see the witness to the covenant.

It is along these lines that we must understand the phrase "a kingdom of priests." The words mean not that all of Israel formed a priestly class but that the entire people had a ministry and that this ministry, on the one hand, was a participation in the kingship of their God and, on the other, was priestly inasmuch as this people was set apart and bidden to pray, to intercede for the other peoples, to offer sacrifice, and to make their Lord known to all humankind. The people was thus a holy people, that is, a people living in close ties with its Lord; its chief mission was to tell other nations of this intimate relationship. Thus, just as Moses was sent to tell a discouraged people that they were a kingdom of priests and a holy nation that had the special mission to tell others of God's closeness to Israel, so Christ chose his apostles and sent them out to the lost sheep of Israel.

These two readings, from the Gospel of Matthew and the book of Exodus, are richly instructive for us, and this at two levels.

First of all, they are instructive with regard to universalism. A certain universalism is already implicit in the texts when the book of Exodus shows us a people chosen for a mission and when St. Matthew tells us of the first stage in the apostles' mission, a stage that will soon be replaced by the proclamation of the kingdom to all the peoples of the world. The role of Israel was to bear witness that it was a holy nation, and it was to do this for all the nations of the world. In like manner, the Church can never become a self-enclosed entity, for her missionary vocation and her apostolate to all humanity are part of her very being.

The second area in which the texts are instructive is that of "priesthood." The Second Vatican Council, in its Dogmatic Constitution on the Church (nos. 10–11), has emphasized the priestly character of the entire new people of God. After stating that Christ is the one true Priest, the Council shows that others participate in his priesthood in two essentially distinct ways. In other words, the entire people of God is priestly, but the priestliness is of two kinds. There is a priesthood of the faithful, which is a true priesthood and not merely so called by analogy. But this priesthood is essentially different from the ministerial priesthood, or priesthood received through ordination.

The entire people of God is called to be missionary, to intercede, to offer sacrifice, and yet their activity is not the same as that of the ministerial or ordained priesthood. The latter is a special participation in Christ's priesthood; it is higher in degree and possesses essentially different powers. The ordained priest is commissioned to make the mysteries of salvation present and operative here and now; the faithful, as priests, can share intimately in the mysteries thus rendered present and operative.

This careful explanation by the Council and this renewed understanding of the priestly character of the entire people of God are very important. The Church is not only an institution, a hierarchic body.

It is also a single unified reality, although unity does not eliminate distinction and organization. Each member has a place and a missionary function; each member prays, teaches, and offers the one sacrifice according to a given place and position.

Believers are thus invited to reflect on how they think of the Church and their role in it. Each person must face the fact that one cannot be truly a Christian unless one carries out one's mission as someone chosen and sent in accordance with God's plan.

Psalm 100, used as the responsorial psalm after the first reading, sings our gratitude to the Lord for all that he has made of us: "Know that he, the LORD, is God. / He made us; we belong to him. / We are his people, the sheep of his flock."

Saved by the Death of Christ (Rom 5:6-11)

Paul is filled with amazement at the mystery of our salvation, for he sees God accomplishing it, not when we were already justified, but when we were still sinners. The sending of the Son into the world was thus the work of the freely bestowed love of the God who loved us before we loved him or could love him.

It is against this background that Paul views our present justification. For if God did all that for people who were still sinners, much more, now that Christ has washed us in his blood and reconciled us to God, will we be saved by the life of the risen Christ.

This is the reason for our boasting. God is the source of our pride and joy, because now we are reconciled with him and we are sure that he is saving us.

Paul's basic thesis that our salvation is utterly unmerited clearly lies behind the theology of this passage. As far as daily living is concerned, however, only one point in the passage is absolutely basic and essential: we must really live out the paschal mystery of death and resurrection. It is precisely in this, and not in a multiplicity of observances, that the greatness of our Catholic religion consists; the latter, after all, are but means to help us achieve our real goal, which is to live in close union with Christ and his mysteries.

Even though we are sinners, we do not lose hope. The past is the guarantee of the future, for if God concerned himself with us when we were sinners, then surely, now that Christ has died for us and despite the weaknesses that persist in us after our rebirth, God continues to love us. We can regard ourselves as saved in hope, in the hope of something that is certain.

Twelfth Sunday: Proclaim the Will of God

Do Not Fear People (Matt 10:26-33)

Today's gospel is a lesson on what the disciple should be. Jesus has chosen his apostles; they are his messengers. How should they act when they meet with opposition? Today's reading is an answer to this question.

A basic principle is this: Do not be afraid. We speak here of the Christian rather than of the apostles Christ chose, because it was for the Christians of his day that Matthew was writing. What he is saying to them he says to all of us.

There is nothing to fear, because when we proclaim the teaching of Christ, we are making an act of confidence in the effectiveness of his work that is being revealed to others. We must therefore not fear those who can kill the body, but only him who can cast both body and soul into hell. Christ is uncompromising here. Christians must choose; they must also realize that Christ cannot save the person who does not have the courage to profess faith. Besides, what is there really to fear? God takes care of us; nothing happens that he does not will. He watches over his creatures, even the least of them, even the very birds of the air.

This first attitude, which is not in any proper sense negative, since it is already an act of faith in divine Providence, must be accompanied by another: the readiness to confess the Lord, to acknowledge before others the demands made by the Father. If we do this, Christ himself will defend us when we come before the Father for judgment. In all their actions Christians must keep the last day in mind; their value judgments must be related to the judgment they know God will pass on their actions.

The Persecutors Will Fall (Jer 20:10-13)

This reading tells us of the prophet's response to persecution. Faced with a plot against him, he trusts unwaveringly in the Lord's help; he asks the Lord to avenge him against his enemies; finally, he bids us praise the Lord who saves the poor.

Jeremiah is telling us of his own experience, and it is very much like what Jesus anticipates for his apostles and for all of us. When Jeremiah answered the call to be a prophet, he did not do so blindly, for the Lord told him in advance of the kind of conflicts he would have to face. The Church does the same thing today when she accepts adults into the catechumenate after telling them of the difficulties they must meet with; later, at the candidates' baptism, the triple renunciation and the triple profession of faith will again remind them of what the future holds.

Jeremiah will be especially tested, for he will have to meet opposition without the support of a family (he must be a celibate; 16:1-4) or of friends (15:17; 16:8). He provides us with a detailed description of the sufferings that his persecutors inflict on him (15:11; 17:16; 18:20; 20:7-9), and we should not imagine him facing all these trials unshaken. On the contrary, he is almost overcome with discouragement (15:18; 20:14-18). And yet, amid it all, he goes on preaching the word of the Lord.

He has very great confidence in the Lord (15:16) and voices it in his prayers (15:15; 17:14, 18). He is sure that he is being heard and therefore urges us to praise the Lord: "Sing to the LORD, / praise the LORD, / for he has rescued the life of the poor / from the power of the wicked" (20:13).

The teaching given in these readings is one that we need today. Not all of us live in countries where not only our faith but our very lives are seriously threatened, but in every life there are moments when we must stand up to others on behalf of our faith. This may happen within the family; it may even happen between husband and wife. Then we must have the strength and courage to keep the promise we made when we professed the faith and to renounce forever what we then renounced. If we refuse, for example, to be dishonest in business, our professional life may be rendered more difficult, we may lose friends, or we may be less well off. The Catholic who is a business executive, the Catholic who has many friends, will often be persecuted and forced to confess the Lord.

Let us therefore meditate on today's readings, stir up our courage, deepen our trust in divine Providence, and learn to pray to God and praise him for the strength he gives us so that we may persevere in his ways and confess him before others. Everyone must face one's own special kind of martyrdom; it may be a hidden martyrdom, but it nonetheless has its value and greatness.

Where Sin Was, Grace Now Abounds (Rom 5:12-15)

The force of this passage may be very much weakened by our contemporary outlook and by various theological inquiries whose dubious findings have gotten out to some of the faithful and made them skeptical about original sin. The parallelism that St. Paul sets up between Adam and Christ now seems to us rather weak, because the word "Adam" signifies not an individual but humanity in general. Though our translations do not register the fact, there are many passages in which Scripture uses the word "Adam" to mean humanity in general.

Without entering here into theological discussions that have thus far not reached any satisfactory conclusions, and though I believe it is difficult not to think here of the sin of an individual (despite the theories currently being circulated about the sin of the world),* I think that in any case the Apostle's comparison remains fully valid. In other words, even if its historical basis is removed, it keeps its full force if we look less at what would then be a simple image and more at the reality being expressed.

The whole passage can be summed up in this very simple comparison between the free gift of grace and sin. The sin of one human brought death to humankind, and the grace given in a single human, Jesus Christ, is given to all humankind, but the grace is given in far greater abundance. God's gift and sin follow different measures.

Thirteenth Sunday: Receive the Lord

Whoever Receives You Receives Me (Matt 10:37-42)

Today's gospel contains some important themes. One such is the necessity of taking up our cross if we are to follow Christ (see Twelfth Sunday, Year C). The central point of the reading, however, is indicated by the context afforded by the Old Testament reading, namely, that we must receive the Lord. It is on this point that we shall dwell briefly.

In the commandment to be receptive we must not see simply a moral precept; there is more to it than that. Christ strongly emphasizes "the one who sent me." There is an identification of the one we

---

* It is not clear which theories Nocent means: the meaning of original sin? collective versus individual sin? the historicity of Adam?

receive and the one who sent him; to accept the person, moreover, is to accept his teaching and his word. Consequently, there is an identification of Jesus with the one who sent him, and there is an identification of the apostles with Jesus who sends them. The Lord is thus laying a heavy burden on his disciples: they must take his place and let others see that they are indeed one with him who sent them.

At the same time, we must respect the differences that do exist. Evidently the kind of identity that exists between Jesus and the Father who sent him cannot be simply transferred to the relation between the apostles and Jesus who sends them. In the former case, the Persons are distinct but have a single nature. The apostles, on the other hand, are identical with Jesus neither in nature nor in person; they are simply invested with his powers. When we receive an apostle, we receive him insofar as he is sent by Christ; we acknowledge his authority even while we register and recognize his personal defects. Here we have the basis of Christian teaching on the apostolic and priestly ministry: those whom Christ sends are to be received because they are his messengers, whatever be their personal moral elevation or lack of it.

In the Church there are prophets as well as apostles. Jesus tells us that if we receive a prophet, we will be rewarded. The same holds if we receive a righteous person, and even if we receive the lowliest of the disciples of Jesus. Observe that Jesus is not speaking here of the charitable welcome we are to give to every human being. What he is focusing on here is the acceptance of a messenger as a messenger, a prophet as a prophet, a righteous person as a righteous person, and a disciple as a disciple. We are thus being bidden to be discerning and to make objective value judgments on the persons we receive.

Receive the Holy One of God (2 Kgs 4:8-11, 14-16a)

The first reading offers an example of the kind of reception being urged upon us. The story is simple and might have been written in our own day. A woman intuitively realizes that the prophet who is visiting them is truly a holy man of God, a person who is very close to the Lord. She therefore receives him with special marks of kindness, and Elisha promises her a reward.

These texts—the Old Testament reading and the gospel—tell us how individuals should be received in the Christian community: how God's ministers should be received, but also how each and every one of our brothers and sisters should be received. Recent study of the Scriptures has given us a better understanding of what it is to receive someone "in the name of the Lord."

Every baptized person has received some special mission; in any event, he or she is clothed in Christ. We must therefore receive each person in a Christian manner, not simply out of human courtesy, but as a joyous duty, knowing by faith that we touch Christ himself.

The duty of receiving others is not limited, however, to hospitality. Receptiveness is, more importantly and more profoundly, an openness to the other. It means that when we offer our hospitality we do not also impose on others our way of looking at things but instead open ourselves to them and try to enter into their persons, especially if there is something about them that we do not find congenial. We must try to understand, even if we cannot always approve. When we thus open ourselves to everyone, though without necessarily making our own all that they say and do, when we try to understand without passing a negative judgment, we are not only acting in a moral way but also building the Church and the kingdom.

We Died with Christ and Now Live with Him (Rom 6:3-4, 8-11)

St. Paul has exalted the new life and the new world that Christ has brought into existence. In the present reading he develops the theme further.

The passage we hear proclaimed today develops on the basis of a brief theology of baptism. In baptism we were immersed in the death of Christ and buried in the tomb with him, but we were also raised up with him so that we might live a new life. It is through baptism that we share fully in the paschal mystery of the Lord, for the sacramental sign is a likeness to Christ's death and resurrection but also contains the full reality and operative power of that death and resurrection.

From the moment of baptism on, our life is a new one, and its whole direction is new. Since we have become Christ and have been clothed in him, and since he died to sin and now lives for God, so we must die to sin and live for God. That is what Christian life is: a dying to sin and living for God in Christ.

The doctrine is simple and logical; its application proves difficult, a task that must constantly be begun anew. Every individual baptized in Christ is called upon to engage in certain basic activities: changing one's outlook, making one's value judgments accord with one's new being. But the difficulty of this kind of life is only one side of the coin. Those who make the effort at constant adaptation so that they may live up to what they have become know that it brings hope and enthusiasm, peace and joy. We must all want to taste this peace and joy and not let ourselves believe that it is reserved for some kind of "specialist" in the Christian life. It is, on the contrary, the ideal toward which all who have chosen Christ must strive.

Fourteenth Sunday: The Lord Is Humble

Gentle and Lowly in Heart (Matt 11:25-30)

This passage was used earlier for the feast of the Sacred Heart (Year A), but here, with the help of the first reading, we approach it from a different angle. We see Jesus as the humble Messiah. In considering him thus, we shall try to forget such instances in which the humility and gentleness of Jesus are treated in an insipidly sentimental way. What we want to do is to put ourselves to school with Jesus because he is humble and because humility is, in God's plan, the condition for access to the secrets of revelation. Those who are not humble and lowly do not receive the revelation.

The words of Jesus are a classical prayer of blessing. First there is the exclamation of praise: "I give praise to you, Father, Lord of heaven and earth." Then the reason for the exclamation is given: "for although you have hidden these things from the wise and the learned you have revealed them to little ones."

The Father expressly wishes to hide the plan of salvation from the wise and the learned and to reveal it to the little ones. We find this same will taking concrete form at many points in the gospel. Only the Son, and those to whom the Son chooses to reveal him, can know the Father. To receive this revelation from the Son, a person must set aside all human wisdom and become "a little one." We must also set aside human wisdom if we are to recognize the Son present in our midst through his miracles and words.

All this means that if we want to know the Father and the Son, we must become pupils in the school of Christ. We must become his disciples, that is, become gentle and lowly in heart like him. If we do, we will find rest and peace, even while we carry the Lord's yoke.

A Humble King (Zech 9:9-10)

The Messiah who comes among us is humble, as Jesus himself tells us in the gospel. In this passage the prophet Zechariah bids us rejoice at the coming of the king. The prophet's language is poetic and may possibly reflect a community liturgy in which the people of God proclaimed their joy. In any event, the prophet is trying to prepare the people to be receptive.

The king is portrayed as "a just savior." These two words doubtless expressed a traditional ideal for a king, but we may ask whether they do not have a special connotation here. As we just indicated, there was nothing new about the idea that a king should be a just savior. But the adjective "just" certainly acquired a new wealth of meaning in, for example, Isaiah's fourth song of the Suffering Servant, where the latter is said to be "just" because he is the object of divine concern, so much so, indeed, that the Lord makes him victorious (see Isa 53:11-12). The prophet Zechariah seems to be using "just savior" with the same messianic meaning. The adjective "humble" (or "meek" or "lowly") likewise reminds us of Isaiah, who has the Lord say that "This is the one whom I approve: / the afflicted one, crushed in spirit, / who trembles at my word" (Isa 66:2).

This Messiah who comes in poverty and humility refuses the kind of mount that the great people of the world would use and prefers to ride on an ass. The prophets were critical of the use of horses in processions, for they saw them as the embodiment of the warrior's pride and aggressiveness (see, e.g., Isa 2:7). Even back in the book of Genesis, the liberator is described as one who "tethers his donkey to the vine, his donkey's foal to the choicest stem" (49:11). The Messiah who comes in humility will establish peace, breaking the bow of war.

Today's readings encourage us to become pupils of Christ and to learn two lessons from him. First of all, Jesus portrays himself as gentle and lowly in heart, a humble king. We too should banish from our lives all doctrinal pride and every authoritarian, domineering, and triumphalist approach to the Church. There are in the Church doctrinal and institutional structures that may not be tampered with or bent to suit our liking, but this does not mean we must present them to others with the proud and boastful inflexibility that people often show with regard to human doctrines and power structures. The Church, her teachings, and her institutions should be presented to people firmly, indeed, but also gently and in a spirit of humility.

A further lesson is that all theological reflection should be marked by the humility proper to doctrinal study. This does not mean that we are to give up on penetrating more deeply into the mysteries of God. It means simply that prayer and humility are the basic conditions needed in the study of doctrine. Similarly, the proclamation of the truth should be characterized by humility. We who proclaim the truth are weak, and we proclaim only the little that our defective humility has allowed us to grasp of the mysteries of God, Christ, and the Church.

To Live, Put to Death the Disorders of the Sinful (Rom 8:9, 11-13)

When we first hear this passage, we may find ourselves somewhat at a loss. The writing is clear, but the sentences are compact, and it is not easy to follow the development of the thought. On the other hand, once we do grasp the line of thought, we hardly need to go into the details of the passage.

The Spirit of God and Christ is within us, and consequently we live in the Spirit. Because we live with the Christ who dwells in us, we are dead to sin and have our life from the Spirit of him who raised Jesus from the dead. We are therefore in debt now, not to the flesh, but to the Spirit, and therefore ought to live according to the Spirit.

It is important that we correctly understand the opposition St. Paul is setting up between flesh and Spirit. In Paul's mind, "flesh" is a theological and religious term, not a biological or metaphysical one. As he elsewhere expresses it in this same Letter to the Romans, the "flesh" is the "sinful body" (6:6). These last words might suggest sexual sin to us, but we must put that out of our minds, for the "sinful body" is meant to sum up the historical situation of humanity. "Sinful body" designates the creature as one who has rebelled against God and succumbed to sin and who is now doomed to death. Christ is distinguished from the rest of us precisely in that he took flesh that was like the sinful flesh but was, in fact, without sin (Rom 8:3). The Spirit, on the other hand, is the divine Spirit; the Spirit of God is power itself.

This opposition between "flesh" and Spirit enables us to grasp the full lesson St. Paul is teaching us in today's liturgy. Christians live in union with God and the Spirit. Their baptism has, in principle, removed them from the sphere of the sinful flesh; they now live a life that is the Spirit's gift. This new situation entails radical consequences in daily living. They must be wholly dedicated to the struggle against the ascendancy of the sinful flesh, from which they have indeed been liberated, but to which the remnants of weakness still incline them; they must put to death the disordered actions of the sinful self so that they may be able to live. In other words, Christians must actualize in themselves the paschal mystery of crucifixion, joining Christ in the destruction of all evil in themselves so that they may rise from the dead and live with Christ.

Fifteenth Sunday: The Efficacious Word

Receive the Word (Matt 13:1-23)

Two points are made in this Sunday's gospel, but the more import-ant of them, as indicated by the Old Testament reading chosen to accompany the gospel, is the reception and effectiveness of the word. This is also the point with which the passage begins.

Jesus here uses the parable of the sower. We are quite familiar with it, and there is no point in reviewing it in detail. The exegetes maintain that we must distinguish, as far as Jesus himself is concerned, be-tween the parable and its explanation. The celebrant is free to omit the latter and to read only verses 1-9, but the explanation is important, even if it represents the reaction of the evangelist rather than the words of Jesus. It is important because it shows us how the early Church thought about the word of God, about its effectiveness de-pending on the soil into which it fell, and about what we might call the catechetical technique of Jesus himself.

The focus of the parable is on the seed and the soils into which it falls. The sower plays a necessary but secondary role; Jesus is con-cerned, not with the sower, but with the seed that yields various results and with the different kinds of soil that receive it. We see seed being sown on four different kinds of ground, and we are familiar with the value set on the various crops produced. There are failures and successes. The successes must be judged in relation to the failures, and vice versa.

As we said, there is no need for a detailed commentary on each part of the text. In any case, the gospel really provides its own com-mentary, doubtless one that Matthew himself is elaborating for the sake of the Church he is addressing in his gospel. We shall come back to this point. The important thing is for us to get a grasp of the parable as a whole, since it sums up the results of Jesus' own ministry and (in Matthew's eyes) the results of the apostolic missions of his own day. The summary is an honest one and begins with the deficit side of the ledger. The first three results are poor or at least mediocre. This was true in Jesus' time; it was true in Matthew's day; it is true in our own day.

The parable is precisely a parable, and to insist on every least detail would be to go astray. To see in the "sower" only Christ would be to give the figure too much importance in the story. St. Matthew is concerned to present the situation of the Church in his own day; his account, however, also reflects the situation in our day as well. Matthew is a realist but not a pessimist. The last of the four soils is good soil; the word is heard and bears abundant fruit. The emphasis at the end is not on the precise value to be assigned to the fruit; the purpose is rather to stir the Church to wonder and thanksgiving.

The Word of God (Isa 55:10-11)

This short passage from Isaiah is a hymn of praise to God for the effectiveness of his word. The word is, in Semitic fashion, treated as a material thing. Second Isaiah intends to express himself as forcefully as he can because he wants to strengthen the courage of his demoralized countrymen. The exile had been a heavy blow for them, not only in material and patriotic terms, but in religious terms as well. It seemed to them that the Lord had ceased being faithful to them and that his promises had gone unfulfilled. Given this situation, we can better understand the way in which Isaiah speaks, putting the effectiveness of the word in the strongest possible terms. The Lord sends his word as an act of goodwill, and because he is the Lord, his word is and must be efficacious. The power of the Lord is everlasting, even if at times it is a power that seems to fail.

This Old Testament reading sheds further light on the gospel pericope. The parable of the sower, as a summary of the situation of the Church and her missionary effectiveness, should not render us pessimistic but, on the contrary, rouse our confidence in the word of God. The problem implicit in the gospel parable is still a problem for the reflective Christian of today; in fact, the problem seems more acute than in St. Matthew's time. After so many centuries of evangelizing activity by the Church, has the kingdom of God really spread? How many Christians in the various countries of the world really believe in the kingdom and its presence? The number of unbelievers remains vast; people's vices are permanent and even seem to have become more refined. Christians reading the parable with these thoughts in the back of their mind might well feel a deep anxiety.

But such a reading does not come to grips with the power of God and of his word. The Lord continues to be the Lord, and his power and the power of the word remain fully effective, despite appearances. We must go on, in blind faith, preparing the soil and preaching the word of God. We must also develop catechetical methods and use the most up-to-date means of communication, but the faith that we must intensify in order to encourage ourselves is not faith in these means and methods but faith in the efficacy of the word that we receive and proclaim in an attitude of adoration and prayer.

It is perhaps precisely here that we can perceive our age going astray. The efficacy of the word does not depend on our activism, but it does depend, to a certain extent, on the quality of our faith and our prayer. It is amazing, is it not, that after so many centuries and despite all the means we have at our disposal, we seem to have advanced no further than the point the Church reached in apostolic times! This relative failure is undoubtedly to be attributed to a lack of faith and of profound prayer. A "relative failure," because we must read any such summary with minds receptive to the Spirit of God. If we do so, our reading can be stern and demanding, but it will also be optimistic, because we know that God's word does not return to him fruitless. To deny this would be to deny God.

The response to the responsorial psalm gives voice to this optimism in words derived from the gospel. So does the psalm itself:

> You visit the earth, give it water;
> you fill it with riches.
> God's ever-flowing river brims over
> to prepare the grain.
>
> And thus you provide for the earth:
> you drench its furrows;
> you level it, soften it with showers;
> you bless its growth. (Ps 65:10-11)

Creation Longs to See God's Children Revealed (Rom 8:18-23)

This reading bids us change our habits of judging and our way of seeing the world. The world is not what we think it is, that is, simply a world subject to cosmological laws that make it an agreeable place but also a place difficult to live in because of the struggle going on between the opposing elements and causing catastrophes from time to time. For living things too, the world is an unbalanced environment. In his poem on the golden age, the prophet Isaiah foresees the world being made over in unity so that the lion and the lamb may live together in it. Humanity itself is often plagued by inner contradictions; the body is no longer simply the outward manifestation of one's soul, but a law of opposition now holds sway and must be eliminated.

We must, however, look at this present situation in the light of the future. There is simply no proportion between the disorders of the present time and the glory that God will soon reveal in us. Moreover, the whole of creation yearns with every fiber of its being to see this revelation of God's children. And by "creation" here we mean not just Christians and not just human beings; we mean the universe in its entirety. The whole universe, now affected by sin, awaits its liberation. Meanwhile, we and all creation with us must pass through time and the pains of birth; we must be willing to groan in travail, but with a hope in our hearts that does not disappoint. For while we have already received the Spirit, we still await the completion of our redemption.

What Paul gives us here is, in fact, a description of our state as Christians and of the state of the world as a whole. This is why the progress of the world cannot be a matter of indifference to Christians, since this progress is a sign that the world is being rebuilt and gradually restored to unity. The disorders we experience should not be allowed to destroy our hope. Instead, we must accept the dissatisfaction every creature feels as a sign of the future toward which we are moving and of which the Spirit has already given us a pledge and foretaste.

Sixteenth Sunday: The Patient Justice of God

The Justice That Saves (Matt 13:24-43)

Today's passage from St. Matthew's gospel is full of substance and leads us in different directions. We must first reflect on the passage in its entirety; then, oriented by the main theme in the first reading, we can focus our commentary on the intention that should guide us in our meditation on this day.

It is easy to see that, as so often, St. Matthew takes St. Mark as his source but then freely rearranges the material. He brings together various parables with the same theme, namely, the final judgment that shall be given when the kingdom reaches its full form. In the latter part of the passage, we find something we have already met elsewhere: a short statement about Jesus' use of parables in speaking to the multitudes and a commentary on one of the parables to the disciples. The wealth of material in these verses should not be allowed to distract our attention in different directions. The liturgy does not ask us to meditate on why Jesus uses parables or to reflect on the parable as a literary genre. The Old Testament reading makes it quite clear what we should focus our attention on: the long-suffering patience of God, his merciful judgment, and his gift of conversion to those who have sinned.

The parable of the weeds is the most important one in the series. Jesus himself explains it in a commentary. In addition, this parable is complemented by the other two parables, one of which tells us of the kingdom's growth by comparing it to a mustard seed, which is the smallest of all seeds but becomes a great tree, and the other of which brings out the same process of growth by comparing the kingdom to yeast, which eventually causes the whole mass of dough to rise.

If Jesus speaks in parables, he does so in order to fulfill the prediction of the prophet: "*I will open my mouth in parables, / I will announce what has lain hidden from the foundation of the world*" (v. 35). It is not possible to determine who the prophet was to whom St. Matthew is referring, but we do find the words themselves in Psalm 78: "I will open my mouth in a parable / and utter hidden lessons of the past" (v. 2). That which "has lain hidden from the foundation of the world" doubtless means the mystery of the kingdom, which is now revealed, but only to the disciples.

The other two parables emphasize chiefly the slow growth of the kingdom. We might even say the inexorable growth, in which humanity plays no part. Only the power of God, who creates all things, explains this growth that nothing can prevent. People live just lives or lives dominated by evil, but meanwhile the kingdom continues to grow, and the power of God brings it to maturity. In these two parables of growth we catch a glimpse of the long-suffering, creative patience of God as he brings to perfection a work—the plan of salvation—that he had conceived from all eternity for humanity's sake.

This same patient expectation is brought out in the parable of the weeds, which is the center of today's gospel.

The field is properly sown and with good grain: the Son of Man has sown the children of the kingdom in the field of the world. During the night Satan comes and sows weeds; the result is confusion in the world as the good and the wicked grow together. The superficial mind even finds it hard at times not to judge God: How can he let evil thus grow great? Why, the evil seem at times to be more prosperous materially than the good! These are everyday problems and not just for simple people. Why does God let things go on unchecked?

The "accusation" is true. God does allow what he has sown to grow: his adopted children, those to whom he has given baptismal grace, those whom the Spirit has transformed into the image of his Son. But at the same time he allows the weeds to continue their growth, the weeds he did not sow and could not possibly have sown. But God is simply waiting patiently. The world must go its way, and God allows it to do so. He is waiting for the harvest; meanwhile, good and evil are so intermingled in this world that it is better not to intervene too soon, lest the good be uprooted along with the evil. The kingdom, however, is constantly growing, like the mustard seed, like the yeast spreading through the dough. The Lord is waiting for the kingdom to reach maturity.

In recording these parables, St. Matthew was certainly well aware of the state of the community for which he was responsible. He could see the community growing like the mustard seed—starting as a tiny seed, then becoming a large tree. He was aware that the yeast was at work in the mass of dough, but he could also see the weeds mingling with the good grain. The situation was undoubtedly a problem for his faithful, as it is for us today, and it was no simple matter to allay their doubts and to rekindle their faith in divine Providence. His purpose in the gospel, therefore, had to be to show the dynamics of the kingdom and how the kingdom was growing despite the enemies and failures; he had to rouse the community to reflect on its own responsibility as it waited for the great day of God's coming.

You Judge with Clemency (Wis 12:13, 16-19)

God's love for the human beings he created is a constant theme throughout the Old Testament. The history of salvation that we can now read and that we know is continuing and will be continued by us makes manifest to us the love God has for us.

Today's first reading is a meditation on the justice or righteousness of God throughout history. History is a long succession of merciful acts on the part of the Lord who is Israel's leader. God's righteousness as manifested in history proves to be quite different from the righteousness of people or the righteousness of the law. God is concerned about everything, and he thus makes it clear that when he judges, he judges with full knowledge of every case. His righteousness has its origins in his power, and his sovereignty over all things makes him patient with all. He has plenty of time at his disposal. Humans, because their power is limited, repress those who oppose them; God alone, because he created everything and holds sway over all, can be patient and can judge mercifully. One sentence in this reading casts a brilliant light on today's text from the gospel: "you gave your children good ground for hope / that you would permit repentance for their sins."

The responsorial psalm sings of God's mercy: "But you, O God, are compassionate and gracious, / slow to anger, O Lord, / abundant in mercy and fidelity; / turn and take pity on me" (Ps 86:15-16).

The Holy Spirit Prays in Us (Rom 8:26-27)

The most marvelous fruit of the Spirit's presence in us is the possibility we now have of reaching God. The end of the reading for the Fifteenth Sunday (Year A: Rom 8:18-23) reminded us that we possess the Spirit as the firstfruits of salvation. Our salvation in its entirety, however, continues to be an object of hope. To hope for what we do not yet see is to await it perseveringly.

This last statement brings out the difficulty of our present situation, for we are pulled, as it were, between what we already possess and what we hope for; since the latter is full and definitive salvation, we must sigh and pray and ask for it. Of ourselves, however, we are incapable of praying rightly. At this point the Spirit intervenes and helps us in our weakness, which is not necessarily a moral weakness but arises rather from our deficient sense of the spiritual and our lack of hope.

The strongly felt tension between what we now have in our grasp as a beginning of the definitive reality and the definitive reality itself, which is not fully guaranteed us, is not such as to leave us in peace, for we are too weak to be patient amid such a tension. We even feel incapable of the energetic reaction that is prayer. Our finiteness prevents us from penetrating the plans of God, while the prison formed by our bodies threatens to keep us from reaching the goal of our deepest desires.

The Spirit therefore prays in us, and this intercession for us is in perfect accord with God's plans. What God wants is that the plan of salvation be carried out and that he be glorified. Just as the Spirit unites Christians with one another in a single community and makes one being of them, so his oneness with the Father allows him to know the Father's plans and to ask him for what is best for us as we live through the complex process that is the re-creation of the world in unity.

Seventeenth Sunday: Choose the Real Treasure

Sell All for the Real Treasure (Matt 13:44-52)

The real or true treasure is the kingdom of God, of which Jesus speaks, as usual, in parables. The Lord here uses three such parables in an effort to help his hearers understand what the kingdom is. The three are: the treasure hidden in a field that a man sells all he has in order to buy; the merchant who comes upon a fine pearl and sells all he owns in order to buy it; the net that is cast into the sea and emerges containing all kinds of fish, of which only the good fish are kept, the rest being thrown away. To these three we may add a fourth, which is to be found in verse 52: the scribe who has become a disciple of the kingdom and is compared to a householder who brings forth from his treasure things new and old. In fact, however, verse 52 is rather a conclusion to the preceding series of parables, although this conclusion is presented in the guise of an opening for a parable.

The first two of today's three parables are fully parallel. Both concern a precious object, for the sake of which a person sells every other possession. The two individuals in question, however, represent two different situations. In the first, a man who is not wealthy sells what little he has in order to acquire the treasure; in the second, the subject is a merchant, presumably a man of means. In this second parable we think spontaneously of the rich young man whom Jesus called to follow him: "Go, sell what you have, and give to [the] poor and you will have treasure in heaven" (Mark 10:21).

The two parables offer perfectly clear models for all who wish to be Christians in more than name. The danger is that we may think of them simply as parables and fail to see the radical demand they proclaim. They are telling us that no one can be part of God's kingdom without the kind of definitive renunciation that allows for no compromise: one must either sell all or not belong to the kingdom. The kingdom requires a positive acceptance; it cannot be acquired by neutrality. The tepid, whom God vomits from his mouth, are not admitted into the kingdom.

The third parable gives a brief but stern description of those who during their lives do not do all they can to win the kingdom and are therefore not among the "good fish." As fishers open their nets and choose the good fish and reject the bad, so it is with the kingdom; those who are rejected will experience "wailing and grinding of teeth." This is not the first time Jesus threatens punishment to those who do not accept and live by the word. He uses the same language in the first gospel when explaining the parable of the weeds in the field (Matt 13:42).

This group of parables on the kingdom—the sower, the weeds, the mustard seed, the yeast, the treasure, and the pearl—ends with the parable of the net and the good and bad fish. A general conclusion follows: "Do you understand all these things?" When the disciples answer that they have indeed understood, Jesus states the lesson in a form that might be taken, as we indicated, as the beginning of a further parable. He speaks once again of a treasure, but a treasure of a different kind than in the earlier parable of the field. Here the treasure is contained in a householder's box in which the well-off proprietor keeps certain objects. A person who has become a disciple of the kingdom now resembles such a householder. Concretely, the scribe, the disciple of the kingdom, is the disciple of Jesus who has heard and understood the parables of the kingdom, for the disciple now possesses new things and old. The new is the Gospel teaching, the Good News. This new is, however, closely connected with the old, that is, with what the Old Testament had taught through the law and the prophets; Jesus has come not to eliminate but to fulfill that teaching. Those who understand the parables of the kingdom and sell all they have in order to become disciples possess the wealth of the gospel that is grounded in Old Testament teaching and that they are now called on to proclaim in turn.

Ask for the Real Treasure (1 Kgs 3:5, 7-12)

The requirements of the kingdom suppose that the person who seeks to possess it has the true wisdom for which Solomon asked when God appeared to him in a dream and said: "Ask something of me and I will give it to you." Solomon asked for "an understanding heart . . . to distinguish right from wrong."

In reading this passage from the Old Testament, we are dealing once again with a liturgical reading of a text. If we make a purely exegetical reading of this passage, we must see as its intention the desire to legitimate Solomon's succession to David's throne. Because this successor prays humbly to God, the latter gives him the qualities that make a good king. When, however, the Church reads the passage in today's liturgy, she is not concerned with the political purpose behind the text. Her concern in the liturgy is rather with the desire a person who wishes to be in the kingdom must cultivate: the desire for a heart that is docile to God's word.

The responsorial psalm (some verses from Ps 119) makes this liturgical interpretation clear: "I have said, 'O Lord, my portion / is to obey your words'" (v. 57) and "The unfolding of your word gives light, / and understanding to the simple" (v. 130). As the gospel makes clear, if people are to belong to the kingdom, there is a gift they must have, namely, a wisdom that comes only through listening to God's word.

Become the Image of God's Son (Rom 8:28-30)

God's love for us wants but one thing for us: that we be like the image of the Son. That has been the goal of the whole divine, centuries-long strategy.

That God should mean such a goal for us is a grace. He calls us to it; it is he who must destine us for it. This same chapter of Romans has already emphasized the presence of the Spirit in us (Sixteenth Sunday). The Spirit makes it possible for us to pray; he even prays in us. Thanks to the operation of the Spirit, the Son is constantly and dynamically present in us. St. Paul likes to express this interior presence of Christ in forceful ways; for example, "I live, no longer I, but Christ lives in me" (Gal. 2:20), and "to me life is Christ" (Phil 1:21).

The language of today's passage from the Letter to the Romans causes us a certain difficulty, however: God "predestined" us to be in his Son's image; "And those he predestined" to this, "he also called."

We must not look in the Scriptures for a treatise on predestination or read into St. Paul the theological problems that arose later on, especially from the time of St. Augustine. Neither is this the place to show both the clarity and the confusion that theology has brought to the question.

For purposes of our meditation on the text, we must first of all change our habitual way of looking at it. Paul is speaking not of individuals but of a people, and this realization immediately changes the whole perspective. A second misunderstanding has to do with the language Paul uses. It disturbs us because of our ideas of freedom; we tend to question God's justice in this matter of predestination. In fact, however, "predestination" and "predestining" are words that convey an idea of anteriority, but this anteriority in no way eliminates freedom. The "pre" (= "before") in the word "predestination" says that the initiative comes from God. In other words, we were not chosen because we wanted to be but because God freely took the initiative and chose us. But while the initiative comes from God and not from humanity, this does not mean that humanity remains inactive. "Predestination" accents the divine initiative, but it also implies a free, active response. St. John sums up the whole meaning admirably when he writes, "We love because he first loved us" (1 John 4:19).

The passage reminds us also of the process whereby we are divinized and glorified. God foreknew us, that is, he loved us; he "predestined [us] to be conformed to the image of his Son," that is, he took the initiative in bringing about such a transformation. Our response of active faith gained for us the gift of being "justified," that is, of sharing in God's life and therefore in his glory.

Eighteenth Sunday: A God Who Feeds People

For a better understanding of today's passage from St. Matthew, we must consult chapter 6 of the Fourth Gospel, the discourse on the bread of life.

We shall reverse our usual procedure and start with the first reading, from the Old Testament. This will help us in grasping the meaning of the gospel text and St. Matthew's intention.

Be Filled (Isa 55:1-3)

In approaching the gospel text, we must always bear in mind that the evangelist is writing for Christians. He and his readers share the experience of the signs given by Christ, and his purpose is to help them understand and enter into that experience more fully. Now, St. Matthew is writing chiefly for Jewish Christians, and he is here offering them an account that must bring to mind what they know of God's plan from the Old Testament.

If we look through the Old Testament, the passage most like our present passage from St. Matthew is to be found in the Second Book of Kings, when the prophet Elisha multiplies loaves of bread (2 Kgs 4:42-44). There is a point-for-point parallelism between the two texts.

Matthew 14:16-21	*2 Kings 4:42-44*
[G]ive them some food yourselves.	Give it to the people to eat.
Five loaves and two fish are all we have here.	
Those who ate were about five thousand men, not counting women and children.	How can I set this [twenty loaves of barley, and fresh grain in the ear] before a hundred?
[He] gave [the loaves] to the disciples, who in turn gave them to the crowds. They all ate and were satisfied, and they picked up the fragments left over— twelve wicker baskets full.	Give it to the people to eat, for thus says the LORD: You will eat and have some left over.

Being filled is an idea that is entirely human but is at the same time linked to the goodness of God in his covenant. The idea recurs often in the Old Testament. In the psalms, for example, we read: "My soul shall be filled as with a banquet" (Ps 63:6); "But Israel I would feed with finest wheat, / and satisfy with honey from the rock" (Ps 81:17); "I will greatly bless [Zion's] produce; / I will fill her poor with bread" (Ps 132:15). On the other hand, people experience situations in which to eat is not to be filled and satisfied: "They will eat but not be satisfied" (Hos 4:10); "You shall eat, without being satisfied" (Mic 6:14); "you have eaten, but have not been satisfied" (Hag 1:6).

In today's celebration Isaiah speaks of a food and drink given by God in fulfillment of the covenant in which his goodness is so manifested. The passage gives us a glimpse of how superior the food is that the Lord wants to give: "Why spend your money for what is not bread; / your wages for what fails to satisfy? / Heed me, and you shall eat well, / you shall delight in rich fare. / Come to me heedfully, / listen, that you may have life."

Psalm 145, which serves today as the responsorial psalm, has been used from very early times as a prayer before meals: "The eyes of all look to you, / and you give them their food in due season. / You open your hand and satisfy / the desire of every living thing" (v.v. 15-16).

They Ate Their Fill (Matt 14:13-21)

It is easy to see that St. Matthew, like St. John, here draws inspiration from the texts of the Old Testament. He models his own account on those texts, because Old Testament events are "types"—not "examples," but rather points of departure and events that anticipate in a lesser way, and are fulfilled by, what Christ does.

The evangelist offers his community an account that they read against the Old Testament background but also in the light of their experience of the Eucharist. It is not accidental that Matthew here describes Jesus' actions in the same terms he will use in describing the Lord's actions at the Last Supper (Matt 26:26-29).

For the Christian community, the account of the multiplication of the loaves is situated on a line between the Old Testament anticipation and foreshadowing and the later definitive fulfillment by Christ, that is, the multiplication of Christ's nourishing presence in the eucharistic bread and wine, a multiplication that still occurs and is experienced by the community. At the multiplication of the loaves, Jesus is present with his disciples, as at the Supper, and the disciples serve as his instruments in the distribution of the bread, as they will later when they celebrate the Eucharist themselves. Evidently, then, the whole atmosphere of this account is inevitably eucharistic for the Christian reader, whether of the early Church or of today. At the same time, the meal of the crowds for which the bread was multiplied also signifies, in the eyes of the believing community, the presence of the kingdom and the banquet at the end of time.

The account of the multiplication of the loaves also clarifies the definitive covenant that is soon to be established. It shows that this covenant will be a gift of God, a gift symbolized and expressed by a munificence exceeding anything humanity can expect or imagine. The situation at the end of Jesus' life will be tragic and beyond any human resolution. The Lord alone can bring that resolution, but he will use his apostles in providing the world with the food of the eternal covenant.

Today's passage from St. Matthew's gospel is very helpful for our understanding of a truly liturgical proclamation. For the event narrated has a basis in the Old Testament for its telling; it will reveal its full meaning when Jesus later institutes the Eucharist; it continues to be proclaimed in the Christian community at the moment when the sign given at the Supper is repeated and makes the bread of life a present, efficacious gift.

Who Can Separate Us from the Love of Christ (Rom 8:35, 37-39)

On the preceding Sunday we saw how St. Paul regards us as justified, glorified, and transformed into the image of the Son. Under such conditions the judgment we must someday face should not worry us. Nothing can separate us from Christ! Using expressions habitual with him, Paul enumerates the things that might be thought able to separate us from Christ but that, in fact, are powerless to do so. The last one he mentions, the sword, occurs only here. Perhaps he was thinking of the executioner. The Apostle also quotes Psalm 44:22, "It is for you we are slain all day long, / and are counted as sheep for the slaughter." Yet we conquer all these things. Nothing can keep Christ from loving us and God from showing his love for us through Christ.

Nineteenth Sunday:
Face the Obstacles and Advance toward the Lord

Bid Me Come to You (Matt 14:22-33)

Before coming to the main story, this passage first mentions two points that are not without their own importance. The first is this: Now that the miracle of the multiplication of the loaves is over, Jesus bids his disciples enter their boat and set sail. Why does he thus force them to leave the scene? St. Matthew gives no reason, but perhaps an explanation is to be found in St. John. At any rate, the latter tells us that after witnessing the miracle, the crowd wants to take Jesus and make him their king (John 6:15). It may be, then, that Jesus did not want his disciples to be aware of this desire on the part of the crowd and be tempted to join them.

The second point is that, as in St. John's account, Jesus withdraws into the hills by himself to pray. It has been observed that the area is not, in fact, a hilly one. It seems, then, that the phrase "into the hills" is a notation with a spiritual meaning rather than a physical one. In other words, St. Matthew uses "hills" to designate a place where an important event is to take place. Both in the Old Testament and in St. Matthew's gospel, the hill or mountain is the preferred place for encounters with God and for theophanies. St. Luke too shows us Jesus praying in the hills (Luke 6:12; 9:28-29).

Now to the main part of the story. Jesus had stayed on the shore, and the boat was now a good distance from the land and was being beaten about by the waves, since the wind was against it. Suddenly Jesus is there, walking on the water toward the disciples. The disciples are fear-stricken; their faith is not yet such as to make them instinctively realize that Jesus is master of the elements.

There are really two central points to the story. One is that Jesus manifests himself as God and Lord of the elements. The other is to show the level of faith of the disciples and especially of Peter, and then their common profession of faith: "Truly, you are the Son of God."

St. Matthew alone tells us of Peter walking on the water. The other two evangelists who tell the story (Mark and John) mention only Jesus as walking over the waves. Peter's request to Jesus reveals his faith but at the same time his inadequate trust: he wants to go to Christ but also wants Christ to call him as a proof that it is truly he and not a phantom: "Lord, if it is you, command me to come to you on the water."

Stand before the Lord as He Passes (1 Kgs 19:9a, 11-13a)

The Old Testament reading reports an event somewhat like that of the gospel, one that brings the elements into play on the occasion of a theophany. Like Moses, Elijah must meet the Lord on Sinai and experience the fury of the elements. But the Lord is not to be found in these furious elements—not in the strong wind or earthquake or fire. Only in the soft breeze is Elijah able to perceive the presence of God. He then covers his head and stands at the entrance of the cave, for no one can see Yahweh and live (cf. Exod 33:20-33).

Psalm 85 provides us with a commentary on this text and its meaning for us today. The refrain suggested for our use expresses our desire: "Let us see, O LORD, your mercy, / and grant us your salvation" (v. 8). If our desire is to be satisfied, we must bear in mind that an encounter with God, even in the depths of the heart, cannot be self-centered, though it is indeed highly personal; it must bear fruit for the world. That is precisely the deeper meaning of the "contemplative" life:

> I will hear what the LORD God speaks;
> he speaks of peace. . . .
> His salvation is near for those who fear him,
> and his glory will dwell in our land. . . .
>
> Also the LORD will bestow his bounty,
> and our earth shall yield its increase.
> Justice will march before him,
> and guide his steps on the way. (85:9-10, 13-14)

We are called, then, to meet the God who comes to us so that we may go to him. That is the meaning of today's gospel for the Church and for each of us: to recognize Christ and to go to meet him with great trust, through whatever storms. The Church and each baptized person are always obliged to this. To the extent that he had faith, Peter was able to walk on the waters. Jesus assures us, moreover, that anyone who believes in him will do the works that he, Jesus, does (John 14:12). Jesus even goes on to say, "and will do greater ones than these, because I am going to the Father." "Greater works," because we must complete the work of Christ and make it coextensive with the universe. "Greater works," because Christ, seated at the Father's side, sends his Spirit to help the Church without ceasing.

I Could Wish Even to Be Accursed for the Sake of My Kin, the Jews (Rom 9:1-5)

A certain preparation is evidently needed if a person is to accept and receive Christ. One step in such preparation is to reject idols. What nation could be better prepared than Israel? They have been given the adoption, the glory, the covenants, the law, the worship, and the promises of God. The patriarchs belong to them, and, above all, it is from their race that the Christ has been born. Israel has all it needs in order to understand the mind of God and to become part of Christ's new people. Yet all that has not kept them from not receiving Christ! For Paul, this is reason for an immense feeling of sadness.

The Christian cannot refuse to acknowledge the riches of the Jewish people, whom God has so loved, and to be saddened, with Paul, that they have not believed in Christ. We must be united with them at least through love and prayer.

Twentieth Sunday: A House for All Peoples

Israel, but All Believers as Well (Matt 15:21-28)

To grasp Matthew's intention in this passage, we have only to read it attentively. His intention is to bring out the universality of salvation. Why this emphasis? Because very likely his readers, who would be chiefly Jewish Christians, were jealous of their privilege as chosen people of God.

In the gospel passage it is a non-Jewish woman who asks Jesus for a miraculous cure. Her request brings a protest from the disciples, who are still too much preoccupied with externals. Jesus' answer to them is evidently important to Matthew: "I was sent only to the lost sheep of the house of Israel." This harsh answer would content the Jewish Christians of Matthew's day, as it would have satisfied the Jews who were Jesus' disciples.

Immediately, however, the woman makes a humble and moving profession of faith. Jesus is evidently touched by her attitude and persistence and says to her: "O woman, great is your faith! Let it be done for you as you wish."

The Gospel is preached even to the Gentiles, and salvation is theirs if they believe. That is the chief point being made in today's gospel. Membership in the chosen people is neither sufficient nor necessary, since those who are not members can attain salvation if they actively believe. Their faith overcomes every obstacle.

For us today, the most important lesson, one that we should receive with gratitude, is to be found in the attitude of the woman who perseveres in her entreaty with all the clear-sighted determination her faith gave her. In her we see a sureness of hope that shames us. This Canaanite woman is willing even to be called a "dog" by comparison with the children of the house, that is, the Jews, but she insists that she too can receive a favor from Jesus if she believes in him, as she certainly does.

A House of Prayer for All Peoples (Isa 56:1, 6-7)

We may ask why the author of this passage is so concerned with the religious situation of foreigners. The answer is that their vast numbers could not but be a problem for the Jews and also for the foreigners, who felt excluded from the life of Jerusalem even though they lived there.

The author reminds his readers that salvation depends first and foremost on the person's attitude and not on membership in a people. The important thing is to "[o]bserve what is right, do what is just." But even foreigners can do this if they become servants of the Lord, observe the Sabbath, and accept the covenant. All who do this will be led to the holy mountain of the Lord. They will find happiness in the house of prayer, and their holocausts and sacrifices will be accepted.

This prophetic statement is extremely important, for it witnesses against the popular nationalistic view of salvation with its claim to reserve the covenant and acceptable prayer to the Jews. This is why the prophet has the Lord say, "my house shall be called / a house of prayer for all peoples." This text is, of course, not the only such text in the Old Testament or even the first. In the book of Amos we already find Yahweh bringing, that is, guiding, the Philistines from Caphtor and the Syrians from Kir. The same prophet, like Isaiah today, makes it clear that if foreigners can be saved, it is on condition that they be subject to the Lord (Amos 1:3–2:3). We see foreigners coming to Jerusalem in order to experience the salvation that comes from God and his law, and, with Isaiah, we see them turning to the living God (Isa 45:14-17, 20-25). Egypt and Assyria are converted (Isa 19:16-25). All nations and tongues are brought into unity by the Lord (Isa 66:18-21).

The Jews as a people, however, were far from accepting this kind of universalist vision; the dangers of corruption that they had experienced during their captivity pressured them into turning in upon themselves. The result was a strong spirit of exclusiveness (see Ezra 9–10); today's stance in Isaiah served in some measure as a corrective.

The responsorial psalm (Ps 67) voices the same universalism. We Christians sing the psalm while bearing in mind all that the word "catholic" means as applied to the Church.

> O God, be gracious and bless us
> and let your face shed its light upon us.
> So will your ways be known upon earth
> and all nations learn your salvation.
> Let the peoples praise you, O God;
> let all the peoples praise you.

All Peoples Can Obtain Mercy (Rom 11:13-15, 29-32)

Paul uses forceful language, and we can imagine the deep feeling of the Apostle as he wrote the lines we read today. He is convinced of the divine call accorded the Gentiles and of his own mission to them, so much so that he utilizes these facts to stir the Jews to jealousy and to conversion. The Jews were, in fact, in a painful position. They had refused belief and were now rejected; the covenant once given to them has now been given to the Gentiles. The world has been reconciled to God, and the Lord has not restricted his privileges to the people he had once chosen. But St. Paul also envisages the return of the Jews, a reintegration into the new people of God, a gift of life out of death as God's life is given to those who formerly did not believe.

There is thus a twofold movement reflected in Paul's words. On the one hand, the Gentiles, who formerly did not share the life of God, now possess that life through faith and conversion. On the other hand, the Jews, who had been chosen, are now dead as far as life in God is concerned, because they did not accept the Word whom God sent, but they too are still being offered a share in the divine life and can pass from death to life.

St. Paul here shows the principle at work in the divine plan of salvation: disobedience gives the Lord the opportunity to be merciful to the Gentiles and to continue offering that same mercy to the Jews.

This presentation of the plan of universal salvation is very important for us today. We are, of course, quite ready to deny any spirit of racial exclusivity. We must indeed continue to assert, as a matter of faith, the unqualified necessity of entry into the Church in order to be saved, but we are also aware of how this statement must be nuanced. The result is that we are pulled in various directions. The division that we now—thank God!—realize is a scandal is real, and it cannot be eliminated by simplistic attitudes. We must therefore suffer it and be able to wait in patience. The kind of patience meant here presupposes an openness and a dialogue that do not seek to jeopardize the truth but rather to understand the other party and to look for expressions of our faith that will not in any way endanger that faith but will make it more accessible to those who have not always understood it or whom we have not always recognized and accepted.

In any accounting, the universality of salvation remains a great mystery, for it expresses the infinite, mysterious will of the God who wants all people to be saved and who looks within each soul to its faith and its longing for him. These interior realities transcend any verification by human means and are known only to the infinitely wise God. Nevertheless, there exists the divine imperative: "Go into the whole world and proclaim the gospel to every creature. Whoever believes and is baptized will be saved" (Mark 16:15-16).

Twenty-First Sunday: Firm Ground

On This Rock I Will Build My Church (Matt 16:13-20)

The liturgical proclamation of a text from Scripture is not meant as a course in dogmatic theology. It would therefore be out of place here for us to investigate all the implications of Jesus' well-known words to Peter. Nonetheless, the proclamation is important and should make us desirous of attaining a better and deeper understanding of words so decisive for the living reality of the Catholic Church. Their grandeur and seriousness are in no way lessened by the fact that they have been interpreted at times in a tendentious way or used for purposes alien to their true meaning.

Two questions of identity are raised in the text. On the one hand, Jesus asks whom the people that meet him take him to be. On the other, Jesus elicits a confession of faith from Peter and, on the basis of it, gives him a new identity.

There are few objections raised against the first part, that is, the confession of Peter. The second part, however—the promise to Peter—has inevitably occasioned doubts. It is easy to imagine the evangelist forcing the words of Jesus in order to give a basis for the actual situation in the early Church and to confirm it by tracing it back to Jesus himself. In addition, there is a fact that must be taken into account: While the confession of Peter is to be found in each of the other gospels (Mark 8:27-30; Luke 9:18-21; John 6:69), the promise made to Peter occurs as such only in Matthew; similar statements may be found in Luke, but only in other contexts (cf. 22:32, "I have prayed that your own faith may not fail; and once you have turned back, you must strengthen your brothers"), and in the passage of the Fourth Gospel in which the Lord appoints Peter as shepherd (John 21:15-17).

Matthew may indeed have introduced this whole account here in order to highlight the promises made by Jesus. This does not, however, prove that the account is fictional and must be attributed to the evangelist himself as an invention for apologetic purposes. Moreover, as we have just indicated, passages of the other gospels contain the essential elements found here in Matthew. In addition, we must take into account the literary genre of this typically Semitic passage; in the light of it, it seems evident that Jesus gave Simon the name Peter with all the symbolism attached to the name.

There is a further problem that lies outside the scope of this liturgical commentary: Does the promise apply only to Peter personally or does it extend to his successors? There are two chief reasons for holding that the promise extends to Peter's successors and disciples. The first is that the work of redemption confided to the Church was meant to perdure; how, then, could Jesus limit to Peter a help that was indispensable for the operation and mission of the Church?

The second reason is the continuous tradition of the Church from the beginning; traces of this tradition are to be found even in the redaction of the gospels. Far from being inventions to meet current needs, the gospels reflect the attitude the disciples adopted from the moment when Jesus made Peter head of his Church. Many of the gospel narratives, independently of the section we are reading today, emphasize the person of Peter and manifest a general conviction that was never to be denied: Peter received the promise from Jesus for his successors as well as for himself.

It is also to be noted that after the death of Peter (of which no text speaks), all went on as before, and there is no evidence that the still young Church fell into disarray when it lost its first visible head years before the composition of Matthew's gospel. At various times in history, the transition to a successor was not an easy one, but the law of succession and the promises attached to it have never been called into question.

To express the nature of the firm support he intends to give his Church and its visible head, Jesus uses the symbol of the rock. It is a natural enough symbol; it is also typically biblical, and frequent in the Old Testament. It is applied to God himself; he is called Israel's "Rock of . . . salvation" (Deut 32:15). Jesus applies Psalm 118:22 to himself and thus calls himself a cornerstone: "The stone that the builders rejected / has become the cornerstone" (Matt 21:42).

A further point to be noted is that in the Bible the giving or changing of a name confers a particular mission on the person. It is to this end that God changes the names of Abram (Gen 17:5), Sarai (Gen 17:15), and Jacob (Gen 32:29). So too, when Jesus gives Simon the name Peter, he indicates clearly what he expects of his disciple and what he is bestowing on him. Jesus also makes the meaning explicit: "upon this rock I will build my church, and the gates of the netherworld shall not prevail against it" (Matt 16:18).

Peter also receives the keys of the kingdom. The first reading in today's liturgy explains the meaning of this symbol: Peter is receiving an almost absolute power; there exists no higher power after God's own (Isa 22:22). It is for Peter, as God's steward, to judge to whom he will open the gates of salvation and to whom he will close them. It would be a mistake to interpret this power solely as the power to govern; it contains also, and above all, the power to define and protect faith and morality.

The power to govern finds expression rather in the phrase "bind and loose," although "government" here is chiefly spiritual in nature. The point is that there is complete harmony between the decisions of the Church and those of God. What is bound on earth is bound in heaven, and what is loosed on earth is loosed in heaven. "Bind and loose" means to condemn or absolve, forbid or allow. This promise, made here to Peter, will also be made to the other disciples (Matt 18:18); it is a power that Peter shares with his collaborators. Christ's statement in St. Luke, "Whoever listens to you listens to me" (10:16), confirms that this power belongs to the other disciples and also that its exercise is ratified by Christ, in whose name it is used.

A Peg in a Sure Place (Isa 22:19-23)

God chooses his servant Eliakim to replace the usurper in the governor's chair. Each detail in the passage has its meaning. Thus, God will put a robe and a sash on Eliakim, and commit the authority into his hand. Such a statement says the same thing twice, for God gives Eliakim the insignia of power together with the power. The governor's basic role is to be a father to the inhabitants of Jerusalem and the house of Judah. He is truly God's vicar.

The governor will carry on his shoulder the key of the house of David. At that period the key was an iron bar that was carried on the shoulder for practical reasons but also as a display of authority. The person with the key had full authority to open and shut. The house of David is a name for the kingdom that has originated in the covenant between God and his people; the chosen servant is here God's steward.

The servant will be as strong and stable as a peg fixed in solid ground. Why is the image of a peg used? To understand, we must look at another passage in the book of Isaiah (33:20), in which the prophet describes the return to Jerusalem and compares the city to a tent that will be immovable because its stakes cannot be pulled up.

A primary lesson we may take with us from this Sunday's readings is Peter's faith in Jesus and in his divinity; it was on account of that faith that the promise was given to him. So too, the security that the Church has is a gift given not because of any merits on her part but because of her faith. At difficult moments in the Church's life, the passages read in today's celebration should encourage us, not to overlook difficulties or to ignore the human defects of the Church, but to deepen our faith and to pray that the faith of the Church in God's power may grow ever stronger. Her trust is that the Lord is with her and that she has nothing to fear if she really believes in him who can do all things.

The lesson, then, is that the Church is invincible in her very weakness. Her strength consists in her faith in the power of God who is with her. Such faith is also the source of the active optimism that should mark every member of the Church in which Christ's Spirit dwells.

From Him and through Him and for Him Are All Things (Rom 11:33-36)

St. Paul here provides us with a fine model for the prayer of thanksgiving. In the preceding verses he has brought out all that God has done for the Jews and the Gentiles and concluded that if all people have been prisoners of sin, this was in order that he who sets them free and renews them might be able to show his love for them. As we contemplate this attitude of God, we are led to understand the depths of his wisdom and knowledge. His love for us is like an abyss, so impossible is it to grasp fully its depth and quality.

The riches of God is a theme dear to Paul. He puts us on guard elsewhere against presuming upon the kindness of God because it is so rich (Rom 2:4). In Christ, God has filled us with the riches of speech and knowledge (1 Cor 1:5). These riches we must make known to the Gentiles (Eph 3:8). We are never left destitute, for out of his riches God supplies for our every need (Phil 4:19). The mystery of salvation, hidden in God through the ages, has finally been revealed, for God has chosen "to make known the riches of the glory of this mystery among the Gentiles" (Col 1:27). Christ's word dwells in us richly (Col 3:16). God's riches are his possession but are meant to be poured out on us.

But God's riches are an abyss, and at times they seem foolishness to us (1 Cor 1:25). In the last analysis, God's wisdom is identical with Jesus Christ, for it is in him that the treasures of divine wisdom are hidden (Col 2:3). Also hidden in him are all the treasures of knowledge, since anything we can say about God is already verified in Christ.

Today's passage ends with a short doxology: "from him and through him and for him are all things." The Letter to the Colossians contains a similar but expanded doxology: "in him were created all things . . . / all things were created through him and for him. / He is before all things, / and in him all things hold together" (Col 1:16-17). St. Paul has the knack of putting in a few words a wealth of theology that needs to be prayed through and that shows us the kind of prayer he himself must have loved and practiced.

Twenty-Second Sunday: The Suffering Required of the Disciple

Renounce Self and Follow the Lord (Matt 16:21-27)

This scene follows Peter's confession at Caesarea Philippi. Now that the disciples, through Peter, have manifested their faith in Jesus, Jesus no longer hesitates to foretell his passion. St. Matthew shows us Christ foretelling his suffering on three occasions (16:21; 17:22-23; 20:17-19). These predictions are clearly climactic moments in the public ministry, and the whole text leads up to them, for in these predictions Jesus is foretelling the paschal mystery of his death and resurrection.

He is not understood, even though he has spoken in such clear terms. He has not simply foretold what is going to happen; he foretells what "must" happen, that is, he speaks of a mission he cannot but carry out. At his baptism in the Jordan, he has been designated by the Father as beloved Son, the one who is loved precisely because he does the Father's will. He is the Son who is also Servant and Priest, the Son who gives his life in sacrifice in order to do the Father's will and save humanity. He cannot escape from this mission that requires so much suffering of him but that is also represented as glorious.

Peter has acknowledged Jesus to be the Son of God and the Messiah, but he does not accept all the consequences of such a faith; he does not yet understand its full implications. His thoughts are those of a mere human; he does not comprehend God's plan of salvation. Herein we see, as it were, Peter's still divided personality: he is a person of lively faith, but he is also weak. When St. Luke (chap. 22) and St. John (chap. 21) bring out this paradox, they thereby emphasize the fact that Peter's status as "rock" or solid foundation is a gift of God and independent of the personal weakness of this apostle who must strengthen others in their faith.

Jesus now goes a step further and teaches his followers what a true disciple's attitude must be. We are all familiar with his words, for they have so often been repeated—and so often ignored in practice! St. Matthew may here be assembling statements originally made on several occasions; in any case, their effect is more powerful by reason of the repetition.

"[D]eny himself, take up his cross, and follow me": these are the three fundamental attitudes. "Deny himself" should not be understood to mean simply a moral attitude and an outward change of ways. It implies a complete conversion, a shift in values that takes place not only in the conceptual order but also in the depths of the person. Peter had been rebuked for thinking like a mere human being rather than like God. The lesson for us is that we must change our human valuations of the way of salvation and adopt the way of salvation that God wants us to follow. Even our very way of understanding Jesus must change, so that we will see him as he really is and not as we would like him to be. The same applies with regard to the Church in our day; if we are to understand her, we must deny ourselves, stop seeing her as we would like her to be, and see her as she really is in God's plan.

"Take up his cross" is likewise often understood in too narrow a fashion, as though it meant simply accepting poor health, moral and social difficulties. In fact, the phrase seems to have a broader and more positive meaning of sharing with Christ in the work of saving the world. Our attitude must be paschal. We must "follow" Jesus, which means, first and foremost, to share with him the burden of saving the world. This attitude is one we must cultivate each day and in even the smallest matters. Our role is an important one, and we must always bear in mind the greater, paschal meaning of the little "crosses" in our life.

The disciple must also risk his or her life. To do so for God and the salvation of the world manifests the courage of a true disciple. Here again, however, we should not think solely of risking bodily life or sacrificing the possible successes that attend on others' lives. The expression "lose one's life" means something more than that. The real point is that one so believes and follows Jesus that one entirely abandons the self, for God's thoughts are not ours. Disciples must be willing to live according to God's plan and to work as the Lord wishes for the salvation of the world. In other words, we give ourselves—not in the ways we had anticipated, but as God wishes; his ways may not be the same as we would have chosen.

All this, however, leads to glory, and Jesus bids us focus our attention on the glory that the Father will give the Son and in which we too will share, according to each one's works.

I Am Insulted and Mocked (Jer 20:7-9)

This passage is part of the "confession" that Jeremiah speaks to his Lord. Here we see the prophet "duped" by the Lord and unable to resist God in the situations in which God involves him. "[Y]ou were too strong for me, and you triumphed." The prophet now finds himself caught up in insurmountable difficulties. He is forced to preach a violence and destruction that do not correspond to his temperament; yet these positions are forced upon him from above. For this reason he has become a laughingstock and the object of mockery.

In these circumstances the prophet experiences discouragement and is tempted to stop following the Lord's commands and speaking in his name. He is no longer his own person but lives a life that is not truly his own; he experiences an alienation from himself. Yet he cannot free himself from God. There is a burning fire within him that he cannot control. The person of the prophet disappears, as it were, and the Lord speaks in and through him, but at the cost of martyrdom to the prophet. Jeremiah has become the very model of self-denial for the sake of doing God's will.

What the prophet is really doing is yielding to the love of God. It is of this that the responsorial psalm (Ps 63) sings. Like David, the prophet thinks of himself as "walking in a dry, weary land without water," but he also knows that "your loving mercy is better than life," and therefore "my lips will speak your praise." He clings to the Lord with all his heart, and the Lord sustains him.

Offer One's Person and Life in Sacrifice (Rom 12:1-2)

Jeremiah had been a model for the sacrificial life of the Christian. Now St. Paul in his turn exhorts Christians to offer their lives in self-denial. For him, however, the model of self-denial for the sake of doing God's will is Christ himself. Christians must set aside their own ways of thinking, not in order to conform themselves to the present world but in order to know and do God's will. It is in this course of action that renunciation of self consists. But that course of action is also authentic worship and adoration of God. There can be no genuine adoration and contemplation without this self-denial, the nature and quality of which we now understand better.

The same love that led the Son to give himself as a fragrant sacrifice to God (Eph 5:2) should lead God's adoptive sons and daughters to the same kind of self-surrender. The Old Testament had, of course, already known this kind of sacrifice acceptable to God (Sir 35:1-3), and we have just seen in Jeremiah's "confessions" a similarly generous and unconditional surrender of self to God. Now it is those who have been transformed by the Spirit in their baptism who are bidden to renounce themselves after the manner of him in whom they have been clothed in the sacrament of rebirth. The Spirit has given them a new birth; now their person and their very mentality must likewise be renewed.

It follows from this that Christians no longer own themselves. They have surrendered their own lives in order to be witnesses to God's will.

Our age is rediscovering the prophetic stature and quality of the Christian. It is important, however, that we not look on this prophetic quality in terms solely of mission and of claims upon others. At the foundation of all truly prophetic action there is, and must be, the denial of self in order to be the messenger of God's will. In other words, there can be no authentic prophecy unless one does God's will in the details of one's own life, just as there is no genuine worship going on in a congregation that is not basically determined to submit to God's plan for it.

The authentic Christian prophet, then, is the person who, despite charges of conservatism and clericalism, does not seek to flatter the desires of worldly people but dares to proclaim the truth and the message as it really is. We saw how Jesus harshly rebukes Peter for seeking to hold him, Jesus, back from his passion and the doing of the Father's will in an utterly self-denying way. The Christian is sometimes forced to speak, for there are silences that amount to surrender and compromise. In these circumstances Christians should, like Jeremiah and despite their fear of the consequences, feel themselves unable to resist the urging of the Spirit given them at baptism.

The period in which we live needs Christians who are prophetic, but prophecy must be inseparable from the attitude of the servant who gives his or or her life. Without fanfare or ostentation, this servant lives a life that is strongly and solidly grounded in truth and wholly given over to God, through renunciation of personal views, for the sake of establishing God's kingdom.

Twenty-Third Sunday: Correcting Others

Win Your Brother Over (Matt 18:15-20)

This passage from the First Gospel enables us to enter into the internal life of an early Christian community and to see the practice

138 Sundays Two to Thirty-Four in Ordinary Time

of correcting others that the great monastic lawgivers would later try to establish in the families they had founded.

If we are properly to understand the duty of correction, we will do well to begin with the final verses of the passage. They show us that we are dealing with a community, a local Church.

"[W]here two or three are gathered together in my name, there am I in the midst of them." To "gather in the name of Jesus" means, for St. Matthew, to form a Church. Consequently, in his view and in accordance with Jesus' words, a Church is identical with those who have gathered in the name of Jesus. Such a gathering of two or three is assured that Jesus is present in its midst; for the Church this means the presence of the glorified Lord. St. Matthew will later record Jesus' final words: "I am with you always, until the end of the age" (28:20).

It is because he is thus present that Christ can say, in the preceding verse, "if two of you agree on earth about anything for which they are to pray, it shall be granted to them by my heavenly Father." It is because people gather in Jesus' name and because Jesus is therefore present in their midst that God hears and accepts their prayer. Later on St. Matthew will report another saying of Jesus: "Whatever you ask for in prayer with faith, you will receive" (21:22).

This local Church, in which the Lord lives and hears the faithful who pray to him, is made up of the baptized. These men and women, however, continue to be human beings, so sin is possible and does occur. This situation requires internal correction. The community cannot simply allow one of its members to live a life that is a contradiction to what the community represents. But the primary reaction to the situation is not rejection or reprobation but brotherly and sisterly love. There can be no evading some decisive action in the name of the Body that is the Church.

The action required must be carefully taken. Jesus is fully aware of this and therefore proposes three stages in the fulfillment of the duty of correcting others. The first is for a member to approach the other privately and try to achieve persuasion. What a joy if the other listens, for "If he listens to you, you have won over your brother"! This, then, is the first step to be taken out of the community's love.

If sinners are convinced that they are right and will not admit the real character of what they do, or if they are convinced that the rebuke springs from subjective motives, then the corrector should take one or two others from the community along. Perhaps this united front will have an effect. The other may be impressed and come to realize the seriousness of the situation.

If sinners still do not understand and remain obstinate, then out of love for them and for the good of the community, the corrector must appeal to the community. This appeal may in turn lead to a painful but necessary decision: If sinners refuse to heed the Church, they must be regarded as "a Gentile or a tax collector." They have no sense of the Lord's presence in the community and are a living offense to God therein present.

The Church has this power of judging, of binding and loosing, as the Lord puts it. His words echo a rabbinical maxim that he is using to establish, not, it seems, the doctrinal power of the Church, but its "disciplinary" power, that is, the power of maintaining order and protecting the community. A judgment of God corresponds to the judgment of the Church when the latter binds and looses. Sinners who are unwilling to change their way of life are condemned by the Church but also by the Lord himself, for it is in the Lord's name that the Church acts. The Church knows that its decision is matched by God's.

Warn the Wicked (Ezek 33:7-9)

The Old Testament knows of a similar duty. Thus Ezekiel understands that the Lord is imposing it on him: "You, son of man, I have appointed watchman for the house of Israel." Israel has forgotten its obligation of fidelity to the Lord. A new exile threatens, and Ezekiel is his people's only hope: he must continue to make clear what justice requires and to rouse his people to conversion. God makes him a watchman—in fact, the last protector who can still do something to lead people back to the right path.

God, of course, is always offering his forgiveness, but the sinners must acknowledge who and what they are. Someone must warn them of the death that threatens. That is Ezekiel's role. If the prophet does not do his duty, he will be responsible for the sinners' death; if Ezekiel does not bid sinners abandon their evil ways, the evil will die in their sins. If, however, Ezekiel warns them but sinners do not listen, sinners will die in their sins, but the prophet will save his own life, for God would have called him to account for his neglect of sinners.

Love Fulfills the Law (Rom 13:8-10)

Love perfectly fulfills the law that requires the Christian to exercise internal correction. This is the conclusion we can draw from the present reading, which chance has joined to the first reading and the gospel. Correcting others pays the debt of love we owe. The debt itself is a permanent thing, for we must constantly love our neighbor.

We are introduced here to the mystical dimension of the Christian community, where the greatest commandment is the commandment of love. The gospel for the Thirtieth Sunday (Year A) will give us the words of Jesus as reported by St. Matthew: "You shall love your neighbor as yourself" (Matt 22:34-40). When Christians exercise charity, they bring the law to its fulfillment, as Jesus did by dying for us (Rom 10:4). To love one's neighbor is thus not only to fulfill an obligation but to enter upon the way of Christ himself, to imitate him, and to live as he did.

The conditions of modern life and civilization do not allow us to imitate exactly the procedure here recommended by Jesus, but the spirit of what he says is incumbent on us all. The reaction of Christians when confronted with a neighbor's sin should always be inspired by this passage, for the stakes are the life of our neighbor. If we divulge the sin without first having tried in a sensitive way to correct the person according to the possibilities open to us in our day, we show that we have not understood the meaning of love. On the other hand, if we allow the whole community to be endangered and if we do not accept to be a sentinel over the life of the Church, we are refusing to love our neighbor.

Correcting others has nothing to do with playing the informer or with a fanatical righting of wrongs, still less with the deadly habit of prying and being always ready to denounce without an ardent desire to heal above all. Our gigantic institutions, which are no longer human in their scale, make it difficult and often impossible to exercise correction in a serene way, although such an exercise is a sign of spiritual vitality in a people that is led by the Lord. At least, each of us must ask ourselves what our own duty is and not be self-satisfied when it comes to our attitude toward a sick member of the community.

Twenty-Fourth Sunday: Forgiveness

Forgive Seventy Times Seven Times (Matt 18:21-35)

This passage must be read in the context of the community, that is, the Church. It deals with the forgiveness of offenses and with the Christian requirement of community and forgiveness and sees these directly in relation to the kingdom. The pericope is thus not simply offering an exhortation to morality but teaching us what Christian community must be in its relationship to the eternal kingdom.

Jesus begins his parable with the words: "The kingdom of heaven may be likened to a king." It is not our task here to engage in historical criticism of the details of the parable, for a parable has nothing to do with historical truth. The improbability of the amounts of money is unimportant; in fact, the improbability helps give the parable its shock value.

Nor is there any point to giving an explanation of a parable that is quite clear in itself. It is so clear, indeed, that every reader can identify with the wicked steward! In addition, the ending, "So will my heavenly Father do to you, unless each of you forgives your brother from your heart," reminds us immediately of the petition in the Lord's Prayer: "And forgive us our trespasses, as we forgive those who trespass against us."

Forgiveness and mercy are basic attitudes that every Christian in the Church must have. They are, and must be, characteristic of every Christian who truly wishes to follow Christ. The Church, when all is said and done, is a community of forgiveness and mercy.

Forgiveness of Neighbor and Forgiveness of Sins (Sir 27:30–28:7)

The Old Testament knew the obligation of forgiving one's neighbor. The first reading for this day is clear enough, and its content may be easily summarized as follows: Anger and wrath are condemned without reserve. Each of us must bear in mind our own fleshly condition and our weaknesses; if we do, we will find it difficult to condemn others and withhold our forgiveness. After all, we are all members of the same community of weak people. Moreover, how can we pray that our own sins be forgiven if we ourselves do not forgive others? Life under the covenant presupposes a respect for the commandments and a willingness to forgive without holding grudges.

We Live and Die for the Lord. Why Judge? (Rom 14:7-9)

The verses read today from the letter to the Romans show a fortuitous but real correspondence with the first reading and the gospel.
The main point that Paul is making here is that whether in life or in
death we belong to the Lord, since Christ has become Lord of both
the living and the dead. In this context more than elsewhere, the use
of the title "Lord" underscores the unlimited power Christ has won
through his death and his resurrection glory. "Lord of both the dead
and the living" expresses his unconditioned domination of the entire
universe. The same formula is to be found in the Acts of the Apostles
(10:42), the Second Letter to Timothy (4:1), and the First Letter of
Peter (4:5).

If we accept the Gospel, embrace the faith, and receive baptism,
we are accepting the lordship of Christ: "we live for the Lord." But
then, all of us alike are under the same lordship, and if we are all
servants of one and the same Lord, why do we condemn one another?
"Why then do you judge your brother? Or you, why do you look
down on your brother?" says St. Paul in the verse immediately following today's passage, and he goes on to show why such condemnation of one another is unthinkable: we must all appear before God's
judgment seat and render an account of ourselves.

In the community of the Church, then, each person must forgive
the others and stop passing judgment on them. In some cases, one
individual may certainly wrong another. But we must also remember
that a certain pluralism and variety is quite legitimate and that one
person may be trying to serve in one way, another in another. We
have no right to demand a uniformity that is cut to our measure and
our personal views. We do not have the duty of judging our neighbors, but, on the contrary, must appear, just as they must, before the
tribunal of the Lord. It is to the Lord that we have all been subject
during our lives and in our death; it is to him that we have promised
service.

The responsorial psalm (Ps 103) sings of the Lord's forgiveness of us:

> He will not always find fault;
> nor persist in his anger forever.
> He does not treat us according to our sins,
> nor repay us according to our faults. (vv. 9-10)

Twenty-Fifth Sunday: God's Thoughts and Value Judgments

Do You Begrudge My Generosity? (Matt 20:1-16)

The phrase we have just used as a title for this section on the gospel of the Twenty-Fifth Sunday can be misleading to the reader. It must also be admitted that the Old Testament reading for the day can direct our thoughts along the wrong lines as far as an understanding of the gospel is concerned.

The workers of the eleventh hour have been a subject of inexhaustible discussion. The exegetes have labored to explain the behavior of a boss who flouts all our social principles; preachers likewise find themselves in difficulty when they must explain this parable of Jesus to people habituated to the idea of social justice. The theologians, for their part, try to avoid having to find a footing on such treacherous ground and seek rather to follow a different line: we cannot comprehend God's thoughts, for they are not the same as ours.

Two points must be kept in mind as we attempt an explanation of this pericope. The first thing to be remembered is the literary genre of parable. In a parable, details are secondary; the primary concern is the main point being made. In the present parable, the main point is that the last will be first. The parable affirms this principle with an illustration that may seem improbable or even be an example of social injustice.

The second point is that the parable must be situated both within the overall teaching of Christ and in relation to the circumstances in which it was spoken. Two circumstances in particular need to be emphasized here.

Jesus often observes that the chosen people has not proved faithful and has refused to accept him. God's choice is therefore now fixed upon a new people: the Church that is in process of being formed. Over against the Jewish people, which had been God's favorite for centuries, the Church, a worker of the eleventh hour, sees itself overwhelmed by gifts from God. St. Matthew is the only evangelist to report this parable, and he may have had good reason for doing so, namely, to bring home to Jewish Christians the importance and unique situation of the Church. The people formerly chosen by God has now been replaced by a new people, a people of the eleventh hour.

There is a further viewpoint that Jesus adopts and that St. Matthew finds opportune to make part of his catechesis. To understand this further point, we must recall the parable of the prodigal son, which is a parallel to the present parable (see below). The real issue is thus the acceptance and forgiveness of sinners. Like Jesus in his time, St. Matthew is having difficulty persuading his community to welcome Gentiles, who are treated as though they too had always been worshipers of the true God.

These two viewpoints—that of the new people that now takes first place and that of the sinner who is treated like the faithful servant—seem to be closely connected. It is along this line that we are invited to understand the parable.

First of all, we must put the parable into its context. It follows Peter's question at the end of the preceding chapter: "We have given up everything and followed you. What will there be for us?" (Matt 19:27). Jesus answers him by telling him that his disciples will sit on twelve thrones and judge the twelve tribes of Israel. He then ends with the statement, "many who are first will be last, and the last will be first" (Matt 19:30). Jesus is here speaking of the latecomers, who are the disciples; even though they come last, they will sit on twelve thrones and judge the twelve tribes of Israel, who were the first to come. The reason the apostles receive this preference is that they have left everything to follow Jesus.

Yet the words of Jesus (Matt 19:30) need some further explanation. "Many who are first will be last, and the last will be first" is a vision of things that cannot be understood solely by reference to the apostles. It yields its meaning only when related to the kingdom of heaven. That is why the Lord continues with a parable concerning the kingdom.

The liturgical proclamation of today's gospel begins, unfortunately, with chapter 20 and omits the last verse of chapter 19, that is, the verse that leads over to the parable of 20:1-16. Verse 1 of chapter 20 actually begins with the connective "for," showing the continuity with chapter 19. Our parable in chapter 20 ends, moreover, with a repetition of the statement in 19:30.

We may now turn to the parable of the prodigal son in St. Luke and relate it to St. Matthew's parable. The parable of the Pharisee and the tax collector (Luke 18:11) should also be related to the first two. By these comparisons we can gain a fuller understanding of the parable of the workers at the eleventh hour.

In the parable of the prodigal son, the elder son complains bitterly at not receiving what his disloyal brother receives, although he, the elder brother, has always been faithful. He does not understand why the prodigal son should receive anything at all; in other words, his anger is due not to the fact that he, the faithful son, has not received enough but to the fact that his brother, a sinner, should be given anything at all. He does not agree that his brother should be forgiven, and we even sense a certain contempt in his attitude.

This same contempt may be glimpsed in the objections of the workers who had come at the first hour, "These last"; in the words of the elder son, "your son"; and in the words of the Pharisee with regard to the tax collector, "this tax collector." It is this contempt for the sinner and for the worker who comes at the last hour that Jesus intends to reprove and correct. The workers are protesting, not so much because they do not receive more than the worker of the last hour, but because the worker of the last hour is rewarded at all. They do not want to see this neighbor of theirs welcomed at all.

The parable certainly is not to be understood as justifying what we today see as a form of social injustice. What it does insist on is the necessity of welcoming and not condemning the sinner. Contempt for the sinner only makes it impossible to understand the action of the householder and the forgiveness given by God. The parable thus has for its focal point the goodness and forgiveness of God. It emphasizes God's acceptance of those who receive his messenger; among the latter, the disciples take first place and will even sit and judge the twelve tribes of Israel.

A person who refuses to regard a sinner as a brother or sister, or the converted Jew who feels contempt for the Gentiles who enter the Church, cannot possibly enter into and adopt the outlook of God. Similarly, those who are satisfied with their own uprightness and imagine that it gives them a right to privileges cannot understand the thinking of God.

The parable thus is not to be explained in terms of purely human justice. Neither, however, does it offer a theology of some incomprehensible divine justice. Its aim is to bring out something quite different: the fact that Jesus has been sent to save sinners and that those who receive him with faith become the first in the kingdom.

My Thoughts Are Not Your Thoughts (Isa 55:6-9)

The prophet is not talking about a God whose behavior is arbitrary and to whom we must submit even though we do not understand him at all. This text, like the parable of the workers at the eleventh hour, has frequently served as the basis for commentaries that urge us to accept trials or comparisons we find hard to admit. Yet we need only read the text attentively and we will see that it is not speaking at all of a God who complacently acts in his own peculiar way, so that we cannot possibly understand his decrees.

If we grasp the real meaning of the Isaian text, it will help us gain a better understanding of today's gospel. These verses of Isaiah have a quite specific context: the prediction of a new Jerusalem and of a new and eternal covenant (Isa 55:1-4). The Lord creates a new people. To enter into that people, a person must be converted: "Let the scoundrel forsake his way, / and wicked his thoughts; / let him turn to the LORD for mercy; / to our God, who is generous in forgiving" (55:7).

What does God mean, then, when he says that his thoughts are not our thoughts nor his ways our ways? Does he mean that his mental categories are alien to ours? That his justice has nothing in common with ours? It does not seem so. We are to read the Isaian statement rather as an assertion that God's mercy is infinite. Our justice condemns, but God's justice pardons, because his thoughts are beyond ours. The responsorial psalm (Ps 145) expresses the idea well: "[His] greatness cannot be measured. . . . The LORD is kind and full of compassion, / slow to anger, abounding in mercy. . . . The LORD is just in all his ways" (Ps 145:3, 8, 17).

For Me to Live Is Christ (Phil 1:20c-24, 27a)

"Christ will be magnified in my body, whether by life or by death." A preferable translation would be: "The glory of Christ will be manifested through me." "In my body" is a literal translation of the Greek text, but "body" stands here for the person or that individual's existence.

Christ's glory is manifested in the Christian's earthly existence, because through baptism and the Eucharist the Christian has been wholly incorporated into Christ. Christ's glory will continue to be manifested by Christians in the life to come, because then they will share Christ's risen life. The communion of Christians with Christ is such that whether Christians are alive or dead (in terms of earthly life), Christ's glory will always be manifested in them.

At the same time, however, while the Christian is indeed incorporated into Christ, even while on earth and is already identified with Christ, death will make possible a more perfect communion with the Lord. In his Second Letter to the Corinthians, Paul writes: "we know that while we are at home in the body we are away from the Lord, for we walk by faith, not by sight. Yet we are courageous, and we would rather leave the body and go home to the Lord" (2 Cor 5:6-8). Nonetheless, here in the Letter to the Philippians Paul hesitates when it comes to choosing death or earthly life, and he ends by choosing to stay on earth, since his presence is useful to his disciples.

Christians have an obligation to lead a life worthy of the gospel that Christ preached, for they are incorporated into Christ and must show forth in their life the glory of their Lord.

Twenty-Sixth Sunday: Repent and Live

Sinners Are Saved by Faith and Repentance (Matt 21:28-32)

The passage proclaimed today may seem to be made up of disparate pieces, with the first part having nothing to do with the second. In addition, the first part may seem to be proposing a simple case of morality and telling us that what counts is not intentions or words but actions. The chief priests and the elders evidently had no difficulty in recognizing that the man who truly did his father's will was the one who actually did it, even though he had begun by refusing to do it. This is fine, but such a very simple lesson on obedience seems a bit disappointing.

We may also feel some dissatisfaction that Matthew should follow the parable with a conclusion that seems to have nothing to do with it. The impression of discontinuity is one many people have; some missals and lectionaries, for example, leave a space between the parable on the two sons and the saying of Jesus. These various difficulties bid us read the text carefully and put it into its context.

Jesus has entered the temple and is teaching there. The high priests and the elders of the people question him, asking by what authority he teaches. Jesus answers with a question: "Where was John's baptism from? Was it of heavenly or of human origin?" The others were in a dilemma. If they answered, "Of heavenly origin," they would be putting themselves in the wrong for not having believed John. If they answered, "Of human origin," they might anger the crowd, who believed John to be a prophet. The high priests and elders are therefore forced to be evasive: "We do not know." Jesus in turn refuses to answer their question to him (Matt 21:23-27).

It is at this point that today's pericope begins. Its context, then, is the faith and obedience that Jesus' challengers are unwilling to risk. Jesus does not leave matters there but proposes the parable of the two sons. The one refused to go into the vineyard but then repented and went; the other said he would go but did not. We can now see the point of the second part of the passage: John came and they did not believe him, but the tax collectors and prostitutes repented and did believe. The Pharisees, on the one hand, and the tax collectors and prostitutes, on the other, are like the two sons with their different responses.

It is clear, then, that if we are to understand today's parable and its conclusion, we must take into account the section immediately preceding. The questioners of Jesus did not believe in John; to this extent they resemble the first son, who refused to obey. That son repented, however, and did obey, while the high priests and elders refused to be converted even after seeing the prostitutes and tax collectors repenting and believing John. Consequently, the prostitutes and tax collectors will go before them into the kingdom of God.

The parable of the two sons sent into the vineyard reminds us of the parable of the murderous vineyard workers, which follows immediately on today's passage in St. Matthew's text. In the latter parable we find the same refusal to accept Jesus and believe in him, a refusal that even involves a hatred and leads to the condemnation of Jesus.

The point being made is that we must receive Jesus with faith. To accept him means not only to accept him with our minds but to act accordingly. Faith and action—that is the lesson of today's gospel. Faith in action—that is, faith that leads to conversion and a life based on faith.

Turn from Your Sins and Be Saved (Ezek 18:25-28)

This oracle is a call to conversion: "if he [the wicked person] turns from the wickedness he has committed, and does what is right and just, he shall preserve his life"; and again: "since he has turned away from all the sins that he has committed, he shall surely live, he shall not die."

We are listening here to a dialogue between God and his people. The people find the Lord's ways strange. Why? The prophet has explained God's view of personal responsibility both in sin and in the avoidance of sin. God does not, however, take pleasure in the death of a sinner; he desires rather that the sinner should live, but this means that sinners must change their ways. Thus, conversion is a possibility offered to humanity, and at the same time, it pleases God. On the other hand, the just can prove lacking in fidelity, and if they do, they will die. Infidelity is no less possible than conversion. It is precisely here that Ezekiel's hearers find God's ways to be strange. But the Lord answers their criticism: If the just turn away from righteousness, become evil, and die in this state, then they die because of their wickedness and because they have not used the means God gave them for attaining life.

The Old Testament text leads over to the gospel of the day. Both deal with the rejection of God and the refusal to be converted; at the same time, conversion is always possible. The danger lies in one's tendency to be inconstant and to let one's dispositions change. The problem of fidelity is thus a very basic one: we can say yes but then not follow up on our decision, or we can say no but then be converted.

Our thoughts today, then, should focus on God's offer of salvation to us. What he did in the past, he still does in our time. On the other hand, we must also be concerned with our own constancy in love and fidelity to the Lord if we are really serious about entering the kingdom.

Evidently the just have no easy path to walk. They must be upright and faithful in their response to God; breaks in continuity are always possible, and against these they must guard. The responsorial psalm (Ps 25) asks that God would forgive us our sins and grant us the light we need:

> O LORD, make me know your ways.
> Teach me your paths.
> Guide me in your truth, and teach me;
> for you are the God of my salvation. . . .
>
> Remember your compassion, O LORD,
> and your merciful love,
> for they are from of old. . . .

Good and upright is the LORD;
he shows the way to sinners.
He guides the humble in right judgment;
to the humble he teaches his way. (vv. 4-5, 6, 8-9)

_____

Have the Mind of Christ (Phil 2:1-11)

St. Paul continues to emphasize the closeness of our communion with Christ; he tells us here that it is such that we ought to share the thoughts and sentiments of Christ. Communion with Jesus is impossible without an accompanying close union among all who live by and through him. It is in Christ that we must encourage one another. This theme of mutual encouragement is a favorite of Paul.

In a manner we might think merely diplomatic, but which is, in fact, spiritual and soundly theological, the Apostle manifests his desire to see Christians solidly united with one another. It would be his greatest joy as an apostle and a pastor to see this unity flourish. Paul was probably aware of dissensions in the community at Philippi; these would be caused by the ambition of some members or by their striving for their own welfare and advantage. The true Christian outlook, however, is to regard others as better than oneself.

In order to make this last-named attitude understandable, Paul appeals to Christ and his attitude. His description will be forever the greatest theological depiction of Christ's self-emptying on the cross:

Christ Jesus . . .
   though he was in the form of God,
   did not regard equality with God
   something to be grasped.
Rather, he emptied himself,
   taking the form of a slave,
   coming in human likeness;
   and found human in appearance,
   he humbled himself,
   becoming obedient to the point of death,
   even death on a cross.

Paul is here summing up the whole mystery of redemption that began with the incarnation. The expressions "human likeness" and "found human in appearance" do not imply that he was only seemingly a human; Paul is simply making the point that while Christ genuinely made the human condition his own, he did not share humanity's sinfulness.

The mystery of redemption did not stop with the cross, however. The paschal mystery of Jesus, which is the center of Christian life, is a mystery of death but also a mystery of resurrection to glory:

> Because of this, God greatly exalted him
>> and bestowed on him the name
>> which is above every name,
>> that at the name of Jesus
>> every knee should bend,
>> of those in heaven and on earth and under the earth,
>> and every tongue confess that
>> Jesus Christ is Lord,
>> to the glory of God the Father.

Paul is here telling how Christ was enthroned in glory, received the name of Lord, and had his lordship proclaimed by the entire universe.

This hymn may have served originally as a liturgical acclamation. In any case, it has been adopted into the Christian liturgy and used on Good Friday and on other occasions.

The description of the course of Jesus' life, death, and glorification has a practical meaning for Christians who live in close union with Jesus: Christians are to imitate in their own life the phases of Jesus' life.

Twenty-Seventh Sunday; The Fruitless Vineyard

He Will Lease His Vineyard to Others (Matt 21:33-43)

This passage still confronts the exegetes with some important problems. Some have seen in the passage a narrative composed by the Christian community in order to describe the advances God had made to his people up until the time when he finally sent them his Son. The parable would thus be a way of relating the life of Jesus to the overall history of Israel; it would show the failure of the advances God had made and how finally he transferred his favor to a new people. In thus making the Christian community the originator of the parable, the exegetes have no intention of denying the role of the Holy Spirit in the redaction of this short history of Israel, Christ, and the new chosen people.

We cannot go into the problems of literary criticism that are involved here, but we may note that other exegetes do not accept the approach just indicated and think rather that we look to St. Mark's gospel for an earlier and more original form of a parable that St. Matthew then took and elaborated for the catechesis of his own community.

We shall not make a detailed comparison of the accounts of Mark and Matthew, but we must note that there are some important differences. In St. Mark's parable (12:1-12), a single servant is sent on each of two occasions before the son of the house is finally sent. Each of the servants is maltreated, the second more so than the first; the tenants are becoming exasperated at the owner, and when the son comes, they kill him. In St. Matthew's parable, two groups of servants are sent, the second group being larger than the first; both groups are cruelly treated, and the son pays for his mission with his life.

We may think that St. Matthew wishes to remind his readers of the fate suffered by the various prophets when they came to the vineyard, that is, to the people of Israel. When the Son, Jesus, finally comes, he too is put to death by the Jews. St. Matthew intends, as so often in his gospel, to emphasize the responsibility of the chief priests and elders of the people, whom Jesus is addressing here, just as he emphasizes the responsibility of the Pharisees.

The general conclusion drawn by both Matthew and Mark is the same: the workers or tenants deserve death, and the vineyard will be let out to others. St. Matthew adds, however, that the new tenants must make the vineyard bear fruit. The former tenants should have had fruits to give to the owner, and they did not; the new tenants will have the same obligation. They must give him the fruits "in their season"; in other words, there will come a time when they will have to render an account of their work.

St. Matthew seems to have wanted to call attention to the way in which Israel had received the prophets and the divine warnings they brought with them. Israel did not produce the fruits God wanted and expected; they were responsible for the death of the Son when finally the Father sent him. St. Mark brings out the same point.

The exegetes think that, as so often when the words "Did you never read in the Scriptures . . . ?" occur, the community is introducing a quotation from Scripture. In this case the Scripture cited is: "*The stone that the builders rejected / has become the cornerstone.*" St. Matthew, in any case, goes on to say, "[T]he kingdom of God [not 'the kingdom of heaven,' as is his wont] will be taken away from you and given to a people that will produce its fruit." Here again, Matthew insists that the new people of God must produce fruit.

The Lord's Vineyard Is the House of Israel (Isa 5:1-7)

This remarkable poem sums up the entire history of God's fidelity to his people and its many manifestations, on the one hand, and the infidelities of Israel, on the other.

The movement of the passage is clear. The owner of the vineyard does everything he can for it, but the vineyard is a failure. The inhabitants of Jerusalem and Judea are asked to pass judgment. What more could the owner have done? All the inhabitants must certainly understand the harsh way in which he will now treat the vineyard. All that is left to do is to indicate the real-life situation that is being reflected in the parable. Finally the prophet does this.

The passage is a poetic description of God's love for his people and of the infidelities that he receives in return. The people are forced to pass judgment on themselves and to recognize themselves in the fruitless vineyard that deserves only to be uprooted: "The vineyard of the LORD of hosts is the house of Israel."

The teaching of this Sunday is important for the Church of our day. The great fault of the first workers in the vineyard, that is, the first people of God, was that they did not bear fruit. They did not listen to the prophets; they were unfaithful. Now the vineyard has been let out to a new people, the Church.

But the Church—the community for which St. Matthew is writing and every community—must remember that it too is expected to bear fruit. In the time that elapses between the establishment of this new people of God and the day of the Lord's return, the Church must see to it that it does bear fruit. The fruit consists first and foremost in its love and deeds. The Church must be a docile instrument in the Lord's hand and not act as owner of the vineyard rather than as simple tenant.

The responsorial psalm (Ps 80) voices the regrets of Israel: "Then why have you broken down its walls? / It is plucked by all who pass by the way. / It is ravaged by the boar of the forest, / devoured by the beasts of the field" (vv. 13-14). The psalm also gives fine expression to the prayer of the new people of God who are the new workers and must make the vineyard bear fruit as it should: "God of hosts, turn again, we implore; / look down from heaven and see. / Visit this vine and protect it, / the vine your right hand has planted" (vv.15-16).

The God of Peace Will Be with You (Phil 4:6-9)

In this passage St. Paul is trying to teach the Philippians to acquire peace of soul through prayer and the practice of the Christian virtues. If they are to be at peace, they must pray in a spirit of thanksgiving while also making their petitions known to God. If they do that, they need not be anxious about anything.

Does it sound as if the Apostle were living apart from the world, or as if he were unrealistic in his approach to actual life? But this very letter makes it clear that this is not the case. He not only reminds the Philippians that he is a prisoner condemned to death but also knows the difficulties at Philippi and the rivalries and disputes in the community. Nonetheless, he tells them they should be enjoying the peace that God gives. It is not an inactive peace; life in Christ is always a struggle, as the very virtues Paul lists make clear. If they put into practice the instruction he gives them, the God of peace will be with them.

Twenty-Eighth Sunday: The Banquet of the Lord

Those Invited to the Wedding Feast (Matt 22:1-14)

This parable is also found in St. Luke's gospel (14:16-24), but once again we find Matthew modifying it to meet catechetical needs. The basic meaning remains the same as in Luke, but Matthew's additions make the parable more suited to, and effective for, his catechesis, which is addressed to converts from Judaism. Without going into details, we shall simply point out what is most important for us and indicate what led Matthew to change and amplify the story.

In Luke, the man issuing the invitation is a rich man; in Matthew, it is a king who is giving a wedding banquet for his son. Later on, Matthew will modify the parable so that those who reject the invitation are Jews. In his eyes, then, the king is God himself.

In Luke, the invitation is given when the time for the banquet has come, and the invitation is carried by a single servant. In Matthew, the king repeats his invitation and on both occasions sends several servants.

Matthew wishes here to remind his readers of the prophets, who were sent repeatedly by the Lord and who not only met with rejection but were mistreated (a detail Luke does not have). In the parable of the vineyard (21:33-43), Matthew had already followed a similar pattern in order to bring out the same point, that is, the rejection of the Lord by the people of Israel; in this parable too, messengers were sent twice.

It is because of the rejection and mistreatment of his servants that Matthew's king grows angry, sends troops to punish, and finally destroys the city. Matthew may here be influenced by the book of Isaiah (5:1-7) and by his earlier parable of the vineyard workers who did not produce fruit and were punished by the owner.

The second invitation is not addressed to those originally singled out but to everyone on the streets: the poor, the disabled, the blind, the lame. Here, as in the parable of the vineyard, the invitation finally goes out to people who had nothing to do with the king (the vineyard will be let out to new custodians). Israel has not accepted the invitation or welcomed the messengers of the owner, who was looking for fruit from the vineyard; now the vineyard will be given to others, and others will receive the invitation to the banquet.

There is a part of the story that is found only in Matthew. Here the king comes into the banquet hall and finds a guest who has no wedding garment. The king's displeasure seems strange, since he had invited everyone without exception to come! This sort of inconsistency, however, is of no consequence in a parable. It is due simply to the fact that Matthew wants to get across a new point of teaching. Here again there seems to be a parallelism with the parable of the vineyard. In the latter, Matthew emphasizes the fact that the new tenants must bear fruit. He is warning Christians not to relax and take pride in the fact that they were chosen to replace the Jewish people; like the Jews, Christians too are obliged to bear fruit.

In today's parable, Matthew's concern at this point is the same. The Jewish people have not responded to God's invitation, and after punishing them and destroying their city, the king invites people who had no right to an invitation. But if they accept and enter the banquet hall, they must be wearing a wedding garment, that is, they must do God's will. The invitation by itself is not enough to save, any more than is the mere fact of becoming the new tenants.

It seems beside the point to inquire here into the exact meaning of the statement: "Many are invited, but few are chosen." When we grasp the general meaning of the parable and understand Matthew's method and purpose, the conclusion proves to represent simply St. Matthew's desire to combat a tendency among his Christians to sit back and enjoy their position as the new chosen people. They are therefore being warned that it is difficult to enter and remain in the banquet hall.

The Banquet of the Saved (Isa 25:6-10a)

We must not forget that despite the warning at the end of the parable, Matthew's basic purpose is to encourage: All who want to follow the Lord can be saved. No matter how wretched they may be, all are invited to the banquet; all can and must acquire a wedding garment.

The reading from Isaiah also concerns an eschatological banquet to which we are all invited. The poem is part of the section known as the "Apocalypse of Isaiah" (chaps. 24–27). In today's passage, the particular subject is the messianic banquet (the last day and the reward it brings are represented in the Old and New Testaments as a banquet).

All peoples are invited to this "feast of rich foods and choice wines, / juicy, rich food and pure, choice wines." But the banquet, though depicted in terms of luxury, has its spiritual aspects too: sadness and sorrow will be no more and death will be forever destroyed; the Lord will wipe away the tears from every face and take away the reproach of his people.

What Isaiah is describing is the new Jerusalem, the long-hoped-for banquet of salvation: "let us rejoice and be glad that he has saved us." "You have prepared a table before me / in the sight of my foes. / My head you have anointed with oil; / my cup is overflowing" (Ps 23:5, the responsorial psalm).

We Catholics must, of course, keep in mind that it is for the celebration of the Eucharist that we gather on this Sunday. Consequently, both the poem of Isaiah and the parable of St. Matthew have a special connotation for us. Each of us has received a call to which we had no right. If we are to share the eucharistic banquet, which is a sign and foretaste of the eternal banquet in the kingdom, we must have a wedding garment. This does not mean only that we examine our conscience with regard to serious sins we may have committed. We must also not be overconfident; we must see how open we are to others. Have we by our manner of life or by our self-centeredness rejected an invitation being offered to us? This is quite possible, even after we have entered the banquet hall to share in the feast.

Bear with Everything by the Power of Christ (Phil 4:12-14, 19-20)

These lines describe the detachment that should mark the life of every Christian. Detachment does not mean, however, that we should not help others in their need. Paul thanks the community for having done so; God will reward them for it. The passage ends with one of the beautiful doxologies we find so frequently in the letters of St. Paul.

Twenty-Ninth Sunday: The Primacy of God's Service

Give to Caesar What Is Caesar's (Matt 22:15-21)

The teaching of this Sunday touches on religion and politics, a subject of vital interest to many today. It is important, therefore, to show the relevance of the readings. We shall be brief but shall also try to help the reader reflect on the problems raised. The answer suggested by the readings is not always the one some would like to hear.

"Then repay to Caesar what belongs to Caesar and to God what belongs to God" is often understood as an answer that fits right in with today's world: two separate domains, each self-enclosed, with the parish priest staying in the sacristy and the politician in the assembly chamber.

As a matter of fact, the two halves of the statement are not treated as of equal importance in the gospel. Jesus is indeed saying that Caesar must be given what is his. He also says, however, that God must be given what is his, and it is this second half that the evangelist concentrates on and emphasizes.

For the contemporaries of Jesus, his statement was an invitation to see in him the Messiah and to acknowledge the presence of the kingdom of which he is Lord. Those who questioned him, however, did not understand that the one they were questioning was the Lord of the kingdom, the one to whom everything belonged.

But even while asserting that in him the kingdom is present, Jesus also makes it clear that his kingdom is not of this world and is not to be compared with the kingdom over which Caesar rules. Jesus' kingdom is spiritual: "my kingdom is not here" (John 18:36). Jesus is not a political Messiah, and his rule is not of the political order; he is thus not a competitor of Caesar. On the other hand, Caesar is not independent but must be subject to Jesus, now that the latter's divine rule has been established. This is so because God's plan is one and undivided, and all created things have their place in it.

Against this background, Jesus' statement "repay . . . to God what belongs to God" is an invitation to believe in and submit to this Messiah, Jesus, who has come to establish a kingdom of a kind his contemporaries cannot understand. He will establish his kingdom by fleeing any takeover of political power and by handing himself over to his enemies, that he may suffer and die and sacrifice his life and rise gloriously from the dead. His victory over sin and death will be the foundation of the kingdom that all believers are called to enter.

"Repay to Caesar what belongs to Caesar" is evidently not on the same level as the second half of the statement; it does not express one-half of reality, with the statement about God expressing the other half! In bidding his hearers give Caesar what is Caesar's, Jesus is simply recognizing that everyone must have a certain concern for the political and social well-being of one's country. At the same time, however, he is stripping political authority of any claim to be divine; it must simply exercise a responsibility that is from God. God wills that people should organize the life they live during their time on earth.

Rendering to Caesar what is Caesar's is also a manifestation of fidelity to God himself, since God wills that we be concerned for our society. Consequently, rendering to Caesar what is his becomes a partial fulfillment of our more basic duty, which is to render to God what is his. The fulfillment of the latter duty has an influence on the measure and manner in which we fulfill our duty to Caesar.

The focus of attention in this passage is evidently on the acknowledgment of the only ultimately true kingdom—that which Jesus inaugurated.

I Am the Lord and There Is No Other (Isa 45:1, 4-6)

This reading is of interest on two counts. First, Cyrus is a Gentile, and yet he receives a commission from God. This means that the Lord can distribute his gifts and missions to whomever he wishes, not only to people of the Jewish nation. It also means that the Lord is interested in the human and political life of his people. The second point is that the mission given to Cyrus by God should lead people to realize that there is no other Lord besides the God of Israel. Cyrus has become a mighty king, but his power is entirely from God.

The text is important and helps us understand today's gospel. "I am the LORD and there is no other." This divine claim, uttered at the moment when God is choosing and consecrating Cyrus as political leader, shows that nothing in human history is independent of God. If Cyrus is to be obeyed, it is not because of any merit in him but because he is invested with power by God, because his power is derived from a God who is not unconcerned with people's earthly and political life. This earthly and political life must, however, lead people to justice, peace, and salvation.

The teaching of the Gospel is thus not indifferent or neutral toward the political order, but neither can the political order be neutral toward God. Giving to God what is God's requires fidelity to social and political duties but according to the spirit and requirements of the Gospel, since everything ultimately depends on God. Everyone must live as a human being in the social context in which one finds oneself, but one must do it in obedience to Gospel precepts.

On the other hand, the Church, in proclaiming the Gospel, must remind those in the political sphere of the primacy of God and the need of walking in the way of his commandments, if only for the sake of the human happiness of the community whose well-being is entrusted to them. The two halves of Jesus' statement are thus complementary to each other, but the "Repay to God . . ." takes priority, for from it flows the second obligation, "Repay to Caesar . . ."

A Life of Faith, Love, and Hope (1 Thess 1:1-5b)

Paul is here addressing "the church of the Thessalonians," or, as he might equally well have put it, "the church in Thessalonica." It is worth our while to dwell on the expression for a moment. We modern Christians tend to think of a local church as a part of the universal Church, the latter being the sum total of these local churches. The Apostle thinks of things quite differently. In his view, each local church is a presence of the universal Church, and that is the view the Second Vatican Council took in its Dogmatic Constitution on the Church (no. 26).

The Church is the assembly of those who have been called by God, and it is to this assembly, as found at Thessalonica, that Paul speaks. He addresses Christians whose unity is attained precisely in the form of the Church—their local Church, which is an embodiment of the universal Church. He thanks God for them, for his gifts to them in the past and in the present. They had received God's word, and that word is now active in them, leading them forward in hope toward the return of Christ. The word has not been received in vain but is efficacious; its proclamation has mediated divine power and the action of the Holy Spirit and has produced conviction.

As we hear Paul's words of thanksgiving, we should reflect on how we ourselves receive God's word. Those whose office it is to proclaim the Word should thank God for making it such a powerful instrument.

Thirtieth Sunday: Love of Neighbor

Love Your Neighbor as Yourself (Matt 22:34-40)

It seems pointless to dwell on Jesus' answer to the lawyer's question and on the two commandments of love that are so closely intertwined. A few remarks are nonetheless necessary. The two commandments were well known to the Jews, and in answering, Jesus had only to quote the book of Deuteronomy (6:5) and the book of Leviticus (10:18).

Yet not all the Jews listening to Jesus would have thought of these two commandments as summing up the whole of the law. In fact, we can be sure that many of them did not and that the question, "which commandment in the law is the greatest?" was put to Jesus as a way of trapping him. It represented another attempt to embarrass him. Matthew records several such attempts: "By what authority are you doing these things [teaching in the temple]? And who gave you this authority?" (Matt 21:23-27; see page 148); "Is it lawful to pay the census tax to Caesar or not?" (Matt 22:15-22; see page 157); "Now at the resurrection, of the seven, whose wife will she be?" (Matt 22:23-33). It is after his reply to this last question, a reply that wins the admiration of the crowd, that a new trap is now laid for Jesus.

Everything in the Law and the Prophets, that is, in the whole of Scripture, depends on these two commandments of love. In Matthew's eyes, the two commandments are on an equal footing, and one cannot put one of them into practice without also observing the other. All other precepts depend on these two. Jesus is not the only one to assert the necessary and unalterable connection between them. St. John, for example, will write: "If anyone says, 'I love God,' but hates his brother, he is a liar; for whoever does not love a brother whom he has seen cannot love God whom he has not seen" (1 John 4:20).

The gospel is here setting forth the essential basis of Christian life, for this life can be authentic only when these two commandments are observed. In the Fourth Gospel, Jesus will say: "This is how all will know that you are my disciples, if you have love for one another" (John 13:35). The New Testament frequently reminds its readers that love of our brothers and sisters cannot be separated from love of God, and vice versa; the unity of the two is a hallmark of the new covenant.

Love the Orphan, the Widow, the Foreigner, and the Poor (Exod 22:20-26)

The Old Testament is very demanding when it comes to love of neighbor, and God shows that he is offended when people fail to attend to, and show love for, their neighbor. God is especially angered at a lack of love for the weak. To this group belong the foreigners in Israel; special concern is owing them because Israel itself had once been in the same position. The widow and orphan are also among the weak; if Israel fails in love for them, the Lord will make those neglectful of them perish by the sword, leaving their wives widows and their children orphans.

An Israelite must show compassion to a fellow Israelite. Today's passage instructs a person on how to act when lending money: one must lend it without interest and must quickly return any pledge given against the loan.

The striking thing in all this is the way in which God enters the picture as soon as the neighbor is harmed. Without saying so explicitly, the text makes it clear that when one does wrong to one's neighbor, one is also insulting God, and God will soon make his wrath felt.

The New Testament goes further, even if along the same general lines. In the New Testament view, the neighbor is the Lord himself. Once Jesus has accomplished his paschal mystery, Christians will share the same baptism and the same Eucharist. Everything that increases and deepens our membership in the Body of Christ provides further motivation for internal charity.

It would then be incongruous to ask whether today's gospel has a lesson for us in our day! But while we acknowledge that Jesus' teaching here is the necessary basis of our Christian lives, we can grasp and apply that teaching more fully.

The love of God is and must remain the major concern of Christians today as in every generation. Today's Christians must, however, also make use of the means that will enable them to enter more deeply into the mystery of God and his plan of salvation, as revealed in Scripture. Christians should pray more, preferably in the form of communal prayer, where Jesus says that he is present. Christians should also make an effort to intensify their liturgical life, since the liturgy, while not being the exclusive means of union with God, is at least the greatest of these means.

In contemporary society and civilization, love of neighbor takes many forms that drew less attention in the past. Thus, scientific research on behalf of human advancement, politics, and social work are certainly forms of service that can and should be inspired by love of neighbor. Working for the advancement of cultural values and even of material values that serve humanity's welfare is also a way of loving one another; contributions to the spiritual advancement of humankind are all the more a way of loving our neighbor. It is therefore inconceivable that there could be a practice of the Christian religion that would claim to exemplify love of God without also embodying, in one form or another, a love of neighbor. At least such love would have to be shown in prayer for neighbors and in a concern for their needs.

We can never overemphasize the importance of these two commandments for the Christian life. To forget them or to be mindful of them only fitfully is to risk worshiping God in an utterly inauthentic way and receiving the sacraments without any regard for their true meaning.

Turn from Idols and Serve God (1 Thess 1:5c-10)

To understand this passage, we must go back and reread the first five verses proclaimed on the preceding Sunday. Paul's thanksgiving in those verses may be summed up as an utterance of joy at seeing a Christian community that was so obviously chosen by God.

His thanksgiving now continues and expands in a way that may astonish us. He seems to forget humility completely when he says: "And you became imitators of us and of the Lord, receiving the word in great affliction, with joy from the Holy Spirit." This text is very important for a theology of the ministry, for it seems to imply a certain fatherhood on the part of the apostle, who brings children forth into the light of faith. God gives life, and people becomes God's collaborators by using their sexual powers; so too God gives life through his word, and the herald of the Gospel is his collaborator in this new and higher gift of life. The parallelism seems evident.

Paul gives thanks because the Thessalonians had received the word but also because their reputation for faith has spread abroad. He is grateful too that his own coming among them was the starting point for their conversion, their "turning" from idols to the true God. Now they await the coming of the Son who delivers them (and us) from the wrath of God.

Every Christian community should meditate on this passage. We have turned away from idols, but there is always danger that we may turn back to new ones that will keep us from hearing the word of God objectively. Our age is quite familiar with such idols: luxury in all its forms, sexual excess, vague notions of freedom and of human liberation.

Thirty-First Sunday: The Law and Obedience to It

They Speak but Do Not Act (Matt 23:1-12)

The people to whom Jesus is referring here are people in important positions. In Judaism, they were the people in authority, and Jesus acknowledges their position as teachers. The Jews believed that on Sinai Yahweh had given Moses a commission to teach, so that henceforth to take "their seat on the chair of Moses" meant to belong to the esteemed line of those who had been charged with teaching the people.

Others must therefore do as these teachers tell them to; Jesus emphasizes this duty. He also insists, however, that others must not act as their teachers act. His words contain a serious accusation that must be backed up by facts. Jesus has no hesitation about going into details and specifying the major sins of the teachers.

He reproaches them on two counts that must have been subject to easy corroboration by those who were able to observe the lives of these teachers. First of all, he accuses them of leading a double life, because they demand various observances of others that they do not fulfill themselves. Jesus uses the image of a burden tied to a slave's back; he must carry it, while those who put the burden on him do not help him at all.

The second accusation is that they are preoccupied with themselves and trying to draw attention to themselves. That is why they wear very large phylacteries (a kind of amulet, which was not, however, an expression of superstitious belief but was intended to remind them of God's law and their duty of observing it). They also wear long fringes on their garments (at the four corners of his cloak a Jew tied a kind of cord, which again was to be a reminder of the commandments of the Lord). They covet places of honor and the respectful salutations given to them. Above all, they love to be called "rabbi" or "teacher."

Jesus lists these faults in a straightforward and not unironic manner; he does so in order to inculcate in his disciples an attitude diametrically opposed to that of the Pharisees. St. Matthew may be reporting the words of Jesus as a lesson to those who exercised some authority in his community. Jesus himself is putting his disciples on guard chiefly against the last of the faults that he lists: the desire to be called "rabbi," with all that the title implies. Jesus' disciples are not to let themselves be called rabbi because they are all brothers and sisters and have only one true teacher, Christ, just as they all have but one Father. In consequence, the greatest among them is to be the servant of all (see page 272). The passage ends with a saying we have already met: "Whoever exalts himself will be humbled; but whoever humbles himself will be exalted."

Watering down the Law (Mal 1:14b–2:2b, 8-10)

Once again, the liturgy of this day chooses a text, not for its own sake and on its own terms, as an exegete would who takes into consideration the whole rich context of the passage, but in order to highlight what the gospel of the day teaches concerning those who have authority in the Church.

From the opening words, the passage is a stern reproach to the priests who do not observe the law but impose it on others. But if they do not take seriously their obligation of glorifying the name of the Lord, the Lord will turn his very blessings into a curse. These people have made of the law, not a guide that would help people to live aright, but a stumbling block for the multitude; by so doing, they have perverted the covenant. The prophet Hosea had earlier uttered the same reproach against the priestly caste: "Since you have rejected knowledge, / I will reject you from serving as my priest" (Hos 4:6; cf. vv. 4-6).

God alone is Father, and sole Father of all, because he created all. His fatherhood is the basis of unity with God and each other in the community that is the people of God. Brothers and sisters must not be faithless to one another. The text is probably alluding to divorce, or marriage with a woman who worships Gentile gods, or something of the kind. The liturgy today simply reads the text in the light of the gospel and is uninterested in such allusions.

Sharing the Gospel and Our Very Selves (1 Thess 2:7-9, 13)

The whole of Paul's teaching has the Good News, the Gospel, for its focus. Those who teach must communicate not their own teaching but that of Jesus. This teaching, moreover, cannot remain purely conceptual; apostles must give themselves along with the Good News, putting their own person on the line both by practicing what they preach and by showing great concern for the members of their community.

The Letter to the Thessalonians uses a number of expressions that are rather rare elsewhere in St. Paul's writings. We sense that he is filled with enthusiasm and tender affection for the Thessalonians, who probably have shown a great change in their lives since their contract with him. He reminds them that he gave himself to them without reserve in his preaching and how he treated them as would a nurse who is wholly concerned for the children she must nourish and educate. He even goes on to say explicitly why he is so happy with the Thessalonians: they received the word of God from him for what it really was—not a human's word, but God's word at work in them. But in all this, Paul feels no personal elation or pride, since all the good he accomplished has been the work of God's grace.

In the ecclesial community all have priestly responsibility but of different kinds and degrees. The layperson as such is responsible for the reign of internal charity in the community and for the advancement of each and all. The responsibility requires laypeople to be upright and not to lead a kind of double life in which, on the one hand, they follow Christian practices but, on the other, show a lack of charity and mutual love as they push their way to the first places, even in Christian organizations that are devoted to work for the good of the community. The temptation to Pharisaism exists even there!

The teaching of today's liturgy is, however, addressed first and foremost to those who are appointed to teach others and have a priestly responsibility in the narrower sense. The sometimes very harsh and often unjust attacks upon the Church with regard to these people are a trial indeed, but they can also be for her the occasion of a searching examination of conscience. None of us lives a life that is perfectly in accord with what we teach or profess; that will doubtless be the case until the end of time, and we cannot require that a priest or catechist be perfect. But the people do have the right to expect that their spiritual leaders will at least be seeking holiness, not so much for their own sake as for the sake of those whose welfare has been entrusted to them.

The service of the community should come before everything else. Ostensibly people look less for honors nowadays, and persons of rank are less concerned about titles, yet pride evidently makes its way in by other and more subtle paths. Many have no desire to be called "rabbi," but they do claim to be teaching "their own" doctrine, and it is not always the doctrine of the Gospel and the Church. This kind of self-assertion often lurks behind a facade of democracy or even bohemianism and an external pseudo-friendly attitude of "letting it go"; it is simply a new kind of pride and self-sufficiency.

It is not always easy to preach the Gospel objectively and to be faithful to teaching that makes its authoritative demands on us. The lesson of today's liturgy is that we must all honestly review our inner attitudes and not be too ready to believe that the reproaches of Jesus are irrelevant to us moderns.

Thirty-Second Sunday: Watch and Wait

Stay Awake, for You Know Neither the Day Nor the Hour (Matt 25:1-13)

The parable contains only the essential points needed for the story. Thus Jesus has deliberately omitted any description of a wedding as celebrated in his day. Doubtless, in accordance with almost universal usage, the bridegroom would come to the young girl's home in order to claim her and take her to his house.

In what sense is one group of virgins "foolish" and the other "wise"? The first reading helps us to an answer. The "wise" virgin's wisdom is not primarily a human wisdom but a wisdom born of meditation on the mysteries of God and, in this context, specifically on the mysteries of the kingdom. The lamp symbolizes this wisdom that must be cultivated by meditation, reflection, and one's way of life.

Such wisdom does not come in a day. The person must know how to wait (the bridegroom does not come immediately), to store up wisdom, and to keep her lamp properly trimmed. The symbolism of the parable is crystal clear.

The bridegroom comes at night. In the Scriptures, the night is the time of God's comings, according to a tradition that reaches back into earliest Hebrew history. Thus, it is in the night that the Lord liberates his people (Exod 11:4; 12:12, 19). To some, the night and the Lord's coming bring salvation; to others, such as the Egyptians, they bring death. The New Testament regularly portrays the return of Christ at night (Luke 12:39-40; Matt 24:43-44; Mark 13:35-36; Luke 12:20).

Those who wait must not sleep but keep vigil, for the bridegroom comes unexpectedly (Matt 24:27; Luke 17:24).

The theme of the "door" is also full of meaning. We know how the New Testament makes use of the theme: it tells us that we must "enter through the narrow gate" (Luke 13:24; cf. Matt 7:13). We recall too that when the destroying angel passed over Egypt, a mark was left on the doorposts of the Hebrews so that they might be spared.

Vigil, night, door—these are paschal themes, connected with liberation and entry into the kingdom. In today's parable the door is closed against the virgins who did not keep vigil and did not trim their lamps properly. Their cries are useless; the hour for the feast has come, and they are excluded. The moral admits of no exceptions: "Therefore, stay awake, for you know neither the day nor the hour."

Watch, and Find Wisdom (Wis 6:12-16)

The first reading describes wisdom in poetic terms. Its theme is that our entire lives should be spent in pursuit of wisdom.

Wisdom is easily discerned by those who love her, and she may readily be found by those who seek her, because she is radiant and visible. It is worth looking for her, because she is unfading. Such are the fundamental attributes of wisdom. This wisdom is not an esoteric doctrine reserved for an elite, but something within the reach of all, provided they are willing to seek her out. When people do search for her, she takes the initiative and presents herself to them; they will find her sitting at their door if they rise early to seek her. The quest of wisdom should be the main preoccupation of a human being; we should think only of her and be watchful on her account.

Without going so far as to regard this wisdom as a person, the Church has seen in her a prefiguration of Christ and his grace. It is not hard to see the justification for such a transposition. Wisdom, Christ, grace—all three seek out those who are worthy of them; all three graciously appear to people and meet them at every point; all three present themselves whenever we think of them.

Psalm 63, the responsorial psalm, sings of God as the object of humanity's desire and search:

> O God, you are my God; at dawn I seek you;
> For you my soul is thirsting.
> For you my flesh is pining. . . .
>
> When I remember you upon my bed,
> I muse on you through the watches of the night.
> For you have been my strength;
> In the shadow of your wings I rejoice. (vv. 2, 7-8)

The Church uses this same passage of the gospel for the Common of Virgins. We may note too that the symbolism of the gospel passage recurs elsewhere, inasmuch as the Church gives the newly baptized candles that they are to keep lit in their lives.

During vigils, and especially during the Paschal Vigil, the Church thinks unceasingly of Christ, her Spouse, who will come to lead her into his kingdom. The chief concern of the Church, therefore, is that the faithful should keep their lamps lit and never be caught by surprise at Christ's coming to them. The chief concern of the faithful should be to seek the wisdom and light of Christ and to keep ever alight the lamps they received at baptism so that with Christ they may enter the banquet hall of the kingdom.

God Will Bring Forth Those Who Have Fallen Asleep in Jesus
(1 Thess 4:13-18)

St. Paul is trying to instill hope into the Christians of Thessalonika. His message, in brief, is that the resurrection of Christ is what gives meaning to every Christian life and that God will take to himself those who have died with Christ. We died with Christ in baptism; we shall also share his resurrection.

The confusion in the minds of the Thessalonians provides Paul with an occasion for describing what will happen at the end of time. He works with images, but his point is clear. His essential teaching is that all, whether already dead or still living when Christ comes, will be taken up with Christ into glory.

This teaching will evidently be comforting only to those who have a deep faith in Jesus and his resurrection. It is a source of strength to those who are trying to live in union with the Lord and who want to reach the goal of all human life: perfect union with God. Quite often people think of the resurrection simply as a matter of personal survival and turn it into an end in itself. They forget that we put on Christ in baptism in order that we might glorify the Father by being restored to what his creatures were intended to be, and more.

The resurrection of all humankind and their appearance before the Lord will put an end to the history of the world. St. Paul looks upon this great event without fear and even regards it as the greatest possible source of strength to people in their earthly life as they see their dear ones die and are compelled to ask themselves what life is all about. Paul's answer to the questions of the Thessalonians is permanently valid.

Thirty-Third Sunday: Fidelity to Duty and Work

You Have Been Faithful in Small Things: Enter into the Joy of Your Lord
(Matt 25:14-30)

If we look to the basic meaning of the first and third readings for this day, it is difficult to connect them, even in a broad fashion. Why, then, was this particular reading from the Old Testament selected? If, on the other hand, we allow the first reading to determine what the major point of the third reading should be in the context of this celebration, the connection is much clearer. We have here, then, another example of a liturgical reading of the Scriptures as distinct from a strictly exegetical reading.

Were we to approach the gospel pericope as exegetes and situate it in its context in St. Matthew's gospel, we would have to say that the central point being made is the need of watchfulness and the need of making the money produce interest before the master returns. Yet the first reading has nothing to say about watchfulness or the Lord's return. In that reading, the main concern is with the fruits produced by the toil of a worthy wife. It seems, then, that on this Sunday the emphasis should be on fidelity and on dedication to duty and work. This does not prevent us, of course, from putting this fidelity and dedication into the perspective of the Lord's return and of watchfulness in preparation for the last day.

The evangelists at times report a parable of Jesus but interpret it to meet the needs of their faithful who find themselves in a new situation. Why should not the Church be able to do the same in the Liturgy of the Word, so as to meet the needs of today's faithful?

There is no point in discussing the details of the parable; the main lines of it alone are of interest to us. Certainly the parable is as rich in instruction for the Church of our day as it was for the first Christian communities. The entire emphasis is on the service every Christian owes to God. Because Christians are servants, it is their duty to make profitable use of the gifts given them for the good of the community and the kingdom. The parable makes it very clear that it is not enough simply to give the gift back to God in the form in which we received it.

At times we run into Christians who think of their Christian life in terms of a strict contract between God and themselves: "I observe strictly what the commandments require of me; I do not see why I should do more." This attitude is perhaps more common than we think, even if it is rarely expressed in such a cold and forthright way. There is a kind of Christian minimalism that takes refuge in the commandments of God and of the Church. At times we find people who are willing to develop only a favorite talent, and this for their own sake, not for the sake of the community.

The master's answer prevents all possibility of misunderstanding: We are all servants and have no choice in the matter. It is not enough for us to preserve what was entrusted to us; we must make it bear fruit in the service of God and others. The baptismal grace that has made us adopted sons and daughters must grow and may not simply be left in its original state; we may legitimately aspire to intensify it, because that is our duty.

Such an attitude is inspired by love and gratitude. It springs also from our awareness that we are called to collaborate in spreading God's kingdom and preparing for the unexpected coming of Christ.

A Worthy Wife Is a Precious Jewel (Prov 31:10-13, 19-20, 30-31)

Our contemporaries should not be displeased by this fine portrait of an ideal woman, and yet the liturgy is not interested in the advancement of women.[†] What the liturgy concentrates on is the skills the woman places at the service of the community; it is for these that she wins the praise of all who experience the fruits of them. Her foresight, her ability, her charity to others make her a model of these qualities; she does not let her talents lie fallow but uses them for the good of all.

Although it is not entirely easy to interpret the readings within the overall framework of the Sunday, today's Liturgy of the Word has its value. It urges persevering work upon those to whom the Lord has given talents for the good of the human community and the Church. Above all, it reminds all Christians of their duty to rise above a merchant's ideal of the Christian life. Christians cannot be satisfied with the minimum required of them but should seek to make their gifts bear as much fruit as possible. Otherwise they may see taken from them the minimum they sought to preserve with little effort and little love.

If We Are Watchful and Sober, We Will Not Be Taken by Surprise (1 Thess 5:1-6)

The expression "day of the Lord" has become unfamiliar to modern Christians; they may never even have heard it. Yet it is a phrase with specifically Christian connotations and should be a source of specifically Christian attitudes.

The gospels have made us familiar with a day of the Lord—of which Amos had spoken long before: 5:18-20—that is terrifying and

---

[†] Actually, the image from Proverbs will strike many as sexist.

will, according to Jesus, come suddenly like a thief in the night (Matt 24:43; Luke 12:30). The world goes its way unthinkingly, as though the day of the Lord would never come. St. Paul reminds the Thessalonians of what Jesus had said before him. But true Christians need no reminder; they will not be taken by surprise, since their whole life is a vigil, an expectation of Christ's return. The baptized are no longer part of the world of darkness; they are children of the light and the day. As such, they must always be vigilant, and this watchfulness requires detachment so that they may be ready for Christ's coming.

St. Paul's teaching here moves beyond anything our imaginations might suggest to us about the last day and the parousia. It speaks of the true meaning of Christian life, which is wholly directed toward the day of the Lord. Because we do not keep this day in view, we concentrate rather self-centeredly on our own death. Because we do not keep in mind the final victory that Christ will share with his disciples, we get distorted value judgments about the things of this world and give them an undue importance.

Our Lord Jesus Christ, King of the Universe

The Son of Man, the Shepherd Who Will Separate the Sheep from the Goats (Matt 25:31-46)

The liturgical year ends with a vision of glory. The final retribution of humanity's deeds is part of the picture, and it may be, at times, that the inclusion of the judgment hides somewhat the glorious splendor of the coming of the Son of Man.

Let us leave aside the literary problem posed by the description of the Son of Man's triumph and go directly to what St. Matthew wishes to teach us in this passage. If we read the text in an objective manner and if we listen to it proclaimed in the Lord's behalf or, more accurately, by the Lord himself today, it seems clear that the judgment rendered by the King of glory is based solely on love. His norm of judgment is: "whatever you did for one of the least brothers of mine, you did for me." Here the Lord sets down only one requirement for entering his kingdom: love of neighbor.

How are we to take the expression, "one of the least brothers of mine"? The meaning of the love required for entering the kingdom depends on the object of the love, and Christ here seems to rank the object quite low, as it were. It is difficult to identify these "least" who are Christ's brethren. In St. Matthew, as in the other New Testament writers, the term "brother" is applied to members of the ecclesial community (Matt 18:15, 21, 35; 23:8).‡ The word is, however, also applied in a much broader sense to include all human beings (Matt 5:22-24; 7:3-4). Finally, the disciples too are called "brothers" (Matt 12:50; 28:10).

In our text the expression is even more specific: "one of the least brothers *of mine.*" In this case there can be no doubt that the disciples are meant. This is confirmed by other passages: "And stretching out his hand toward his disciples, he said, 'Here are my mother and my brothers'" (Matt 12:49); "Go tell my brothers to go to Galilee, and there they will see me" (Matt 28:10).

In what sense are they the "least"? The expression is one used elsewhere of the disciples, although it can also be applied to Christians generally. It may help to look quickly at the other texts in which St. Matthew uses the expression. "[T]he least in the kingdom of heaven is greater than he [John the Baptist]" (11:11). Jesus is here speaking of John the Baptist, whom he calls the greatest of those born of woman. In this greatest-least comparison, the reference is really not to the person of the Precursor himself. Rather, two situations are being compared: before the coming of the kingdom and after the coming of the kingdom. The person—any person—who belongs to the kingdom is in an entirely new situation; the time of the kingdom is superior to all that went before. "I give praise to you, Father, Lord of heaven and earth, for although you have hidden these things from the wise and the learned you have revealed them to the childlike" (Matt 11:25). In this context "the childlike" or the "least" evidently means the poor and the lowly. (In another context—"See that you do not despise one of these little ones. . . . [I]t is not the will of your heavenly Father that one of these little ones be lost" [Matt 18:10-14]—"little ones" clearly means "children.")

There is another text that will prove even more enlightening: "whoever gives only a cup of cold water to one of these little ones to drink because he is a disciple . . ." (Matt 10:42). The sense is clear. We are at the end of the missionary discourse, and Jesus has just said to his disciples: "Whoever receives you receives me, and whoever receives

‡ It also translates a Greek word that is gender inclusive here.

me receives the one who sent me. Whoever receives a prophet because he is a prophet will receive a prophet's reward, and whoever receives a righteous man because he is righteous will receive a righteous man's reward" (10:40-41). As in the text of today's gospel, the context is one of retribution and of attitudes to envoys. "And whoever gives only a cup of cold water to one of these little ones to drink because he is a disciple—amen, I say to you, he will surely not lose his reward" (10:42). The equivalence of "little one" and "disciple" is evident. People are to welcome the disciples in the name of Christ.

It is clear that a homily that emphasizes exclusively the requirement of love and the need of openness to others is leaving out some important factors and is likely to give a false impression. The point of the passage is that we must receive the messengers of Christ, who are in fact other Christs; it is to Christ that we give the glass of water when we give it to his messenger. The attitude being inculcated is not only one of charity but one of receptivity that is based on faith. We are to receive not only the person sent by Christ but his word and teaching as well.

The Lord Will Judge between Sheep and Sheep (Ezek 34:11-12, 15-17)

We must not lose sight of the purpose of today's readings. All deal primarily with a king who comes to judge. He is, however, a king and a judge who has no match on earth. He is not content to acquit or condemn but is concerned chiefly to save and give rest. He is a judge who searches for the lost sheep; he cares for the wounded sheep and restores the strength of the sheep that has grown weak. Such a shepherd is the Lord who comes on the last day; he is the truest of all shepherds. His judgment justifies people and establishes justice once more.

We Christians know that our sacramental life is preparing us for the judgment that the King of shepherds will render. God has prepared a place for us, and we advance toward it without fear. "The LORD is my shepherd; / there is nothing I shall want. / Fresh and green are the pastures / where he gives me repose" (Ps 23:1-2).

The Final Reign of the Glorious Christ (1 Cor 15:20-26, 28)

This passage is part of St. Paul's instruction on the resurrection of the dead. In it he speaks of a kind of great apocalypse. We are given a grandiose fresco of the resurrection in which, in Christ, all rise, but in proper order. Then comes the grand finale, when Christ hands over his royal power to the Father, after having finished his work by destroying the last of the enemy powers. Now God is all in all.

This handing over of power to the Father does not mean that Christ's kingship is a temporary condition and ceases when history comes to its end. These statements of Paul are rather a way of saying that all of Christ's activity and even his paschal mystery have no other purpose than to make God the head of all creation once again. The kingdom of God is now fully established.

We may not be well prepared for understanding today's readings; their style may be unfamiliar to us. Nonetheless, the teaching of Matthew and Paul to their communities remains relevant to us today. The time of the Church and the historical time allotted to each of us derive their meaning from the judgment that will come at the end of time, when all things will finally be subjected to God's royal power. We must spend the time given us in loving God and our neighbor, in receiving his word and those who proclaim it, and living in expectation of the final judgment. We must also bear in mind, however, that this final judgment is primarily a justification of humanity and the act by which the world's reconstruction is completed and not primarily a condemnation of the wicked. We must endeavor to live with loving faith, heeding those whom Christ sends us and putting their words into practice.

Year B

In the following table, the general theme of each celebration and the particular theme of each reading are indicated. If the second reading is connected with the general theme of the day, it will be commented on together with the first reading and the gospel (these second readings are marked by an asterisk in the following list). If the second reading does not fit in with the theme of the day, a heavy line separates the commentary given from the preceding.

Year B		
Sunday 2	*The Call of God*	
	John 1:35-42	Come and you will see
	1 Sam 3:3b-10, 19	Hear the call and obey
	1 Cor 6:13c-15a, 17-20	Our bodies are the members of Christ
Sunday 3	*Be Converted and Believe*	
	Mark 1:14-20	Repent and believe in the gospel
	Jonah 3:1-5, 10	Turn from your evil ways
	*1 Cor 7:29-31	Live free
Sunday 4	*The Teaching of God*	
	Mark 1:21-28	Teach in the name of the eternal God
	Deut 18:15-20	I will put my words into the mouth of the prophet
	1 Cor 7:32-35	The unmarried woman and the concerns of the Lord

Sunday 5	*Overcoming the Forces of Evil*	
	Mark 1:29-39	He healed the sick
	Job 7:1-4, 6-7	Humanity and its suffering
	1 Cor 9:16-19, 22-23	The duty of proclaiming the Gospel
Sunday 6	*We Are Lepers*	
	Mark 1:40-45	If you will, you can make me clean
	Lev 13:1-2, 44-46	The unclean person must dwell alone
	1 Cor 10:31–11:1	Christ our model
Sunday 7	*The Forgiveness of Sins*	
	Mark 2:1-12	The Son of Man has authority to forgive
	Isa 43:18-19, 21-22, 24b-25	God forgives sins
	2 Cor 1:18-22	Our yes to the glory of God
Sunday 8	*The Marriage of God to His People*	
	Mark 2:18-22	The bridegroom with us
	Hos 2:14b, 15b, 21-22	I will speak tenderly to my spouse
	*2 Cor 3:1b-6	Ministers of a new covenant
Sunday 9	*The Meaning of the Sabbath*	
	Mark 2:23–3:6	Jesus, Lord of the Sabbath
	Deut 5:12-15	The Sabbath, a holy day
	2 Cor 4:6-11	The life of Jesus manifested in our bodies
Sunday 10	*Evil Overcome*	
	Mark 3:20-35	Satan conquered
	Gen 3:9-15	The promise of victory
	*2 Cor 4:13–5:1	We believe, and so we speak
Sunday 11	*The Growth of the Kingdom*	
	Mark 4:26-34	The seed sprouts
	Ezek 17:22-24	The tree planted by God
	2 Cor 5:6-10	Pleasing the Lord

Sunday 12	Lord of the World	
	Mark 4:35-41	The wind and the sea obey him
	Job 38:1, 8-11	Here shall your proud waves be stayed
	2 Cor 5:14-17	A new world
Sunday 13	God, Author of Life	
	Mark 5:21-43	I say to you, arise
	Wis 1:13-15; 2:23-24	God did not make death
	2 Cor 8:7, 9, 13-15	Give what you have received
Sunday 14	The Prophet Rejected	
	Mark 6:1-6	A prophet without honor
	Ezek 2:2-5	A people impudent and stubborn
	2 Cor 12:7-10	Strength in weakness
Sunday 15	Chosen and Sent	
	Mark 6:7-13	The Twelve are chosen and sent
	Amos 7:12-15	Prophesy to my people Israel
	*Eph 1:3-14	Chosen before the creation of the world
Sunday 16	The Flock Gathered	
	Mark 6:30-34	Sheep without a shepherd
	Jer 23:1-6	The shepherd gathers the remnant of the flock
	*Eph 2:13-18	Brought near in the blood of Christ
Sunday 17	We Are Filled with the Bread of God	
	John 6:1-15	The multiplication of the loaves
	2 Kgs 4:42-44	They shall eat and have some left
	Eph 4:1-6	One body, one Lord, one faith, one baptism
Sunday 18	Believe, Then Hunger and Thirst No More	
	John 6:24-35	Go to Christ and you will not hunger or thirst
	Exod 16:2-4, 12-15	A rain of bread
	Eph 4:17, 20-24	Live as a new person

Sunday 19	The Bread That Has Come down from Heaven	
	John 6:41-51	I am the living bread
	1 Kgs 19:4-8	In the strength of that food
	Eph 4:30–5:2	Walk in love, as Christ loved us
Sunday 20	Eat the Bread, Drink the Wine, and Live Forever	
	John 6:51-58	My flesh is food indeed and my blood is drink indeed
	Prov 9:1-6	Come, eat of my bread
	Eph 5:15-20	Understand what the will of the Lord is
Sunday 21	Live with the Lord Whose Words Are Spirit and Life	
	John 6:60-69	To whom shall we go?
	Josh 24:1-2a, 15-17, 18b	Die rather than abandon the Lord
	Eph 5:21-32	This is a great mystery, Christ and the Church
Sunday 22	Keep the Commandments of the Lord	
	Mark 7:1-8, 14-15, 21-23	God's commandments and human traditions
	Deut 4:1-2, 6-8	Observe the commandments of the Lord
	*Jas 1:17-18, 21b-22, 27	Act on the word
Sunday 23	The Messianic Age	
	Mark 7:31-37	He makes the deaf hear and the dumb speak
	Isa 35:4-7a	The ears of the deaf shall be unstopped, and the tongue of the dumb shall sing for joy
	Jas 2:1-5	The poor shall inherit the kingdom
Sunday 24	The Sufferings of the Servant of God	
	Mark 8:27-35	The Son of Man must suffer much
	Isa 50:4c-9a	I gave my back to the smiters
	Jas 2:14-18	Faith without works

Sunday 25	*The Son of Man Handed Over*	
	Mark 9:30-37	The Son of Man handed over
	Wis 2:12, 17-20	Condemned to a shameful death
	Jas 3:16–4:3	Peacemakers
Sunday 26	*Preach and Heal in the Lord's Name*	
	Mark 9:38-43, 45, 47-48	Cast out demons in the name of the Lord
	Num 11:25-29	May the Lord make everyone a prophet
	Jas 5:1-6	The corruption of riches
Sunday 27	*The Unity of the Human Couple*	
	Mark 10:2-16	No human being must separate what God has joined
	Gen 2:18-24	The two shall now be one
	Heb 2:9-11	Jesus and those he consecrates have one origin
Sunday 28	*Abandon All You Have*	
	Mark 10:17-30	Sell what you have and follow Jesus
	Wis 7:7-11	Regard riches as worthless
	Heb 4:12-13	The living word of God
Sunday 29	*The Life of Christ, a Ransom for Many*	
	Mark 10:35-45	The Son of Man gives his life for many
	Isa 53:10-11	The Servant will justify many
	*Heb 4:14-16	Jesus, the High Priest, has been tested
Sunday 30	*Messianic Signs and Faith*	
	Mark 10:46-52	Lord, let me see!
	Jer 31:7-9	The blind and the lame will be consoled
	Heb 5:1-6	Jesus, a Priest forever

Sunday 31	The Great Commandment	
	Mark 12:28b-34	No greater commandment than love of others
	Deut 6:2-6	You shall love the Lord with all your heart
	Heb 7:23-28	The eternal priesthood of Christ
Sunday 32	Give What You Have to Obtain Life	
	Mark 12:38-44	The poor widow has given more than all the others
	1 Kgs 17:10-16	The widow gives what food she has
	Heb 9:24-28	The unique sacrifice of Christ
Sunday 33	The Last Days	
	Mark 13:24-32	The elect, gathered from the four quarters of the world
	Dan 12:1-3	He comes to save his people
	Heb 10:11-14, 18	Having offered his sacrifice, Jesus leads to perfection those he has sanctified
Our Lord Jesus Christ, King of the Universe	Christ's Rule over the Universe	
	John 18:33b-37b	As you say, I am a king
	Dan 7:13-14	To him was given dominion and glory and kingship
	*Rev 1:5-8	Ruler of kings on earth

Second Sunday: The Call of God

Come and You Will See (John 1:35-42)

I think it important to emphasize the fact that Christ chooses his future disciples in the milieu in which they live and in the social and professional situation proper to them. Those called to follow Jesus are human beings like other people, living in a certain context and devoting themselves to their trade or profession. This, however, does not prevent them from attending to the essential thing: the meaning of their own lives and the meaning of their people as a whole.

The men in question have attached themselves to John the Baptist as other Jews might to one or another rabbi. But now Jesus passes by, and a radical change is underway in the lives of the two disciples who happen to be accompanying John at the moment. John is entirely without egotism in his doctrine and spirituality; he has been forming disciples, not for his own benefit or according to his own desires, but for the sake of Jesus and the renewal of the world. Consequently, he points Jesus out to his disciples, and he does so in terms that leave no doubt in the minds of hearers who were well acquainted with the Scriptures: "Behold, the Lamb of God" (John 1:36). In other words, here is the man of whom Isaiah spoke (chap. 53).

We must not forget that John the Evangelist reflects the thinking of the early Church. For the Christians of that time, John the Baptist was the supreme witness to the fulfillment of the Old Testament promises. He was the link between the Old Testament period and the new age inaugurated by Christ, and he brought his own disciples to Jesus because that new age was now beginning. The first two disciples did not miss the meaning of John's words and of Jesus' person. Andrew says to his brother Simon, "We have found the Messiah" (v. 41), and brings his brother to meet Jesus; a new disciple himself, he immediately goes and gets another to join him! Jesus then looks at Simon and says: "You are Simon the son of John; you will be called Cephas" (v. 42).

It would take too long, and not be very profitable, to analyze in detail all the words of the passage. It is important, however, to emphasize, as we have done on other occasions, the care with which St. John uses words.

Take, for example, the question Jesus asks when he sees the two disciples following him: "What are you looking for?" (v. 38). John puts the same question on Jesus' lips on two other occasions. One is the moment in the garden when the soldiers come to arrest Jesus, and he asks them, "Whom are you looking for?" (18:4). The other is when Mary Magdalene at the tomb of Christ hears a man who looks like the gardener ask her, "Whom are you looking for?" (20:15). These questions are, in fact, a manifestation of Jesus' knowledge of what is in the heart. He knows the answer before it is given, but he provokes it.

Or take the question of the future disciples: "where are you staying?" (1:38). They are not simply asking for the address of the man whose teaching they intend to follow. For St. John, the word "stay, dwell, abide, remain" (Greek: *menein*) has a more profound meaning, as we can see from several passages of his gospel: "Whoever eats my flesh and drinks my blood remains in me and I in him" (6:56); "neither

can you [bear fruit] unless you remain in me" (15:4); "Whoever remains in me and I in him" (15:5; cf. vv. 7, 9). We should recall especially the Prologue: "And the Word became flesh and made his
dwelling among us" (1:14).

All this is an invitation to us to go beyond the simple material
meaning of the words and discover the doctrinal themes at work.
When Jesus bids the would-be disciples to "Come, and you will see"
(1:39), we must remember that "seeing" for St. John is the starting
point of faith and a new attitude. "[M]any began to believe in his
name when they saw the signs he was doing" (2:23); "What sign can
you do, that we may see and believe in you?" (6:30); "this is the will
of my Father, that everyone who sees the Son and believes in him
may have eternal life" (6:40); "Now many of the Jews who had . . .
seen what he had done began to believe in him" (11:45); "If you know
me, then you will also know my Father. From now on you do know
him and have seen him" (14:7); "Then the other disciple also went
in, the one who had arrived at the tomb first, and he saw and believed" (20:8).

We too are meant to cultivate these attitudes: seeking, coming,
seeing, believing. We have been called by Christ; we must become
the children of God.

Hear the Call and Obey (1 Sam 3:3b-10, 19)

The Old Testament gives a moving example of God's call in the
story of the boy Samuel. There are many such calls reported throughout the Old Testament, calls to enter into the service of the people as
a whole. These calls are always imperious, yet they leave the human
being free to answer or not answer; that is why the Lord can complain,
"I called and you did not answer, / I spoke and you did not listen"
(Isa 65:12).

Before answering, however, one must be sure it is indeed the Lord
calling; this is part of the story of Samuel. Even though he lives in
the sanctuary itself, he is not certain that it is God he hears, and so
he is mistrustful, or he cannot believe that God really wants to enter
into intimate dialogue with someone like himself. God's call often
means suffering for the person chosen. The Servant (Isa 41:8; 43:10)
shows the world what it means to hear God's call and to answer it
without reserve.

The responsorial psalm, Psalm 40 (same as in Year A), shows the kind of response God wants: "Then I said, 'See, I have come. / . . . I delight to do your will, O my God'" (vv. 8, 9). "I waited, I waited for the LORD, / and he stooped down to me; / he heard my cry. . . . He put a new song into my mouth" (vv. 2, 4).

Our Bodies Are the Members of Christ (1 Cor 6:13c-15a, 17-20)

This is an important passage. It shows us that Paul is unaware of any "taboo" in regard to the body; he sees only the body's dignity, and it is this that serves him as a basis for prescribing the conduct that Christians should observe. "Dignity," however, is here not primarily a moralist's term; for Paul, it springs from an ontology. Concretely, the dignity of the body is due to the fact that every Christian is incorporated into Christ, so that each person's very body is a member of Christ himself.

Paul is certainly not obsessed by fear of impurity, but impurity does seem to him to be especially opposed to membership in Christ and to the fact that we have become temples of the Holy Spirit. Nor, despite Paul's words about every sin but fornication being outside the body, do I think he concentrates too much on sins of impurity. (Did Paul have no knowledge of drug use? Was drunkenness rare in his day?) Rather, the point is that Paul is vividly aware of human destiny; he knows that we do not belong to ourselves, that our bodies are for the Lord, and that our true life is in eternity. For these reasons, we must preserve the integrity of our bodies. We do not belong to ourselves because our calling has made us temples of the Spirit and our baptism has incorporated us into Christ.

Paul is deeply impressed by the unity that exists between the Christian and Christ and by the unity that should exist among Christians themselves. To bring out this unity, he does not hesitate to use the example of a prostitute and her client (vv. 15-16): If a man joined with a prostitute becomes one flesh with her, much more does he become one with Christ, where the unity is spiritual. Through union with Christ, humans are divinized and become temples of the Spirit. We have been bought at a great price and must therefore glorify God in our bodies.

We might well ask whether an education based on this text, properly explained, would not be more successful than hours of sex education and depth psychology. Paul here presents us with a true analysis of what we are; we ought to reflect deeply on it.

Third Sunday: Be Converted and Believe

Repent and Believe in the Gospel (Mark 1:14-20)

In St. Mark, the Good News, or Gospel, is the person of Jesus himself, to whom one must cleave through faith. When a human being comes face-to-face with the Gospel that is Jesus himself, two things are required: repent and follow Christ in an act of faith.

"Repentance" and "conversion" are two words for the same reality. The most important thing in repentance is conversion of the heart. The prophets of the Old Testament had been chiefly concerned with this interior conversion.

Hosea, for example, acknowledges a conversion as fruitful only when it is a profound, love-inspired conversion of the heart (6:1-6). Isaiah, for his part, emphasizes the uselessness of outward worship, or *cultus*, if it does not express an interior conversion (1:11-15). Sins that are scarlet can become white as snow—but only by walking in God's ways (1:16-20).

Following Isaiah, all the other prophets are unwearying in their stress on interior conversion. Jeremiah has perhaps the most striking formulas for bringing out the need of such conversion; one must, for example, plow fallow ground and circumcise the heart (4:1-4). Ezekiel has more to say than the other prophets about the cultic regulations connected with repentance, but he is no less emphatic than they about conversion being a condition for true life (Ezek 18:31). The Israelites are stubborn and a "rebellious house" (2:4-7), but the Lord will put his Spirit upon them so that they will repent of their ways (36:26-31).

Jesus too, when he calls for repentance, emphasizes the interior conditions of a true conversion. In fact, the evangelists offer us very rich perspectives on repentance as preached by Jesus. We must obey the commandments and seek the kingdom of God and his righteousness (Matt 6:33); we must make an energetic effort to change our ways. Above all, however, the act of conversion comprises humility and a confident turning to God amid the consciousness of our own weakness (Luke 8:13). The Lord always retains the initiative in a conversion, as is made clear by the attitude of the father as he awaits the return of his erring son: the father sees him coming and welcomes him with great forgiveness (Luke 15:11-32). So too, the real shepherd goes in search of his lost sheep (Luke 15:4).

Conversion is followed by adherence to Christ through faith. Conversion and faith are closely related attitudes. Thus, in the Acts of the Apostles we see conversion being followed by baptism (2:38). Conversion is required for baptism, but this is in part because a true conversion already involves an adherence to Christ (3:19), although the fullness of such adherence comes in baptism itself as a gift of the Spirit.

In today's gospel, St. Mark gives a brief picture of the apostle who is called by Christ, but he also gives a picture of persons who are called. First, the apostles. A first point that must be emphasized is that in their call Jesus takes and retains the initiative; it is he who approaches these men and calls them.

In the Old Testament, when God calls, he does so in order to send someone to carry out a mission. God's choice is entirely his and cannot be justified by merely human considerations. Examples abound; all follow the same pattern: the person chosen is chosen not for his own sake but for the sake of a mission. This is true of Abraham (Gen 12:1); it is true of Moses (Exod 3:1-12); it is true of prophets like Amos (Amos 7:15), Isaiah (Isa 6:9), Jeremiah (Jer 1:7), and Ezekiel (Ezek 3:1-11).

Mark also calls attention to the attitude of those who answer Christ's call: they agree unhesitatingly to change their whole way of life. They set out on a new road by an act that is a brutal, almost unthinkable rupture with their past.

"Follow Jesus" is an expression frequently found in the New Testament; it occurs over thirty times, being used chiefly by St. Matthew. If we look at the words as they apply strictly to those who were being called to be Jesus' disciples, we may note the following passages: "'Come after me, and I will make you fishers of men.' At once they left their nets and followed him" (Matt 4:19-20; cf. Mark 1:18; Luke 5:11); "immediately they left their boat and their father and followed him" (Matt 4:22); "Follow me, and let the dead bury their dead" (Matt 8:22); "Follow me," says Jesus to Matthew (Matt 9:9; cf. Mark 2:14; Luke 5:27-28); "whoever does not take up his cross and follow after me is not worthy of me" (Matt 10:38; cf. Mark 8:34; Luke 14:27; John 12:26; the same expressions occur again later on: Matt 16:24; cf. Luke 9:23); "If you wish to be perfect, go, sell . . . [and] come, follow me" (Matt 19:21; cf. Mark 10:21; Luke 10:28; 12:33; 18:22).

Those whom Jesus thus calls he intends to make "fishers of men." In other words, their vocation will be to go and call others in turn.

The gospel also applies to the ordinary person who is called. We should bear in mind that St. Mark is writing his gospel at a time when the Church is already established, although it is admittedly still in its beginnings and the evangelist is undoubtedly thinking primarily of those with the special calling to be apostles with Christ. Yet he is also thinking of his fellow Christians. That is to say, the calling of the apostles has become applicable to every person who wishes to enter the Church and live Christ's life therein. One must leave the Gentile or Jewish milieu to enter the Church. More specifically, Jews must leave the Jewish community and cast their lot with those who had been Gentiles.

Underlying the proclamation of this account in today's liturgy there is a realistic view of a close continuity between the call of the disciples and life of the Church today. Each of us has received and is constantly receiving a call to repent and follow Christ.

Turn from Your Evil Ways (Jonah 3:1-5, 10)

Nineveh repented, and the instrument of its conversion was Jonah, a Jew sent by God to the Gentiles of that great city. But the prophet went despite himself; he was afraid of the Gentile city and initially ran off in the opposite direction. But the Lord had his way, and almost incredible adventures led Jonah against his will to the place where he was supposed to preach conversion. Jonah succeeded where the prophets before him had failed. Indeed, the conversion of Nineveh was almost instantaneous: "the people of Nineveh believed God"; their conversion was manifested by signs of mourning and especially by the fact that they "turned from their evil way." As a result, God did not inflict the punishment he had threatened.

This passage, when taken together with the gospel, teaches two lessons: the lesson of obedience to a mission and the lesson of conversion. The two lessons add up to a program that every disciple of Jesus makes in a spirit of trust in the Lord and his strength.

The responsorial psalm is taken from Psalm 25 and asks God to make his ways known to us and to lead us in the truth. To this petition for guidance from God is added praise for the God who saves us: "Good and upright is the LORD; / he shows the way to sinners" (v. 8).

Live Free (1 Cor 7:29-31)

The second reading for today is an exception in that it happens to fit in with the other two readings. It teaches that we who are called to leave all and follow Christ must lead lives of complete freedom from all things. The basic reason for following Christ in this unconditional way is that time is limited. That is why we must leave everything—boat, nets, parents—why those who are married must live as though they were not married; why those who mourn must act as though they had no cause to mourn; why those who rejoice must live as though they had no cause to rejoice; why those who buy must act as if they owned nothing; why those who deal with the world must act as though they had no dealings with it. Christians have no time to dally along the way as they go about their mission; they must be ever intent on following Christ, because the world as we know it is passing away.

We must not think that St. Paul is showing contempt for marriage, which elsewhere he speaks of as a great mystery (Eph 5:23-33; 1 Cor 7:2-5). He is not saying Christians have no right to feelings or that they are to be indifferent to suffering and joy. He is not arguing against private property or teaching contempt of the world. Such interpretations would mistake the thrust of his teaching.

The point St. Paul is making is that, given the presence of the kingdom and the short time a person has to live, the Christian must make a pragmatic value judgment and live in complete detachment. We must love the values inherent in this world, we must love creation, we must work for the advancement of the world, but we must do so with detachment, standing back from all of these things. This is the characteristic attitude of the saints, whose lives are sometimes distorted in the telling because we attribute to them a contempt for the world, when, in fact, they are simply judging the temporal and transient in the light of Christ who is eternal.

Fourth Sunday: The Teaching of God

Teach in the Name of the Eternal God (Mark 1:21-28)

We should not let our attention be too much taken up with the evil spirit that Jesus casts out in today's gospel. In the light of the first reading, greater interest is to be accorded to Jesus' teaching. This is not to deny, of course, that the kind of exorcism Jesus practices is connected with his teaching and gives it extraordinary authority. The evangelist notes the connection but also brings out the fact that it is secondary to the teaching proper. For, in fact, the crowd is not struck chiefly by the exorcism and violent dispelling of the demon; the words of the crowd as recorded by Mark concern rather the teaching: "What is this? A new teaching with authority. He commands even the unclean spirits and they obey him" (v. 27).

Both word and action highlight the authority; that is the point St. Mark wants to make. Jesus is manifesting himself as Messiah, and his teaching differs from that of others not only by its content but by the fact that it is linked to an effective power from on high. His teaching thus manifests his person and the fact that he has been sent from God.

St. Mark notes at the beginning of the pericope that Jesus' teaching impressed his hearers because he spoke with authority and not like the scribes. The account of the exorcism conveys something to us of the same impression. Jesus is not satisfied with words, nor does he give his hearers a catechesis that he could have learned in a rabbinic school, where the concern was to explain the law. On the contrary, his teaching is new in the sense that it seems to come directly from God and is confirmed by acts of power, such as the exorcism. In another context John writes, "The words I have spoken to you are spirit and life" (6:63); these words provide one of the Alleluia verses for the Sundays of Ordinary Time.

Jesus has accustomed us to powerful words that find further expression in action; this pattern of word-and-action has carried over from the gospel into the sacraments of the Church. In the latter case, the combination is one that Pope St. Leo the Great often speaks of in his sermons as "sacred sign and example" (*sacramentum et exemplum*), that is, an efficacious sign and at the same time an example that conveys a lesson or a teaching to us. The words provide a succinct description of the whole life of Jesus as well as of the Church's sacraments.

The authority of Jesus is acknowledged by the evil spirit, who cries out, "I know who you are—the Holy One of God!" (v. 24). Thus it is that both the teaching and the actions of Christ show him to be the Messiah, and his reputation spreads throughout Galilee.

Word and sacrament—this phrase sums up, now and until the end of time, the Church's activity to which she is commissioned by Christ and the Father. The two together represent the new teaching that astonished the crowd, according to Mark's account, and led people to faith throughout Galilee. The two also represent the teaching of the Church, whereby, under the guidance of the Spirit of Christ, she carries on the teaching of him who was sent by the Father. We are too accustomed to this kind of teaching and are less sensitive than the crowds in Galilee were to this entirely new manner of communicating God's word; it is teaching that has little in common with ordinary teaching, which is notional and conceptual in character.

The Church must indeed endeavor to prove the validity of her teaching and must engage in scholarly study of the truth and the message she is commissioned to transmit. She may not, however, be satisfied with mere study; her teaching must be primarily an action, a transmission from God of a power that renews the earth. That is what a sacrament is, and that is what the word of the Church has always been meant to be.

I Will Put My Words into the Mouth of the Prophet (Deut 18:15-20)

Moses offers himself as the model by which the Israelites will be able to identify the prophet who is to come and whom God will raise up for us. Moses reminds the people that at Horeb they had bidden him ask the Lord to appoint someone to serve as intermediary between them and the Lord and that the Lord had promised a prophet. Moses himself had served as the first intermediary, the first in the line of prophets, who are people chosen from among their colleagues. God, not the people, does the choosing of each prophet, and his way of choosing often proves disconcerting. He guides his people and chooses those who are to be sent in his name.

What is to be the role of the chosen prophet? "[I] will put my words into his mouth; [the prophet] shall tell them all that I command" (Deut. 18:18). This means that God looks upon the prophet as another self. People must therefore heed the prophet's words; not to listen is to refuse God, and God will demand an accounting of this refusal. The prophet must speak exactly what God says; otherwise, the prophet will betray the mission.

Who is the future prophet who is like Moses? We know that in Jesus' time such a prophet was expected, for John the Baptist sends his disciples to ask Jesus whether he, Jesus, is the awaited prophet (John 1:21). It becomes clear, when Jesus asks his disciples who people think he is, that people were expecting a new Elijah or a new Jeremiah

(Matt 16:14; for Elijah, see also Matt 11:14); in short, a prophet was indeed expected to come soon.

Jesus, for his part, acts like a prophet, that is, one who speaks on behalf of God: "But I tell you . . ." St. Luke reports Jesus as saying, "[W]hoever receives me receives the one who sent me" (9:48; cf. Matt 18:3; Mark 9:37; John 13:20). In the Fourth Gospel, Jesus frequently refers to the One who sent him: "the one whom God sent speaks the words of God" (3:34); Jesus has come to do the will of him who sent him (4:34); in all things he seeks the will of him who sent him (5:30); his teaching is not his own but his who sent him (7:16). Evidently, then, he is presenting himself as the long-expected mediator. If he speaks as he does, it is in order that people may believe that the Father has sent him (11:42). Eternal life consists in believing in the one who has been sent (17:3), for in the last analysis he who sends and he who is sent are one.

Jesus clearly thinks of himself as doing what is expected of the great prophet whom God had promised to raise up from among his people. Consequently, the reading from Deuteronomy does much to bring home the full significance of the gospel pericope from St. Mark.

Today the Church carries on the prophetic function of Christ. The Lord puts his words into her mouth, and she teaches in the name of the Lord. The whole revelation has been given, and the task of the Church in her teaching is to make it known by explaining it and, under the guidance of the Spirit, drawing further conclusions from what Christ and the Father have revealed to us in the Scriptures. For us Catholics, the Church alone can interpret the Scriptures with absolute authority; it is in and through her that the Scriptures manifest to us their authentic meaning.

To say this is in no way to play down the charisms that existed in the past and that, according to the Church herself, still exist today.[1] But the prophetic role connected with the charisms is today, as in St. Paul's time, subordinate to revelation and to the Church. The Church is guided in her development and adaptation by the Spirit of Christ, but she is also helped by the charisms. The latter have only too often been viewed with distrust; today we are more open to them, although the concrete manifestations of them must still be examined to determine whether they are truly from God.*

---

* Perhaps Nocent is referring to the beginnings of the Catholic Charismatic Renewal.

The responsorial psalm is from Psalm 95. The response is from verses 7-8, "If today you hear God's voice, harden not your hearts."

The Unmarried Woman and the Concerns of the Lord (1 Cor 7:32-35)

As read here apart from their context, St. Paul's statements regarding the dedication of one's life to the Lord may appear one-sided and insufficiently mindful of the sacrament of marriage, concerning which he himself elsewhere writes, "This is a great mystery" (Eph 5:32). It is easy enough to put today's pericope back into its context, however, and to read it as it should be read.

St. Paul is addressing the community of Corinth, with which previous readings have already familiarized us. We know how rich this community was in persons and gifts; we also know that it had its troubles, inasmuch as its responses were not always those that its gifts should have elicited. In a new Christian community of this kind, the sexual problem was bound to make itself felt. St. Paul does not, however, spend a lot of time discussing serious situations in which his only response can be to condemn, situations involving incest and fornication (5:1-5; 6:12-19).

Whenever a Church that is enthusiastic about its faith and its Christian life finds licentiousness being practiced by some of its members, there is always the likelihood of a reaction to the other extreme. So it was at Corinth. Paul has received a letter telling him that a group within the community has chosen the unqualified position that there must be abstention from marriage: "It is a good thing for a man not to touch a woman" (7:1). In response, St. Paul makes some needed distinctions and takes up the various possible states: married people, widowed individuals, celibates, etc.

St. Paul makes it clear that his own preference is for what we today would call the "consecrated life." Does this preference betray a certain scorn for marriage or a negative vision of a state of life that he seems to consider only as a means of retaining one's moral balance: "it is better to marry than to be on fire" (7:9)? Quite the contrary. We receive the impression that Paul regards the way God set down in the book of Genesis as being the natural and normal way of life for humanity; he even emphasizes the practice of intercourse for husbands and wives (7:5).

It does seem to me, however, that if we limit ourselves to the First Letter to the Corinthians, we will not easily grasp the very positive view Paul has of marriage. To this end, we must also read the Letter to the Ephesians (5:21-33), where we find Paul expressing his admiration for the sacrament of marriage. He sees marriage as symbolized in the union of Christ with his Church and gives the spouses a primordial role in the building and extension of the kingdom.

In today's reading, Paul's emphasis is more on the eschatological dimension of Christian life. He would like to see Christians truly free, not for selfish fulfillment, but for the sake of a more direct and constant union with God and for the service of others. This kind of freedom from all things gives the person dedicated to God the ability to go wherever the Lord calls.

The First Letter to the Corinthians, when taken together with the Letter to the Ephesians, gives us the basic Christian teaching on marriage and virginity. Virginity is seen as a gift in which a person renounces the way of matrimony that Providence has established. It is a response to a divine choice and a step forward into what is humanly unknown, but a step taken in the conviction that the Lord is ever present and will guide his disciple.

The problem, in a sense, is only with the starting point: Does this person really have the charism of virginity? There are signs that argue against it. Paul, for his part, knows of no commandment from the Lord in this matter, and he has no desire to trap anyone. Humility, prayer, love, and devotion to neighbor will bring the light needed to discover God's choice.

Fifth Sunday: Overcoming the Forces of Evil

He Healed the Sick (Mark 1:29-39)

Today's gospel acquaints us with two facts. The first is that the Good News is gradually spreading and that healings symbolize the radical newness that the Good News represents, for it is the good news of spiritual healing, resurrection, and new life. The other fact is that the crowds do not look beyond the material sign to its real meaning. (This is, unfortunately, always the case, and yet, while the Church should not be preaching to empty bellies [St. Augustine's phrase], her primary aim must be spiritual healing, not raising the standard of living.) This situation, and the conflict it embodies, runs through the whole of Jesus' public life.

In this passage of Mark's gospel we find Jesus healing the sick and, in particular, driving out demons. What is the significance of the healing of Peter's mother-in-law? Mark uses a word that may provide a clue when we compare this passage with the Letter of St. James, where the same word occurs. We are told that Jesus "helped her up," and the fever left her. The Greek word represented by "help up" is *egeiro*. Now St. James, in speaking of the sacrament of the sick, uses the same word: "the prayer of faith will save the sick person, and the Lord will *raise* him *up*" (Jas 5:15). The Greek verb *egeiro*, in its active form, has a number of meanings: wake, rouse; raise, help to rise; relieve; restore to life. In our view, we should not try to limit the word to a single meaning but should utilize the various meanings. The mother-in-law of Simon Peter gets up and begins to serve the guests. This is very much like what we find in the sacrament of the sick, where the person is healed to join once again in the Christian assembly.

Jesus heals; his coming is a sign of life, and life in turn is a sign that the kingdom is present. The Good News is the news of life, and we must not make that life either exclusively spiritual or exclusively physical. That is the kind of mistake the crowds make when they see only the material side of Christ's gifts to them. When that happens, the Lord leaves them; he withdraws from them.

In this passage of Mark, Jesus moves on to another place, and we sense a certain disillusionment about his going. The crowd seeks him out only because it wants physical healings, but Jesus must concentrate rather on preaching the Good News: "For this purpose have I come" (v. 38). In the parallel passage Luke has "for this purpose I have been sent" (4:43), thus specifying "have come" as "have been sent," that is, by the Father. Mark seems satisfied simply to emphasize the fact that Jesus' primary purpose is to preach the Good News, not to perform physical cures.

The "messianic secret" plays a part in this passage, as elsewhere. This is a favorite theme of St. Mark. The demons, of course, recognize Jesus for who he is (v. 34), as the possessed man in the synagogue had (1:24). Jesus does not wish, however, to be acknowledged solely because of physical healings; these are but signs that should lead to faith, and faith must go further. Therefore he imposes silence.

People must discover only gradually who Jesus is, and they must not be motivated chiefly by their own material interests. The healings he performs are meant to prod people into asking who Jesus really is. If they once recognize him to be the Messiah, they must then go a step further and accept him as the Messiah who must die and rise from the dead for the salvation of the world and whom they themselves must follow in death and resurrection.

Humanity and Its Suffering (Job 7:1-4, 6-7)

This passage from the book of Job raises in a brutally direct way the problem of human existence and suffering. People often have a one-sided impression of the book of Job, as though it preached a passive submission to the will of God. As this passage shows us, however, the book is about a normal man with violent reactions to suffering. He is a man who rebels angrily against the injustice of his lot and complains bitterly about his human state. He has known months of emptiness, and his nights are times of misery. And ahead lies death, after a life that passes as swiftly as a weaver's shuttle moves. But though he cannot solve the problem raised by his physical and spiritual suffering, Job has not despaired. He knows that he can encounter God and that God is mindful of him.

Job doubtless had no conception of an afterlife, and his cry concludes with a phrase we could not accept: "I shall not see happiness again" (7:7). And yet he knows that God is mindful of him. God is mindful indeed. Eventually he sends his Son to proclaim the Good News of life and to bring, not necessarily a cure of present ills, but a life that will last forever.

The real solution to the problem of suffering is to be found not in a philosophy of simple resignation but in the absolute certainty that any and all suffering is part of building a new world with Christ, who himself died but then rose from the dead. Sin, as a consequence, has been forgiven, and there is the prospect of a new life whose full energies are hidden from us as yet and whose joys we can only try to imagine.

The Duty of Proclaiming the Gospel (1 Cor 9:16-19, 22-23)

Paul depicts himself as all the prophets had before him: as a person who cannot renounce preaching the Word. He cannot renounce it, not only because God has chosen him, but also because of what his mission means to other people. To preach the Gospel is to be the servant of all, so as to win over to Christ as many as possible. It is to be all things to all people for the sake of saving some. That is the purpose of preaching; in the last analysis it is meant to bring people into contact with God and his salvation.

Preaching is thus not primarily a matter of teaching doctrine or teaching anything at all; it is a matter of touching people in such a way that they enter into close contact with the Lord who speaks the word through his apostle. In order to carry out his mission, Paul is determined to be utterly free and at the service of all. He renounces his right to a salary; he eagerly lives with others and shares their way of life. He is not the kind of teacher who remains apart from and above those he instructs. He teaches a way of life, and this kind of teaching is communicated only through example, through becoming all things to all people.

Sixth Sunday: We Are Lepers

If You Will, You Can Make Me Clean (Mark 1:40-45)

Today's gospel could well be the subject of a lengthy commentary, since it raises a number of problems. But to go into such problems in connection with the Sixth Sunday of Ordinary Time would be to lose sight of the real meaning the passage has within the liturgical celebration. For this reason, we shall make a few brief remarks, by way of a digression, in order to satisfy those who are intrigued by certain statements. These remarks, however, are not the main concern; we shall quickly leave them behind and concentrate on the essential point of today's message.

The same story is found in the other Synoptic Gospels (Matt 8:2-4; Luke 5:12-16). The moment in Jesus' life at which the event takes place is different in the different gospels, since each evangelist uses the story when it fits in best with his catechetical presentation of the life of Jesus.

The passage confronts us once again with the "messianic secret," as Jesus forbids the leper to make his cure known. The cure of the leprous is one of the signs of the Messiah (Matt 11:5), but Jesus wants to avoid having the Jews mistake the meaning of his coming. He has no desire to establish an earthly kingdom, as the Jews expect the

Messiah to do. On the contrary, if people want to understand the real meaning of his mission, they will find it in his passion and death. Jesus was evidently quite justified in imposing silence on the leper, for once the leper spoke of the cure, Jesus could not openly enter a town without crowds running to him for miracles.

Christ does send the former leper to the priests and urges him to follow the prescriptions set down by Moses for his legal purification. Thus, while he does not want the thoughtless crowd to know of the cure, he does not seem to have wanted to keep it a secret from the priests. The priests were presumably more enlightened, and when the leper went to them to testify to his cure, he would make it known to them that the Messiah had come.

This passage of the gospel touches all of us closely. Spiritual leprosy is a reality in every age; that is why the fathers make frequent use in their preaching on the various gospel pericopes that speak of leprosy.

The Unclean Person Must Dwell Alone (Lev 13:1-2, 44-46)

The Old Testament, as we know, considers leprosy not only as the most terrible of afflictions but also as a legal impurity.

We should not let the book of Leviticus put us off entirely. Admittedly, its subject matter is not what we would expect in an inspired book, but we would be wrong if we saw there only the juridical details. If we look beyond the latter, we will find interesting teachings on sin and the mercy of God and on the means of atoning for sin, especially through sacrifices. Moreover, the concepts of the book are not purely culture-bound and reflective solely of a now-dead civilization. If we look more deeply into the thought of the book, we will find the same teaching that God had given to Moses along with the law.

It was taken for granted in the Old Testament that sickness was connected with sin; in fact, so deeply rooted was this assumption that Jesus would later find it necessary to insist that a direct link was not always present. Furthermore, the Old Testament regarded leprosy as the very type, or fullest visible form, of divine chastisement. We should observe here that the assumption of a connection between sickness and sin was not peculiar to the people of the Old Testament; many other cultures have taken the same view of sickness. Be that as it may, people who wished to be acknowledged as cured had to present themselves to a priest and confess their sin. The book of Job, we may remember, likewise gives a "moral" vision of leprosy; that is, leprosy is regarded as sent by the Lord (Job 19:20-21) and as cured by the Lord (Job 5:18). Leprosy rendered impure the person afflicted with it. It is quite understandable that the seriousness of the illness and its contagious character should have led people to cast out any persons afflicted with it and to regard them as impure in the eyes of the law. Such is the situation in the background of today's gospel passage.

We shall not insist further on this background, despite the cultural interest it may have for us, because today's liturgy does not dwell on the point. The message today is not that we should be divided into the pure and the impure. Rather, the point is to show us that sin is what separates and that the power of God can heal us.

Both leprosy and sin separate us from others. Too often today, sin is considered to be an entirely personal matter; its necessarily social character is overlooked. For, in fact, every sin is necessarily social in its bearing; even if the sin is hidden, it influences the world and the Church. That is why tradition has insisted on the confession of sin to the Church, for which that sin created a spiritual "crisis." The value of excommunication was that it emphasized this social aspect of sin, the separation that sin caused. But whether or not one's sin is known, the sinner is, in fact, someone "separated." The ancient monastic rules also provided for "excommunications"; these were inspired by the fear that a guilty monk might morally contaminate the community, and they were also a punishment intended to make the guilty person reflect on his sin.[2]

At the same time, sinners and their sin should never be thought of apart from the mercy of God and the divine power to heal. In today's passage from St. Mark, Jesus sends the healed leper to the priest. Jesus does not say whether he thinks of the leper as a sinner whom God has punished; his chief reason for sending the man is that the priest and his associates may be forced to acknowledge the presence of the messianic age. Henceforth, leprosy can be cured because the Lord who pardons and heals is now present.

St. Matthew emphasizes the faith of the sick. Jesus uses his authority and power in order to bring into the open the priests' stubborn refusal to accept any testimony that may speak in favor of Jesus.

St. Luke, who has his eye on Gentile readers, wants to emphasize the power of Christ, who heals people by freeing them from sin. St. Mark, as we have seen, is more interested in stressing the presence of the messianic age and on bringing out the true nature of the king- dom. The messiahship of Jesus has nothing to do with the coming of a restored earthly kingdom.

The lesson being taught on this Sunday is not a useless one, for the Church is still made up of sinners who are looking for healing. The first reading and the gospel pericope should guide us in our quest for salvation by making us more fully aware of the social aspect of our sins as well as of our responsibility in today's world. Other people accept the fact that a Christian is a sinner, but the Christian cannot simply accept it; in fact, only by not accepting it can one be a Christian despite one's sin.

The Christian is a person with a deep faith in the Lord's power to heal. Christians are aware of their responsibility and are able to evalu- ate properly the things of this world. They know that, if they ask for God's mercy, they will be pardoned, but that their earthly life will not thereby become a paradise. For when the Lord pardons, he does not promise a life of happiness in the earthly sense; to think that he does is to misunderstand the messianic message of Jesus. When Christ forgives sin, he does, however, heal us interiorly and gives us access to the life that constantly enlivens his Church.

Christ Our Model (1 Cor 10:31–11:1)

St. Paul has already emphasized to the Corinthians his disinterest. He has pointed out that in order to be all things to all people, a person must be free. The freedom in question is not simply a freedom from material concerns or even from attachment to human beings. It is also—and this is the point Paul is making in today's short pericope—a more continuous and radical liberation in which all of our actions are dedicated to the glory of God. Whether we eat or drink or do anything else, we must do it for God's glory.

Paul is thus not afraid to speak of the need to be free. He empha- sizes it several times in the First Letter to the Corinthians: "Am I not free?" (9:1; cf. 9:1-12); "Everything is lawful" (10:23) for one who is fully dedicated to God's glory. But though there may be no interior obstacle to using this freedom, charity may at times bid the apostle not to use it, precisely so that he may continue to be all things to all people. Paul is very much aware of the limitations that charity sometimes imposes on an individual, and he insists on them in today's passage: "Avoid giving offense, whether to the Jews or Greeks or the church of God" (10:32).

In all this, the Corinthians can take Paul as their model. The real model, however, is Christ, whom Paul seeks to follow in everything. Of what is Christ a model? Of self-sacrifice to the will and the glory of the Father, for the sake of saving everyone. If we are to imitate Paul in his quest of freedom (as limited by the bidding of charity), we must look beyond Paul and follow Christ, who did not hesitate to lay down his life for the salvation of all.

Seventh Sunday: The Forgiveness of Sins

The Son of Man Has Authority to Forgive Sins (Mark 2:1-12)

Despite the startling character of the miracle and the unusual circumstances in which Jesus worked it, the narrative is concerned primarily with the forgiveness of sins. That is the main point, and the evangelist doubtless described the scene in order to highlight this central issue: sin is forgiven. The witnesses are utterly amazed; they glorify God and claim that they have never seen anything like it. That is the first step toward the assent of faith, for what the sign is showing is the power of Jesus and the mystery of his person.

The scribes realize what is going on, and they tell themselves that only God can forgive sins. In fact, Jesus claims and exercises two powers, one of which (healing) is the sign of the other (forgiveness of sins). The second is essential, since Jesus has come to save. What good would his coming do, then, if he did not forgive sins?

Jesus is the Lamb who takes away the sins of the world. Thus, this story, like others of the same kind, is an attempt to bring to light the true person of Jesus. The scribes are aware of the danger Jesus represents to them; they can take Jesus' words, "Your sins are forgiven," only as a blasphemy, for they realize that, in a sense not yet fully clear to them, Jesus is claiming equality with God.

At the time when St. Mark was writing, the power to forgive sins was being exercised in the Church. Perhaps the evangelist was highlighting the power of Jesus in order to help his readers understand the power he had left to his Church.

God Forgives Sins (Isa 43:18-19, 21-22, 24b-25)

In this passage, forgiveness is presented as a form of renewal: We are to forget the past. God says that Israel has treated him as a servant and weighed him down with the sins of his people. Yet he forgives and will no longer remember their sins!

The New Testament throws light on what God says here through Isaiah, for according to the New Testament, forgiveness is an act by which God creates anew. In its full form, then, forgiveness is an eschatological reality: "Behold, I make all things new" (Rev 21:5). The whole purpose of the coming of Jesus and of his paschal mystery was to renew the world. St. Paul, for his part, writes, "So whoever is in Christ is a new creation: the old things have passed away; behold, new things have come" (2 Cor 5:17).

The Christian is thus uniquely privileged in not having a past! God's forgiveness means that God no longer remembers our sins. Despite our ingratitude, despite the fact that we have treated him like a servant, he wants to forget and, in keeping with his covenant plan, to forgive and make us new beings. This determination of God to forgive is perhaps his most incomprehensible aspect. St. Paul was deeply impressed by this mystery: "God delivered all to disobedience, that he might have mercy upon all. . . . How inscrutable are his judgments and how unsearchable his ways!" (Rom 11:32-36).

The responsorial psalm sings of the God who helps people on their sickbed and brings them healing: "In my integrity may you have upheld me, / and have set me in your presence forever" (Ps 41:13).

Our Yes to the Glory of God (2 Cor 1:18-22)

The community at Corinth was not fully convinced by Paul's first letter, and the saint was offended by certain attitudes of the Corinthians concerning which we have no direct information. He did not return to Corinth but sent Titus in his stead. Through the latter he learned that peace seemed to have been restored in the community and that tempers had been chastened. Therefore, he writes to them again. In our present passage he writes in the first-person plural, showing that he, Silvanus, and Timothy are agreed.

The Corinthians may have offended Paul by saying that he did not preach a clear and sincere message but that, on the contrary, he spoke and acted with duplicity. Such, at least, is the background the letter suggests. If so, Paul does not attempt to justify himself, nor does he make repeated claims to have spoken and acted in a straightforward way. For his own teaching and actions, he refers simply to the teaching of Christ. Christ was not yes and no, for he was the very incarnation of truth and taught us that we should speak a clear yes or a clear no, without ambiguity (Matt 5:37).

In this passage, then, Paul is claiming to be a genuine apostle. The authenticity of his mission has God himself as its guarantor, since it is God who chose and consecrated the apostles and put his seal upon them. The seal is a sign that something is authentic. Consequently, the anointing by the Spirit and the gift of the Spirit are the two sources from which the Apostle's evangelizing activity draws its value. That is what the community at Corinth must ever keep in mind.

Eighth Sunday: The Marriage of God to His People

The Bridegroom with Us (Mark 2:18-22)

The gospel for this Sunday provides a good example of the liturgical reading of a biblical text. The passage invites the exegete to go into the importance of fasting and the way Jesus thinks of it. In today's liturgy, however, the first reading provides the context within which the gospel is to be read and tells us that in reading Mark, we are to concentrate chiefly on the presence of the Bridegroom and on the behavior this presence suggests. In other words, Jesus' answer to his questioners is not to be taken as a facile defense of his disciples, who do not fast, but rather it bids us think in symbolic terms, which we must now try to specify.

A narrowly exegetical approach might lead us, as it has led others, to challenge the authenticity of the passage as perhaps having been inserted in Mark's text as a justification for the practice of fasting in the early Christian community. Such an interpretation (which in any case is completely hypothetical and lacks any real basis in the text) bears no relation to the liturgical proclamation of the passage.

The passage speaks to us of the presence of the Bridegroom and of his disciples' attitude while he is present and after he has gone. The element of fasting appears as secondary in relation to the prediction of Jesus' departure, a departure Jesus himself seems to foresee as marked by violence.

The overarching context for the whole account is the presence of the kingdom. The various cures that Jesus works (vv. 2 and 3) are signs of the kingdom, as Jesus elsewhere tells the disciples of John the Baptist (Matt 11:5). They are "signs of the times" (Matt 16:3). The kingdom, however, means the presence of the Bridegroom, that is, of the definitive covenant, which is described as a marriage. The "marriage" in this instance is not simply a juridical entity but a personal relationship: God is united to his people as his people are to him, and when his people are unfaithful, God is jealous.

The prophet Hosea was the first to compare the covenant to a marriage. Jeremiah will then use the same image (2:2, 20), as will Ezekiel (16:1-43, 59-63). Isaiah too will make poetic use of it (54:4-8; 61:10; 62:4).

The covenant is made eternal by Christ, whose coming is the most important step toward making the marriage fully real (Matt 9:15; Mark 2:18-22; Luke 5:33-39). St. John thinks of John the Baptist as "the best man" (3:29). We know how often Jesus describes the kingdom as a wedding feast that a king prepares for his son (see, e.g., Matt 22:2).

Since the covenant is here and the kingdom has begun, there can be no question of fasting. Let those fast who do not realize that the Bridegroom is present and that a marriage is to be celebrated. But, we may ask, how is it that John the Baptist and his disciples fast? Is not John being illogical, since he also proclaims the kingdom? No, he is not illogical, for he fasts precisely as a preparation for the coming of the kingdom. Jesus is really anticipating the full reality of the kingdom; his attitude here and his approval of what his disciples are doing are further signs that the kingdom has begun.

Jesus then moves on to a new point: "the days will come when the bridegroom is taken away from them" (Mark 2:20). The words are an evident allusion to his own violent death. (The Bible elsewhere uses the expressions "take away" or "cut off" to indicate a tragic death: Isa 53:8; Jer 11:19; Matt 24:40; Luke 23:18; John 19:15.)

The important thing here, however, is not how the Bridegroom will cease to be present but the very fact of his future absence. His absence will be a sign to the disciples that the time for fasting has come. We must, moreover, not take "fasting" in a narrowly literal way but interpret it more broadly to include the sufferings of the disciples and the persecution they will undergo. In addition, the fast in question is not necessarily associated with mourning, since the Bridegroom who departs from the disciples rises and ascends to heavenly glory.

Thus the fast will be accompanied by expectation of the Bridegroom's return and will therefore be of a festive kind.

It is against this background that the Church established her custom of the nocturnal vigil spent in fasting and prayer, with the vigil and the fasting ending in the celebration of the Eucharist. The great examples were the vigils of Easter and Christmas.

The pericope from Mark ends with two short parables: the parable of the old garment that cannot be repaired by sewing new cloth onto it and the parable of the old wineskin that cannot be used for new wine. The two parables are closely related to each other and to what precedes. The point being made is that the kingdom that is now present is a new creation; it introduces a new world in which people must rid themselves of an outmoded outlook and acquire new attitudes.

Such a change is no easy matter. It is difficult to keep and renew customs that are really inadaptable but to which, nonetheless, people cling more than they do to charity. It has always been so, and so it is today. We know how St. Paul was forced to be constantly shaking up his contemporaries who were too attached to customs that were without a point. Recall, for example, the dispute about circumcision (Gal 5). Jesus began a new era in history, and we live in a new dispensation.

Clothing often serves as a symbol in Scripture, especially in the Old Testament. Shining garments, white as snow, appear in Daniel's vision (7:9) and again in Jesus' transfiguration (Matt 17:2; Mark 9:2-3; Luke 9:29); the angel at the tomb, when Mary and Salome come to anoint Jesus' body, is likewise wearing shining white garments (Matt 28:3; Mark 16:5; Luke 24:4; John 20:12). The image of a worn-out garment as representing a decaying civilization is used in Isaiah: "The earth [will] wear out like a garment" (51:6). Psalm 102 develops the same poetic image more fully:

> Long ago you founded the earth,
> and the heavens are the work of your hands.
> They will perish but you will remain.
> They will all wear out like a garment.
> You will change them like clothes, and they change. (vv. 26-27)

Thus those who listened to Jesus were familiar with the image. So too, in a country where viticulture was important, everyone had a background of experience for appreciating the little parable of the old wine and the new wineskins. They could grasp the point that the institutions proper to the old law would not serve for the renewal of the world through the new covenant.

Jesus is not urging his contemporaries to abandon ascetical practices; on the contrary, he himself (Matt 6:16-18) and the early Church (Acts 13:2; 14:23; 2 Cor 6:5; 11:27) recommend them. Moreover, he claimed to fulfill the old law, not to abolish it (Matt 5:17). What he is urging, then, is a new attitude of freedom and openness that goes beyond the letter of the law.

This new outlook joins ascetical practice to the joy of the eucharistic banquet, which is a sign of the kingdom. Jesus is proclaiming a new life in which Catholics, who have put on Christ, accept trials and testings; try to maintain their balance with the help of ascetical practices, in which they are not attached to the letter but to the spirit; and constantly test their own adaptation to the new dispensation that Jesus has established through his paschal mystery.

In this we have an extremely valuable lesson for life in the Church today. The most important thing, we are being told, is faith in the presence of Jesus and his new covenant. This faith is constantly finding expression in the Church: in the gathered assembly, in the prayer group, and especially in the celebration of the Eucharist. At such moments the members become aware ever anew of the presence of Christ the Bridegroom with his new and eternal covenant. This presence, which we grasp through faith, is absolutely basic to the Church and to the life of each individual; from it come joy and freedom. Yet to attain such a constant faith and to be able to enter into the covenant and meet the Bridegroom, we need asceticism; ascetical practices enable us to concentrate more fully on essentials.

I Will Speak Tenderly to My Spouse (Hos 2:14b, 15b, 21-22)

Faith in the presence of the Bridegroom with his new covenant, while requiring a new outlook, also makes dialogue with God possible. Hosea had already made this point. When he presents Yahweh as husband of Israel, he makes us privy to an overwhelming religious experience in which Israel received the revelation of God who loves. Hosea gives us access to this experience by way of his own experience.

The people of Israel could look back to all that their God had done for them in rescuing them and establishing them as a nation; for Israel, God was truly a covenant God. And yet the Israelites remained a weak people who allowed themselves to be seduced by the less demanding gods of Canaan, whose worship flattered the instinctive urge to drunkenness and sexual expression.

Meanwhile, the prophet had his own special experience. At the Lord's command, he took a prostitute as wife, but the woman, named Gomer, abandoned him (Hos 1:2). In the passage we read today, Hosea links the two experiences, his own and that of his people, when he tells us of God's words to his unfaithful spouse: "I will lead her into the desert / and speak to her heart."

For us today, the dialogue is that of God with his Church and with each of us. In this dialogue God constantly renews us; we become a new garment, new wine: "She shall respond there as in the days of her youth, / when she came up from the land of Egypt."

Christians, despite their infidelity, do not have a past weighing upon them. Moreover, the mystery of their liberation by divine love is ever alive, ever renewed: "I will espouse you to me forever." Three times the Lord repeats his "I will espouse you to me," and each time it is accompanied by new gifts. "I will espouse you to me forever": the Lord asserts his intention of being faithful to his covenant; he is always with us and always will be with us, ever searching us out. "I will espouse you in right and in justice, / in love and in mercy": these are the gifts specific to the covenant, which establishes social justice and love in human society. "I will espouse you in fidelity, / and you shall know the Lord": there will be an intimate union between God and us; we shall be able to draw close to him as we acknowledge his constant gifts and as we experience his fidelity and our own.

These statements of God in Hosea describe the life of the Church and of each Christian: the primacy of God's love for us and our love for him (our love being inseparable from love for others as well). Other things—various observances, rituals, customs—are not to be neglected, for they help in a measure to foster love and fidelity; the sacraments, in fact, even give the grace to love and to be faithful. But the chief thing in the life of the Church and the individual should be the profound sense of God's loving presence.

Ministers of a New Covenant (2 Cor 3:1b-6)

St. Paul speaks to the Corinthians with assurance and firmness. The assurance is not grounded in his own abilities but comes from

God, who has made him minister of a new covenant. The Apostle depends not on his personal qualifications but on God. All the apostles are "ministers" of a new covenant; that is, they are "servants" of this new covenant.

In two other places Paul emphasizes the humble and demanding role of servant that is his. "What is Apollos, after all, and what is Paul? Ministers through whom you became believers, just as the Lord assigned each one" (1 Cor 3:5). Here Paul has been obliged to intervene when the community was divided by clannish allegiances. Later on he is forced to write to the Corinthians once again: "For we do not preach ourselves but Jesus Christ as Lord, and ourselves as your slaves for the sake of Jesus" (2 Cor 4:5).

The apostle's role is to implement the covenant between God and humanity, the marriage of God with his people. Thus the idea of the covenant links this second reading with the first reading and the gospel. It is in Jesus Christ that the covenant of which the apostles are servants is fully realized. The Spirit of the new covenant gives people a new heart and leads them in a love that goes beyond the letter of the law, and it is this Spirit of Christ that the apostolic ministry serves (2 Cor 3:8). "[T]he law of the spirit of life in Christ Jesus has freed you from the law of sin and death" (Rom 8:2).

The Corinthians, then, are Paul's "letter of recommendation," for they are now new creatures united to the Lord in a new covenant. In fact, the whole community at Corinth is Paul's letter of recommendation, since he became their father in Jesus Christ through the Gospel (1 Cor 4:15).

Ninth Sunday: The Meaning of the Sabbath

Jesus, Lord of the Sabbath (Mark 2:23–3:6)

The evangelists found it necessary to take up the question of the meaning of the Sabbath, since at times (as is the case with St. Matthew, for example) their readers were Jewish Christians. The latter, while celebrating Sunday, also observed the Sabbath, at least in the early days of the Church. (We should not forget that down to the fourth century all Christians worked on Sunday; the day of rest for them, as for everyone else, was Saturday.) The evangelists were also addressing Gentile converts to Christianity, for whom the Jewish Sabbath observances would be of little if any intrinsic interest; yet the question of the Sabbath was, in fact, of concern even to them, inasmuch as they, no less than the Jewish Christians, could slip into a legalistic mentality when it came to outward observances.

St. Mark's position is quite clear: the Sabbath is made for humanity, not humanity for the Sabbath. He would find no difficulty in coming out with such a straightforward statement, since his gospel was meant for converts from Gentile religions, not for Jewish Christians. Some exegetes have maintained that Jesus himself did not utter these words about the Sabbath; they could have been more easily uttered at a later date and especially in a community of former Gentiles.

The two stories told in today's pericope—the disciples plucking grain on the Sabbath, and Jesus curing the man with the withered hand on the Sabbath—create a conflict between Jesus and the Pharisees. Consequently, they provide an opportunity for him to voice his mind about the Sabbath and the Jewish attitude toward it.

We must not, however, exaggerate the difference between the position of Jesus and that of the Pharisees. Nowhere does Jesus show contempt for the Sabbath; nowhere does he tell people not to observe it; nowhere does he speak of celebrating some other day of the week. Moreover, he tells us that he came to fulfill the law, not to abolish it. In fact, when we read the present passage from St. Mark's gospel, our impression is that it is telling us of something far more important than a conflict between Jesus and the Pharisees.

"The Son of Man is lord even of the sabbath" (Mark 2:28). The Lord, however, is above the law. Consequently, while the Sabbath was instituted so that humanity might honor the Lord while contemplating the Lord's great deeds at leisure, and while the weekly rest was instituted for that same purpose and so that work might be interrupted and the family strengthened, the Lord himself is above this law that he instituted on humanity's behalf. In fact, anything bearing directly on the very life of humanity itself is more important than the law. Where healing is required or charity is called for, the law can and should be set aside.

This amounts to saying that Christ is not destroying or abolishing the Sabbath law; he is simply telling people how it is to be applied. Did those present on this occasion understand what Christ meant by calling himself Lord even of the Sabbath? Did they understand that life is more important than the observance of the letter of the law? It seems they did understand and yet could not accept Christ's prin-

ciples. Instead, they go off to find the Herodians and plot the destruction of Jesus.

The Sabbath, a Holy Day (Deut 5:12-15)

It is evident from this text that a social and religious law was being
established. The Jewish people had experienced enslavement in
Egypt. Now that they were free, they were being given a weekly
opportunity to recoup their strength at two levels or in two ways: as
weak human beings, by enjoying a weekly rest they had not known
in Egypt, and as a chosen people, by strengthening the bonds of a
community that had God for its center, and this by adoring him for
his wonderful deeds and for all he had done for his people. The new
institution was thus both social and devotional.

The Sabbath and its observance has always been a distinguishing
mark of Judaism. At times we outsiders have been overly critical of
the Jewish Sabbath observances. The observances are a fact and the
pious Jew respects them, but the important point for the Jew is not
the observances as such but the worship of God, the development of
community and family, and respect for the poor, whom the Jew visits
on the afternoon of the Sabbath. The biblical theology of the Sabbath,
as understood by the devout Jew, is altogether admirable and can be
totally integrated into our theology of Sunday, even though the Christian Sunday is in no sense simply a transposed Jewish Sabbath.[3]

To Jews, the Sabbath is the feast that celebrates their liberation. It
is a kind of weekly Passover and recalls the exodus from Egypt and
the liberation from bondage. The Sabbath is the day of the one who
has been freed.

The texts read on this Sunday are extremely important. It is a paradox that in our day the people with the most legalistic attitude
toward the weekly observance are the Christians. Observant Jews
have a very rich theology of the Sabbath. They are not content to
abstain from work but engage in fervent public and private prayer
and do works of mercy, such as visiting the sick. The Sabbath reminds
them of how they became a people after the liberation from Egypt
and the reestablishment of the nation.

Some Christians tend to be much more legalistic, seeing only the
obligatory practices. And yet Sunday is not simply a transposition
of the Jewish Sabbath; in fact, as we have already pointed out, Sunday

rest was possible and prescribed only in 357, under Emperor Constantine. What Sunday should be for Christians is a summons to center their life once again on the fact that they have been freed by Christ's resurrection, on the building of a new world and of God's kingdom, and on the expectation of the last day.

The celebration of the Eucharist, which actualizes the paschal mystery, does not exhaust the positive side of Sunday. To the Eucharist must be added the effort to perfect the domestic community, the parish community (or the group), and our awareness of others, of the sick, the poor, the lonely. Sunday has unfortunately lost much of its meaning for the Christian. The Christian ought not be described by others as someone who "goes to Mass" but as someone for whom Sunday is a day of prayer, a day of community, a day of charity.

The Life of Jesus Manifested in Our Bodies (2 Cor 4:6-11)

We are familiar by now with the difficulties Paul met in his relations with the Corinthians. He found in them a kind of pretentious intellectualism and a quite pronounced philosophical pride. This was serious enough, but it was accompanied by a pride in relation to faith and to preaching. In short, the whole community of Corinth was permeated by a pride that Paul wished to correct. It is this situation that accounts for the somewhat pessimistic tone of his second letter.

We carry a treasure—the light that the Lord has given us—but we carry it in worthless earthen vessels. Preachers, then, are simply spokespersons for the Lord. Yet, as spokespersons and authentic witnesses, they should make the life of Jesus manifest in their very bodies. The Corinthians, however, were tempted to focus their attention entirely on the resurrection and glorification of Christ and to reject everything else. They were tempted, that is, to move apart into their own world, but it was an illusory world without weakness, temptation, and suffering. They thought of themselves as a group of chosen souls who lived solely by the Spirit and the resurrection of Christ. They ended up making the world of the cross and the world of the resurrection contradict each other.

St. Paul puts things into proper perspective. Preachers bear witness in their very bodies to the *kenosis*, or "emptying," of Christ, to the humiliation of the cross and passion and suffering. But it is this passion, this suffering, that actually gives life. That is why Paul can say to the community of Corinth: You seem to be rich, and think you are already living in the kingdom and by the Spirit; I, for my part, live in weakness and poverty, but through the suffering of Christ I bring life; I even bring life to you.

We must not, of course, turn the letter into something it is not meant to be and require that every preacher of the Gospel bear all the marks of suffering of which Paul speaks. On the other hand, we ought to read the passage in the light of the community and the Church today. As it confronts the modern world, should not the community and the Church show that it bears the marks of Christ's sufferings and that it is a life-giving community and Church? The contrast between world and Church can only be where Paul puts it: I (community, Church) am weak, suffering, and afflicted, but I actively accept this lot in order to bring you life.

There are many conclusions to be drawn from such an attitude on the part of the Church, and it would be worthwhile for contemporary society to draw them. But it can do so only if the Church does manifest the signs Paul lists and in which he sees the source of life for the community at Corinth.

Tenth Sunday: Evil Overcome

Satan Conquered (Mark 3:20-35)

Two incidents, unconnected in themselves, come together in this pericope. Jesus' friends and family come to seize him; there is an interruption as Jesus is forced to answer those who accuse him of expelling demons by the power of Beelzebul; finally, the incident of the family's coming is concluded. But though the two incidents seem unrelated, there is, in fact, a certain link between them, as we shall see.

Obviously, the miracles that Jesus worked could not pass unnoticed, and the publicity disturbed the scribes and the family of Jesus himself. He was increasingly surrounded by crowds of people, so much so that he and his disciples could not even eat in the house of which Mark often speaks and in which Jesus lived when he was at Capernaum. It was especially the exorcisms Jesus practiced that drew the attention of the religious leaders. In Jewish thinking, authority over demons, such as Christ possessed, could come either from God, as a power given by him to one of his messengers, or from the devil. The crowds are more credulous and incline, without thinking much about it, toward the first solution: one who expels demons and works so many miracles can be sent only by God. The leaders and scribes are of another mind, and they show it in this passage.

Jesus' answer amounts to an assertion that he has been sent by God. He does not answer the question directly, but his argument leads indirectly to a description of what he truly is. In his reply he uses two examples: the kingdom divided against itself and the strong man's house.

The kingdom and the family divided. The answer, Jesus is saying, is quite simple: If Beelzebul, the prince of demons, expels demons, then Satan's kingdom is at odds with itself, and he has lost the struggle. If enemies are at odds with themselves, they will surely lose the battle. Satan's "house" or family, according to the scribes, is bent on destroying itself!

The strong man's house. No one can enter a strong man's house and steal his possessions without first binding the strong man. That is what Jesus is doing. Satan is the strong man who has taken possession of the world, and Jesus is binding Satan so as to recover the world from him. As of now, Satan's rule is coming to an end; that is the point of the exorcisms. The Messiah is now here, and the new kingdom, foretold by John the Baptist, has begun.

The scribes, for their part, are "guilty of an everlasting sin," because, despite the various proofs Jesus has already given of his being sent by God, they refuse to believe. They not only refuse to believe but also accuse Jesus of doing what he does with the help of an impure spirit. They thus commit a serious and unforgivable sin of blasphemy, for by refusing to accept God's messenger, they refuse salvation. Such a refusal, springing as it does not from weakness but from a perverse heart and bad faith, cannot be forgiven; it is an everlasting sin.

At this point Mark returns to Jesus' family, which is looking for him. His mother Mary is there. St. Mark names her first, as he always does when the Blessed Virgin comes on the scene with others. We need not put any special emphasis on the phrase "your brothers and your sisters," since it is a known fact that among the Semites "brothers" could be cousins or other relatives as well as blood brothers and sisters. Thus, in the gospel itself, St. Matthew calls James and Joseph the brothers of Jesus (Matt 13:55) although they are the sons of a Mary who is not the mother of Jesus (Matt 27:56).

Jesus' reply with regard to his mother and brothers and sisters might suggest that they do not do the Father's will. In fact, Jesus is saying nothing of the sort. They are not excluded when he looks around and says: "whoever does the will of God is my brother and sister and mother." He thus shows how close a bond is forged between himself, the Father's messenger, and those who do God's will.

Is this passage relevant to us today? It is, for though we may think quite differently of the devil today (short of denying his existence), it is certainly not possible to ignore the forces that are constantly assembled in the struggle against the Church. It is a struggle in which the Church can hold her own because she knows Christ is with her; she knows that hell itself cannot triumph over her. This does not mean she enjoys a triumphalist kind of security. She must always be on guard, and she must purify herself each year (as one of the Lenten prayers says). In her sacramental ministry the Church carries on the work of Christ, but she is by no means to be equated *per se* with Christ.

The Church explicitly rejects all triumphalism. She is engaged in a constant struggle with the powers of evil. In that struggle she knows she can win; the members know that at their side in the conflict stands the Leader who himself conquered temptation during the forty days he spent in the wilderness. What disciples must do is live close to Christ; in order to do this, they must believe that Christ is God's messenger, and they must do the Father's will so that they too may be worthy of having Christ call them brothers and sisters.

The Promise of Victory (Gen 3:9-15)

Everyone is familiar with the text and sufficiently knowledgeable about its literary character and about the essentials of its teaching. The account is a psychological and religious analysis of the phenomenon of temptation and sin, but it also contains a promise of victory. The victory will be God's victory, but it will be shared by humanity as well. People may yield to the devil's tempting, but they will always receive the grace to overcome, with the weapons of Christ, the very demon who earlier led them astray. That statement describes the history of salvation in the constant experience of the Church. The Lord conquers sin through the action of sinful humanity; he conquers the forces of evil through humanity's very weakness.

The account in the book of Genesis is grounds for optimism, once we read the Genesis story in the light of the book of Revelation, which describes the victory of the Lamb and the victory we too hope for at the end of time. The Church attributes to the Blessed Virgin a special place in the struggle and in the winning of the victory. Christ's incarnation, to which she gave her consent, brought us a Savior who shared all our struggles and sufferings, except for sin itself, and who conquered death by rising from the dead.

The response to the psalm (Ps 130) sings of the victory over evil: "For with the LORD there is mercy, / in him is plentiful redemption" (Ps 130:7).

We Believe, and so We Speak (2 Cor 4:13–5:1)

The second reading, as we know, was not deliberately chosen to fit in with the other two readings. Nonetheless, it can, without forcing the meaning, be related to the others if we think of the major theme of the latter as being the victory over evil.

St. Paul tells us of his struggles and sufferings and weakness. The thing that keeps him going amid the trials that he accepts and offers up for the Corinthians is his faith in Christ as the risen Lord who has conquered death and evil. Paul believes that he himself will rise as Jesus did; both Paul and the readers for whom he offers his struggles will be with the Lord.

At the same time, Paul tells us, we must have a clear vision of what our present life means. Even if our outward self is undergoing decay, the interior self is being renewed each day. It is Christ—the Christ who while on earth expelled demons and conquered them for good through his passion and death—who daily renews us interiorly. St. Paul is here sharing his own experience with us, and it is a valuable lesson for us.

Our basic need is the faith that will enable us to pass an untroubled judgment in the discernment of true values and to see that the trials of the present time are little in comparison with the eternal glory for which they are preparing us. We must fix our gaze, not on what is visible, but on what is invisible and eternal. Christ's victory over the devil and evil is so great that our very bodies, though they are corrupted by sin and must be destroyed, will rise up and live forever.

It is this experience based on faith and this unshakable optimism that St. Paul wants to communicate to us.

Eleventh Sunday: The Growth of the Kingdom

The Seed Sprouts (Mark 4:26-34)

In today's gospel reading, Jesus tells us two parables: the parable of the seed that a man sows and that grows without his knowing how, and the parable of the mustard seed, which is tiny yet produces a great tree. Then Jesus explains why he uses parables.

Two points in the parable of the seed call for our attention. One is that the seed in the ground develops through stages. The other is that when the sower has done his work, he pays no further attention to the seed but goes about his ordinary business; the seed grows without his intervention, which is called for again only at the harvest.

The lesson of this parable must have been clearer to Jesus' contemporaries than it is to us. For the image of the sickle would immediately remind them of Joel's prophecy concerning God's judgment (Joel 4:12-16).

While the seed is growing, the sower is inactive as far as the seed is concerned; time passes without his paying any attention to the seed. What was Jesus' point in telling this parable? On the one hand, he wished to proclaim the judgment of God, which is evoked in the image of the sickle; he is saying that the kingdom is near. On the other hand, however, there is nothing in the parable itself to indicate this nearness. It must be, then, that in using the example of the sower, who, after sowing, patiently waits for the harvest, Jesus is putting us on guard against a wrong interpretation of the seeming silence of events as regards the kingdom. The seed indeed grows without the intervention of the sower, but the growth is a sure sign that the harvest is coming. The period in which the Lord seems disinterested in what he has sown is precisely the period preceding the harvest and the sudden coming of the kingdom.

The second parable, that of the mustard seed, is also found in Matthew (13:31-32) and in Luke (13:18-19). We are not interested here in the question of which account was historically the first. The way in which Mark presents the parable bids us attend to one point in particular: the fact that the tiniest seed becomes a shrub that is larger than all the others in the garden and in which the birds can make their nests.

The tree is a sizable one if it can shelter the birds and their nests. The tree has been taken as a sign of the kingdom and of the powerful king who protects his subjects. Thus the book of Daniel speaks of a vision of a great tree in whose branches the birds of the air dwell; the tree represents King Nebuchadnezzar (Dan 4:9-27). The book of Ezekiel likewise describes a great tree in which the birds of the air dwell; this tree represents the Egyptian pharaoh (Ezek 31:6). The point of Jesus' parable would thus be that the kingdom already prepared has a king and offers refuge to all who enter it. The kingdom of God grows slowly but is moving toward its majestic completion. The hearers of Jesus must grasp the importance of the time in which they are living. They are seeing the kingdom being prepared; the kingdom is growing, though the seed and the growth are hardly visible; for all its small beginnings, the kingdom is indeed coming in majesty.

But why does Jesus teach with the aid of parables? Mark tells us that in public Jesus spoke only in parables but that in private he explained everything in detail to his disciples. This means that the parable differentiates what Jesus wants to say to others from what he wants to say to his disciples. Why so? Because the people of God have not accepted God's messenger and Jesus does not want to further blind a people who reject the light. Therefore, he communicates God's message in such a way that only those who possess the key to the parables can understand it. This key Jesus gives only to the disciples, because they have followed him.

St. Mark is writing for the Church of his own day. The chosen people have by now rejected both the message and the messenger; it was this situation that led to the use of parables. In the prophet Isaiah, Mark finds evidence that such was God's will: Jesus speaks in parables "that 'they may look and see but not perceive, / and hear and listen but not understand, / in order that they may not be converted and be forgiven'" (Mark 4:12, citing Isa 6:9-10). In other words, for Mark the use of the parable is a form of punishment inflicted by divine Providence and a measure provoked by the attitude of the chosen people, who refuse to see. Because they refuse to see, everything is presented to them in parables that only those who have accepted Jesus in faith can understand.

The Tree Planted by God (Ezek 17:22-24)

We mentioned this passage above as a parallel to the parable of the mustard seed that becomes a great tree. We need only read the whole passage in Ezekiel to see that the image is of a king who will come and protect his subjects. Is it worth the trouble of trying to pinpoint the precise identity of this king? Identifications have, in fact, been attempted, but it is not clear that the terms of the prophecy really apply to any of the persons selected. In any event, our concern is to look beyond the historical reference and see the prophecy of the Messiah and of a new kingdom.

The image of the tree is not used much in the New Testament, and yet when St. Mark does use it, we must think that he does not do so by chance. He chose it deliberately, and it serves very well Jesus' purpose in speaking to the crowds only in parables, whereas he was able to speak openly to his disciples.

Does the text have any meaning for us today? Yes, it does, provided we take the parables as wholes and do not get lost in details. An example of getting lost in a detail would be to emphasize the majestic size of the tree and to see in it the power of the Church, to think proudly of how the Church has developed and grown through the centuries and become a powerful body.

Two points about the parables seem of primary importance to me. One is the divine initiative in the extension of the kingdom; the other is the patience we need and the spiritual vision of events that occur in the Church.

Once the seed is planted, it develops. It is the Lord, however, who sustains and stimulates this development. He is the Sun who makes all plants germinate and grow. There are lessons to be drawn from the parable by the Church of today and each of us. The lesson is not, of course, that we are to neglect missionary activity and wait for God to do everything. The lesson is, rather, that we must have faith in the divine initiative and look upon prayer and contemplation as more important than the effectiveness of our works. We have developed catechetical activities and techniques; the various works of the apostolate have made use of the modern means of communication. Yet the use of all of these means has not produced spectacular results. Perhaps the fault is in our lack of the contemplative mentality and in our excessive trust in human means that are not supported by prayer.

The parables also invite us to wait patiently for the time of growth and for the harvest and to learn how to judge aright the events that affect the Church. We sometimes get the impression that the Lord is not concerned about his Church, that he is absent. Our judgments on events are usually quite subjective; we are incapable of properly interpreting our experiences. And yet, if we are indeed unable to read the meaning of events, the reason is simply that we are insufficiently contemplative. We are not spiritual enough, and so we interpret the difficulties the Church faces and the needs that must be met if the kingdom is to grow as a politician or a business executive would interpret them. But the kingdom of God does not depend for its extension solely on our methods; divine Providence often judges things quite differently than we do. Only a humble, contemplative vision of reality can lead us to a proper judgment of what divine Providence is doing in the events God is using for the extension of his kingdom.

Pleasing the Lord (2 Cor 5:6-10)

This reading tells us how we should conduct ourselves in our present life of faith. We walk in faith and do not see. We are, in fact, both far from the Lord, because we are still in the body, and near to him, because we believe.

Our aim must be to please the Lord. St. Paul links this intention of pleasing God with the final judgment, when everything will be revealed and all will individually receive what they have deserved by their actions while they were still in their bodies.

A text like this helps us to properly understand what Paul means when he says that we are saved by faith alone and not by works. We refer the reader to our earlier explanation on the Ninth Sunday of Ordinary Time. That we should be irreproachable on the day of judgment is another favorite theme of Paul's (see 1 Thess 3:13; 5:23; 1 Cor 1:8; Phil 1:10). We must work for our salvation while being ever mindful of the judgment (Phil 2:12) at which the Lord will individually reward all people according to their works (Rom 2:6).

Paul presents the life of the Christian as lived in view of the last day. It is a life lived in the darkness of faith, a life in which, knowing as we do the real meaning of our existence, we seek in all things to please the Lord.

Twelfth Sunday: Lord of the World

The Wind and the Sea Obey Him (Mark 4:35-41)

We would considerably diminish the lesson contained in this reading if we were to see in it nothing but a demonstration of Christ's power over the elements. There is far more to the passage than that.

If we are to understand what the passage is saying, we must reflect on how the Scriptures think of water and the sea. In the book of Genesis, the primeval waters must be tamed before the world can be created (Gen 1:6-10). The Lord himself made the sea and all that is in it (Ps 95:4; cf. Ps 146:6; Amos 5:8; Jonah 1:9). He established its boundaries and shut it in with doors (Job 38:8); he assigned the sea its limits (Prov 8:29).

The people of the Bible, many of them fisherfolk, loved the thought of the water that the Lord causes to exist and out of which (according to the cosmogony of antiquity) so many animals emerge; the water that the Lord causes to part in the book of Exodus; the water in which so many great living things dwell, including "Leviathan you made to play with" (Ps 104:26). They loved especially the thought of the sea and had a grandiose idea of it. Psalm 107, which provides the responsorial psalm after the first reading, is a fine poem about the sea; it brings home to us the splendor of the sea but also the sacred fear it inspires.

Against this background we can perhaps better understand the amazement of the disciples when, amid their terror at the storm, they see Jesus calm the waters. They express this amazement in the form of a question, but it is really an exclamation of praise: "Who then is this whom even wind and sea obey?" If we bear in mind the associations that the sea must have had for them, we can better understand their stupefaction.

The story is valuable to us in our day. We are quite ready to give theoretical acknowledgment of Christ's divinity and God's power, but are there not circumstances when our instincts get the upper hand and we become distrustful and unbelieving?

The fact that Jesus is asleep while the storm rages plays an important part in the story. To these men, a storm at sea is the greatest danger they meet in their work; nothing could make them more fearful, even despairing. And yet the Lord lies there asleep in the stern! They wake him and cry out in their fear: "Teacher, do you not care that we are perishing?"

Here again, the story has a very modern ring to it. Jesus sleeps; God seems unconcerned with us as we try to ride out our storms. How can God allow the abominations of the past and present? How can we put up with his failure to intervene, especially since, being God, he is supposed to be good? These are the angry questions we hear every day, even from Christians. God is sleeping!

Christ's answer is a harsh one: "Why are you terrified? Do you not yet have faith?" As a matter of fact, when Christ is undergoing his passion, the faith of his disciples will be so weak that Peter will not have the courage even to acknowledge that he knows Jesus. Even at the resurrection Jesus will find his disciples still hesitant to believe in the saving event and the new life it brings. The fathers of the Church in their time will see the Church shaken by storms within as well as without. And it is certainly true—is it not?—that at times we are tempted to think that Jesus is asleep in the boat that is his Church and pays her no heed. There is indeed a problem, but Jesus tells us here that it is a problem of faith. We shall come back to this point and endeavor to answer the questions we ask ourselves, or others ask of us, about the apparent sleep of Christ amid the storms of our day.

Here Shall Your Proud Waves Be Stayed (Job 38:1, 8-11)

Job is the very model of the person who is tried by sufferings of every kind. His friends, however, do not grasp his situation and stir him up to rebel against the Lord. The Lord then appears to Job amid the storm and reminds him that he, the Lord, created the very oceans. This vision gives us a better understanding of what sea and storm meant to biblical people, but the passage is admirable as well for its literary quality and its theology.

The Lord tells us that he created the sea and assigned it its boundaries, but he sets limits to the flow of the waves: "Thus far shall you come but no farther, / and here shall your proud waves be stilled." He can do all this because he is Creator of the universe in its entirety. But we must not stop here, with the material world. God also directs the course of each individual's life; everything that happens to us is controlled by his providence.

But it is precisely for this reason that the questions mentioned earlier arise. Why does a child suffer? Why does the young father of a family die? Why are dishonest people rich and good people impoverished? Everything seems to say that God is asleep and has no concern for humans.

There can be no answer to these questions except one inspired by faith, and faith is what we lack. God knows what he is doing. He knows what it is he allows to happen and why he does not intervene visibly, here and now, to check people's ill will. Time belongs to him; he is the one who sees justice done and who sanctifies people. By permitting trials and suffering, he gives his followers the opportunity to deepen their faith and detachment. Faith alone, then, supplies an answer. Can faith disappoint? If any believer is disappointed, it is because of a lack of trust in God.

Psalm 107, which supplies the responsorial psalm, gives fine expression to God's power: "He stilled the storm to a whisper, / and the waves of the sea were hushed. . . . / Let them thank the LORD for his mercy, / his wonders for the children of men" (vv. 29, 31).

A New World (2 Cor 5:14-17)

St. Paul here shares some of his personal religious experience with us. He tells us of the emotions that well up in him when he thinks of how one human has died for all and how all have therefore overcome death. All humans are so linked to Christ that they die with him in order to rise from the dead with him. This reality ought to become the focus for every Christian's life.

If we are to be truly alive and real Christians in Christ, we must receive the life Christ gives us, which is Christ's own life as one who has died and been raised from the dead. This life in turn becomes the basis for a Christian's entire conduct: we are humans who cease to live solely for ourselves, fettered by our instincts and our self-centered way of judging everything, and must instead ground our life in the dead and risen Christ. Christ must live in us.

In light of this truth, all of Paul's human experience fades into the background. He must now see things differently. He cannot judge his neighbor as he did before but must look on others as those who have died and been raised up in Jesus Christ. The same can be said for his way of knowing Christ: his relationship to Christ is a relationship to the Christ who died and was raised up and now communicates a share of his own life.

In short, we find ourselves in a new world. The old world has passed away. This idea of the old being gone and having been replaced by the new is a favorite of Paul's. We see, in faith, a new creation (2 Cor 5:17; Gal 6:15: Col 1:19-20) that has Christ for its center (Eph 2:15). Like Isaiah before him (43:18; 65:17), St. Paul urges us to put the former things out of mind.

Such is the enthusiastic vision Paul offers us on the basis of his own religious experience. It is a grandiose but also demanding vision: the world, humanity, humanity's judgments, humanity's behaviors—all these are to be new. That means that everything in our life must be reviewed and revised, for the past is dead; it must be forgotten so that we can build anew in Christ.

Thirteenth Sunday: God, Author of Life

I Say to You, Arise (Mark 5:21-43)

There are several points of interest in today's gospel, but all can be subsumed under one heading: faith gives life. In order to show the necessity of faith, St. Mark reports two miracles: the cure of the woman with the flow of blood and the raising of Jairus's daughter.

These miracles are responses to faith, and yet we may at first sight be dubious about the quality of that faith. Jesus' reputation has spread abroad. Does not the woman with the flow of blood take him simply for a famous and powerful wonder-worker? Does the ruler of the synagogue, forgetful of his position because he is distracted by the impending death of his child, really believe in Jesus?

To us and our way of thinking (which has something to say for it), it is not very clear that there is genuine faith. We tend to distrust the kind of confidence these people show. We might think, of course, that Jesus is here satisfied with the remote beginnings of faith and wishes to clarify and confirm it by working miracles. This is often the case in the Gospel of St. John, where a cure does not always follow upon faith but sometimes precedes and leads to it.

To the evangelist, however, the faith of the woman and of Jairus can be regarded as of the right kind. To the woman, who had defied the prescriptions of the Jewish law for someone in her condition, Jesus says, "Daughter, your faith has saved you. Go in peace and be cured of your affliction." His statement says two things: faith has saved the woman, and she is cured. That is, there are two healings—one bodily, one spiritual. We should also note that St. Mark has already said that the woman was healed at the moment she touched Jesus' garment, because "power had gone out from him." But this observation is of little moment. The important thing is that Jesus wishes to give salvation and life to those who believe.

Jesus manifests the same will in regard to Jairus's daughter. The ruler asks for the healing of his daughter; news is then brought to him that she has died, but he does not lose faith. Jesus enters his house and raises the child. Then, as so often in Mark, he bids the bystanders say nothing about the miracle.

God Did Not Make Death (Wis 1:13-15; 2:23-24)

The book of Wisdom has its own vision of death: death is an accident, for God is the author solely of life. The thought is the same as in the book of Genesis, where death, we are told, entered the world because of the devil's jealousy, or, as St. Paul would put it later on, because of human disobedience (cf. Rom 5:12; 6:23; 1 Cor 15:21).

It is not too difficult for us to see the relevance of these two readings to our own situation. The miracles reported by St. Mark have two lessons for us: one is that faith saves; the other is that Christ wants to make people new and indeed to create a new world in which, as the book of Revelation tells us, there will be no sicknesses and no tears.

What is the quality of the faith we find, not only in others, but in ourselves? We know what we should believe about the person of Jesus. But when we pray, does our faith touch him as he really is? Do not many of us find ourselves reaching for some "pure" faith when we pray? Do we think that our faith is less pure if we look for some blessing from God? Do we think that the prayer of petition is less noble than the prayer of praise, and do we find ourselves practicing only the latter? If we do, we are forgetting that to expect something from almighty God is a way of praising him. We must therefore avoid proudly seeking a "pure" faith and realize that God can draw people to him in various ways that are not always as direct as we might think.

The second point that concerns us in these readings is that the Lord wants to give life and to build a new world. Do we as Christians look upon death differently than they do who have not received the gift of faith? Jesus' words about Jairus's daughter, "The child is not dead but asleep," are repeated elsewhere in the New Testament. They show us that from the very beginning, Christians understood death to be a passage to a new life. When St. John recounts the raising of Lazarus, he tells us that before going to Bethany, Jesus said, "Our friend Lazarus is asleep" (John 11:11). In what may be a fragment of an early Christian hymn, we read: "Awake, O sleeper, / and arise from the dead, / and Christ will give you light" (Eph 5:14).

St. Paul elsewhere speaks of "those who have fallen asleep in Christ" (1 Cor 15:18). Moreover, when Jesus raises someone from the dead, Mark habitually uses the word "awaken" (Greek: *egeirein*) for "raise up"; the risen are those who have been "awakened" (Mark 6:14; 12:26). Other writers of the apostolic age use the same verb for the resurrection of Christ himself. It seems clear that from a very early point Christians thought of death as a passage to a new life.

This, then, is the second lesson of the day: death is a passage to life; Christ is the Author of life and wants to communicate life to us.

Give What You Have Received (2 Cor 8:7, 9, 13-15)

The occasion for the Second Letter to the Corinthians was a material need: the Church of Jerusalem was in serious financial straits. In the verses that precede the present passage and in verse 8, which is omitted from the reading, Paul asks the Christians of Corinth to contribute to the collection that will be made, but he accompanies the request with numerous reservations. In addition, the community at Corinth had its problems, as we know, and Paul had had to reproach the Christians there; now, to encourage them, he looks beyond the immediate question of the collection and speaks of the many graces the Corinthians have received. He mentions them: the faith, the word and knowledge of God, and the fervent love communicated to them by Paul himself.

These blessings should encourage the Corinthians to be generous in turn and to show love for the community at Jerusalem. But St. Paul also appeals to the example of Christ, a spiritual example that has nothing to do with money but that nonetheless will encourage the Corinthians to see where their duty lies. Christ emptied himself; being rich, he became poor for our sakes so that his poverty might enrich us.

Applying this spiritual example to the present problem, Paul speaks of the generosity the Corinthians should show in material things. The point is not that they should burden themselves but that they should do what equality in the community requires. They should give what they can spare; the favor may well be returned in other circumstances. Such a charitable exchange of material goods is not isolated from the sharing of spiritual blessings that the various communities should likewise exchange. Solidarity among the communities relates to both the spiritual and the material goods that each shares with the others.

The passage is very relevant to us today. It can give our generosity in material things a new dimension. It tells us that a complete openness to others, both spiritual and material, is essential to genuine poverty, that authentic poverty is a matter not simply of giving away material goods and being detached from them but also of being spiritually open to others and sharing with them what we have received. The passage thus encourages us to reflect on what we mean by the "equality" of which Paul speaks and that our contemporary world applies too exclusively to social and material conditions. If Christianity is to collaborate in building an egalitarian society, it can do so only by adding a necessary corrective, that is, by making the sharing spiritual as well as material. Christians know that by reason of their baptism they now live a new life that requires value judgments different from those of this world.

Fourteenth Sunday: The Prophet Rejected

A Prophet without Honor (Mark 6:1-6)

The account is not one to make us optimistic, but we must accept it as a faithful reflection of the situation that will eventually bring Jesus to his death. St. Mark shows that despite Jesus' miracles and teaching, his mission is apparently a failure. Jesus expresses this in a proverb of the day: "A prophet is not without honor except in his native place." Those who heard him did not get beyond the outward, human facts about him: he is the carpenter's son, Mary's son, and brother to James and Joses and Judas and Simon. The opposition to his new way of life and the scandal people take at the change in him are such that Jesus is unable to work miracles in their midst. He is astounded at their lack of faith and resigns himself to preaching elsewhere.

A People Impudent and Stubborn (Ezek 2:2-5)

Can the first reading give us a lead as to how we may understand the Gospel better?

Ezekiel is being sent to a rebellious people who have turned their backs on the covenant and whom the Lord is attempting to convert. Ezekiel himself later on describes (in chap. 20) the disordered state of Israel. Today's passage shows that the most serious aspect of the whole situation was the impudence and stubbornness of this people whom God loved.

Ezekiel will bring God's word to the people; in addressing them, he will use the familiar prophetic opening: "Thus says the LORD God." Even if the people do not accept God's word, they will at least know that a prophet has been sent and is among them. They will know it, whether they end up listening to and heeding his word or whether they will be converted only by the punishment sent them for being unwilling to listen and remaining obstinate.

The circumstances in which Ezekiel carried out his mission were the very ones Jesus later met. He was there in the midst of his people, but his words and deeds did not make them see that he had been sent to them with a mission. Thus Jesus had the same experience as all the prophets before him.

This drama is still going on. Do people accept the Creed without changing it? The works of Jesus as recorded in the gospel and the works he now accomplishes are plain to see, but there are eyes that do not see and stubborn hearts that are closed to God's word.

This tragedy of the failure to understand goes on in various forms. To refuse Jesus' teaching as mediated by the Church is not the only way of failing to understand him. People also reject Jesus by identifying the Church with its form at a particular period of history and refusing to let the Church adapt and be what she should be in today's world. People reject Jesus by closing their ears to criticism that may admittedly take an excessively bitter form and yet may be inspired by the Lord, who wishes his Church to change some of her ways. The failure of his own to receive Jesus is repeated more often than we think.

Strength in Weakness (2 Cor 12:7-10)

St. Paul here alludes to revelations he had received. These could have made him proud, but the Lord prevented him from yielding to pride by humbling him with a "thorn" in the flesh that might have led people to think of him as under Satan's influence rather than as a messenger of God. In Paul's day, nervous disorders, like many illnesses, were regarded as caused by the demon. That is why Paul thanks the Galatians for not spitting at him (that is the literal meaning of Gal 4:14) in a gesture meant to exorcize a person who was sick or blind and therefore regarded as under demonic influence.

There is no point in trying to determine just what the "thorn" was of which Paul speaks. It has been suggested, without proof (what proof could there possibly be?), that the "thorn" consisted in sexual temptations. In all likelihood, it took the form of some humiliating, chronic illness that upset those who listened to Paul and might well cause them to refuse him a hearing. They would ask themselves: Is he really from God (the Galatians received him as an angel of God; Gal 4:14), or is he under the influence of Satan?

The Lord refuses to free Paul from this "thorn" that causes him to share the cross of Christ by humiliating him and then making him strong in his very weakness. For amid his weakness, the power of Christ dwells in him. He is strong because he is weak, since his weakness leaves room for the very power of God who is in him to exercise itself. The humiliated, crucified Jesus had the full power of the Spirit within him, and at the very moment when he was suffering and seemed powerless, he was lifting the world from its sin into the life of God.

A life marked by persecution, coercion, and suffering of every kind is not regarded by the Christian as reason for discouragement or despair; rather, it is a life that draws strength from the indwelling Lord. Weakness and suffering enable Christians to clear a space within themselves where the power of Christ can dwell.

Fifteenth Sunday: Chosen and Sent

The Twelve Are Chosen and Sent (Mark 6:7-13)

The theme of choice recurs several times on the Sundays of Ordinary Time. On the Fourth Sunday (Year A) we are told that God chooses the weak (1 Cor 1:26-31); on the Eleventh Sunday (Year A) we read of the choosing of the priestly people and of the twelve apostles (Matt 9:36–10:8; Exod 19:2-6). The theme was evidently an important one to the early Church, and we should go back to the Sundays just mentioned for further discussion of the points that will be made briefly here.

What is it that characterizes today's pericope compared with the others on the same subject? The first reading, and the second as well (which happens to fit in with the other two), tells us that the main point being made by the liturgy in its use of this gospel passage is that God has the initiative when it comes to choosing people. He chooses them, and he does it before the creation of the world; he does it too without taking into account the qualities we humans judged indispensable.

The first thing, then, that we ought to emphasize in the passage is the fact of the choice, together with the delegation of authority and powers. Jesus speaks as one with authority and not like the scribes (Mark 1:22), but the same cannot be said of the Twelve. Their mission and their activity depend on their having been given power. It is in the name of Jesus that they do what they do.

The purpose of their mission is to proclaim the Gospel and to call people to conversion. This short statement sums up the Church's real mission, and we must reflect deeply on it. The Second Vatican Council was very much aware of the fact that the Church is by its nature missionary; though the Church possesses a permanence, it is nonetheless always on pilgrimage and must not acquire too much baggage. The bishops must be concerned about all the Church and make sure that they all carry out their mission of preaching conversion.

Prophesy to My People Israel (Amos 7:12-15)

This reading will enable us to understand better why the gospel pericope was chosen. Amos is preaching at Bethel and has caused a scandal by attacking the immorality, the sacred prostitution, and the social injustice that he finds at the shrine and that have infected even worship itself. Amaziah, the priest of the shrine, asks Amos to leave.

The prophet's answer is the most important part of this little passage. In it he tells of his calling: he is a simple herdsman, but the Lord has taken him away from his regular tasks, from "following the flock." He has had no preparation for his mission; the Lord has come and taken him nonetheless. "I was no prophet, nor have I belonged to a company of prophets. I was a shepherd and a dresser of sycamores."

Despite this background and lack of preparation, the Lord calls him and tells him: "Go, prophesy to my people Israel."

Chosen before the Creation of the World (Eph 1:3-14)

This passage from St. Paul does not directly take up the theme of the other two readings, but it does deal with the same subject to a certain extent. "[God the Father] chose us in him [our Lord Jesus Christ], before the foundation of the world, to be holy and without blemish before him. In love he destined us for adoption to himself through Jesus Christ."

The passage is the hymn with which the Letter to the Ephesians begins. It reminds us that we have been blessed in Christ, who is the source and center of all grace. We were predestined, not because of any merit on our part (cf. 1 Cor 1:27-29), but simply because God so willed it for his own glory. He has revealed to us the mystery of his will and purpose, and we are given a knowledge of his plan of salvation. A "mystery," as St. Paul uses the word, is thus quite the opposite of what we are accustomed to mean by it. As we use it, it means something hidden and incomprehensible; for St. Paul, on the other hand, it means a revelation of God's plan, which is eternal and has been hidden until now but has been revealed by Christ and taught to us so that we can experience its reality.

Concretely, the mysterious plan of God is to bring everything together under one Head, Christ. God wishes to rescue the world, which had been created in unity, and to restore it to an even greater unity.

The lesson being taught us on this Sunday is clear. The apostles are chosen, but so are we all chosen, and the choice in every instance is a manifestation of God's merciful love. He chooses us for his own glory and predestines us to be his children. He also chooses us for the great mission that he initiates and that consists in uniting the world under the headship of Christ. To proclaim the Gospel is to proclaim the kingdom, that is, the unification of the world under one Head, Jesus, for the glorification of the Father. No one is worthy of undertaking such a work; God chooses those whom he wishes, regardless of their preparation, and even takes them away from the place of their habitual labors.

The fact that God chooses even people who are unprepared does not mean that we should neglect the human and theological potentialities of those who feel themselves called. It simply means that God's choice is utterly free. Consequently, our judgment of those who are called should be prudent; the judgment requires great spiritual discernment.

Sixteenth Sunday: The Flock Gathered

Sheep without a Shepherd (Mark 6:30-34)

The narrative is quite brief. The disciples return from an apostolic journey; Jesus takes them into solitude so that they can rest, but the crowd seeks them out. When Jesus sees the crowd, he is filled with pity for them because they are like sheep without a shepherd, and he begins to instruct them in detail. The theme of the passage as read in the liturgy is sheep without a shepherd, whom Christ wishes to evangelize.

The passage tells us, then, of the anxious concern Jesus feels for the crowds. The evangelists like to point out that the crowds follow Jesus (see Matt 4:25; 8:1, 18; 12:15 and parallels; 13:2 and parallels; 19:2; 20:29; Mark 1:33, 45; 2:2; 3:20, 32; 4:36; 5:21, 24; 9:14; Luke 7:11; 8:45; 11:29; 12:1; 14:25; 19:3; 23:48; John 12:18). We read that Jesus is moved by the sight of the crowd (Mark 9:36; 15:32) and that the crowd is struck by wonder at Jesus (Matt 12:23; 21:9; Mark 12:37; John 7:12, 40) and has a great desire to hear his teaching (Mark 11:18; 12:37; Luke 5:1, 15). This desire for teaching, along with the desire to be cured and to see miracles, is what draws the crowds after Jesus.

Jesus' mission is to teach. He teaches in the synagogues (Matt 4:23; Mark 1:39; Luke 4:44) and in the towns (Matt 11:1). He himself can say at the end: "Day after day I sat teaching in the temple area" (Matt 26:55; cf. Mark 14:48-49; Luke 22:52-53; John 18:20).

What is the character of his teaching? He teaches with authority (Matt 7:29) and says that the Father has told him what he is to teach (John 12:49). All those who are of good faith must acknowledge that he teaches truly the way of God (Matt 22:16; Mark 12:13-14; Luke 20:21). He also teaches in parables, however (Matt 13:3, 35; Mark 4:2; Luke 8:4). His teaching is new and is confirmed by actions: he commands the unclean spirits and they obey him (Mark 1:27). His hearers ask themselves where he gets this teaching of his and what the wisdom is that has been entrusted to him; they exclaim in wonder at the mighty deeds he accomplishes (Mark 6:2).

The reason why St. Mark says so much about the teaching of Jesus is that his gospel is meant as a catechesis, perhaps for use during the Eucharist of the Jewish-Christian community. This purpose explains Mark's care throughout the gospel to show Jesus confirming his teaching by miracles.

When Jesus is moved at the sight of a crowd that resembles sheep without a shepherd, his first reaction is to teach them. In his eyes, the primary function of a shepherd is to communicate the Father's teaching.

This attitude of Jesus should make us stop and reflect. In our day we are tempted to assign the Church's shepherds many roles that often do not leave them time to teach and to prepare themselves for teaching. St. Mark, on the contrary, sees teaching as the first and foremost task of Jesus the Shepherd. What Jesus teaches has, moreover, been entrusted to him by his Father. In fact, what Jesus teaches is precisely that God is a Father and that he loves people and wants to save them. At the same time, today's passage from Mark shows that Jesus was especially concerned to teach his disciples, who would themselves later become teachers of others. He explains his parables to them because they accept him with faith.

It is by teaching the sheep that Jesus gathers them together. This is an aspect of his teaching that must be emphasized. He does not give an abstract religious instruction that stimulates the hearers to discussion. Rather, he teaches with authority and confirms the teaching received from the Father by miracles. His teaching is filled with power and creates a new people. The crowds gather around him and share his teaching with one another by telling one another of their impressions; slowly they form a united flock on which Jesus bestows his love and for which he prepares future shepherds.

The Shepherd Gathers the Remnant of the Flock (Jer 23:1-6)

The theme of the shepherd occurs frequently in the Bible, and this is only to be expected when we recall the kind of life led by many of the writers and readers of the Scriptures. The patriarchs were shepherds; King David himself was called from tending the flocks. Today's text from the prophet Jeremiah was written against the kings who misgovern the people of God. Evidently, then, "shepherd" must be taken in a wide sense to include prophets, kings, and even those who misused their authority. Jeremiah is not the only one to write against evil "shepherds"; both Isaiah (56:10-12) and Ezekiel (24:2-10) attack them vehemently. The Lord's basic reproach to such rulers is that they neglect his people and are not really concerned about them. Isaiah speaks of these rulers as blind; Ezekiel speaks even more strongly, accusing them of the selfish abuse of their power: they act as shepherds to no one but themselves.

God himself intends to act as the shepherd of his people, for he is deeply concerned about them. His work will consist first and foremost in gathering the scattered sheep and bringing them to pastures where they will become fruitful and multiply. This divine intervention for the sake of gathering the scattered sheep is a theme that is also to be found in Isaiah (31:8-10; 40:11) and Ezekiel (34:11-16).

In order to effect this gathering, God will provide his people with shepherds. In this promise we have a prediction of the Messiah whose name will be "The Lord our justice" (Jer 23:6). The same idea may be found, expressed in almost the same terms, in the prophet Ezekiel (34:23-24). Another name, "a just shoot," is used of the Messiah in the book of Jeremiah (33:15) and is repeated in the prophet Zechariah (3:8; 6:12) and the New Testament (Heb 7:10; 1 John 3:9).

The model shepherd, so fully described in the Old Testament, re-appears in the New and is concretely embodied in Jesus. The tenth chapter of the Fourth Gospel develops the theme. The Letter to the Hebrews mentions it (13:20) in the context of Christ's high priesthood. The First Letter of Peter speaks of Christ as the shepherd who continues to lead his people and sees him coming on the last day as the great Shepherd (2:25; 5:4). In Revelation we find a strange mixing of themes of lamb and shepherd: "the Lamb who is in the center of the throne will shepherd them / and lead them to springs of life-giving water" (7:17); we also see the Lamb, in his role as shepherd, being followed wherever he goes (14:4).

The First Letter of Peter describes us as scattered sheep whom the shepherd gathers: "you had gone astray like sheep, but you have now returned to the shepherd and guardian of your souls" (2:25). The theme of the shepherd naturally calls to mind the theme of gathering, for the shepherd makes his voice heard, and the sheep follow him. It is under this image that Zechariah anticipates the gathering of the nations: "I will whistle for them and gather them in" (10:8).[4]

The responsorial psalm for today is inevitably Psalm 23, the song sung by the newly baptized when, after their baptism and confirmation, they go in procession to the eucharistic celebration for the first time. Consequently, there can hardly be a homily on the Good Shepherd that does not speak of the Eucharist, to which he leads us in order to feed us and to form us into a single people.

Psalm 23 was the subject of frequent patristic commentary.[5] For St. Cyril of Jerusalem, the psalm is a prophecy of Christian initiation:

> Blessed David, too, tells you of the power [of this mystery] when he says: "You have prepared a table before me, in the face of those who persecute me." . . . To what does he refer but to the mystical, spiritual table that God has prepared for us? . . . "You have anointed my head with oil."

He has anointed you on the forehead with oil, in the form of the seal you have received from God, so that you are imprinted with the seal and are now consecrated to God. "And your cup intoxicates me like the best wine." You see here mention of the chalice which Jesus takes in his hands and over which he gives thanks and says: "This is my blood."[6]

St. Ambrose offers the same explanation in his commentary on the psalm when addressing the newly baptized:

Learn again what kind of sacraments you have received. Listen to what holy David says, for he, too, under the impulse of the Spirit, foresaw these sacraments. He rejoiced and declared that he lacked for nothing. Why? Because one who has received the body of Christ will never again be hungry. How often have you not heard Psalm 22 and failed to understand it! See how well it applies to the heavenly sacraments.[7]

The fathers thus regarded Psalm 23 as a synthesis of sacramental catechesis, and the psalm had an important place in the ritual of Christian initiation in the early Church. We shall limit ourselves here to two further passages from the fathers that bring out their pastoral concerns. St. Gregory of Nyssa writes:

By all these means he [Jesus] teaches the Church that you must first become a sheep of the Good Shepherd through a good catechesis and through initiation into the pastures and springs of Christian teaching so that you may he buried with him and die with him in baptism, and yet not fear such a death. For this death is not death proper but a shadow and likeness of death. . . . Then he prepares the mystical table. . . . After this he anoints your head with the oil of the Spirit and brings the wine that rejoices the heart and fills the soul with sober intoxication.[8]

St. Cyril of Alexandria says that in this psalm

converts from Gentile religions, having been taught by God and spiritually fed, acknowledge the giver of the salutary food and call him their Shepherd and Nourisher. . . . They have for leader not a mere saint, such as Israel had in Moses, but the Prince of shepherds and the Teacher of teachers, in whom are hidden all the treasures of wisdom and knowledge.[9]

Brought Near in the Blood of Christ (Eph 2:13-18)

Today's second reading can be considered along with the other two. It tells us that this Lord who is a shepherd has united Israel and the nations into a single people; in his own flesh he has destroyed the walls that separated them.

It is in a baptismal context that St. Paul says this, for earlier in this second chapter of the letter (vv. 1-10), he shows us that the baptized have been raised to new life in Christ. Now he adds that although at one time they were far from God, they have now been brought near to God and to each other through the blood of Christ. Christ the Shepherd has made the two peoples one, and the one people has become a single new person. Peace now is a reality for the people of Israel as well as for the converts from Gentile religions. The two peoples who have become a single new person can draw near to the Father in the power of the one Spirit.

We had gone astray, but now we are led by a Shepherd who has given his life for us. We have become a single people and have access to the Father in the one Spirit.

Today's entire liturgical celebration is thus endowed with a special unity. The Lord stands before us who have gone astray and need a guide; he stands before the peoples of our time as they seek for some unity to their lives. Everyone wants unity within oneself; human groups seek for unity; the peoples of the earth are looking for common ways of thinking and for a common life. There is only one hope of succeeding in this manifold quest for unity, and that is to find unity in Christ, who as Shepherd has shed his blood in order to bring the peoples of the world together in unity and peace.

We must not delude ourselves: Without faith in this one Shepherd, there can be no unity and no peace. All other ways are illusory. Every Christian, certainly, must be convinced of this truth. Moreover, when faced with our lost and groping world, each Christian has the responsibility, in some measure, of a shepherd; we must show others the way. But at this point we must be on guard: The world is not looking for our theories, any more than it wants an "easy" religion. It wants the true way, and there is only one true way that leads to lasting life, the way shown us by Christ's cross. Only the blood of Christ can give peace and unite people on a common road.

The problem of unity among Christians and, more generally, of unity among the nations has but one answer: Christ. It is to be found only in one source: the blood of Christ. There is no getting around the fact that human life will achieve fulfillment only by passing through the crucible of trials accepted with joyous love. The Christian, in shepherding others, has no other solutions to offer. If we were to show them another, more humanly acceptable path, we would be creating a costly illusion. We have many examples of such false guidance. When "shepherds," unwittingly acting in an evil manner, point people toward other ways, they are dooming them to failure, for they are pointing toward false joys and a false unity. The only true peace and unity are those to which the Spirit of Christ leads us.

Seventeenth Sunday: We Are Filled with the Bread of God

The Multiplication of the Loaves (John 6:1-15)

In Year B, the continuous reading of St. Mark's gospel is interrupted, and from the Seventeenth to the Twenty-First Sundays, the sixth chapter of St. John, on the Bread of Life, is read instead. It will be of great interest to see how the understanding of this sixth chapter is conditioned, Sunday after Sunday, by the accompanying reading from the Old Testament.

In this first pericope the crowd follows Jesus, and the evangelist tells us the reason: they had seen the signs Jesus gave by healing the sick. This opening statement already gives the ensuing narrative a messianic dimension. It is followed almost immediately by a further observation that hints at the sacramental character of what is to follow: "The Jewish feast of Passover was near." We must bear in mind, of course, that John's catechesis is addressed to Christians; the latter could not but think of the Eucharist when they read that the multiplication of the loaves was thus so closely linked in time with the Passover.

We observed a moment ago that the reference to the healing of the sick gives a messianic coloring to the events and discourses to follow. This messianic dimension is further accentuated by the way John concludes the multiplication, for while the Synoptic Gospels pass directly to the event of Jesus' walking on the water, John reports the crowd as saying: "This is truly the Prophet, the one who is to come into the world." They wish, therefore, to make him their king.

Even before the discourse on the Bread of Life, John insinuates that the miracle of the multiplication was an anticipation of the Eucharist and part of the progressive revelation Jesus was undertaking. Thus he notes, before the miracle, that Jesus "himself knew what he was going to do."

It has been claimed that in this passage of his gospel, John intends to evoke in a systematic way the memory of episodes during the exodus. In any case, the evocation follows not the chronology of events as recorded in the book of Exodus but rather the chronology adopted in the book of Wisdom, when the latter speaks of the manna (16:20-26). John's narrative also refers to the book of Numbers (11:13), from which there will be some citations in the following verses.

The situation of God's people in the desert is not the only reference to the Old Testament. Surely the story of the loaves being multiplied by Elisha was also in St. John's mind. In that story (2 Kgs 4:42-44), as in St. John, the loaves were of barley. In addition, Elisha's servant raises an objection almost identical with that of Philip: "How can I set this before a hundred people?" (2 Kgs 4:43). Finally, as in St. John (6:12-13), there is a reference to bread being left over: "when they had eaten, there was some left over" (2 Kgs 4:44).

In telling the stage-by-stage story of the journey through the desert, the book of Numbers emphasizes the fact that the people could not possibly save themselves; the Lord was the one who saw to that. Moses, for example, objects that he cannot feed six hundred thousand people (Num 11:21-23); he estimates that all the fish in the sea would not be enough to feed such a multitude. In the book of Exodus (chap. 16), enough manna falls to feed everyone.

It would be an exaggeration, of course, to say that John's account of the multiplication of the loaves is woven with allusions to the eucharistic celebration. At the same time, readers who had read the accounts of the institution of the Eucharist and were participating in the eucharistic gatherings must inevitably have seen in the account as a whole a desire on John's part to present the story of the multi-plication as a prophecy of the Eucharist. Here, as in the Eucharist, Jesus takes bread, gives thanks, and distributes it.

When Jesus performs the miracle of the loaves and fish, the food he supplies proves to be too much, but at his bidding the disciples gather up the remnants. Does John intend some symbolic meaning when he says that twelve baskets of fragments were collected? If so, what was this symbolic intention?

The crowd fails—tragically, we might well say—to understand the deeper significance of the miracle. They see only a sign that their nationalistic messianic longings are to be satisfied.

They Shall Eat and Have Some Left (2 Kgs 4:42-44)

We have already referred to this passage in commenting on the gospel pericope. It is useless to go further and try to determine the locality of the wonder and the details of the event. Its meaning is the important thing. There was evidently a disproportion between the twenty loaves and the hundred who were to eat them, just as in the gospel. It is not clear whether the author of the text wanted to glorify Elisha and create a legend about him or whether he sought rather to emphasize humanity's impotence and God's ready intervention.

The two passages read today do not lead us to a proximate meditation on the Bread of Life. The accent is rather on Christ's mysterious preparation for the discourse, as he stirs in the crowd a desire for a more than material nourishment. More specifically, at this moment he wants them not to go astray by thinking of salvation in nationalistic terms when they are forced to recognize the power of God's messenger. Jesus is not the messiah imagined by the Jewish people of his day, but the crowd does not see this. He therefore withdraws into the hills by himself. For the evangelist, this means that Jesus withdraws to pray in solitude and silence.

The readings for this Sunday already show us the true Messiah who heals and the true Prophet who has power to feed the crowds. Since we have faith, we are prepared to take the next step and accept the consequences of what Jesus does here, for we already know the sequence and its teaching. But even if we stay simply with the first fifteen verses of chapter 6, we are already being invited to enter the ways of God and to acknowledge his power and his determination to share in the life of people.

The responsorial psalm (Ps 145) after the first reading bids us sing: "The eyes of all look to you, / and you give them their food in due season. / You open your hand and satisfy / the desire of every living thing" (vv. 15-16). The rest of chapter 6 will spell out what is meant by these words of the psalm, but we already think of the Eucharist as we sing it.

One Body, One Lord, One Faith, One Baptism (Eph 4:1-6)

Life in Christ is not a matter simply of receiving the sacraments. On the contrary, the sacraments point us to a way of life. We must live and act in accordance with what we have received. The unity that exists in Christ's Body is not only the result of moral activity but an epiphany or manifestation of what each individual has become, an outward expression of the radical inner transformation of his person by the sacraments, a manifestation of what the new creature really is. Humility, gentleness, patience, mutual loving support, the desire for peace—these are not simply virtues plastered onto life but the normal expression of the person who is now part of a single Body due to the action of one and the same Spirit.

This splendid text, so clear but also so theologically profound and solid, deserves frequent meditation. Without this solid base, life becomes weak for Christians; they are in danger of succumbing to mythical thinking and to the superstition of ritualistic magic. The sacraments have nothing magical about them, however; they require of us a real commitment, as baptism evidently does in linking us to the one Body by the power of the one Spirit. Only one kind of life and action is possible thereafter.

Eighteenth Sunday: Believe, Then Hunger and Thirst No More

Go to Christ and You Will Not Hunger or Thirst (John 6:24-35)

In this continuation of chapter 6 of the Fourth Gospel, we read the beginning of the discourse of the Bread of Life. Jesus delivers the discourse in the synagogue at Capernaum (6:59), where the crowd has found him, across the lake from where the miracle of the loaves had occurred.

As is usual with St. John, the discourse begins with an ambiguous statement: the crowd seeks Jesus because it has been filled, not because it has seen signs. In other words, what draws the crowd to Jesus is not the proclamation of the kingdom but the fact that he gave them their fill of material food. The ambiguity proper is in the word "eat." The crowd has eaten bodily food but has not understood the further "eating" of which the bodily food and the bodily act of eating were meant to be a sign. To put it another way, the crowd has failed to perceive the ambiguity, or the deeper meaning behind the surface meaning, in Jesus' taking bread and distributing it.

As far as the crowd is concerned, the food that Jesus gave them disappeared once they ate it. Consequently, they ate, saw, touched the sign, but they did not understand the sign or what they were doing. Such is the crowd's state of mind. Jesus takes advantage of the fact that they have at least come after him to tell them that, in addition to the food that perishes, there is another food that does not perish but endures to eternal life. He thus enunciates the theme of his discourse.

The first part of the discourse continues as far as verse 34. In the pericope for Mass, verse 35 is included. It clarifies what has preceded, but it also begins a new development that will not be read until the next (Nineteenth) Sunday.

With the opening words of Jesus, we pass from perishable earthly food to a food that endures to eternal life. The latter is linked to the person of Jesus; it is a food "which the Son of Man will give you. For on him the Father, God, has set his seal." Does the crowd understand who this "Son of Man" is? It seems not, since later on in the gospel (12:34) they will still be asking, "Who is this Son of Man?" But whether or not the crowd realizes it, Jesus is the Son of Man who has been appointed by the Father to carry out his will; the Father has set his seal upon him through the intervention of the Spirit (John 1:32).

The crowd evidently does not grasp the full implication of Christ's statement. They do, however, sense that Jesus is speaking of some sacred reality in which they are to share through their activity, that he is pointing a way to them and telling them of something God wants done. But, for the Jews, "the works of God" mean chiefly actions that have a material, visible dimension: prayers, fasts, ascetical practices, proselytizing, etc. For this reason, their response to Jesus' opening statement is a question about external activities: "What can we do to accomplish the works of God?" Jesus' answer is direct and to the point: "This is the work of God, that you believe in the one he sent." He proposes here an activity that his hearers were surely not expecting, since it is entirely interior. At the same time, however, Jesus does not speak in abstract concepts but shows the concrete form this interior action must take: believe, and believe specifically in the one God has sent.

The crowd now realizes that there is a connection between Jesus and the messenger who bears God's seal. They ask for a sign; that is, they have failed to grasp the meaning of the multiplication of the loaves. Another point they instinctively grasp, however, is that there is a connection between the messenger and the eternal food. That is why they remind Jesus of the manna in the desert. Their ancestors had been given a food from heaven; what sign can Jesus offer?

The mention of the manna allows Jesus to advance a step and to mention the true bread. The bread Moses gave was a perishable bread and a prefiguration of something further. Jesus offers the true bread that the heavenly Father gives.

At this point Jesus goes further and speaks of the true bread as identical with himself. "the bread of God is that which comes down from heaven and gives life to the world." Then, when the crowd cries, "Sir, give us this bread always," he makes the identification completely explicit: "I am the bread of life." Anyone who comes to Jesus and eats will never be hungry or thirsty again. Jesus is referring to the messianic banquet, and his hearers probably had some inkling of his meaning. They knew the prophecy, "They shall not hunger or thirst" (Isa 49:10). This imagery had often accompanied God's declarations that he would send a Messiah to liberate his people (cf. Isa 55:1-3; 65:13). The same language later appears in Revelation (7:16).

Thus does the discourse unfold, through a series of ambiguities. We must accustom ourselves to John's way of structuring the discourses of Jesus. There is a food that perishes, but there is another that endures to eternal life. The manna is not truly a heavenly food; it is the Father who gives the heavenly food; he gives his Son who is the Bread of Life. People must believe in the person of the Son; to do so is to do the work of God. Whoever believes in the Son will not hunger or thirst.

A Rain of Bread (Exod 16:2-4, 12-15)

This account is not the work of a single author but has undergone important revisions. The scholars have seen the Yahwist source behind verses 4-11, while they regard verses 12-14 as the work of the Priestly source. As far as the liturgical proclamation of the passage is concerned, the fact that the account unites two different traditions is of no particular significance.

For our spiritual understanding of the passage and our understanding of the gospel, the points we should bear in mind can be summed up rather briefly. The situation of God's people in the desert is desperate and leads them to a complaint that is proof of their lack of faith. And yet, even while the people murmur because they lack confidence in him who brought them out of Egypt and through the Red Sea, they still have a lively hope in God's goodness and action on their behalf;

this hope is almost a subconscious reflex with them. The manna falls from heaven, and the quail cover the ground. Now this gift of God also brings a further test of faith: Will the people accept what God gives on his terms? He intends to "test them, to see whether they follow my instructions or not." God is giving them this bread from heaven as bread for their journey toward the promised land.

It would have been impossible for St. John, addressing as he was a believing community, to recount Jesus' words about the Bread of Life without recalling the manna.

The responsorial psalm, Psalm 78, recalls the manna and praises God for it:

> [H]e commanded the clouds above,
> and opened the gates of heaven.
>
> He rained down manna to eat,
> and gave them bread from heaven.
>
> Man ate the bread of angels.
> He sent them abundance of food. . . .
>
> So he brought them to his holy land, /
> To the mountain his right hand had won. (vv. 23-25, 54)

Live as a New Person (Eph 4:17, 20-24)

We continue here the reading of the Christian charter as contained in the Letter to the Ephesians (the reading of which began on the Fifteenth Sunday). Chapter 3 of the Letter to the Colossians (vv. 5-15) closely resembles this fourth chapter of the Letter to the Ephesians. Both are concerned with unity among the baptized. We who are baptized have taken up a new way of life and must not live like the Gentiles. At this point (Eph 4:18-19), St. Paul gives a list of the attitudes characteristic of the Gentile, but these verses are omitted from the liturgical selection: hardness of heart, religious ignorance, etc. St. Paul sums it up as "futility" and warns us not to be led astray by it.

We must, then, put aside the old self that still exists in us and be guided instead from within by a renewed spirit. In this last phrase Paul is clearly alluding to baptism, which has utterly transformed the life of the person who has received it and who has become a new person through rebirth from water and the Spirit. The Letter to the Colossians voices almost an identical idea: "you have taken off the old self with its practices and have put on the new self, which is being renewed, for knowledge, in the image of its creator" (3:9-10). The Christian has been created as one who is holy and just in truth, after the image of God; we must therefore lead our life under the guidance of the renewed self.

All this is perfectly obvious. How sad to think, then, of what the world could be if Catholics remembered, in act as well as in thought, what they truly are and are meant to be. What power they would have in the present situation to remove the burden of the new en-slavements we are constantly accepting! No truly good and viable civilization can be built apart from the spiritual renewal of outlook that should be exemplified in and promoted by the baptized in Christ.

Nineteenth Sunday: The Bread That Has Come down from Heaven

I Am the Living Bread (John 6:41-51)

This time the Jews have understood Jesus' statement about himself and the heavenly bread. They realize that he is identifying himself with the heavenly food he offers. This scandalizes them, however: "Then how can he say, 'I have come down from heaven'?"

Jesus is clearly aware of the question in their minds. How could they—or we—help asking it? There are, of course, the miracles Jesus does, the healings, and especially this most recent miracle of the loaves. But the crowd does not really understand. They look upon Jesus as a prophet who is to restore their kingdom; they cannot locate what has happened at the level where it belongs.

Jesus then goes on to say: "No one can come to me unless the Father who sent me draw him, and I will raise him on the last day." To understand Jesus and move toward him is a gift from the Father, and the person who receives this gift of faith and does come to Jesus will be raised up for eternal life. The gift of faith requires a responsible attitude on our part: we must listen to the Father's teachings, since "Everyone who listens to my Father and learns from him comes to me."

It is important to emphasize at this point that as Jesus speaks to the crowd, the context is that of the desert in which the manna fell and the crowd complained (Exod 16). The crowd in those days did not follow the Father who drew them to him with signs and teaching. Now they complain against the Son, in whom they are willing to see only the son of Joseph. The drama is thus repeated—a drama of unbelief and refusal to follow the paths of salvation opened by God. This time Jesus sharply rejects their attitude and declares himself to be what he truly is: the bread that has come down from heaven.

Jesus now explains what he has been saying. In his explanation he begins with the manna that had prefigured the Eucharist and explains that, while the Father gave manna to the Hebrews when they complained against him in the desert, the manna was nonetheless only an earthly food, and, consequently, those who ate it eventually died. The same holds for the people who have eaten the miraculously multiplied loaves, for these too are but a prefiguration of the true bread that is yet to be given. Whoever eats this last will live forever, but it is a bread that is only foretold, not given as yet. The reason for the delay is that the bread is the flesh of Christ, and this he does not and cannot give here and now. But he will certainly give this flesh in the future, and therefore he will give the bread as well, for he will one day give his life, his flesh, himself, for the life of the world.

In this last statement we see the condition required if the promised flesh is to have its saving power. It is Christ's flesh and must be handed over, given up, for the life of the world. The reference is to the sacrifice of the cross, as in the account of institution in the First Letter to the Corinthians: "my body that is for you" (11:24).

At this point in the discourse on the Bread of Life, we have passed from the bodily food that secures bodily life, the manna and the multiplied loaves, to that which such bodily food signifies: the everlasting food, the flesh of Jesus that gives eternal life.

In the Strength of That Food (1 Kgs 19:4-8)

In this passage Elijah is the very model of a person who is discouraged and beaten down by opposition and persecution. He is fleeing from the outraged Jezebel when an angel appears to him in a dream. On awakening, he finds a meal ready for him: a cake baked on hot stones and a jar of water. This is a divine intervention like those Israel experienced during the exodus when God fed his people with the manna and the quail (Exod 16:9-16). The same kind of miraculous food is now given to Elijah so that he may continue his journey. With his strength renewed, the prophet walks on for forty days and forty nights until he reaches Horeb, the mountain of God, where he will meet the Lord.

It is odd that patristic tradition did not eagerly lay hold of this tradition as a prefiguration of the Eucharist, since the forty days and the miraculous food were parallel to the forty years in the desert and the manna. In today's liturgy, at any rate, we are evidently meant to see in the story a figure of the Eucharist, no less than in the story of the multiplication of the loaves.

Psalm 34, a psalm traditionally used in the eucharistic celebration, provides a suitable responsorial psalm for today's Old Testament reading: "The angel of the LORD is encamped / around those who fear him, to rescue them. / Taste and see that the LORD is good" (vv. 8-9).

Walk in Love, as Christ Loved Us (Eph 4:30–5:2)

The reading on the Eighteenth Sunday reminded us of the new life that is ours in Christ. In this passage Paul continues his exhortation. We must not grieve the Holy Spirit of God, who has marked us with his seal in anticipation of the day of redemption. While the letter seems to have in mind people recently baptized, it applies just as well to the entire Christian community. St. Paul lists the attitudes and actions that can grieve the Spirit within us, and it is to be noted that these attitudes are chiefly ones that disturb the life of the community: bitterness, wrath, anger, and so forth. We must develop attitudes contrary to these and be kind to one another, tender-hearted, forgiving of one another. We must walk in love like Christ, for the Christian must be an imitator of God.

Twentieth Sunday: Eat the Bread, Drink the Wine, and Live Forever

My Flesh Is Food Indeed and My Blood Is Drink Indeed (John 6:51-58)

The gospel reading continues the discourse on the Bread of Life. On the preceding Sunday we heard Christ assert his claim to be the Bread of Life that has come down from heaven. With verse 51 we begin the third section of the discourse, in which the statement just referred to is developed, namely, "I am the living bread that came down from heaven; whoever eats this bread will live forever; and the bread that I will give is my flesh for the life of the world."

Jesus' language leads his hearers to question him. In this manner of development we see a characteristic procedure of St. John. It can be seen, for example, in Jesus' conversation with the Samaritan woman, where misunderstandings about the "water" lead to new questions (John 4:5-42). It can also be seen in the conversation with Nicodemus; here the latter misunderstands Jesus and asks: "How can a person once grown old be born again? Surely he cannot reenter his mother's womb and be born again, can he?" (John 3:1-21). At this point in chapter 6, a similar misunderstanding leads once again to a question: "How can this man give us his flesh to eat?"

Jesus did not give a direct answer to the Samaritan woman or to Nicodemus. Neither will he give a direct answer here to the question asked him by the Jews; instead, his answer will take the form of re-affirmation but with explanations. St. John does not, however, put on Jesus' lips the sacramental explanation of the gift of his flesh, the explanation we find Jesus giving at the Last Supper and Paul repeating in the First Letter to the Corinthians: "This is my body that is for you." Had Christ done so, his hearers would not have understood him.

While Jesus does not explain how he will be able to give his flesh to eat, he does explain clearly what the significance is of eating his flesh and drinking his blood. The effect of such actions will be a union with Christ, analogous to that which exists between Jesus and his Father. Jesus will dwell in them, so much so that whoever eats the flesh of Jesus will live because of him. In this passage we can, once again, easily see the allusion to the violent death of Jesus. The union with Jesus, by reason of which he lives in us and gives us life, leads finally to our resurrection on the last day.

Here again, as in the account of Lazarus' resurrection, we can see John's method at work, the method whereby misunderstanding leads at last to a grasp of the real meaning of Jesus' words (cf. John 11:23-27). In our present passage, Jesus explains what is meant by the life he gives by referring back to the manna. The manna was a bread for everyday life, and those who ate it finally died. The bread that is the flesh of Jesus is a food that gives eternal life. In fact, the dwelling of Jesus in us and of us in him is eternal life.

Come, Eat of My Bread (Prov 9:1-6)

It cannot be maintained that in the book of Proverbs, wisdom, concerning which we read some beautiful lines in today's Mass, is a divine person, and specifically Christ. While fully realizing this, the liturgy nonetheless follows the commentaries of the fathers and sees in this wisdom a prefiguration of the Eucharist. This is why the text has been so frequently used in liturgical celebrations. In the old Office for Corpus Christi, for example, the first antiphon at Lauds was the opening verse of the present pericope.

The house being built is Jerusalem, and it is in Jerusalem that wisdom sets her table. We may recall the words of Psalm 23 (sung during Christian initiation): "You have prepared a table before me / in the sight of my foes" (v. 5).

The fathers, as we noted, had a high regard for this passage on wisdom, since they saw in it a prefiguration of the messianic banquet and of the Eucharist. St. Cyprian, in one of his letters, links the passage from Genesis on the prefigurative offering of Melchizedek with our present passage on the banquet that wisdom prepares: "Solomon speaks [in the book of Proverbs] of the wine mixed, that is, he prophetically announces the chalice of the Lord with its wine and water."[10]

Origen, in his commentary on the Song of Songs, writes:

> We said earlier that the friends of the bridegroom are to be understood as referring to the prophets and all who have served the word of God since the beginning of the world. The Church, or the soul that clings to the word of God, asks them to lead her into the wine cellar, that is, the place where wisdom has mixed her wine in the bowl and whither, through her servants, she invites all who are ignorant: "Come, eat my bread, and drink the wine I have mixed." This is the wine cellar and banquet house in which all who come from east and west recline at table with Abraham, Isaac, and Jacob in the kingdom of God. . . . Into this wine cellar the Church, and each soul, desires to enter by becoming perfect, there to enjoy the teachings of wisdom and the mysteries of knowledge, as though these were a savory food and a wine that rejoices the heart.[11]

Finally, St. Ambrose says: "Do you want to eat and drink? Come to the banquet set by wisdom, who invites all with a great proclamation: 'Come, eat my bread and drink the wine I have mixed for you.'"[12]

Psalm 34 has been chosen as the responsorial psalm. Though less expressive in this context than Psalm 23 would be, it does tell how nothing is lacking to those who seek God, whereas the rich go empty-handed and hungry.

We are constantly being invited to this table of wisdom that Christ prepares for us, even though, because we live for Christ and share in his suffering, we, like Paul, are considered fools by the world around us. If we eat this bread and drink this wine, we will, as today's reading from the book of Proverbs says, "Forsake foolishness that you may live; / advance in the way of understanding." Wisdom invites us to eat her bread and drink the wine she has mixed for us; in the light of today's gospel, we identify wisdom with Christ, who invites us to eat his flesh and drink his blood. If we accept the invitation, we will be fools in the eyes of the wise of this world, but wise with Christ in a world that rejects his invitation.

Understand What the Will of the Lord Is (Eph 5:15-20)

St. Paul continues to instruct us on the subject of the new life. He sees it as an ongoing reality situated between the baptism that renewed us and the moment when we enter into glory. He wants us to make the most of this time given to us, for dangers beset us, since the days are evil. New Christians have to live in a Gentile milieu, and this brings with it the possibility and risk of slowly and almost imperceptibly falling back into Gentile ways.

Paul is accurately describing our situation today. It must be acknowledged that many Christians lead a Gentile life, a life tinged by certain Christian practices but unmarked by any Christian wisdom or even any search for such wisdom. It is in such a context as this that we must seek to know God's will. Prayer in all its forms is the means of finding wisdom and of preserving it once found.

St. Paul here presents a picture of what the liturgical gatherings of his day must have been like. Christians must have done a great deal of fervent singing of psalms, hymns, and spiritual songs. Thanksgiving must have been the dominant ethos—thanksgiving offered to God the Father in the name of our Lord Jesus Christ. In this same context, St. Paul states the ideal of constant prayer: pray always and for everything. This means a type and method of prayer that will enable us to be in constant union with God and thus to exist in a

Gentile milieu yet live according to the wisdom proper to our new life.

If we create such a vital milieu for ourselves, we shall be able to know God's will for us and put it into practice, as we pray we may do in the Our Father: "Your will be done on earth as it is in heaven."

Twenty-First Sunday; Live with the Lord Whose Words Are Spirit and Life

To Whom Shall We Go? (John 6:60-69)

In today's Mass we read the end of the discourse on the Bread of Life. We are made witnesses of the drama and of the division it caused, even among the disciples of Jesus. "This saying is hard; who can accept it?"

The passage contains a dialogue between Jesus and his disciples. They had their part to play in the multiplication of the loaves, but the subsequent discourse involved chiefly the crowd in a dialogue with Jesus. Now that the discourse is ending, the disciples come into the foreground once again. That is to be expected, since they are in a far better position to grasp the last part of Jesus' address to the crowd and to lay hold of its basic meaning. Even within the group of disciples, however, some are not yet able to believe fully and to accept the deeper meaning of Jesus' words. They lack an essential faith in Jesus as messenger of the Father. Otherwise, even if they had not fully grasped what he was saying in the discourse, they would have accepted him as did the disciples who elected to stay with him.

The important thing in this concluding section is the introduction of the "spiritual" element; we must, however, understand that this "spiritual" is utterly "real"! In fact, for St. John, there is a very close relationship between the spirit and what is real and true. The realm of the spirit is absolute reality, as opposed to the flesh, which is a secondary kind of reality. In other words, for Jesus and St. John, the spirit (or the spiritual, as we would say) is real par excellence, whereas material things (the flesh, for example) exist only in the phenomenal order.

This contrast occurs several times in St. John. In his conversation with the Samaritan woman, Jesus links "spirit" and "truth" (John

4:23). In the dialogue with Nicodemus, when the latter cannot understand how one can be born again, Jesus explains that it is a question
of being born from above through water and the Spirit (John 3:5-7).
So now, in the sixth chapter, Jesus says, "It is the spirit that gives
life"—the spirit is reality and truth, while the flesh is powerless. If,
then, the words of Jesus are life-giving, it is because in them spirit
and truth reside. Earthly food is simply material, while spiritual food
is reality and truth. The Spirit alone can give life. Christ is from above,
but he has taken flesh, and this flesh is now a means of union with
him. No one can accept this, however, unless he "sees" Christ. But
to "see" him and believe in him is itself a gift from the Father.

At this point there arises the dramatic crisis that will separate the
other disciples from the Twelve who remain faithful to Jesus. In his
moving answer, Peter says to Jesus: "Master, to whom shall we go?
You have the words of eternal life." In other words: We know that
you are spirit and life and that you possess the words of truth. Peter
then goes on to express the faith of the Twelve: "We have come to
believe and are convinced that you are the Holy One of God." To the
Twelve, who remain faithful, unlike the other disciples and the scandalized crowd, Jesus is not only the Holy One of God; his words also
give eternal life.

Today is the last of the Sundays (Seventeenth to Twenty-First, Year
B) on which the sixth chapter of St. John is read. It seems useful, now
that we have seen the whole series, to give a brief overview here:

- Verses 1-15 (Seventeenth Sunday): Multiplication of the loaves;
  Jesus is hailed as the great prophet, and they want to make him
  king.

- Verses 26-35 (Eighteenth Sunday): The Jews misunderstand; they
  follow Jesus because they have eaten a perishable food, whereas
  they should be asking him for a food that is eternal. The manna
  was perishable food; the Father gives a heavenly bread, which
  is Jesus himself, the Bread of Life.

- Verses 41-51 (Nineteenth Sunday): Jesus is the bread from
  heaven. But is he not Joseph's son? No one can come to Christ
  unless the Father draws him. People must listen with faith to the
  teaching of God as transmitted by his messenger. This means
  people must also believe in the messenger who comes from

heaven. Those who ate the manna have since died; those who eat this bread from heaven will live forever. The bread to be given is Christ's flesh for the life of the world.

- Verses 51-58 (Twentieth Sunday): Christ is both the bread and the giver of the bread. Therefore he gives his very self, his flesh and blood. Eat the flesh and drink the blood of Christ, and the result is that he dwells in us and we in him. This flesh is to be "given" for the life of the world (an allusion to the Eucharist).

- Verses 60-69 (Twenty-First Sunday): Conclusion. To understand Jesus' message, one must be called by the Father. The words of Jesus are spirit and life: the spirit gives life while the flesh is powerless. Earthly food perishes, but the food from above, that is, the Spirit, brings eternal life. The true bread is spiritual food.

Die Rather Than Abandon the Lord (Jos 24:1-2a, 15-17, 18b)

The people have gathered at Shechem at Joshua's summons. Shechem is the place of the covenant, but the gathering in this case does not seem to be for worship. The people are summoned because they must make a definitive choice. Joshua delivers a lengthy discourse in which he recalls all that God has done for his people, beginning with the call of Abraham. His kindness to the people has been great indeed, and he has bestowed on them blessings they did not earn. Now they must choose. The people's answer is clear: to die rather than abandon the Lord. The people in their turn recall what the Lord has done, and they come to the conclusion that they wish to serve the Lord because he is their God.

All this is prefatory to the renewal of the covenant. In his address (which should be read in its entirety), Joshua does not gloss over the difficulties the people must face and the many temptations to infidelity that they must overcome. His predictions were, in fact, to be realized, and the soft life in Canaan would corrupt the people.

We too are faced with a choice. When we celebrate the Eucharist, which is the sacrament of the new covenant, we are forced to choose and to say, with the faithful disciples, "to whom shall we go?" or, with the Israelites, "Far be it from us to forsake the LORD." Every sharing in the Eucharist implies such a decision, for each time that the Church celebrates the Eucharist, she renews her covenant with the Lord, protests her faith in him, and draws the faithful with her in her act of unconditional fidelity.

In response to this first reading, we sing in Psalm 34, "Who is it that desires life / and longs to see prosperous days?" (v. 13).

This Is a Great Mystery, Christ and the Church (Eph 5:21-32)

As he continues his disquisition on the Christian's new life, St. Paul comes to the family and domestic life. In order to give a theological basis for the mutual relations of husband and wife, the Apostle lists the duties of each and bases his statements on the union and relations of Christ and the Church.

It was not difficult for Paul to portray the Church as the spouse of Christ. When the prophet Hosea had wanted to describe the requirements of the covenant, he appealed to the image of God as husband and the chosen people as wife, and he developed the theme in a realistic manner (Hos 2:18-22). As for Paul, in his Second Letter to the Corinthians, he also depicts Christ as husband and the Church as wife (11:2). In today's passage he sees Christ as the Head and the Church as the Body—a new way of expressing the unity existing between God and his people, and an entirely new metaphor. But the new image is not an artificial product of Paul's own imagination. According to the book of Genesis, the wife is the body of her husband (3:23-24). This is why, after citing a passage from Genesis (2:24), Paul says that the mystery of the union of man and wife is a great one, for he thinks, as he quotes Genesis, of Christ and the Church.

The words, "This is a great mystery, but I speak in reference to Christ and the church," are not easy. The Apostle seems to mean that the kind of union being depicted in the book of Genesis, the reality contained in such a union, prefigures the union of Christ and the Church, while the latter represents the ideal of every marriage. The union of man and wife, as defined in Genesis, is a "type" that finds its fulfillment in the union of Christ and his Church, while every marriage lives up to its ideal if it resembles the union of Christ and the Church.

The Apostle is thus giving us here one aspect of his theology of the Church. But he also tells us something about conjugal life by comparing it to the union that is the very basis of the Church's life.

The words, "This is a great mystery," have made Christians think of the sacrament of marriage, simply because "sacrament" (*sacramentum*) was the traditional Latin translation of the Greek word for "mystery" (*mysterion*). Such an interpretation extends somewhat the real meaning of the text. It is more correct to see in the text an image and ideal of marriage, a way of understanding fully the reality that the Church will later define as the "sacrament" of matrimony. That is how the Council of Trent interpreted the text when it said that in the passage from the Letter to the Ephesians, Paul "intimated" or "hinted" (*innuit*) that Christ, through his passion, merited the grace by which the natural institution of marriage is perfected and the spouses are sanctified.[13]

Twenty-Second Sunday: Keep the Commandments of the Lord

God's Commandments and Human Traditions
(Mark 7:1-8, 14-15, 21-23)

It seems quite normal that the new Christian community should find itself in concrete difficulties caused by the opposition between the ways it is abandoning and those it wishes to acquire. The Old Testament and Judaism were not alone in feeling tempted to take refuge in traditional practices and observances and to soothe the pangs of conscience thereby. Christianity did not have to wait for modern times to experience this temptation; the early Church was quite familiar with it.

St. Paul shows us that legal purity and the observances of the law led to attitudes that needed to be tested. The problem keeps cropping up in the Acts of the Apostles, the Letter to the Galatians, the First Letter to the Corinthians, and the Letter to the Romans.

The Letter to the Galatians shows us that Peter was daunted by people's reactions. He had been in the habit of eating with Gentiles, but the arrival of some of James's entourage caused him to draw back from the Gentiles out of fear of the party of the circumcised. He chose thus to act like other Jewish converts, and for this Paul opposed him vehemently (Gal 2:11-14).

Chapter 10 of the Acts of the Apostles shows Peter facing this same problem, but now he learns from a vision how he is to act. He enters the centurion's house, even though, as Peter himself recalls, a Jew was forbidden to do so.

St. Paul finds it necessary to emphasize that traditions concerning food are quite secondary. "'Food for the stomach and the stomach for food,' but God will do away with both the one and the other"

(1 Cor 6:13). In his Letter to the Romans he shows balanced judgment with regard to the same problem: "the kingdom of God is not a matter of food and drink, but of righteousness, peace, and joy in the holy Spirit" (Rom 14:17). He goes on, however, to exhort his readers to circumspection for the sake of the "weak": "For the sake of food, do not destroy the work of God. Everything is indeed clean, but it is wrong for anyone to become a stumbling block by eating" (v. 20).

These various problems of the early Church enable us to understand better what St. Mark is teaching his faithful in today's gospel. In this pericope Jesus finds himself under attack from the Pharisees because of the way he handles human traditions. He insists on the principle that it's not what goes into a person from outside but what comes out of a person's heart that defiles. What are some of these defiling things? ". . . evil thoughts, unchastity, theft, murder, adultery, greed, malice, deceit, licentiousness, envy, blasphemy, arrogance, folly." To those who invert this order of values he says in outraged tones, "You disregard God's commandment but cling to human tradition."

Observe the Commandments of the Lord (Deut 4:1-2, 6-8)

The commandments and decrees that Moses transmits in God's name are a sign of the Lord's love for his people. They bring out the two major aspects of the covenant he is establishing with the Israelites. On the one hand, God chooses this people, leads them, protects them amid the many difficulties they encounter, and constantly proves his fidelity to them. On the other hand, God's fidelity calls for humanity's fidelity to him in return; concretely, people must hear and keep the commandments; they must observe them in their entirety without adding or subtracting anything from them.

This, then, is how people should respond to the fidelity of God. If they hear and accept the law, if they meditate on it and observe it, they will contribute to the carrying out of God's plan of salvation. If and when Israel thus responds, she will show herself to the Gentiles as a great and wise people. The law is thus meant not as a crushing burden but as a leaven and a source of enthusiasm for Israel, which will find in the law both salvation and greatness.

"LORD, who may abide in your tent, / and dwell on your holy mountain? / Whoever walks without fault; / who does what is just" (Ps 15:1-2).

Act on the Word (Jas 1:17-18, 21b-22, 27)

There is an illusion that constantly tempts us, as St. James points out. It is the temptation to be satisfied with hearing the word and not to put it into practice.

This word is a gift from above, a marvelous present from God: it gave us a new birth. The Christians to whom James writes were the very first to benefit by this gift of the regenerative word. But despite the objective efficacy of this word, it is not enough simply to hear it; one must welcome and accept it with docility. Since the word is a law, this means that one must put it into practice. Here St. James tells us quite clearly what it means to practice our religion and sweeps away all the intended or unintended illusions cultivated by Christians who think they can take refuge in religious practices and traditions. "Religion that is pure and undefiled before God and the Father is this: to care for orphans and widows in their affliction and to keep oneself unstained by the world" (v. 27).

The message given us in today's readings is a profitable one and needs frequent repetition. The point made is not that we should be contemptuous of, or regard as hypocritical, all traditions and customs; that would be a puerile attitude. The point is, rather, that we must be constantly purifying the way we live and practice our religion. Our worship may not be worship in spirit and truth; it may be tainted with legalism, or it may have degenerated into a refuge.

There can be a false kind of sacramentalism that unconsciously uses the sacraments as a dispensation from the practice of charity. This description is doubtless too harsh, but it does point to the confused state of mind into which Catholics can fall. They may come to imagine that the practice of the sacraments and other observances can save them in a magical way and require a lesser love of God and humanity. No Catholic would put things so baldly, but we may hold this view unconsciously. Christ, however, gives us a means of judging whether or not our worship and observance has a solid basis: What comes out of a person may be corrupt.

Twenty-Third Sunday: The Messianic Age

He Makes the Deaf Hear and the Dumb Speak (Mark 7:31-37)

The whole manner of this healing seems strange to us. It was not an oddity in the time of Jesus, for it reflected practices that were more or less part of the medicine of the day.

Once again we find Jesus forbidding those present to speak of the miracle to others. The crowd is evidently deeply moved. Do they perhaps realize that such cures as this are a sign of the Messiah's presence in their midst? We may think so when we listen to their acclamations, which may well be echoes of popular songs of the kind Isaiah presents to us in the first reading. It certainly seems, at least, that this messianic reference is the reason why Jesus bids those present be silent about the cure. It is to be noted that silence is imposed, if not always observed, with regard to miracles considered to be works of the Messiah who was to come: "the blind regain their sight, the lame walk, lepers are cleansed, the deaf hear, the dead are raised" (Matt 11:5).

Jesus forbids others to speak of the miracle when he cures the leper (Mark 1:44), when he raises Jairus's daughter from the dead (Mark 5:43), when he cures the deaf-mute (Mark 7:36), and when he cures the blind man at Bethsaida (Mark 8:26). The reason for the prohibition is that he does not want to reveal his identity before the appointed time; he still has to undergo his passion. He wishes to make himself known only gradually and to faith.

In today's gospel the reactions of the crowd, which St. Mark notes, indicate a certain progress. The crowd exclaims in praise that is directed to what has been done but that says nothing as such about the person of Jesus, although it certainly urges reflection on his identity. We may well ask, however, whether the cry of the crowd is not also the cry of Christians who have been enlightened by the paschal celebration of the death and resurrection of Jesus and who therefore understand the messianic significance of Jesus' action in the light of the later events they have celebrated.

It is to be noted that the rite of baptism has made use of the actions Jesus here performs in curing the deaf-mute.

The Ears of the Deaf Shall Be Unstopped, and the Tongue of the Dumb Shall Sing for Joy (Isa 35:4-7a)

The coming of the Messiah was foretold by Isaiah and fulfilled in Jesus, as his healings bear witness. St. Mark knew of the prophecy and must have thought of it as he wrote, just as his Christian readers must have thought of it. Of course, many stages of history were to pass between prophecy and fulfillment. In addition, now that the Messiah has, in fact, come and has suffered his glorious passion, we find ourselves awaiting a new coming.[14] We go our way in company with the Church, and we are witnesses to the presence of the Messiah and the accomplishment of his saving mission.

Only Christ can give us the light to walk in the right path, just as he alone can cure our leprosy and rescue us from death. These spiritual miracles are constantly being worked for us, and they strike with wonder anyone who witnesses them. We know, moreover, that the liberating miraculous deeds of Jesus are still being done, even though we are not always able to see them or put them into words. Our real difficulty, however, is in interpreting the signs that we do see in our own day. It is the same problem as was faced by the disciples contemporary with Jesus, and this even though twenty centuries of ecclesial experience now lie behind us.

The problem of the first disciples was to see Jesus as he really was and therefore to construct a new and different idea of the Messiah than the one that had always filled their imaginations. They had to try to understand what his miracles really meant. We know that when Jesus first spoke of the eucharistic sign—the eating of his flesh and the drinking of his blood—he met with harsh misunderstanding from many. In our day too, sacramental signs affirm the presence of the kingdom and the Church's progress toward the definitive establishment of that kingdom. With these signs occur many interior miracles as the grace of enlightenment and conversion is bestowed on individuals or groups. These people must now live with eyes fixed on the death and resurrection of Jesus, for whom human existence takes on a new meaning. Far from despising human life, they work for its advancement, but they also see it as related to an invisible goal that transcends any claims humans can make.

The Poor Shall Inherit the Kingdom (Jas 2:1-5)

It can hardly be denied that if James began the second chapter of his letter in this manner, he did so not in a fit of abstraction but because a real situation in his community required him to do so. In his Jewish-Christian community, he saw favoritism at work, perhaps unconsciously, and a consequent failure to live by the Christian ideal. Respect for persons was entangled with faith in Jesus Christ. And this must have been the case even at the celebration of the liturgy.

The words "For if . . ." are simply diplomatic. People were certainly making judgments based on a false scale of values. Yet, "Did not God choose those who are poor in the world?" Paul says the same thing to the Corinthians: "God chose the foolish of the world to shame the wise" (1 Cor 1:27-29). The whole of the Old Testament is very much concerned with the poor, and the prophets are constantly lashing out at those who show contempt for the poor. The gospel shows the same concern, and its "Woe to you rich" and "Blessed are the poor" resound like solemn challenges that sum up the entire Good News.

And yet neither riches nor poverty supply, of themselves, a norm of judgment. The sole norm is love. Those who love the Lord will inherit the kingdom he has promised, for he has made them all rich in faith. Faith is authentic wealth, and love is the passport into the kingdom.

We must all challenge ourselves: What are the values in the light of which we deal with our companions?

Twenty-Fourth Sunday: The Sufferings of the Servant of God

The Son of Man Must Suffer Much (Mark 8:27-35)

On the Twenty-First Sunday (Year A) we read, from the Gospel of St. Matthew, the same account of Peter's confession and the prediction of the passion (Matt 16:13-20). In the context of the Twenty-First Sunday, the emphasis was placed chiefly on the confession of Peter and on the solid foundations of the Church. Today, on the contrary, the emphasis is on the prediction of the passion and on the necessary suffering of Christ.

Jesus has kept his identity secret, not judging it timely to reveal his messiahship. He has frequently ordered bystanders not to spread the news of a miracle, especially when the miracle could be seen as a clear sign that the Messiah had indeed come. Now, at Peter's confession, the veil is lifted, at least for the immediate disciples.

The prediction of the passion leads Christ to tell his disciples the conditions that must be met if they are to follow him. Even though Mark's account is the source of the account in St. Matthew, we may refer the reader to our commentary on the latter (pp. 134–35).

I Gave My Back to the Smiters (Isa 50:4c-9a)

Part of this passage, which is the third poem of the Suffering Servant, was read as a first reading on Palm Sunday.[15] The prophecy is repeated here and brought into relation with Jesus' prediction of his passion and his invitation to the disciples to follow him in accordance with certain necessary conditions.

The Servant's inner attitude is made clear from the opening lines of the poem: he does not rebel and does not flee from the sufferings inflicted on him. In fact, he not only does not seek to escape but even offers his back freely and does not protect his face against blows.

The Servant thus becomes a model for those who want to follow Christ, take up their cross, and not seek to save their own lives. Such discipleship would be impossible if the Lord did not come to the aid of the person who surrenders his life in obedience. Here the prophecy waxes lyrical: The Lord helps his Servant, and the latter becomes invincible, setting his face like flint against his enemies. His strength is chiefly moral; that is, he knows he will not be put to shame, because the One who justifies him is at his side; it is the Lord himself who is his defender.

The Servant sees his sufferings as occurring in a short interval before the last day. The One who justifies him is at hand, and the Servant has no fears about appearing before the Lord's tribunal, along with those who inflict martyrdom on him. It is prayer that enables the Servant to pass safely through all the attacks and to endure them for the Lord. The responsorial psalm (Ps 116) reminds us of how God helps the person who offers himself in sacrifice in order to do God's will: "They surrounded me, the snares of death; / the anguish of the grave has found me; / anguish and sorrow I found. / I called on the name of the Lord. . . . / I was brought low, and he saved me" (vv. 3-4, 6).

In the readings of this Sunday, the Christian's suffering is transformed, and the self-denial involved in following Christ ceases to appear as a mutilation or a purely negative asceticism. Instead, we see it as a sharing in the glorious passion of Christ as he undertakes the redemption of humankind and the rebuilding of the world. The suffering of the Servant of God, that is, of Christ, is a priestly sacrifice. Consequently, as Christians follow the lead of Christ, they share more fully in the priesthood of Christ, who is offered and offers.

From this we see that the only useless suffering is the suffering we do not accept and offer to God; every other suffering is redemptive. If this were not the case, there would be no reason for insisting on the realism of our baptism as a participation in the death and resurrection of Jesus. We would also have to shrug off as unreal and mythical that which constitutes the very heart of Christian life, namely, the fact that we have put on Christ. To deny oneself, then, and to carry one's cross is not to mutilate oneself but, on the contrary, to give one's life a supreme efficacy and thus to win through to glory.

Faith without Works (Jas 2:14-18)

We must show our faith by the way we act. This passage of James will protect us against all the illusions that beset Christian life, for it warns us that the test is not concepts but concrete actions. As we read the passage, it becomes clear that it was meant to be read aloud; its sentences strike like a hammer, and it can leave no one indifferent. Christians who hear it must immediately turn to themselves and examine their own life.

St. James supposes that we know what faith is and to what it is directed. He concentrates on the concrete activity that faith should inspire and directs his attention chiefly to loving concern for others. The theme is also a favorite of John's, but here the style is simpler and more pastoral. A merely conceptual faith does not save, but only a faith that takes concrete form in our lives.

In order to make his point more forcefully, James, like a good preacher, uses an example. The little scene he describes sounds humorous, and yet we know of "good Christians" in our own day who are fine when it comes to principles but are not too anxious to put them into practice. St. Augustine once said, "You do not preach the gospel to people with empty stomachs." A true witness to the faith is not satisfied with preaching it; he or she is on the alert for the needs of others and tries to be of help to them.

For St. James, then, the Christian of his example has only a dead faith: "Faith of itself, if it does not have works, is dead." It is not enough to have faith; you must also act in accordance with that faith. In this, St. James is not at all in disagreement with St. Paul. When the latter says that faith alone saves (Rom 3:28), he is only expressing in a theological formula the fact that the Lord has the initiative in the work of salvation and that he exercises this initiative by giving us the gift of faith; our human actions, by themselves, cannot save us. Faith is a gift of God (Rom 3:27; 4:2-5), and faith is an indispensable condition for salvation (Rom 3:22-28). At the same time, however, Paul emphasizes the fact that Christ saved us through his obedience (Rom 5:18-19); it is precisely for that reason that our own works cannot save us (Rom 3:28). Yet if we are to be saved, we must cooperate and live according to the faith we have received: "we are his handiwork, created in Christ Jesus for the good works that God has prepared in advance, that we should live in them" (Eph 2:10).

Twenty-Fifth Sunday: The Son of Man Handed Over

Jesus the Servant (Mark 9:30-37)

This passage contains the second prediction of the passion. The first is contained in readings we have already seen (p. 134); the second occurs here, in Year B; how Luke presents the message may be seen on the Twelfth Sunday in Year C (p. 326).

In the texts parallel to this one of Mark, the passion is spoken of in the future tense: "The Son of Man is to be handed over to men" (Matt 17:22; Luke 9:44). In Mark, however, it is spoken of as a present event: a literal translation of the Greek would be, "The Son of Man is handed over [or: being handed over] to men," although the slaying of Jesus and his resurrection are put in the future.

As the reader doubtless knows, the words "hand over" are a characteristic verb of the passion narratives. We also meet it in Jeremiah (26:24) and in St. Paul's letters (Rom 4:25; 8:32; Eph 5:2). It is also used in Luke and Paul in the accounts of the Last Supper (Luke 22:19; 1 Cor 11:23).

How are we to take the statement that "the Son of Man is [or: will be] handed over to men"? It does not imply a constraint placed upon Jesus but simply the fulfillment of God's plan, for it is the Father who delivers his Son—the Son of Man—into the hands of his enemies. Here we have a favorite Johannine theme: "God so loved the world that he gave his only Son" (John 3:16). In words closer to Mark's text, St. Paul writes: "He . . . did not spare his own Son but handed him over for us all" (Rom 8:32).

The disciples do not understand the prediction of the passion. So little do they understand it that at this moment, which should have been such a dramatic one for them, they fall into a discussion about who is the greatest among them!

Jesus takes advantage of this discussion to teach them what the ideal of "first place" must be in the community they will constitute. Primacy is first and foremost a primacy in service; to discharge a responsibility will mean that the responsible ones make themselves the least and the servants of all the others. It is possible that disputes had already arisen among the disciples about who would possess authority; we have, for example, the incident in which the mother of the Zebedees asks a special place for her sons (Matt 20:20). It is possible too that the evangelist had met with challenges in his own community and wished here to report the words of Jesus, thus bringing home the true meaning of authority and first places in the Church. We may also ask whether, having just predicted his passion, Jesus is describing himself as the first who is the servant of all by giving his life for all. That is the point he will make again at the washing of the feet, when the passion is at hand.

Today's pericope continues: "Taking a child, he placed it in their midst." The connection of this incident with what precedes is not clear. All the hypotheses offered are possible, but they remain simple hypotheses.

Is there a connection between the prediction of the passion, Jesus' role as servant, and faith in Jesus who insists on accepting the child as the symbol both of innocence and of defenseless weakness? "Whoever receives one child such as this in my name, receives me; and whoever receives me, receives not me but the One who sent me."

In point of fact, this final episode of the child hardly forms part of the theme of this Sunday, which is given over to the prediction of the passion.

Condemned to a Shameful Death (Wis 2:12, 17-20)

The text draws a picture for us of Jesus predicting his passion. Jesus is the killjoy: "He . . . sets himself against our doings" (Wis 2:12). The complaints against the just one are listed. The first is very general: he opposes us. The second is more specific: he reproaches us for our behavior. The third is still more offensive to the Pharisees: he accuses us of betraying our traditions.

This passage, especially the verses read in today's liturgy (vv. 17-20), has been seen as a prophetic announcement of Christ's passion. This view seems justified. In St. Matthew's gospel, though without any express reference to the book of Wisdom, we find the Jews speaking the same language as the persecutors of the just one in the prophecy: "He trusted in God; let him deliver him now if he wants him" (Matt 27:43). Whether or not the Old Testament text is prophetic, it presents at least a prefiguration of Christ, who in his suffering will reach the pinnacle of martyrdom.

The responsorial psalm (Ps 54) expresses the determination of Christ the Servant to offer himself to the Father: "I will sacrifice to you with willing heart, / and praise your name, for it is good" (v. 8).

Peacemakers (Jas 3:16–4:3)

St. James's thoughts about his Christian community are not totally optimistic, and in this a parish leader of our day could often agree with him. There is a genuine wisdom: it comes from God; its fruits are unmistakable, and the most important of them is justice accompanied by peace. The lack of this justice and peace is disastrous for the Christian community and for the world generally. James sees that the life of the Christians he is addressing is not what it should be. Even their prayer is no help in this regard, because what they pray for is material riches and the satisfaction of their instincts.

Twenty-Sixth Sunday: Preach and Heal in the Lord's Name

Cast out Demons in the Name of the Lord (Mark 9:38-43, 45, 47-48)

Today's passage from the gospel contains several themes that have little connection with one another. It gives an impression of a conversation in which Jesus turns from subject to subject according to the questions his disciples put to him.

John asks a question, prompted by his wonder and concern that someone who does not belong to the group should be casting out demons. The answer Jesus gives is important because it can and should deepen the disciples' understanding of their own group. Jesus is telling them that there can be people outside the group who believe in him and can perform exorcisms in his name. There is no reason for hindering such a person. The implicit criterion is that he should not speak ill of Jesus. St. Matthew tells us that the mark of a false prophet is that he does not do the Father's will. It is not necessary that a person belong to the Christian community in order to act in the name of Jesus, provided he believes and observes the commandments.

Jesus is trying to broaden the outlook of his disciples, who may be tempted to seal themselves off as a closed group and to maintain in a spirit of jealousy what they consider to be the exclusive prerogative of the community. This does not mean, however, that it is meaningless to be a disciple of Christ. When someone offers a disciple something as small as a cup of water, he is offering it to Jesus himself. There is a close link between Jesus and the disciples, and this should be further reflected in solidarity within the Christian community. The disciples "belong to Christ" (an expression favored by St. Paul; see Rom 8:9; 1 Cor 1:12; 3:23; 2 Cor 10:7).

The gospel reading now moves on to another area: the question of scandalizing the "little ones" who believe in Jesus. "Little ones" should not be taken as referring only to children. It can also mean the simpler members of the Christian community, that is, those who are less educated and who belong to a lower social class and are materially or culturally poor.

The passage ends with still a third admonition, this one concerning occasions of sin. To attempt a detailed exemplification of Jesus' meaning would, however, distort his message. He never thought of a catalogue of temptations corresponding to a catalogue of sins. His teaching is concerned rather with the unconditional value of the kingdom as compared with anything and everything else. The important thing is to live by the standards of the kingdom and thus to avoid the fire of hell.

May the Lord Make Everyone a Prophet (Num 11:25-29)

The situation of the people of God requires that it possess institutions and that provision be made for its future; there must be continuity between the successive leaders of the people. This is why Moses establishes a council of seventy elders. The Lord takes some of the spirit that rests on Moses and bestows it on the elders. They begin to prophesy, but this phenomenon is passing.

The spirit also comes to rest on two men who were not present at the meeting at which the seventy were appointed, and they begin to prophesy in the camp. This startles a young man, who runs to tell Moses of it; the reaction of Joshua, the minister of Moses, is that the two men should be stopped. Moses' response, on the contrary, shows a fine breadth of outlook: "Would that all the people of the LORD were prophets! Would that the LORD might bestow his spirit on them all!" In this response we see a desire for openness as opposed to rigid traditionalism.

Moses' response represents a reaction against what in our time we might call a proud clericalism. The responsorial psalm (Ps 19) supports such a reaction: "From presumption restrain your servant; / may it not rule me" (v. 14).

The teaching given today is by no means irrelevant and should stir us to reflection in several areas. The readings teach us to be open and to reject all forms of clericalism and ecclesiastical triumphalism. These temptations are real both for the Church at large and for those in the Church who hold authority and exercise power.

A further point is that, while the priesthood of Christ is communicated in forms that are essentially and not only accidentally different, nonetheless, all the baptized are in some sense prophets. Consequently, just as we must not turn the Church in on herself and deny that great things can be done outside of her, neither must those who have received a higher and more important degree of priesthood prevent the faithful from exercising the priesthood that is properly theirs, even though they should exercise it under the control and authority of the hierarchical priesthood.

The problem of scandal should likewise not be neglected. It relates not only to the temptations each of us experience but to the possibility of shocking those whose faith is not properly enlightened. There is, of course, only one truth; this does not mean, however, that everything should be said and taught to everyone without exception and in every circumstance and without regard for the manner in which it is done. We should review our attitudes on this point as on the others made in today's readings.

The Corruption of Riches (Jas 5:1-6)

James speaks harshly; the passage sounds like a homily intended to reawaken consciences. Without regarding it as a party platform, it certainly applies to situations we find today. It has the advantage of avoiding the vulgarity and superficiality to which this kind of criticism often degenerates.

The picture of wealth and the wealthy is unsparing and forthright. Wealth, seemingly so splendid and desirable, unexpectedly vanishes, leaving only a few wretched tatters behind. It seems worthwhile only if we do not put it in the perspective of the last day that is drawing near; if we do view it in this perspective, it proves valueless and even a source of condemnation, since it is too often derived from injustice: wages not paid and crying for retribution; people slain so that the rich might live their life of luxury. The rich often kill the righteous without their resisting; they deprive the poor of their bread and thus condemn them to death. Does "the righteous one" refer to Christ? Certainly it was the wealthy and those living luxurious lives who killed Christ, inasmuch as he bore the sufferings and injustices that are the lot of the poor.

St. James is content with this short description, with this reproach whose "peaceful violence" has rarely been surpassed. He doubtless saw in the Jewish-Christian community situations that called for such a harsh attack. Certainly our own age can meditate with humility on this passage and profit from it.

Twenty-Seventh Sunday: The Unity of the Human Couple

No Human Being Must Separate What God Has Joined (Mark 10:2-16)

Today's gospel passage contains two parts, with no visible link between them. St. Mark is recording various teachings of Jesus under the general rubric of revelation and faith, but he is not interested in there being any further logical link between the teachings. Today's first reading is connected with only the first part of the gospel peri-cope. We are thus invited to emphasize chiefly the first part but with-out wholly neglecting the second. We shall comment on the first part, then go to the first reading, and finally come back to the second part of the gospel.

Mark is recording a debate between Jesus and the Pharisees. The Pharisees begin with an insidious question concerning divorce. The conversation reminds us of a worldly gathering today at which an attempt is made to embarrass a priest with questions regarding civil divorce. It seems clear that St. Mark is glad of the opportunity to provide his faithful with clear instruction on this matter.

The issue, of course, is the Christian view of marriage, which stood in contrast to both the Jewish and the Gentile views of it. Christianity was in conflict with Judaism and Gentile religions alike on the ques-tion of fidelity in marriage.

In rabbinic Judaism, a wife could be guilty of adultery toward her husband, but he could not be similarly guilty toward his wife. To this view St. Mark opposes the clear attitude of Jesus: Man and woman have the same duty of fidelity, so that a man who divorces his wife and marries another is an adulterer. Adultery can be a man's sin no less than a woman's. Jesus is here clearly abolishing the Mosaic law on divorce and promulgating once again the law of God, which is timeless, unlike the Mosaic law, which represented a yielding to temporary circumstances.

Jesus is not satisfied to enunciate a principle; he shows that the Scriptures agree with him, as he gives his interpretation of the text of the book of Genesis: "from the beginning of creation, *God made them male and female. For this reason a man shall leave his father and mother and be joined to his wife, and the two shall become one flesh.* So they are no longer two but one flesh." He is here stating the permanent and indissoluble unity of marriage.

The Two Shall Now Be One (Gen 2:18-24)

The account of creation in the book of Genesis shows man and woman to be equal beings with a common origin. Woman is indeed not "created" in the same way as man, since her being is drawn from his. But the point of the description is to show the human beings as being diversified so that the male receives from God the helpmate he has requested. The account is not saying that the second human being—woman—belongs to a different level or order than the first. On the contrary, Adam is able to say: "This one, at last, is bone of my bones and flesh of my flesh." He then gives her her name: "this one shall be called 'woman.'" The English here reflects to some extent the relation between the Hebrew words for Adam and Eve: Adam is *'ish*, that is, "man," while Eve is *'ishah*, that is, "woman," *'ishah* being simply a feminine noun formed directly from *'ish*.

The book of Genesis goes on to explain the consequences of this "creation" of woman from man: "That is why a man leaves his father and mother and clings to his wife, and the two of them become one flesh." The unity of the couple is being emphasized. We must not, however, read too much into this text. People of early times understood quite well the role of woman as helpmate to man without concluding that polygamy was to be practiced. It was not practiced in the time of the biblical patriarchs. In today's passage from Mark, divorce is the only issue; Jesus says nothing of polygamy. The author or authors of the book of Genesis were interested only in asserting the equality of woman. In human terms, she is not a different kind of being from man and is not inferior to him. She possesses the same nature as he does; she is "part" of him; she is his partner and equal.

Consequently, from the beginning the Church has felt bound to transmit a doctrine that is confirmed by her own experience. In God's plan, woman is joined to man as a helpmate, but a helpmate who is his equal.[†] The union between them is so great and strong that there can be no question of breaking it. None of the reasons given for permitting divorce can counterbalance the ontological fact that is manifested in their being "created" together. The unity of the couple and the requirement of mutual fidelity are not simply moral imperatives required by external convention. Rather, the demand for fidelity flows from what each member of the couple is ontologically for the other. No one has a right to act contrary to this ontological relationship, be it individual, State, or Church. This very fact implies that the requirements of fidelity may demand heroism of the couple.

Surely today's reading will be a subject for salutary meditation by all married people, especially in today's world, in which pagan and erotic views of marriage are gaining the upper hand. It is not simply an external moral code that requires fidelity of spouses but the way in which God himself has planned the world and set man therein, giving him a helpmate who is to be another self to him.

To Such Belongs the Kingdom of Heaven

We come now to the second half of the gospel pericope; as indicated above, it has no connection with the first half.

The words concerning the kingdom and little children have at times been misinterpreted. Jesus is not recommending a vague and naïve attitude to life nor saying that the irresponsibility of a child will take us into the kingdom. He is simply pointing to a single truth: We must be open to the gift of the kingdom. The child here is a model, not of childish naïveté or of the supposed beauty of inexperience, but of receptivity; a child is still open to reality much more than an adult. Children have not yet been hardened by selfishness or closed off by

---

[†] In spite of the effort to counteract a charge of sexism in this passage, Genesis never concedes that the man is also a helpmate to the woman.

pride in their own knowledge and accomplishments; therefore they readily and generously accept what is given to them.

These dispositions are necessary for the kingdom. Children enter the kingdom easily because they are capable of accepting gifts. It is this candor and openness, which has nothing to do with naïveté, that Christ wants to see in those who wish to enter the kingdom.

Jesus and Those He Consecrates Have One Origin (Heb 2:9-11)

He who sanctifies (Jesus) and those who are sanctified (people) are intimately linked with one another: they "all have one origin." This is why Jesus calls them his brothers and sisters. But the perfection of humanity in Christ is the result of a long and painful journey on Christ's part and on ours. Jesus remains the source of all holiness. But it is God's intention to have a multitude of sons and daughters whom Jesus will lead to glory. This plan required that he who is the source of salvation for everyone else should himself first be made perfect through suffering.

This passage contains expressions that we may find quite strange at first hearing, and they need to be properly understood. All of them bring out the reality of the incarnation; they apply to the human nature of Jesus and in no way derogate from his divinity.

Jesus was made a little lower than the angels, but because he suffered and died, he was crowned with glory. This is one of the themes of the Letter to the Philippians (2:1-11; see Twentieth Sunday, Year A). In today's passage, the writer cites Psalm 8:5 in order to give expression to the humbling of Jesus in his human nature.

Jesus has also been brought to his perfection through suffering. He was, of course, perfect in his divine nature. On the other hand, he took to himself a human nature and everything in it, except for sin; he accepted even the consequences of sin, and therefore he was capable of being perfected. His human nature will be made complete and whole, and in this sense perfected, through suffering. Suffering is not in and of itself the source of perfection, but suffering accepted and offered up in accordance with God's plan is such a source. In the case of Jesus, the "perfection" to which he is brought takes the form of his glorification. If such has been the course of Jesus' life, then it must also be the course of our lives, since he gave his life for us, his brothers and sisters.

Twenty-Eighth Sunday: Abandon All You Have

Sell What You Have and Follow Jesus (Mark 10:17-30)

Today's passage from St. Mark offers no special difficulties. Its theme is easily grasped: Wealth makes the attainment of salvation difficult, even when the rich person desires salvation and seems to be seeking it. Jesus then promises a hundredfold, even on earth, to those who leave everything and follow him.

The young man who has great wealth but throws himself at Jesus' feet certainly is desirous of obtaining eternal life. He is eager in his wish to learn from Jesus the means of salvation. He calls Jesus "Good teacher." Jesus answers him with a question, "Why do you call me good?" but does not wait for an answer; instead, he continues by saying, "No one is good but God alone." Jesus is doubtless here taking advantage of an opportunity to emphasize his own divinity and to open the eyes of the rich man. We may also suggest, however, that the adjective "good," which befits God alone, is also introduced because of the commandments that follow and that are a sign of God's goodwill toward his people, since through his commandments he leads them in the right path.

When Jesus lists the commandments, the rich man says that he has observed them since his youth. Well, then, all he lacks is one thing: to sell all he has, give it to the poor, receive treasure in heaven instead, and follow Jesus. At this point the mood changes: the rich man grows heavy of heart and goes away sorrowful.

Jesus now has occasion to develop his teaching on attachments and the kingdom. The example he gives is so extreme, however, that it discourages the disciples when they realize that it is not enough to have surrendered all their possessions. St. Mark is thinking, of course, of all Christians, and not all of them were rich people; even for those who are not rich, there are many obstacles along the road, and these must be overcome. But who is capable of that? Jesus answers the disciples' fearful question by saying: "For human beings it is impossible, but not for God. All things are possible for God."

This passage has at times been interpreted as referring to "religious life," as we understand this term today, that is, to a special path of perfection. But, in fact, Jesus is here addressing all Christians, and that is how Mark understands him. All Christians must renounce what they have and follow the way of detachment, because that is the price of entering the kingdom. Such a teaching confronts the Christian with an immense task, and in the face of it there is only one resource: faith in God who can do all things.

Peter and the other disciples are discouraged; he speaks in their name: "We have given up everything and followed you." We can guess his anxious implication: What good is it all? Jesus then lists the things people must be detached from and promises, along with persecutions, a hundredfold reward in this life. This amounts to saying that it is not possessions as such that are an obstacle to salvation (otherwise they would not be given back to us a hundredfold) but our attachment to them. (St. Mark must have had a twinkle in his eye when he added persecutions to the blessings that will be restored!) Detachment will bring eternal life in the world to come.

Regard Riches as Worthless (Wis 7:7-11)

The choice of this passage is evidently determined by the gospel pericope. We may therefore read it in the light of the gospel, just as we may in turn read the gospel in the light of this reading. This procedure may not be justified according to the strict norms of exegesis, but we have on several occasions in these volumes explained the nature of a liturgical reading of the Scriptures.

The prayer of the wise person, who is now able to regard riches as worthless, shows that this kind of wisdom is a gift and must be asked for. The detachment that wise people now possess is humanly impossible without this gift of wisdom. Like wisdom, poverty and detachment are gifts, but once wisdom is received, all riches become as nothing in comparison with it.

Using the words of Jesus, St. Mark in today's passage teaches his Christians the dangers of wealth but also the dangers of any attachment to earthly things. Those who want to follow the Lord must rise above everything that is transient and set their heart on what abides. They cannot do this unless the Lord gives them his grace.

Too often, as we said above, texts like this are applied only to "religious life," but, in fact, they refer in the gospel to the life of every Christian. We must apply them to ourselves.

The Living Word of God (Heb 4:12-13)

There is always a danger that we may think of the word of God simply as the expression of concepts or ideas. In fact, however, the word of God is essentially something living and active. The writer of this letter expresses this aspect of God's word with the help of a striking image: the executioner's sword.

The Old Testament prophets have already made us familiar with the idea that the word is active and efficacious (see Isa 55:11). It is a power that brings salvation. The word always looks to our real selves; it is not deceived by appearances but lays all things bare. Christians are therefore urged to cultivate honesty in the presence of the word. The Liturgy of the Word is a time of judgment for them but also a time when they are helped to greater holiness and courage. We shall have to render an account of the word spoken to us.

Twenty-Ninth Sunday: The Life of Christ, a Ransom for Many

The Son of Man Gives His Life for Many (Mark 10:35-45)

In the immediately preceding scriptural title for this commentary on the pericope from Mark, I have deliberately omitted the words "as a ransom." I am not trying to emend the gospel. The fact is, however, that the expression "give his life as a ransom" needs to be provided with a context and explained accordingly if it is not to be misinterpreted. It is misinterpreted when the reader imagines a kind of exchange between God and humanity or a contract between God and the victim that he requires if he is to forgive sins. That kind of interpretation makes God's forgiveness conditional upon the death of a victim; it is consequently an insult to the mighty love of God. Yet the expression does suggest that kind of interpretation and therefore needs to be properly explained.

The petition of the sons of Zebedee seems both strange and bold. They already know that Christ must suffer, for he has predicted his passion three times already. Yet they seem quite determined: "we want you to do for us whatever we ask of you." The trouble is that though they want to share Jesus' lot, they want, in fact, to share only his glory and not the sufferings in store for him. (James and John were among the first four disciples whom Jesus called; traditionally, though without any proof, they have been regarded as relatives of Jesus.)

Jesus answers them, but in doing so he uses an unusual vocabulary, and his whole answer is couched in such a special way that some exegetes think that the episode and Jesus' answer were introduced later on as a postfactum prophecy of the martyrdom of James and

John. In any event, the other disciples are indignant at the two brothers for making such a request to Jesus.

Jesus does not answer their petition directly. He tries to make them understand more fully the painful reality of his passion, for they must endure it in their own way, just as he must. Jesus knows that they do not really understand what it is they are asking. He tells them they must drink the cup that he will drink. "Cup" is a frequent image in the Bible; thus, "the cup of wrath," "the cup of salvation," "the cup of blessing" were familiar expressions that pointed to a crucial moment in the life of an individual or a city.

On the other hand, the image of a "baptism" that Jesus must undergo and that his disciples must share would not have been familiar. In itself, the image might have the same content as the image of the cup: a baptism in suffering, an immersion in pain, under the wrathful hand of God. Psalm 109 speaks of a curse as penetrating like water (v. 18). In Psalm 42 the psalmist speaks of the waves and billows of God that pass over him (v. 8). If today's passage from Mark was indeed introduced into the gospel later on, as some exegetes suggest, we could relate this baptism to the forgiveness of sins through the passion of Jesus.

The sons of Zebedee persist in their request and claim that they are prepared to share in Jesus' sufferings. Even so, Jesus grants them only a share in his passion. The sharing in his glory depends not on him but on the Father who prepares places for people. People can only submit to his decisions.

The indignation of the other disciples gives Jesus an opportunity to give further teaching on authority and service. The other disciples are not as bold as the sons of Zebedee, but they doubtless had similar ambitions. Jesus therefore tells them what authority and service should mean for those who are his disciples. Among them, the attitudes of the world are turned upside down. Here authority is a form of service. The great people of the world make others feel the weight of their power; not so among the disciples. Among them, anyone wishing to be great will serve others, and the ones who wish to be first will make themselves the slave of everyone else. ("Servant" and "slave" are two words that mean pretty much the same thing here.)

We may think that this passage was important to Mark in the light of his Church's needs. He wants his Christians to think in terms of service rather than of authority and to realize that the service in question must be given to everyone in the community and will impose a kind of slavery on the servants, since they will be utterly at the disposal of all. No one can undertake such service by one's own unaided powers; it can be accomplished only by God's gift.

Even though there are degrees of service in the Church, with persons at each level putting their talents and gifts at the service of all, all the degrees together form a kind of body of slaves, dedicated to the service of the community at large. In undertaking such service, the disciples will simply be imitating what Christ does before them, for Christ took upon himself the condition of a slave (Phil 2:5-8). In today's pericope, Jesus sums up his situation with utmost clarity: "the Son of Man did not come to be served but to serve and to give his life as a ransom for many."

We can understand what "give his life as a ransom" means, and yet it sounds strange to us. Some theologians, as I indicated earlier, have gone so far as to postulate a kind of exchange: Jesus surrenders his life so that we might have life. Yet how horrible and even blasphemous seems the idea of a God who wishes that one should die as a ransom for sin and who demands this death as the means of liberating others! Certainly, when presented dryly and in bare form as we are presenting it here, this kind of trade seems not only repugnant but utterly unworthy of God and of human beings confronted with God. We must therefore avoid the words "as a ransom," while keeping the valid thought that the words contain.

If we are to understand the text correctly, we must turn to historical fact and not let ourselves be hampered by what may be simply a temporally conditioned image that reflects the social conditions of a country or even the larger world at a particular moment in time. Both the Old and the New Testaments are familiar with the theme of one who suffers and gives up life in exchange—as a ransom—for many. The first reading for today provides us with an example (Isa 53:10-11). The Synoptic Gospels (today's pericope, for example) use the theme, and St. Paul will develop it at length. The first Christian communities liked to think of Jesus as the Suffering Servant who gives his life as a ransom for many. In short, the ideas of redemption (buying back), ransom, and substitution occur frequently. The question is: do they express a theology, or are they simply images that try to approach the reality in a particular way?

In an unqualified form, the theology according to which Christ pays a ransom to God for us all by dying brings us very close to religious myth. It seems more suited to some ancient religion or other in which a god wants an expiatory human victim.

What are the historical facts? By this I mean: what happened in the life of Jesus? We must see his life, not through the spectacles of images, but as it really was. In reality, then, the entire life of Jesus was a struggle—not at the ideological level, but a concrete struggle against all that enslaves humanity, all the imbalances that have become like a second nature. The preaching and examples of Jesus were entirely a manifestation of his will to restore humankind to true freedom—a freedom from sin and guilt. More concretely, we see Jesus seeking to free people from the law. In what sense? Not by abolishing the law (he explicitly says that he does not wish to abolish it), but by showing that it is not per se the way to salvation. In so doing, he comes into conflict with the religious establishment of his country.

Jesus refuses to play the political game that is expected of him, for he refuses to let his mission be interpreted as a political restoration of the nation. Moreover, he refuses to let his mission and powers be co-opted for a political miracle that would bypass the responsibility of people and their free will. He refuses also to let people rest in an easy security in relation to God or to employ magic in their dealings with him. He demands, instead, true love of neighbor, forgiveness of others, humble charity, hidden prayer, and unostentatious austerity.

In all these ways Jesus disappoints and shocks others, and his death will be the outcome of his persistence in his ways. He dies as a prophet who has refused to cater to the desires of the people he teaches. He has disappointed them. Worse than that, he has done a disservice to the cause of well-ordered religion, its priestly caste, and its learned elite.

Jesus dies, and his death is especially meaningful and efficacious because it is a death endured for the sake of the forgiveness of sins. This forgiveness will free the many and lead them to a new life. We might try to bring out the basic direction of Jesus' life by saying that his passion began at his incarnation, for it was at that moment of entering the human condition that he deliberately accepted death. His death, his forgiveness ("Father, forgive them, they know not what they do"), and his resurrection—these mediate the salvation that God has intended for humankind from the beginning.

We must be careful not to put our theology into categories that are temporally and culturally conditioned. Can God in his anger require the death of a human being—his Son—so that others may thereby be ransomed? Does such an idea express a truly theological vision, or does it rather represent theology translated into the cultural language of a particular age?

Let us look for a moment at the Trinity. Does not the Father give himself to people, all of them, so that he may win them? He does not die himself, and his suffering at giving his Son is not identical with the suffering of the Son, but the Father does suffer at the death of the Son. When Jesus dies, we do not have the Father standing as a judge over against the Son who gives himself as a victim in place of all the others and pays on behalf of all the price the Father requires. No! Between Father and Son there is a perfect conformity of wills.

Perhaps John best expressed the point we are making when he wrote: "God so loved the world that he gave his only Son, so that everyone who believes in him might not perish but might have eternal life" (3:16). The same evangelist sees the mystery of the cross as a mystery of the love that is God's very being: "God is love" (1 John 4:16). God is love even at the moment of Jesus' death. At this moment, when Father and Son seem to be so utterly separated, they are, in fact, utterly united in a single love for the salvation of the world. Bloodshed and death are but the signs that express love; it is not the death that saves but that which the death expresses. Yet the death was needed precisely so that the love might find expression and convince the world of its reality.

If we go back now to the words "give his life as a ransom for many," we can see better what they mean, and we can without difficulty overlook the commercial overtones of a "swap" or exchange that the words would normally carry. In this context the words are an imaged way of expressing the reality of the love that the Father and the Son have for the world they wish to save. The Son has been sent into the world, and he dies in consequence of a deliberate attitude of obedient self-surrender that has been his throughout his earthly life. In his death he forgives us all, and in his resurrection he brings us all to victory with him. Thus he frees us all for eternal life.

The Servant Will Justify Many (Isa 53:10-11)

The preceding commentary will enable us to read this text from a Christian viewpoint. For an analysis we refer the reader to the commentary on the Good Friday liturgy.[16]

Jesus, the High Priest, Has Been Tested (Heb 4:14-16)

This reading has likewise already been read on Good Friday; a short commentary on it was given at that point.[17]

The readings of this Sunday require more than passive contemplation. They have consequences for the spiritual life of each individual. Like Christ, we must accept the consequences of our baptism, which puts us in clear opposition to the principles of the world. Baptism makes us strangers and pilgrims on earth, although it does not absolve us of our duty to be concerned about our world.

Like Christ, we are servants, and the more authority we may happen to have, the more we must make ourselves the servants of others. In our service, we must give our lives and we must forgive the offenses of all so that they may believe and live by what they believe. In fact, the thing we must communicate to others is that same desire to serve; then all will share in the kingdom. The divisions among us and the fight to get the first places in the Church are shameful and most unworthy. Each of us should seek to be where the Spirit wants us to be, according to the judgment of the Church. And wherever the Church puts us, she wants us to be servants of the Word, to the extent of sacrificing our lives for all.

Thirtieth Sunday: Messianic Signs and Faith

Lord, Let Me See! (Mark 10:46-52)

Jesus is on the road, moving toward Jerusalem. A sizable crowd follows him. Beside the road sits a blind man named Bartimaeus. These are the circumstances of a miracle that, like all the miracles of Jesus, is a sign that the Messiah is now present.

Jesus is moved to act by the blind man's faith-inspired cries: "Jesus, son of David, have pity on me." The crowd tries to silence him, for they find his cries embarrassing and almost indecent; they hardly sense the faith of the man, moving though it is. But Jesus is touched by it; he stops and has the blind man brought to him. His act is inspired by kindness, but he does not go to the man; rather, he has the man brought to him. His coming, even though he is led by the hand, is a personal act. The intensity of the man's faith can be seen by the way he throws off his mantle, leaps to his feet, and comes to Jesus.

The question Jesus asks seems odd. Why ask a blind man what he wants done for him when he cries out for pity? But just as Jesus wanted the man to come to him and thus prove his goodwill, so he wants the man to express his faith in Jesus in a clear way: "Master, I want to see." Jesus' response is immediate and unhesitating: "Go your way; your faith has saved you." The blind man receives his sight and follows Jesus on his way.

The Blind and the Lame Will Be Consoled (Jer 31:7-9)

This passage from Jeremiah was chosen for today's liturgy because it contains the words, "I will gather them . . . the blind and the lame. . . . They departed in tears, / but I will console them and guide them." But this compassion is simply one of the signs proving that "[t]he Lord has delivered his people, / the remnant of Israel." The blind and the lame as such have but a very secondary role in the passage; they are part of a great assembly of exiles returning from Babylon, to whom salvation is being offered. The "remnant" of Israel is returning from a foreign land, and Jeremiah lists the various categories of people found in their numbers. All these people went away in tears, but now they are returning amid consolation. The Lord ends his oracle with the words, "I am a father to Israel."

The responsorial psalm (Ps 126) is indeed a response to this reading, for it sings of the joyous return of the exiles: "Then the nations themselves said, 'What great deeds / the Lord worked for them!' / What great deeds the Lord worked for us! / Indeed, we were glad" (vv. 2-3).

The theme of this Sunday is a broad one. What profit can we draw from it? The cure of the blind man doubtless makes us think immediately of the light that God gives us, but the first reading does not lead us in the direction of such an interpretation. The following remarks may help us make a synthesis of the important points in the two readings.

In the order of salvation, everything depends on God taking the first step, for in the last analysis, it is he who saves. This was true for exiles whom he freed from Babylon; it was true for the blind man whom Jesus healed. God deliberately reaches out in his goodness and establishes contact with humanity.

At the same time, however, some movement of humanity toward God is also required. Thus the remnant of Israel obeys the call and journeys toward Jerusalem; even the blind, the lame, and the pregnant women take to the road. So too the blind Bartimaeus leaps up and moves toward the Lord. This movement is a sign of a deep faith;

in fact, the blind man has already been crying out so loudly that the crowd tries to silence him. On humanity's part, this kind of faith is the basic element unto salvation.

Salvation is not limited to some immediate, personal cure. The cure of the blind man is a messianic sign; that is, it is a sign of a final age that is still coming. The remnant of Israel journeys to Jerusalem, but that holy city is itself only a sign of an abiding city. In order to enter this abiding city, this ultimate age, people must be converted and must live by faith.

We must be on guard, then, not to stop short at immediate events as though they were an end in themselves. The cure of the blind man is not simply a goal but also a sign of the world to come. Neither must we stop short at the sacramental signs as though the sign were all; the sign is important because it helps us and our world toward the final day and the complete reconstruction of the world.

On this Sunday, therefore, we are urged to deepen our faith by directing it toward the abiding world that is on its way. Every grace we receive should lead us onward to this final day.

Jesus, a Priest Forever (Heb 5:1-6)

In this day and age, a reading on priesthood should not leave us indifferent but should provide an opportunity for clarifying our ideas on a subject that is part of our faith. The priesthood of the New Testament is radically different from that of the Old, not only because it is not hereditary, as the priesthood of Aaron was, but also because it comes through a new mediator, Christ.

"The order of Melchizedek" is only an analogy, and the priesthood of Christ, though prefigured by that of Melchizedek, also transcends it. Much that is said of the high priest in the Old Testament can be said of Christ, but Christ's priesthood is nonetheless fundamentally different: he is the one Priest and need not offer his sacrifice more than once. Because he is both Priest and Victim, he offers but once, and his sacrifice is perfect.

The priesthood given through ordination and the priesthood given through baptism are participations, essentially different among themselves in degree, in the one priesthood of Christ. The priesthood given through ordination is essentially distinguished by its Spirit-given power to make the past mysteries of Christ present and operative.

Thirty-First Sunday: The Great Commandment

No Greater Commandment Than Love of Others (Mark 12:28b-34)

In St. Matthew's account, the scribe's question was: "Teacher, which commandment in the law is the greatest?" The question was meant as a trap, for the Jews used to discuss among themselves which commandment might be said to sum up all the others (see page 160). In St. Mark's gospel, the same question takes a slightly different form, and we have less of a sense that the questioner is trying to entrap Jesus. In fact, the scribe who asks the question even admits that Jesus is right. For doing so, he receives praise and encouragement from Jesus: "You are not far from the kingdom of God."

In his answer, Jesus quotes a passage from the book of Deuteronomy (6:4) that speaks of loving God. It is chiefly in this book that the expression "love God" occurs in the Old Testament; it is less frequent in the other books, but it does occur (for example: Josh 22:5; 23:11; Ps 31:23; Sir 2:10; 7:32). Even the word "love" is quite infrequent, for the Old Testament prefers a related set of terms: fear of God, service of God, seeking the face of God, fidelity. In the passage from the book of Deuteronomy, love of God is linked to a monotheistic faith: "The LORD is our God, the LORD alone" (Deut 6:4). To this love of God, Jesus then adds love of neighbor as a commandment closely connected with it.

The response of the scribe to Jesus' answer is itself a teaching, for it tells us that love of neighbor is more important than offerings and sacrifices.

Jesus' final words are to be noted: "You are not far from the kingdom of God." They reflect Mark's preoccupation with the kingdom that has been proclaimed and is at hand. That kingdom is continually proclaimed when love of God and neighbor rules the community. Surely, that too is a lesson Mark wants his readers to take with them.

You Shall Love the Lord with All Your Heart (Deut 6:2-6)

This is the passage from which Jesus drew his answer to the scribe. It is such an important passage that it became part of the prayer *Shema' Israel*, which the devout Jew recites daily, even in our time. Since the Lord Jesus quoted the text to express a central point in his own teaching, it deserves our meditation; it is certainly also an important point of contact between Christianity and Judaism.

In the book of Deuteronomy, the Lord promises happiness if the Israelites observe the law he is about to give them. In the context, this happiness is doubtless the earthly happiness of Israel as a community. We should not look down our noses at this, since earthly happiness is a good thing, and no authentic spirituality can be totally unconcerned about it, to the extent that it does not become a stumbling block or make a person forget the happiness that will be lasting. This much is certainly true: the observance of the commandments of love for God and neighbor makes a community well balanced and creates in it an atmosphere that is relaxed and joyous.

The love commanded us is love of the one true God whom the text calls "our God." "Yahweh is our God" is a kind of liturgical acclamation that may have been used in various celebrations. Toward the fifth century BC, "Adonai" had become a favorite title for Yahweh; it was forbidden to pronounce the name "Yahweh," and "Adonai" was substituted for it, although the written text continues to read "Yahweh."[18] In the phrase "our God," Israel prayed to the God it regarded as its own special possession.

If the commandments are obeyed, God promises that the land will be fruitful, "flowing with milk and honey." In many countries, a newborn child used to be given some milk and honey; the practice was medicinal but also superstitious to some extent. According to the *Apostolic Tradition*, an adult neophyte received a drink of milk and honey at baptism as a reminder that the promises of God to the patriarchs had now been fulfilled.[19] It is easy to understand how a practice that already existed in handling newborn babies could be given a spiritual meaning and transferred to "newborn" Christians.

The responsorial psalm (Ps 18) sings of love for God. In fact, it is one of the relatively few psalms that uses the verb "love" with God for its object. "I love you, LORD, my strength; / O LORD, my rock, my fortress."

In our day the Church continues to remind the baptized of the fundamental principle on which her, and our, life is built. In our efforts to live by the principle of love for God and neighbor, we should draw strength from Jesus' response to the scribe: "You are not far from the kingdom of God." A community that puts into practice the love of God and neighbor is already an initial embodiment of God's rule.

The Eternal Priesthood of Christ (Heb 7:23-28)

The Letter to the Hebrews continues its teaching on the priesthood (see last Sunday for its beginning). Christ's priesthood is utterly unique, because while death prevented other priests from continuing in their office for ever, Christ lives eternally and has a priesthood that never ends. He lives always and is always making intercession for us.

His priesthood is unique for other reasons: he is holy and utterly without sin, and he therefore has no need to offer first for his own sins, then for the sins of others, and when he did offer for the sins of the people, he needed to do so only once in an offering of himself. Under the law of Moses, the high priests were weak men. In the new covenant, the Son has been brought to his perfection and has been appointed by the Father to be the one authentic High Priest.

Thirty-Second Sunday: Give What You Have to Obtain Life

The Poor Widow Has Given More Than All the Others (Mark 12:38-44)

Jesus calls his disciples to him in order to point out the hidden value of the widow's action. The crowd that passes by and puts money into the treasury is contrasted with the humble widow: many in the crowd make their contribution ostentatiously, while she is simply embarrassed that she can give so little, even though it is all she has.

Today's gospel begins with Jesus' warning against the scribes, who are so preoccupied with wearing distinctive garments and with getting the first places. The contrast between these men and the widow brings out once again the importance of the interior religion that God finds pleasing and acceptable. The lesson was an important one for Mark's Christian community. St. Luke recounts the same incident, for he too thinks it useful to his readers. In order to make the contrast even stronger, Luke omits mention of the crowd and sets the rich men and the widow side by side (Luke 21:1-4).

All these others gave of their abundance; the poor widow gave all that she had.

The Widow Gives What Food She Has (1 Kgs 17:10-16)

As we saw earlier, widows are regarded in Scripture as the special targets of social injustice; they exemplify misfortune and poverty in all its forms. In today's reading, two exemplars of poverty meet: a widow and the prophet Elijah.

In the story, the widow is inspired by faith ("As the LORD, your God, lives . . .") to give what she has to the prophet. The miracle is then performed, because the widow has such faith and because she has given, not any extra food, but the last food she possessed.

The responsorial psalm (Ps 146) reminds us that the Lord "does justice to those who are oppressed . . . gives bread to the hungry . . . upholds the orphan and the widow, but thwarts the path of the wicked."

The Church and the faithful are being urged on this day to examine themselves on two points. The first is their generosity as inspired by faith. All the faithful are members of one Body, and all belong to Christ; their generosity should be inspired by a faith that rises above all calculating attitudes. The second point is that they should be so detached from their possessions that they are ready to give even their necessities, if this is necessary in order to save others. This is the kind of openness and readiness that should characterize a community that truly belongs to the Lord.

Today's gospel also reminds us of the interior dimension in every Christian's life. God's value judgments are not always the same as those of people; he knows people's hearts and can judge them perfectly. It is the intention and manner of giving, not its material value, that makes a gift precious in his sight. Once again, Jesus and the evangelists are calling us to a religion of Spirit and truth.

The Unique Sacrifice of Christ (Heb 9:24-28)

This passage throws important light on both the sacrifice of Christ and the eucharistic celebration. The writer first underscores the superiority of Christ's sacrifice over all others: our earthly sanctuaries are made by humans and are but imitations of the true sanctuary— heaven—into which Christ entered in order that he might stand before God and intercede for us. He is our perpetual intercessor.

Christ was able to enter this heavenly sanctuary because he had a sacrifice to offer. It was a perfect and utterly unique sacrifice: it did not have to be offered anew, because Christ was offering his own blood, not another's. Nor did he have to suffer his passion over and over again, but he offered his sacrifice once and for all, because it was a perfect sacrifice. He will appear a second time, not to offer sacrifice for sin, but to take to himself all those who await his coming.

This unique and infinitely valuable sacrifice of Christ does not prevent the Eucharist from being a true sacrifice. Christ willed that we should offer the Eucharist in memory of him. But this remembering is not simply a psychological act; it is a rendering present and operative of the one historical sacrifice. That sacrifice is rendered present so that the Church and each of the baptized may offer it with Christ, who is always interceding for them. To "renew" the sacrifice of the cross is not to begin it again (it was offered once and for all) but to render it present, in accordance with Christ's own will, so that we may actively share in it.

Thirty-Third Sunday: The Last Days

The Elect, Gathered from the Four Quarters of the World
(Mark 13:24-32)

This and similar passages from the gospel are bound to prove disconcerting to a modern listener. They are so alien to our way of thinking and speaking, and their images are so naïve and fantastic, that we can hardly keep from thinking that we are listening to an unusual poem or to a vision of some gigantic catastrophe as conceived by a genius of the theater. There is danger, then, that the gospel pericope and the passage from the book of Daniel may have no effect on us and that their teaching may pass us by.

There are other difficulties. The exegetes debate the authenticity of the passage in the gospel. More specifically, they ask to what extent the evangelists, especially St. Mark, expanded a teaching that Jesus may well have given in a less imaginative form and perhaps with greater brevity. We shall not explain the various hypotheses that have been constructed, especially since no one of them can claim wide acceptance. It seems clear at least that here, as in other passages, the evangelists have used the teaching of Jesus to meet the needs of their Churches; they have not invented the teaching, but while leaving its substance untouched, they have expanded it and put it into a new framework.

It is difficult, if not impossible, to imagine that we can now determine with certainty all the phrases and expressions that come from Jesus himself. But when everything is said and done, this whole problem should not disturb us. We accept that the evangelists were divinely inspired and that this means not that they were automatons in writing their gospels but rather that the Holy Spirit is responsible for the teaching of Jesus conveyed in writing to later generations.

Since our interest here is not literary, there is no point in examining the details of the description. We may, however, dwell briefly on a few expressions.

"They will see 'the Son of Man coming in clouds' with great power and glory." This description is taken from the book of Daniel (7:13). How does the gospel interpret and make use of this passage from the prophet? In Daniel's vision, beasts are contrasted with "a son of man," who belongs to a transcendent, divine world (although he cannot be further identified). The beasts represent the various world empires that must collapse and give way to the kingdom of God. After Daniel, the symbol of "a son of man" continues to be used but with even greater emphasis on his transcendence. Finally, the expression, transformed now from "a son of man" to "the Son of Man," enters the gospels. We know that Jesus applies the title to himself (Matt 5:11; Luke 6:22; Matt 16:13-21; Mark 8:27-31). According to the Acts of the Apostles, the dying Stephen has a vision of Jesus as the Son of Man (7:55), and in Revelation, the figure of "Son of Man" appears again (Rev 1:12-16; 14:14). For Jesus, the Son of Man is evidently a person— himself!—who gives his life to ransom many (Mark 10:45).

"He will . . . gather his elect from the four winds, from the end of the earth to the end of the sky." According to Jewish belief, all the Jews of the world would be assembled in their own country. The gospel refers rather to all the baptized, who make up the new kingdom. The same image will recur in the *Didache*, a Jewish-Christian writing.[20]

"Amen, I say to you, this generation will not pass away until all these things have taken place." There will be preliminary signs. Here the fig tree serves as a parable from nature. Are its branches becoming tender and is it putting forth leaves? Then we know the summer is at hand. Similarly, when the predicted signs occur, we will know that the Son of Man is at hand. "All these things": the reference is not quite clear; perhaps what is meant is the phenomena described earlier in this chapter, including the destruction of the temple.

"This generation" would literally mean the generation contemporary with the evangelist, but the reference is nonetheless quite vague. For the first Christians, "this generation" included their Jewish contemporaries and the culture that would vanish with the temple, the destruction of the latter being a sign of God's judgment. And yet the parousia in its totality was still in the future; Christians awaited it, but its date was not known. Besides, Jesus himself had said, "But of that day or hour, no one knows, neither the angels in heaven, nor the Son, but only the Father." (This text has its own difficulties. How can the Son be ignorant of what the Father knows, especially since, as Jesus himself says, no one knows the Father but the Son? The exegetes solve this difficulty by distinguishing between the Son in his divine nature and the Son as incarnate, who, in his human nature, did not know the day or the hour.)

What this pericope and the whole of chapter 13 presents us with is an attempt of the evangelist to explain the parousia to his community and to awaken both a desire for it and an attitude of deliberate expectancy.

He Comes to Save His People (Dan 12:1-3)

The first verse describes, in very general terms, a time of catastrophe. Yet it is at that moment that salvation will come to the people, a salvation that Daniel describes as coming in the form of judgment and resurrection. The dead will awaken, some to eternal life, others to eternal shame and contempt. Among the blessed, those with insight and the teachers of uprightness will shine like the stars in the firmament. Daniel is once again asserting here an individual resurrection and retribution for humanity's deeds in this life. This is a theology that is as yet novel in Judaism; it will be accepted and taken over by the New Testament.

The responsorial psalm (Ps 16) says: "you will not abandon my soul to hell, / nor let your holy one see corruption" (v. 10). In these words the psalmist provides the lesson of this Sunday. Our attention should not be absorbed by the frightening details of a great catastrophe; instead, the joy that is to come on the last day should inspire us to hope.

Christians today do not think enough about the parousia, or second coming of Christ; we tend to reflect exclusively on our death and our appearance before the judgment seat of God. This is because we are not sufficiently conscious that we belong to a kingdom that must someday enter its final and definitive state. This does not mean, of course, that we should be uninterested in our individual, personal salvation; it means only that we should view this in the perspective of the final and all-embracing passage of this world to its final state and condition at the last judgment.

The "last judgment" is in any case more than simply a judgment and should not be approached purely in a spirit of fear lest we be punished. It is also God's great act of reconstruction, and we can be sure that God will produce something unimaginably new and great. The Christian expectation of final redemption should take the form of a lively, joyous hope of that great act of reconstruction.

The eucharistic celebration is a pledge that Christ is coming again and that then the new and lasting world will begin. It is also the efficacious power that causes the world to reach its maturity and thus hastens the coming of the end. Every time we celebrate the Eucharist, we await Christ's coming and advance further toward the moment when the regime of sacramental signs will pass away and we will see him face-to-face. This whole spiritual outlook has unfortunately been so much forgotten that we even find it difficult to understand many a passage of Scripture. We tend to wrap ourselves up in a somewhat fearful expectation of our own death and fail to connect our lot with that of the whole Church journeying toward the meeting with the Lord.

Having Offered His Sacrifice, Jesus Leads to Perfection Those He Has Sanctified (Heb 10:11-14, 18)

The doctrine of Christ's one sacrifice and its limitless efficacy continues to be the writer's theme. His point of departure is a comparison with the sacrifices of the Old Testament. The repeated sacrifices of the old law could not remove sin, and the priest was forced to stand daily at the altar. Christ offered but one sacrifice and now sits at the right hand of God. The writer is continuing the line of thought we met last Sunday.

There is one statement, however, in today's passage that deserves our attention: "by one offering he has made perfect forever those who are being consecrated." Does such a statement apply to us, when we have daily experience of our own weakness? The answer is that we understand the writer to be speaking of what Christ accomplished in principle by his sacrifice. That is to say, he has created a situation in which it is possible for us to be perfect, but we must enter into that situation and lay hold of the gift offered.

There is, then, a tension at the heart of all Christian life: Christians are already made holy, and yet they must be constantly striving for the holiness offered them. Consequently, though Christ offered but one sacrifice, our weakness requires that it be constantly made present and operative in our lives. There is no need of another sacrifice for the forgiveness of sins, but Christ himself willed that his own sacrifice be made present to us and, with it, his forgiveness.

Our Lord Jesus Christ, King of the Universe: Christ's Rule over the Universe

As You Say, I Am a King (John 18:33b-37)

The scene is the praetorium, where Pilate is questioning Jesus. We can sense that Pilate is interested in, and even disturbed by, this man who stands before him; he is asking himself who this man may really be. We need not read irony into his question: "Are you the King of the Jews?" Jesus alludes quietly to the inner disturbance Pilate feels: "Do you say this on your own or have others told you about me?"

Jesus does not intend to hide his true rank any longer; he picks up Pilate's words and applies them to himself. But Pilate may still not see his claim correctly. Christ's kingship is of the spiritual order, not the political. His royal authority is spiritual and comes from God; his kingdom does not originate in this world but is given to him by the Father.

Pilate may think of Jesus as a political king, but he is wrong; he is right, however, in saying that Jesus is a king, even if of a different order than Pilate realizes. The exercise of Jesus' kingship consists in bearing witness to the truth. "Truth" here does not mean a philosophy; it means eternal reality, the reality of God himself, as contrasted with transient things. Jesus has been sent to give people the eternal reality that will set them free from the guilt of sin. That is the essential object of the revelation for the sake of which he has become human.

This scene from Jesus' trial is marked by paradox. Pilate acts as judge of Jesus; in reality, Jesus is Pilate's judge. He is the true King and Judge, because he frees people or condemns them, depending on whether or not they accept his testimony about divine truth.

To Him Was Given Dominion and Glory and Kingship (Dan 7:13-14)

In this passage the prophet presents the Lord as the Judge of the last times. For us, this symbolic personage—the son of man who comes before the Ancient of Days—is Jesus the Messiah. We see him exercising dominion and power as the glorious King of all nations and peoples. His rule is eternal and will never be abolished. "The LORD is king, with majesty enrobed. / The LORD has robed himself with might" (Ps 93).

Ruler of Kings on Earth (Rev 1:5-8)

We pass here from the apocalypse of Daniel to the Apocalypse of the Apostle John. In it Christ is presented as King, while in his kingdom we are the priests of God his Father.

The passage is a doxology, a hymn to the King who has freed us from our sins by his own blood and who now gives us his peace. He is the firstborn of the dead and guarantees our resurrection as well. He is the ruler of earthly kings, and now all acknowledge him, the one they pierced, to be their sovereign Lord.

Christ's paschal mystery has borne its fruit, for he has established a kingdom of priests to serve the Father and glorify him. He has established a great kingdom in which all praise the Lord as the Alpha and the Omega.

Today's liturgy in its entirety conveys a vision of glory. Yet unless we are careful, it may lead us astray. When Jesus admitted to Pilate that he was a king, he meant that he was a king very unlike any earthly king. He does not free nations, as a political king might. Pilate might mistake Jesus' meaning; so might we. But then, even the apostles mistook it! On the very day of the ascension they asked him, "Lord, are you at this time going to restore the kingdom to Israel?" (Acts 1:6)! It is not surprising, then, that during his earthly life the crowd should have wanted him for their king (John 6:15).

If Jesus is a king, then all Christians belong to a royal race. How easy then to argue: Every Christian is a brother or sister of Christ and a ruler; the Church is Christ's people and therefore of royal stature; therefore, the Christian and the Church deserve social privileges.

It is indeed possible, even if not in such a crass way, to transform Christ's spiritual kingship into a very earthly and transient type of kingship. But, in fact, our kingship is one of service; every Christian and the Church in her entirety belong to a truly privileged kingdom and therefore have no concern for temporary privileges. Their sole function is to bear witness to the truth, for their royal rank comes to them precisely as messengers of an eternal kingship and kingdom. They bear witness to the King who frees people from the bondage to sin in which even earthly kings and political rulers live.

On the other hand, the spiritual character of this kingship and the fact that Jesus had no interest in political power do not mean that the Church is to live, as it were, apart from the world and cultivate a spiritualist lack of interest in the life of our contemporaries. No, the very fact that Christ is a king forces all who are engaged in the political order to become aware of the ultimate goal that all politics must serve. The true relationship would be stood on its head if we thought that, because Christ is a king, the Church must have political authority in this world! The Church has been tempted at times to confuse the kingship of Christ with an earthly kingship, when in fact Christ's kingship should have led her to remind earthly kings of the limitations and true purpose of their transient power.

It will always be necessary for the Church to study anew the impact Christ's kingship should have on this world. She is not to seek domination herself but rather always to encourage as best she can the concrete efforts being made to liberate the weak and the oppressed. The Church honors Christ's kingship not by seeking any form of earthly supremacy but by encouraging those engaged in the political order to keep ever before them the one, true, eternal King and his eternal rule.

Year C

TABLE OF SUNDAY READINGS

In the following table, the general theme of each celebration and the particular theme of each reading are indicated. If the second reading is connected with the general theme of the day, it will be commented on together with the first reading and the gospel (these second readings are marked by an asterisk in the following list). If the second reading does not fit with the theme of the day, a heavy line separates the commentary given from the preceding.

Year C		
Sunday 2	*Marriage*	
	John 2:1-11	The marriage at Cana
	Isa 62:1-5	The marriage of Jerusalem
	1 Cor 12:4-11	The same Spirit distributes all gifts
Sunday 3	*The Word of God Proclaimed to All Peoples*	
	Luke 1:1-4; 4:14-21	He has anointed me to preach good news to the poor
	Neh 8:2-4a, 5-6, 8-10	Listening to the word of God
	1 Cor 12:12-30	The body and the members
Sunday 4	*A Prophet Speaks to the World*	
	Luke 4:21-30	God speaks to the world
	Jer 1:4-5, 17-19	A prophet to the nations
	1 Cor 12:31–13:13	Charity, the greatest of the three

Sunday 5	*Messengers of God*	
	Luke 5:1-11	From now on you will be catching people
	Isa 6:1-2a, 3-8	Here I am; send me!
	*1 Cor 15:1-11	The message of faith
Sunday 6	*Blessings and Curses*	
	Luke 6:17, 20-26	Blessed are you poor. Woe to you who are rich
	Jer 17:5-8	Authentic riches and security
	1 Cor 15:12, 16-20	If there is no resurrection, our faith is in vain
Sunday 7	*Be Merciful*	
	Luke 6:27-38	Be merciful as God is to us
	1 Sam 26:2, 7-9, 12-13, 22-23	Spare your enemy
	1 Cor 15:45-49	We shall bear the image of the heavenly one
Sunday 8	*The Word and the Heart*	
	Luke 6:39-45	The true disciple
	Sir 27:4-7	The word and the heart
	1 Cor 15:54-58	God gives us the victory through Christ
Sunday 9	*Faith Is Answered*	
	Luke 7:1-10	The faith of a foreigner
	1 Kgs 8:41-43	The prayer of a foreigner in the temple
	Gal 1:1-2, 6-10	Either serve Christ or please people
Sunday 10	*The Gift of Life*	
	Luke 7:11-17	I say to you, arise
	1 Kgs 17:17-24	See, your son lives
	Gal 1:11-19	To preach your son among the Gentiles

Sunday 11	Sin Forgiven	
	Luke 7:36–8:3	Forgiveness and love
	2 Sam 12:7-10, 13	The Lord has put away your sin
	Gal 2:16, 19-21	Christ lives in me
Sunday 12	The Suffering Messiah and Savior	
	Luke 9:18-24	Take your cross and follow Christ
	Zech 12:10-11; 13:1	They shall look on him whom they have pierced
	*Gal 3:26-29	Clothed in Christ
Sunday 13	Follow without Delay	
	Luke 9:51-62	Do not look back
	1 Kgs 19:16b, 19-21	Leave everything
	Gal 5:1, 13-18	Called to freedom
Sunday 14	Joy and Peace	
	Luke 10:1-12, 17-20	Joy springing from mission
	Isa 66:10-14c	The joy and peace of the messianic age
	Gal 6:14-18	Bear in your body the marks of Jesus
Sunday 15	The Law of Love	
	Luke 10:25-37	Who is my neighbor?
	Deut 30:10-14	Live by the word of God
	Col 1:15-20	All things were created through Christ and for him
Sunday 16	God Visits Us	
	Luke 10:38-42	Receive Jesus in your house
	Gen 18:1-10a	God comes and fulfills his promise
	Col 1:24-28	The mystery hidden and revealed
Sunday 17	Ask and You Shall Receive	
	Luke 11:1-13	Learn to pray
	Gen 18:20-32	Pray tirelessly against all hope
	Col 2:12-14	Buried and risen with Christ

Sunday 18	The Passing and the Abiding	
	Luke 12:13-21	Rich in God's sight
	Eccl 1:2; 2:21-23	Leaving one's possessions to an unknown
	*Col 3:1-5, 9-11	Seek the things that are above
Sunday 19	Be Ready to Receive God's Glory	
	Luke 12:32-48	Be ready
	Wis 18:6-9	Called to glory
	*Heb 11:1-2, 8-19	Look for the city of God
Sunday 20	Signs to Be Contradicted	
	Luke 12:49-53	Violence for the sake of the kingdom
	Jer 38:4-6, 8-10	The prophet, a person of discord
	*Heb 12:1-4	Hostility from sinners
Sunday 21	The Whole World at the Feast in the Kingdom	
	Luke 13:22-30	The last will be first
	Isa 66:18-21	Gather all nations
	Heb 12:5-7, 11-13	To correct is a sign of love
Sunday 22	Humble Yourself, and You Will Be Exalted	
	Luke 14:1, 7-14	The one who exalts oneself will be humbled
	Sir 3:17-18, 20, 28-29	Humble yourself and find favor with God
	Heb 12:18-19, 22-24a	You have approached Jesus, Mediator of a new covenant
Sunday 23	Be Free, and Understand the Lord	
	Luke 14:25-33	Renounce your possessions and become a disciple
	Wis 9:13-18b	Wisdom enables us to understand God's will
	Phlm 9b-10, 12-17	Onesimus is to be treated as a brother, not as a slave

Sunday 24	The Lord's Forgiveness	
	Luke 15:1-32	Joy in heaven for a sinner's conversion
	Exod 32:7-11, 13-14	The Lord relents and does not punish his sinful people
	*1 Tim 1:12-17	Christ came to save sinners
Sunday 25	Mammon—Money	
	Luke 16:1-13	The service of God and money are incompatible
	Amos 8:4-7	Greed of the merchants
	1 Tim 2:1-8	Pray that everyone may be saved
Sunday 26	The False Security of the Rich	
	Luke 16:29-31	Final lot of the rich and the poor
	Amos 6:1a, 4-7	A corrupt civilization
	*1 Tim 6:11-16	Keep the Lord's commandments until he returns
Sunday 27	The Dynamism of Faith	
	Luke 17:5-10	The power of faith
	Hab 1:2-3; 2:2-4	The just one who is righteous because of faith shall live
	2 Tim 1:6-8, 13-14	Bear the hardship that the Gospel entails
Sunday 28	Gratitude to God	
	Luke 17:11-19	They have not returned to thank God
	2 Kgs 5:14-17	Naaman returns to glorify God
	2 Tim 2:8-13	We have died with Christ and shall live with him
Sunday 29	The Prayer of Faith	
	Luke 18:1-8	Pray unwearyingly and with faith
	Exod 17:8-13	The power of Moses' intercession
	2 Tim 3:14–4:2	Be inspired by the wisdom of Scripture and proclaim the word

Sunday 30	The Prayer of the Humble	
	Luke 18:9-14	The tax collector is justified by his humble prayer
	Sir 35:12-14, 16-18	The prayer of the humble pierces the clouds
	2 Tim 4:6-8, 16-18	Receive the reward of a winner
Sunday 31	The Compassion of a Loving God	
	Luke 19:1-10	The Son of Man has come to seek out and save what was lost
	Wis 11:22–12:2	The lengthy patience of God, who urges people to conversion
	2 Thess 1:11–2:2	The Lord Jesus, glorified in us
Sunday 32	The God of Life	
	Luke 20:27-38	All receive life from God in the world to come
	2 Macc 7:1-2, 9-14	Raised up for eternal life
	2 Thess 2:16–3:5	The Lord is faithful; he strengthens us and protects us from evil
Sunday 33	The Day of the Lord	
	Luke 21:5-19	Persevere through suffering so as to obtain life on the Day of the Lord
	Mal 3:19-20a	The Day of the Lord, a blazing oven for the wicked, a sun of justice for the good
	2 Thess 3:7-12	Earn your own bread
Our Lord Jesus Christ, King of the Universe	A Crucified King	
	Luke 23:35-43	Jesus crucified, remember me when you come as King
	2 Sam 5:1-3	David, anointed as shepherd and king of Israel
	*Col 1:12-20	In the kingdom of the beloved Son

Second Sunday: Marriage

The Marriage at Cana (John 2:1-11)

The wedding at Cana has already played a part in the Liturgy of the Hours for the feast of the Epiphany, but the approach to the event is different in the present Mass. The main point, of course, is always the same: Jesus' self-manifestation through his first miracle, which is a "type" of the Eucharist.

In this Mass, however, the first reading, as we shall see, provides a context that requires us to take a somewhat broader view of the Cana event. The first reading too is concerned with a marriage (Isa 62:1-5). This does not mean that we are to think of Jesus' action at Cana as being simply a blessing of human marriage. Cana, like the multiplication of the loaves, represents a proclamation of the messianic banquet, which is often compared to a wedding feast. The messianic banquet presupposes a new world, a new wine, a new love, and the new people of God made one in the joy of the kingdom.

We may leave aside the scene itself, though the description of it possesses high literary quality and presents certain difficulties, such as Christ's attitude to his mother: "Woman, how does your concern affect me?" (John 2:4). The important thing for us here is the sign motif: Jesus "revealed his glory" (2:11). The thought is a continuation of the Prologue: "And the Word became flesh / and made his dwelling among us / . . . we saw his glory" (1:14).

The messianic banquet, as we indicated, is often represented as a marriage feast. This is true of the Synoptic Gospels. The book of Revelation speaks of "the wedding day of the Lamb" (19:7). We should note, in this context, that the wedding at Cana took place "on the third day" (John 2:1), that is, on the same day on which Christ later manifested his glory through his resurrection. This wedding feast, therefore, is the wedding feast of the triumphant Christ who came among us and showed the glory that he acquired by shedding his blood and that is still present among us in the Eucharist. He will give us a share in that glory at the wedding feast that is the eschatological banquet at the end of time, when he shall bring all together in love.

The Marriage of Jerusalem (Isa 62:1-5)

The theme of this very beautiful poem is the new creation: Jerusalem will be renewed. The notion of glory runs through it: "All kings [shall behold] your glory" (v. 2); "You shall be a glorious crown in the hand of the LORD" (v. 3). For the poem is proclaiming the messianic age, the time when the successful covenant will be celebrated by a marriage. The poet quite naturally uses marriage symbolism:

the Lord who has rebuilt Jerusalem will marry her. We think immediately of Revelation: "I also saw the holy city, a new Jerusalem, coming down out of heaven from God, prepared as a bride adorned for her husband" (Rev 21:2).

Later in this same passage from Revelation we read that "the old order has passed away" (21:4). It is the time now for wine, not for water; for covenant, not for division. It is the time, not for the forsaken spouse, but for her who is "My Delight," the city which her Spouse, the divine Architect, will rebuild.

Do we find this Mass rather "mystical" and rather far removed from our situation and concerns? I personally do not think the impression is justified; I would say rather that the readings penetrate to the very heart of our problems. For in the last analysis, what we look for, especially today, is a renewal, a new wine, a new world, a renewed love, a transformation of our age. We look for it, and we have a right to look for it; unfortunately, we often go about our looking in the wrong way and end up confusing what should be kept distinct.

The newness we should be looking for is first and foremost our own interior renewal, the new human who comes into being through baptism and the Spirit. We were once water, now we are wine and are judged worthy of the wedding feast. The bride can now be reunited to her Spouse; she is no longer forsaken but the beneficiary of the eternal covenant in the blood of the Lamb whose marriage we celebrate. We are being invited, then, to meditate on this renewal of ourselves, of our institutions, and of everything around us, but we must bear in mind that the renewal will come in its fullness only at the wedding feast on the last day.

The Same Spirit Distributes All Gifts (1 Cor 12:4-11)

No one can prevent political positions, sociological choices, and the laws of anthropology from having their repercussions and exerting their influence even in the Church. St. Paul was probably faced with a kind of "democratic spirit" that did not grasp the deeper meaning of ministries in the Church.

The distribution of these ministries does not point primarily to a hierarchy of officials who may argue about their relative dignity, nor is the distribution primarily a juridical matter. Ministries, on the contrary, are gifts given to certain persons for the service of the whole

community. The bestowal of a ministry is not primarily a legal inves-
titure and a handing over of authoritarian powers. Rather, each minister, depending on rank and office, is to be a mediator and distributor
of gifts to others. In the Church, all offices are ministries or services.

St. Paul here lists some functions that correspond to particular gifts.
He then insists that these gifts have been distributed according to
God's will, that they all come from the same Holy Spirit, and that
they are all given in order to form the one people of God.

The conciliar documents on the Church, the bishops, the priests,
and the laity pay a good deal of attention to the different ministries
and roles. There is need to avoid not only clericalism but a false democratic approach as well. For example, in the liturgical celebration a
great effort must be made to bring out the unity of all who make up
the assembly, but this end is not to be achieved by giving everyone a
uniform and identical role. It is not to be achieved by leaving the
congregation uncertain about who the celebrant is or by preventing
him from assuming his role in accordance with the teaching of St. Paul
in today's passage from the First Letter to the Corinthians.

The celebrant's function, which must be brought out liturgically
by insignia and by the place he occupies, is not primarily hierarchic,
indicating superiority; it is ontological. That is, the entire ascending
activity of the assembly and the entire descending activity of God
necessarily pass through the celebrant. Christ is the primary celebrant
of the liturgy, and the priest represents him. Not to understand this
and to obscure what should be a visible ministry because of the democratic feeling in this or that place is not progress but confusion. We
must accept that the Spirit distributes his gifts to each individual as
he chooses but always for the service of all.

Third Sunday: The Word of God Proclaimed to All Peoples

He Has Anointed Me to Preach the Good News to the Poor
(Luke 1:1-4; 4:14-21)

On this Third Sunday in Year C we begin the reading of St. Luke's
gospel, and by a happy choice the Prologue has been included. A
happy choice, because the Prologue tells us how the evangelist conceived his mission of writing a gospel.

His main concern is clear: the events he is to narrate represent, to
some extent, a break with the past, but they are first and foremost a

fulfillment, since in them what the prophets foretold has been accomplished. Luke is not the first to have written down the message received from Jesus. He is well aware of this, and yet he thinks it necessary that he in his turn should put it in writing for the sake of his local community.

We know, to some extent, the problem that his Church was facing. Luke was writing around 70, and the Acts of the Apostles, which is also his work, enables us to put our finger on his basic concern. Chapter 11 of the Acts of the Apostles shows us the struggle going on between Peter and the Jewish Christians who were finding it difficult to accept the admission of Gentiles to baptism and the Church. By the time Luke was writing, specific positions had been taken, such as those of the Council of Jerusalem (Acts 15),* but this did not mean that the problem had been completely resolved.

People continued to ask about the importance of the Jewish law for the Christian. Jewish Christians continued to attend the temple while also celebrating the breaking of bread. But what of the Gentiles who were entering the Church? Furthermore, if the Church were not to see in Judaism the work of the Lord who had now himself come upon the scene of the world in order to save humankind, would she not be introducing a break pure and simple into the plan of God? Must she not safeguard at any price the unity of the divine plan that was continuing in the New Testament and the Church? The continuous reading of St. Luke's gospel will show that the evangelist's concerns were still keenly felt. The problem he faced in his apostolate was not yet wholly resolved.

Nonetheless, at the beginning of his gospel, Luke asserts the continuity of the Old and New Testaments. He also asserts a transition, although he does not go so far as to call it a complete break with the past.

The passage chosen for today jumps now from the Prologue to the latter part of chapter 4 and to Christ as predicted by the prophet Isaiah. Before we continue with the text, however, it will be helpful to recall briefly what we know about the synagogal liturgy. (In point of fact, we project the synagogal liturgy of the time of Jesus chiefly through the liturgy of our own time and through partial reconstructions.) The liturgy was quite simple in form: first came the word of God and then

* This was not an ecumenical "council" in the sense of a gathering like Vatican II.

the prayer of the congregation. It is the same scheme that we find in chapter 67 of St. Justin's *First Apology*: reading of the prophets and the apostolic writings followed by the prayers of the people.

The later evolution of the synagogal liturgy parallels that of the Roman liturgy: now the service begins with preparatory prayers; after these come the readings. We should note that in the synagogue the Law was read first and then the Prophets. It is to this sequence that Jesus frequently alludes when he speaks of "the law and the prophets."

In our passage today, Jesus attends the synagogue; when the time for the reading from the Prophets comes, he is offered the book. He reads the assigned passage and then, as was customary, comments on it; this was the original pattern of the synagogal liturgy.

The decisive moment, of course, comes when Jesus proclaims that the passage he has read is now fulfilled: "Today this Scripture passage is fulfilled in your hearing" (4:21). He knows that it is of him that the prophet was speaking, and therefore he declares that he himself is the long-awaited Messiah. He has been anointed and sent to preach good news to the poor. The prophecy of Isaiah goes on to list the signs by which the Messiah's coming can be recognized; they are the signs of which John the Baptist is told as he lies in prison. Here, in a solemn manner, during the liturgy of the word in the synagogue, Jesus asserts that the prophecy is fulfilled in himself.

Luke, then, while placing his main emphasis on the coming of the Messiah and the inauguration of a new age, also links this event to the past; in other words, he writes both as historian and as theologian. He has his sources—the entire Christian tradition—and makes perhaps a fuller use of them than the other evangelists do. But he does not write simply as a historian. After all, Theophilus, for whom he writes, already knows a good deal; but it is not enough for him simply to know; he must also make the full commitment of faith. It is to help Theophilus achieve that goal that St. Luke writes his gospel. It is consistent with this that the evangelist is not writing for Theophilus alone or even for Christians alone; he knows that many, including Gentiles, will read his gospel, and that is what he wants.

The prophecy of Isaiah is actualized every time it is read in the Christian assembly of our own day, and everyone who hears it hears it as actualized, according to the role he or she plays in the Church. Each bishop, priest, and deacon hears his own missionary vocation in the Church set before him; so does each Christian, for the prophetic vocation of every Christian must not be forgotten, since it is part of one's commitment to the faith and the Gospel.

Listening to the Word of God (Neh 8:2-4a, 5-6, 8-10)

The first reading is taken, not from Isaiah whom Jesus reads in the gospel, but from the book of Nehemiah, in which we hear of God's word being proclaimed. The choice of this reading is an indication to us that in today's liturgy the emphasis is on the actualization of the word and on the work of proclaiming it rather than on the designation of the person who is to speak it. In the passage from the book of Nehemiah, it is the Torah, or "law" (really, "instruction"), that is being read and that will always be the main focus of the synagogal liturgy. Read the whole ritual as described in Nehemiah and you will see the origin of the Jewish synagogal liturgy as well as of our own Liturgy of the Word.

According to the passage, the people stand to hear the word of God; after it has been read, it is translated so that all may understand, and then a commentary on it is provided. The passage notes that the people weep as they listen to the words of the law, for these words are so many signs of God's love for his people. The whole day was given over to the Lord who spoke to his people, and it was a day of joy.

The responsorial psalm, from Psalm 19, emphasizes the power of God's word: "The law of the LORD is perfect; / it revives the soul" (v. 8). Further on, praise turns into petition: "May the spoken words of my mouth, / the thoughts of my heart, / win favor in your sight, O LORD, / my rock and my redeemer" (v. 15).

Today's liturgy is an invitation to us, early on in Ordinary Time, to meditate on the importance of the proclamation of God's word. This proclamation is like a constantly renewed confirmation of our calling and an active reminder of what we are and must become. We are to listen to the word in faith and pass it on to others.

The Body and the Members (1 Cor 12:12-30)

Paul is seeking to restore some order and, above all, a sense of unity in the church of Corinth, which seems to have been a very lively but also a somewhat troubled place. He seeks to achieve his purpose with the help of the image of a human body. Once he has presented his paradigm, the practical applications become obvious, and his readers will know what they must do if they wish to be true to themselves as Christians.

With the passage of time, however, Paul's paradigm has lost the power it had when he first used it. We must even say that in our day it can serve as only a partial image of the Church. At a very early time, by the third century, in fact, Church law began to develop, and "body" soon came to have juridical connotations. We are familiar today with professional groups that are "bodies," with a single head, the same laws for all, and the same purpose guiding all. The Church is likewise an institution with a single head, a code of law, and a goal. It is, however, more than an institution.

In order to get beyond the factors that would lessen the power of St. Paul's image, we must have recourse to St. John's gospel, chapter 17, where Christ, in his prayer to the Father, asks that "they may be one, as we are one" (v. 22). The word "united" still implies entities that are separate each from the other, whereas we Christians are not simply "united" (in that sense) but have become, through baptism, a single entity. This in no way destroys the personhood of each member: the Father and the Son are distinct Persons and yet they are also "one," a single Being.

The rich gifts bestowed on the community at Corinth should therefore not fragment the community or make its members jealous of one another. St. Paul lists the various gifts and ministries and gives the latter first place among the charisms. He sees no opposition between charism and hierarchy as far as ministries are concerned, since ministries are also charisms. It can even be said that he regards ministries as the most important charisms.

When there is an abundance of varied gifts, Christians, instead of thanking God for the variety of riches, may act so as to tear their communities apart. Pluralism in accidentals, if it is to work, always presupposes a very orthodox faith binding Christians together under, and in, a single Lord.

Fourth Sunday: A Prophet Speaks to the World

God Speaks to the World (Luke 4:21-30)

The passage chosen for today's gospel is hard on the Jews, and we can understand why it made the hearers angry. It is a condemnation of the chosen people for not receiving Jesus as a prophet. Also, all that he does is done for the sake of non-Jews. Like Elijah, he not only responds to the needs of an Israel that rejects him but turns to the Gentiles as well. Jesus has been sent to save, but the salvation is intended for the entire world and not just for the Jews. In fact, it is really not just his rejection by the Jews that convinces him to go to the Gentiles; his very mission is to proclaim salvation to all flesh (cf. Acts 2:17).

The drama being played out here is basic to the entire future of the Church. In reporting the scene in the synagogue at Nazareth, Luke really has in mind the Church's mission. Without giving up on the Jews, the Church had to free herself from her Jewish connections and put aside all nationalistic views so that she might preach the Good News to the entire known world. The Church had to speak to everyone. This was the challenge Paul faced: the Church must not limit herself to the Jewish people, who in any case refused to listen; the prophet's mission is to the world.

The Church has always understood the true nature of her mission, but she has not always found it easy to address the word of God to all nations. In doing it, she has sometimes imposed on various nations the lifestyle and thinking of an alien culture, with the result that the true point of the Christian mission was to some extent lost from view. When the Church has moved onto new terrain, her problem has always been to distinguish the essentials of the Gospel itself from the cultural forms with which she is already familiar. The Church faced this challenge at the very beginning, and she is still facing it today.

We become aware of the problem even as we study the life of Christ. Our study groups and prayer groups are always in danger of confusing the essential with the accidental and of therefore closing themselves off to others. Though the professed aim is to widen the boundaries of the Church, people actually cut themselves off from the Church at large, even in celebrations that should be most open to the universal Church, namely, celebrations of the Eucharist. People want to celebrate the Eucharist in a small group, but they forget that the legitimacy of the small group depends on a firm determination to create not an exclusive group of the "pure" but a living assembly to which every comer is welcome.[†]

[†] At Nocent's writing, small-group celebrations of the Mass were popular. In the twenty-first century some Sunday assemblies seem like small groups, and some Church leaders seem to prefer a smaller, like-minded Church.

Today, this particular gospel pericope has an importance that cannot be overemphasized. We must be open to all; we must not let the universal message be limited to some small group or other but rather preach the Good News everywhere; we must proclaim it to the world at large by trying to distinguish clearly between its essentials and the cultural form that a particular nation or civilization has developed. Salvation is for all—that is what the Savior is insisting on in this passage. If we close our minds and hearts to this truth, salvation may be given only to others, for we may keep the grace of the Lord from entering us.

A Prophet to the Nations (Jer 1:4-5, 17-19)

The life of the prophet Jeremiah (see Jer 36–45) contains a wealth of teaching for us. We see him unable to speak and yet forced to do so by God in the face of the hostility his message arouses on all sides. He overcomes his fear and continues to preach as the Lord commands him: "Thus says the Lord." He has been chosen by God, who takes the initiative without regard for human qualifications and makes of the prophet "a fortified city, / a pillar of iron, a wall of brass, / against the whole land" (1:18).

Jeremiah prefigures Christ, and his life enables us to understand better the life of Jesus, who is the supreme Prophet. Jesus is chosen from among his people; the latter do not accept him, but his determination is unswerving: to proclaim the eternal Father's plan of salvation that has been prepared since the creation of the world. Until the very end of his life, Jesus will be the Prophet who preaches what the Father has bidden him communicate to all people; that is what he has been sent to do.

The attitude of Jesus must find an echo in the attitude of all his followers. According to the teaching of St. Thomas Aquinas, which has been repeated by Vatican Council II in its Dogmatic Constitution on the Church, baptism brings us a share in the priesthood of Christ. This means that the baptized share in the ascendant role of Christ (that of offering sacrifice to the Father) and in his descending role (that of bearing witness among human beings through word and attitude).

All Catholics should examine themselves with regard to their prophetic role. How do they conceive of it? How do they carry it out? Too often they may think of themselves as a prophet, even though they are in disagreement with the norms of holy living as proposed by the Church. Catholics are not given a share in Christ's priesthood so that they can set themselves up against the Church! They are given it so that they may help her to fulfill her task, even while they may respectfully tell her their own views. The criterion of true prophets will always be their basic accord with the Church, even though this may entail suffering and the acceptance of what they personally find difficult to accept.

The prophet's function is to stimulate persons and institutions to reflection and needed change. Often, however, persons and institutions are excessively attached to what they like to think of as "tradition" but what is, in fact, at times a fad or a comfortable way of doing things. It is quite to be expected, therefore, that prophets will not be well received. This is the test that proves the prophets' authenticity. If they rebel, if their enthusiasm dissipates, if they become bitter, if they turn harshly critical, above all if they do not bow to what those in authority require of them or if they even form a group apart from the community and attack the community in a loveless way, then we cannot trust them in their prophetic claims.

Good sense, good judgment, timeliness (which is not the same as opportunism), and respect for others are some of the criteria by which we can know the true prophet. The Church certainly needs such prophets. When St. Catherine of Siena harshly remonstrated the pope, she was acting as a prophet. She said what she was bound to say; but though she used hard words, made concrete criticisms, and kept nothing back, she did so with the deep love of one whose aim is to heal, not to wound.

The texts for this liturgy should make us reflect on the role of the prophet today. Our approach should not be negative but be marked by the moderation that is the sign of authenticity.

Charity, the Greatest of the Three (1 Cor 12:31–13:13)

The community of Corinth must have been a difficult one to lead. It was rich in gifts but also rather turbulent and outspoken in its reactions. In chapter 12, Paul has been speaking of the various gifts, ministries, and activities in the Church. Unfortunately, the gifts, which are meant to strengthen the unity of the Church, have at times been the reason for disagreements. Paul has therefore emphasized the fact that a gift is given not primarily for the benefit of the person who receives it but for the benefit of the entire community. He has listed these gifts that are meant for the service of all and has ended with the gift of tongues. This last, sensational though it is, is not the greatest of the gifts; moreover, there is a way superior to the whole range of the charisms. With this he turns to the theology of charity (love).

Hitherto, Paul has not spoken of any radical difference between the three virtues of faith, hope, and charity, which are bound up each with the others. Nor does he now deny their interaction. He does, however, see in charity the basic dynamism behind all Christian activity and the virtue that must accompany every other gift. If the Corinthians do not live in accordance with charity, of what use are the other gifts that they have received and of which they are so desirous and proud?

The love that Paul is speaking of is not just any "charity"; it is a higher gift given by the Spirit of God. Paul takes the opportunity to write almost a lyric poem on the power and splendor of charity. It is the indispensable foundation for everything else (13:1-3); it is the source of fruitful energy (13:4-8a); it will last forever (13:8b-13), whereas the other two basic virtues will necessarily cease to exist when our definitive encounter with the Lord takes place.

Such is the teaching that is ever vital to the Church's life and that we in turn must call to mind and keep vivid before us. We may be tempted to yield to our yen for the extraordinary and to substitute some new way for the way of charity, a new way that will be more showy—and require less sacrifice. But charity will always provide the basic criterion for separating the wheat from the chaff.

Fifth Sunday: Messengers of God

From Now on You Will Be Catching People (Luke 5:1-11)

It is easy to sense the deep joy that filled St. Luke's soul when he began to write this chapter. He is describing the time when Jesus is beginning his ministry to the crowds, now that he has gathered his band of disciples. Preparations are already being made for the future Church.

Jesus comes forward here as the Master who teaches the crowds. Luke describes the scene, for the moment is an important one: Simon Peter is about to be given his mission, and Jesus will manifest the meaning of the Church and its activity in language that Luke deliberately makes rather solemn. The crowd presses around Jesus, and he gets into a boat that puts out a little from the shore, not so that he may separate himself from the crowd but simply so that he may teach them better. The boat he picks is Peter's. Does Luke see something symbolic in this? Well, at least he does call attention to the fact.

The miraculous catch of fish follows. This is not simply a reward to Peter for his blind obedience. (If the night fishing was so unprofitable, the daytime fishing would be even more so!) It is quite clear, on the contrary, that the catch is leading up to something further. The very fact that so many details of the miracle are given proves that Luke sees it as extraordinarily important. So marvelous is the wonder that Peter and his fellows become quite fearful. Peter falls down and worships God for this manifestation of power. He does so with the humility so typical of him; we may also think, however, that Luke, writing as he was after Peter's later denial, was himself deeply moved, so that he naturally puts on Peter's lips the words, "I am a sinful man."

Then the climax: Jesus reveals to Peter his future activity, and the various disciples, on reaching land, leave everything and follow him. "'[F]rom now on you will be catching men.' When they brought their boats to the shore, they left everything and followed him." Here we already have a picture of the Church and its mission, which will reach its full and mature form after Pentecost. The Lord is already preparing his disciples for their important role of preaching the Good News, healing and saving people, and bringing them into the bark of Peter.

Here I Am; Send Me! (Isa 6:1-2a, 3-8)

Isaiah was affected by his vision, much as Peter was by the miraculous catch. Every contact with God is to some extent terrifying. Isaiah saw the Lord and was therefore sure that he was lost, just as Peter is made deeply aware of his sinfulness. Isaiah is even more deeply affected, because he has seen the King who is Lord of the universe. After the theophany, which despite its aura of majesty is comparable to the event of which St. Luke tells us, the prophet receives his mission and asks to be sent. So too, after revealing his power, Jesus sends Peter to be a fisher of people. The lips of the prophet are purified by a burning coal; Peter repents of his sins.

In its own way, the Old Testament was already preparing for the Church and its mission. At every point it was God who chose people and God who sent them on their missions. Any extension of his rule was always his doing. Psalm 138, the responsorial psalm, implicitly makes this point when it says: "O LORD, your merciful love is eternal; / discard not the work of your hands" (v. 8). The Spirit of the Lord continues to choose people and carries on the work of building up the Church.

In silence of heart and humble acceptance of their spiritual and human condition, people today still encounter the majestic Lord who purifies their lips with a coal; they leave everything to follow Jesus and become fishers of people. This miracle occurs often; we do not see it or even think of it, yet it is a source of life for the Church. Because of it, no persecution has ever been able to kill the impulse that Christ gave to his apostles long ago at the miraculous catch of fish. Christ's words, "You will be catching men," continue to echo in our world today, and nothing can diminish their power.

The Message of Faith (1 Cor 15:1-11)

Being a fisher of people does not mean priding oneself on one's own intellectual resources or one's own psychological or pedagogical methods. The mission of a fisher of people is first and foremost to proclaim the Good News as Christ gave it to us and to help observe it without altering it. The message is absolutely basic: Christ died, was buried, rose on the third day, and appeared, first to Peter, then to the Twelve, and then to a large number of other people. In other words, the message is the mystery of Christ.

It is possible that in this passage Paul's intention is to emphasize the essentials of the message. As we know, the Corinthians were proud of their knowledge and their philosophy. Doubtless they do not go so far as to deny the resurrection, although the current philosophies were not favorable to such a doctrine; the least that can be said, however, is that the Corinthians tended to give priority to human wisdom.

Faced with this attitude, St. Paul reminds his readers of a very simple profession of faith; perhaps it was even the formula in use in that community: "Christ died for our sins in accordance with the Scriptures; . . . he was buried; . . . he was raised on the third day in accordance with the Scriptures." These are historical facts: Christ's death, his entombment, his resurrection. But the facts were also redemptive events: Christ died for our sins, and his resurrection is the pledge of ours. There you have the Christian message. Paul is able to refer to witnesses of the resurrection and of the apparitions of Christ. Christ even appeared to Paul himself, who is an apostle by the grace of God and a preacher of the message of faith.

Sixth Sunday: Blessings and Curses

Blessed Are You Poor. Woe to You Who Are Rich (Luke 6:17, 20-26)

The discourse on the beatitudes is usually thought of as part of the Sermon on the Mount (Matt 5–7; see Fourth Sunday, Year A). Luke, however, introduces the discourse as being delivered on a "stretch of level ground" where many listeners were assembled. If we compare the beatitudes in the gospels of Matthew and Luke, we will find many points in common but also some differences. The exegetes usually conclude to the existence of a common source, unknown to us, on which both accounts drew. We may note the rhythmic style of Luke's four beatitudes and the fact that there are four corresponding curses.

It makes a deep impression to hear Jesus himself addressing the congregation and each of us with the words: "Blessed are you." They are indeed addressed to us, for we honestly seek to follow him. We are weak indeed, yet the four curses seem addressed, not to us, but to those who do not seek him.

"Blessed are you who are poor." Those who are deeply concerned with social problems feel their urge to do good aroused when they hear the Lord thus honoring the disinherited. Nor are they mistaken. We have perhaps too quickly turned the poverty of which Jesus speaks into something spiritual. Recent scholarly study of the Scriptures has shown that Jesus is indeed speaking of material poverty, just as in the corresponding curse he is speaking of material wealth. It is to those who are materially poor that the promise of joy in the future kingdom is given, for, in Luke's view, material poverty leads to a surer detachment. The quest for material poverty in the Desert Fathers and the religious orders has no other purpose; the goal is not asceticism or poverty for its own sake but the detachment from material things that makes it easier to attach oneself to authentic values.

It will be worthwhile to see what Luke's thoughts on poverty are elsewhere in his gospel. A reading of these other passages shows us that what Luke is concerned with is a genuine liberation that enables us to follow Christ without compromise. Thus, later in this same sixth chapter we read: "Give to everyone who asks of you, and from the one who takes what is yours do not demand it back" (v. 30) and "lend expecting nothing back" (v. 35).

Later on, in chapter 11, detachment is presented as a means of acquiring a purer vision of all reality: "But as to what is within, give alms, and behold, everything will be clean for you" (11:41). In chapter 14 Jesus says, "blessed indeed will you be because of [the] inability [of the poor, the crippled, the lame, and the blind] to repay you. For you will be repaid at the resurrection of the righteous" (v. 14). Zacchaeus, a man attached to earthly goods, proves the reality of his conversion when he says, "Behold, half of my possessions, Lord, I shall give to the poor, and if I have extorted anything from anyone I shall repay it four times over" (19:8). And Jesus tells the rich official, "There is still one thing left for you: sell all that you have and distribute it to the poor, and you will have a treasure in heaven. Then come, follow me" (18:22).

The parables that Luke puts on the lips of Christ certainly have to do with material poverty; this is true of the parable about Lazarus the beggar (16:19-31) and of the incident in which Jesus sees the poor widow making her gift in the temple (21:2). When he urges action that involves the "poor," he means those who are materially poor: "[W]hen you hold a banquet, invite the poor" (14:13); "Go out quickly into the streets and alleys of the town and bring in here the poor" (14:21). It is to the really poor that the Good News is preached (4:18), in accordance with the prophecy of Isaiah (61:1-2).

And yet, material poverty is not enough; one must have the heart of the poor, as St. Matthew tells us (5:3). When Jesus speaks of humble service, he tells us, "When you have done all you have been commanded, say, 'We are unprofitable servants; we have done what we were obliged to do" (Luke 17:10). Yet, even such interior poverty is not a value in itself; it is to be sought not for its own sake but as a means of detachment in the following of Christ.

St. Luke has a real fear of riches. He speaks of wealth as "dishonest" (16:9) and shows us Jesus telling the money-loving Pharisees, "[W]hat is of human esteem is an abomination in the sight of God" (16:15). We will recall the abundance of detail Luke uses in the parable of the rich man and the beggar Lazarus and how he describes the reversed lots of the two after death, with the rich man being tormented and Lazarus sitting at the banquet table in the kingdom (16:23-28). In the *Magnificat*, Mary sings, "The hungry he has filled with good things; / the rich he has sent away empty" (1:53), and Jesus later tells the rich, "You have received your consolation" (6:24). And finally there is the great saying: "Where your treasure is, there also will your heart be" (12:34).

In addition, Jesus gives a series of instructions that evidently caught St. Luke's interest: "Take nothing for your journey" (9:3); "Carry no money bag, no sack, no sandals" (10:4); "Sell your belongings and give alms" (12:33). The disciples tell Jesus, "We have given up our possessions and followed you" (18:28). Later on, when describing the life of the early community in the Acts of the Apostles, St. Luke twice mentions that "they had everything in common" (2:44; 4:32).

Such poverty must even sustain indifference to the opinion and respect of others. The disciple must not love the best places in the assembly (11:43) but should take the lowest place (14:10), glad to be scorned for the sake of the Son of Man.

Poverty, then, is an ascetical means to life in the kingdom.

Authentic Riches and Security (Jer 17:5-8)

The first reading presents us with a very simple yet utterly decisive antithesis. The literary procedure is different from Luke's, inasmuch as Jeremiah speaks first of those who are cursed because they put their trust in weak humans; he then turns to those who are blessed and find joy because they put their trust in the Lord. Note the serenity of the detachment foreseen by the prophet; one who trusts in God has nothing to fear.

Many of the psalms praise this trust in the Lord as the way to joy and peace. The psalm chosen as the responsorial today gives poetic expression to this idea:

> Blessed indeed is the man
> who follows not the counsel of the wicked. . . .
> but whose delight is the law of the Lord. . . .
>
> He is like a tree that is planted
> beside the flowing waters,

that yields its fruit in due season,
and whose leaves shall never fade. (Ps 1:1-3).

If There Is No Resurrection, Our Faith Is in Vain (1 Cor 15:12, 16-20)

Faith in Christ as "the firstfruits of those who have fallen asleep" is the principle on which the whole logic of Christian life is based. If Christ be not risen, faith is useless; we are still in our sins, and those who died before us in Christ have perished. If, moreover, it be a genuine truth that the dead do not rise, then Christ cannot be risen!

The reader may be tempted to reproach the author of these volumes for not adverting to modern theologies of the resurrection and to the way some contemporary theologians deal with the mystery, when he comes to discuss the paschal mystery.[‡] Some readers may reproach him on the same counts for this short commentary on the First Letter to the Corinthians. But the liturgy is not interested in hypotheses on the resurrection, be they old or new. Its aim is simply to bring the Scriptures alive; it has nothing in common with the study of the manner of the resurrection or the conditions required for it. The liturgy, like faith itself, is content with the fact. If our hope in Christ related only to our present life, we would indeed be the most pitiable of humankind.

Seventh Sunday: Be Merciful

Be Merciful as God Is to Us (Luke 6:27-38)

We should recall here the passage from St. Matthew that is read in Year A for this Sunday, since in the present passage Luke deals with the same subject and draws inspiration from the same verse of Leviticus: "Be holy, for I, the LORD your God, am holy" (19:2). Luke has changed the slant somewhat, however, for he writes: "Be merciful, just as [also] your Father is merciful" (6:36).

The end of this passage—"the measure with which you measure will in return be measured out to you" (v. 38)—reminds us of the petition in the Our Father: "forgive us our debts, / as we forgive our debtors" (Matt 6:12). The fathers, in commenting on the Lord's Prayer, emphasize the idea that we are the ones who determine the limits of

---

[‡] Nocent does not name who, but several controversial books on the resurrection were popularly available.

God's mercy, which in itself is infinite. Those limits are the ones we ourselves place on the forgiveness we give to others.

It is in this matter of forgiveness that we see the true originality of the Gospel and of the Christian lifestyle. While the world goes its way around them, Christians live a special kind of life; they are not understood and are regarded as fools by those who judge according to a purely human criterion. What a difficult ideal to attain! And yet no one can truly be called a Christian without pursuing that ideal.

Spare Your Enemy (1 Sam 26:2, 7-9, 12-13, 22-23)

The Old Testament reading provides us with a remarkable example of generosity and respect for an enemy's life and person, which is consecrated by God. The story is an attractive one and becomes even more so when we put it into its context. The Lord has already regretted anointing Saul (1 Sam 15:11, 35), and the Spirit of the Lord has already laid hold of David (1 Sam 16:13). David is being pursued by Saul's soldiers. Now Abishai sees, as anyone would, that Saul is in their power; this is providential, and David must take advantage of it.

David's reaction is quite different, for it is inspired by the Lord. He instinctively respects God's action in originally choosing Saul, and he needs far clearer signs before he can bring himself to kill someone who, though his enemy, was once anointed by God. Therefore, he refuses to lift his hand against the anointed king and leaves it to the Lord to see justice done: "The LORD will reward each man for his justice and faithfulness" (v. 23). David will not take the law into his own hands. Thus, whereas Abishai sees the Lord delivering Saul into David's hands, David interprets the event quite differently; he prefers to respect God's plan and to look to God for justice.

This is a splendid story; even today it strikes us as one that does honor to humanity. The Christian of today should have the same respect for God's plan as it affects every created person.

The merciful David has been seen as a prefiguration of Christ. He, David, was the anointed one who foretold the great Anointed One who was to come and who would forgive his enemies from the cross.

We Shall Bear the Image of the Heavenly One (1 Cor 15:45-49)

St. Paul has told the Corinthians how important he thinks the resurrection is, but he has made no effort to analyze how the resurrection took place. He does, however, now attempt to clarify the essential meaning of the resurrection, which is so central to our faith.

His explanation begins with a parallel between the two Adams: the first, a human being who received the gift of life; the second (Christ), a spiritual being who gives life. The first Adam came from the earth; the second, from heaven. But now, through the saving intervention of Christ, human beings, who are of the earth, belong to heaven. We are now in the image of the earthly Adam, but some day we shall be also in the image of the heavenly Adam.

This is a splendidly simple explanation of the doctrine of our resurrection. It tells us that we have a twofold being: we are made from the earth in the image of the earthly Adam, but we have become spiritual in Christ and are now modeled after the image of the heavenly one. The body of Christ was raised up in glory; we shall rise glorious like him.

Eighth Sunday: The Word and the Heart

The True Disciple (Luke 6:39-45)

In this passage, once again, there is a many-sided teaching, and the aspect we are meant to attend to when the passage is read in the liturgy is determined by the first reading. In this light, the primary emphasis in the gospel is on the word that comes from one's mouth and shows what one is. True disciples of Christ are to be recognized by what they say as well as by what they are. For in the first reading, the word one speaks is said to be a norm for judging that person.

What Jesus has to say about the "fullness of the heart" is not to be taken as simple moralism; rather, it tells us something about the "ontology," or very being, of the disciple. If the disciple has indeed put on Christ and has indeed been anointed at baptism with the Spirit, then what the disciple says will make this manifest. The tree is to be judged by its fruits. The whole person of the baptized individual is affected by baptism; the change wrought by baptism and the fact of belonging to Christ involve the entire person.

This does not mean that Christians are to be closed in upon themselves. It does mean that there are ideas and principles they cannot accept and that their exclusiveness in this respect is not imposed from outside but springs from their very Christian being. The baptized must live within the limits set by the Body of Christ to which they belong. Christians live in the world, but they are not therefore free to move in any of the directions the "world" happens to favor. There are even political commitments they will not accept, not because of a discipline imposed on them from without, but because a balanced prudence that is a reflection of God's wisdom bids them not compromise the Body of Christ to which they belong.

In many matters Christians are not dependent on the Church advising them or acknowledging that their attitude is correct. The Christian can speak only as a Christian. At the same time, however, we must recognize that it is not always a simple matter for individuals to judge whether what they want to say is always in keeping with orthodox thinking. When this difficulty arises, they must have the humility to ask advice, not because a law binds them to do so, but because they respect their own religious commitment. They know that others will judge them and the Church by what they say; they will judge the tree by its fruits.

It is perhaps artificial to link what we have been saying with the beginning of the gospel pericope, which states that one blind person cannot lead another. A guide is a person who accepts a responsibility. Not everyone is in a position to accept such a responsibility; Luke may well have in mind certain dangerous prophets who lacked the ability to lead others. That is why he goes on to remind us of the need to submit to a teacher. He himself is surely thinking of Jesus, but we should certainly think of the Church and its teaching authority; to her we must submit, even if this means at times putting up with delays or a lack of understanding or openness. If the disciple puts forth doctrines that are not those of the Church and are dangerous, this person speaks indeed out of the fullness of heart, but it is a proud person speaking, not one who has become a member of Christ's Body through baptism.

Some may regard the judgment we have just expressed as regressive and will not accept it. There can be no question, of course, of canonizing every suppression and every condemnation. Yet there are plenty of illustrious examples of submission to the Church that show us the possibilities inherent in true discipleship. Those who have humbly conformed to what was commanded them have often reached a level of holiness and even of human renown that confounds the rebellious, most of whom end up empty and bitter.

Nor are disciples free to issue severe criticisms and judgments of their neighbor. Here again the mouth speaks out of the heart's fullness. It is pride that leads to harsh criticism and judgment of others, not the spirit of merciful forgiveness that we find in God and Jesus and should find in every disciple.

The word "hypocrite" that Jesus here applies to a certain type of person is itself harsh, even offensive. We must bear in mind, however, that it does not mean quite what it does in modern parlance. For us, hypocrisy means hiding one's real thought and character behind a deliberately adopted but false front. The Hebrew word that lies behind the Greek of the gospel means, rather, persons who are far from God because they are unwilling to discern the truth. Jesus uses the word elsewhere with this same meaning. For example, when the multitudes prove unwilling to discern the signs of the times, Jesus treats them as "hypocrites," that is, people who are blind and incapable of objective judgment and who therefore depart from God's ways (Luke 12:56).

The statements of Jesus that are grouped here (in Luke 6:39-45) were probably made at different times. For St. Luke, they must have been connected in ways we cannot always readily see. In any case, the teaching of this Sunday's gospel is more important today than ever before: true disciples will be known by their outlook.

The Word and the Heart (Sir 27:4-7)

This short passage from Ben Sira, which is subtle in its analysis though harsh in its language, determines the point of view for reading the gospel of the day: "Praise no one before he speaks, / for it is then that people are tested" (v. 7). In three images the writer gives us criteria for testing a person: the sieve and husks, utterances show people's faults; the furnace that tests the potter's vessels, the test of a person is in conversation; the tree and its fruits, speech discloses a person's heart. This last parallel we have already seen in the gospel pericope: disciples are known by their words.

A disciple of Christ must live in accordance with one's profession as a baptized person who has put on Christ. Everything a disciple says and does involves discipleship and therefore Christ and the Church as well. For though we live in the world, we are part of a new creation. This does not at all mean that we can be unconcerned about the world and withdraw into a cocoon so that we may be sure of living in perfect accordance with what we are. On the contrary! If we are really aware of what we are, we will feel constrained to enter more and more fully into the service of the world. This service, however, requires precisely that disciples be what they should be and that their utterances never be inspired by political calculation but be those of persons who have become God's messengers.

God Gives Us the Victory through Christ (1 Cor 15:54-58)

This passage is a very encouraging one for the Christian life. This whole chapter concerns the resurrection, and we have already heard Paul's reflections on the subject (Sixth and Seventh Sundays, Year C). Here he goes into a little more detail.

"When this which is corruptible clothes itself with incorruptibility and this which is mortal clothes itself with immortality. . . ." Paul likes the image of "clothing"; here, as in his other writings, it refers not to a mere external form but implies a real change in the person. Thus when he says that "all of you who were baptized into Christ have clothed yourselves with Christ" (Gal 3:27), he means that we have been reborn and utterly transformed. So here, in putting on immortality, we will again be transformed. The garment of immortality is something heavenly (1 Cor 15:40, 47-49; 2 Cor 5:2). Our lowly bodies, he tells us elsewhere, will become like the glorious body of Christ (Phil 3:20-21).

Given this belief, Christians should think of death in an entirely different way than do people who do not believe and have not been baptized. The words of Scripture, says Paul, will come true for them. Where does Paul get these words? In fact, they do not occur as such in the Bible but are based by Paul on two different passages. The first statement, *"Death is swallowed up in victory,"* derives from, or is based on, the book of Isaiah (25:8), where the prophet writes, "He [the Lord] will destroy death forever." It makes no difference whether or not Isaiah was thinking of a real resurrection; it is with the resurrection in mind that Paul uses them here. The second quotation derives from the book of Hosea (13:14): "Where are your plagues, O death! where is your sting, Sheol!" The oracle is a threat to destroy Israel utterly. Paul turns it into a promise of resurrection and of the integral survival of the Christian. If we read the passage with faith, Paul gives us an overwhelming sense of confidence and security in the face of death.

The thing that makes death fearful for every human being is sin. In itself, death might possibly be a simple transition to a glorious state; it is the sting of sin that makes death hateful to us, while the law reinforces the power of sin because it tells us what is wrong but does not give us the power to avoid doing wrong (Rom 7:7). Instead of freeing individuals from evil, the law only makes them sin more. Christ alone can deliver us from the captivity of the law (Rom 7:1-6) and rescue the human conscience, which is prisoner to evil (Rom 7:14-25). Because of Christ's redemptive action, the law is no longer external to us; the Spirit transforms us and writes the law in our hearts by pouring out God's love therein (Rom 5:5). How grateful we should be, then, to God who gives us the victory through Jesus Christ!

The Christian life, while remaining realistic, should also be fearlessly optimistic, for the Christian has already conquered death in and through the risen Christ. No place, then, for real sadness; nor should any event be able to take away our assurance of winning through to the end. Death after a "life in Christ" can only be a Passover to glory.

Ninth Sunday: Faith Is Answered

The Faith of a Foreigner (Luke 7:1-10)

The story of the cure of the centurion's servant is also found in St. Matthew and St. John, though with differences that are not lacking in interest. St. Luke's intention seems to be to contrast the ease with which a non-Jew believed in Jesus and the difficulties the Jews felt in committing themselves to him. In addition, St. Luke sets the stage carefully and in detail. As a Gentile, the centurion does not himself come to Jesus, for he feels ill at ease and does not dare to approach him. Instead, he sends some Jewish elders for whom he had probably done favors. The elders tell Jesus that the man had built a synagogue for them and was truly a friend of the nation. Finally, when Jesus sets out for the centurion's house, the latter sends word that Jesus should not take such trouble, for he knows that a Jew is not supposed to enter a Gentile's house. It is at this point that the man's faith is manifested in moving words that have become part of the eucharistic celebration in the Latin Church: "I am not worthy to have you enter under my roof. . . . [B]ut say the word and let my servant be healed."

Jesus' response to this is carefully recorded by St. Luke: "I tell you, not even in Israel have I found such faith."

Perhaps Jesus could say the same thing about us, the new people of God, as he says here about Israel. Does he find the centurion's faith among us? This is a question we ought to ask about ourselves and about the contemporary Church on this Sunday. Is it in the Catholic Church that we find the greatest manifestations of faith? Is it in the Christian Churches that faith in God is always seen to be liveliest? Christ's words to the centurion might well be applied to our age as a hard judgment. The fact should make us quite humble. Faith is certainly a gift that must be accepted and cultivated, but in any event it is a gift, and no one can claim it as one's exclusive possession.

The Prayer of a Foreigner in the Temple (1 Kgs 8:41-43)

Solomon built the temple, but to the Israelite mind his action, however praiseworthy, was not unproblematic, because it is impossible to enclose the Lord within a temple; we can neither force him to answer our prayers nor prevent him from answering the prayers of others.

Earlier in this chapter of the First Book of Kings, Solomon had explained to the people his reasons for building a temple (1 Kgs 8:14-21). Then, after praying that there might always be a successor to the throne of David, Solomon prays for the entire people that God would hear them in every circumstance. Finally (in today's pericope), he prays for foreigners as well, that is, for those not of the race of Israel. It is not surprising that foreigners should, in fact, come to the temple, since they too would have heard of the great things God had done and was doing for his chosen people. The Scriptures predicted, after all, that all the peoples of the earth would acknowledge the power of the Lord.

Solomon's prayer thus anticipates the situation we find described in the gospel: the foreigner too, that is, one who does not belong to our religion, may have authentic faith. The fact should not vex us but rather make us praise God, who wishes to save all people. At the same time, it should make us reflect on ourselves. For us, faith has been made easy in so many ways; it has been fed by so many gifts of grace (the word of God, the sacraments). Do not this very ease and these very gifts condemn us for our lack of faith?

Either Serve Christ or Please People (Gal 1:1-2, 6-10)

The Galatians are in trouble. Some individuals seem to be preaching to them a doctrine that is not in conformity with the Gospel. Paul complains of the rapidity with which they have abandoned the Gospel of Jesus that he had preached to them. The real problem lies in the Jewish-Christian milieu and its opposition to Paul's teaching that neither circumcision nor the observance of the Mosaic law were necessary for salvation. Paul therefore feels obliged to remind his readers that he has been sent by Jesus himself whom the Father had raised from the dead. His words to them are stern: There is only one Gospel, and no one, not even an angel, has the right to come preaching another. The Galatians must remain faithful to the Gospel of Christ that he, Paul, has preached to them.

It is difficult for Paul to write in this vein. He is not seeking to satisfy people, however, but to preach the truth as it is. His real interest is in serving Christ, and "If I were still trying to please people, I would not be a slave of Christ."

Except for the contingent circumstances that caused Paul to write this letter, we today face the same problem Paul faced; in fact, it is a problem that the Church, each authority in the Church, and, in the last analysis, each Christian has always had to face. There are moments when fidelity to Christ does not allow us to evade taking firm positions and making firm decisions. The situation of our contemporary world requires that Christians be sensitive to all the anxieties and sufferings of people, but also that they be strictly faithful to the message and teaching of Christ.

The Christian and the Church cannot hold fast to nonessential traditions that are likely to stifle the spirit, on the pretext that if they depart from these, they will displease those who frequently love what they call "tradition" because it answers to their own mind-set, their education, a type of "humanism," a specific culture. Nor can the Christian and the Church agree to moral compromises that are clearly deviations from the requirements of divine revelation; this applies not only to sexual morality but also to aspects of social life and to some kinds of government.

The Church must preach the truths of the Gospel; these are the true and genuine tradition! Therefore, it cannot be afraid of displeasing people by requiring, no matter what, obedience to this essential Gospel. On the other hand, neither can the Church be afraid of people when it comes to adapting to the contemporary world and abandoning what is not essential in its tradition. Judgments on these matters are evidently not easy to make. But we must remember that Christ's Spirit is present to help the Church, today no less than in the beginning.

Tenth Sunday: The Gift of Life

I Say to You, Arise (Luke 7:11-17)

The story of the raising of the widow's son at Nain is found only in Luke's gospel. It is one in a series of episodes that proclaim the gift of life we are all meant to receive.

When John the Baptist sends his disciples to inquire of Jesus who he is, Jesus answers by pointing to his significant deeds; among these is the raising of the dead (Luke 7:22). The raising of the widow's son, recounted just before, is an example of this extraordinary activity (Luke 7:11-17). The prophet Isaiah had long ago predicted that this would be a sign of the Messiah: "your dead shall live, their corpses shall rise" (26:19).

St. Luke notes that Jesus is deeply moved with pity for the poor widow. In his emotion, however, we may see something more than simple pity for the widow's suffering. He is also deeply moved at the thought of the life and resurrection he will give to those who believe in him, a life and resurrection symbolized by the raising of the widow's son. St. Luke most certainly has this broader perspective in mind. In addition, the raising of the widow's son will be a sign to the Baptist that he, Jesus, is the long-awaited Messiah. In short, St. Luke reports this incident in order to strengthen the faith of his readers in Christ the Prophet, the God who visits his people.

St. Luke likes the phrase "God has visited his people." The elderly Simeon uses it (Luke 1:68). Later on, Luke puts the following words of reproach on the lips of Jesus: "you did not recognize the time of your visitation" (19:44). The Old Testament had supplied Luke with the idea and the phraseology. Thus the book of Exodus reports Joseph as having said in Egypt, "God will surely take care of [or: visit] you, and you must bring my bones up with you from here" (Exod 13:19). The psalmist marvels at this visitation and cries: "what is man that you should keep him in mind, / the son of man that you care for [or: visit] him?" (Ps 8:5).

The divine visitation to which Luke refers through Simeon in the temple (Luke 1:68) is the divine coming to redeem and liberate, prefigured in the liberation of Israel and the exodus of the people from Egypt. Jesus is the Prophet who conquers death and gives life.

We should not forget that Luke is writing after the death and resurrection of Jesus. In the account of the raising at Nain, we have resonances of the experience of the early Church.

See, Your Son Lives (1 Kgs 17:17-24)

The Old Testament reading is chosen so as to provide a prefiguration of Jesus' miracle at Nain. The incident chosen is the raising of another widow's son by the prophet Elijah. (The Second Book of Kings has a parallel case: the raising of the Shunammite's son in 4:32-37.)

What is the relevance of this miracle, and of the miracle at Nain, to our lives today?

Scientific progress and a resurgence of Gentile religions have made us forget that life and death are in God's hand. This applies not only to physical life but also to the resurrection and the life in God that will come at the end of time and are prefigured in the miracles of Scripture. It is the Lord who bestows this definitive life on us and thus brings us to our fulfillment. Baptism as new life, and the other sacraments that sustain this life and cause it to intensify until the coming of Christ—these are the realities ultimately meant by the miracles we have been considering, as well as by the resurrection of Lazarus, which prefigures the resurrection of Christ and our own resurrection.

When we think of this gift of life and of the complete fulfillment, in the world to come, of all that we are meant to be, we must not narrow our vision and focus solely on a life given to each of us as individuals. We must think rather of a life that is given to the people of God in its entirety. The Church, which has been commissioned by Christ to raise the spiritually dead, must look to the Lord for her being and life. She is meant to be a sign of resurrection for each individual, and though the reality of the resurrection exists only in promise, she nonetheless gives us real pledges and anticipations of that unending life.

When all is said and done, the whole preaching of the Church rests on a single foundation: the resurrection that is given to people even now (in pledge and promise) and the sacraments that free people from sin and give life to the Church and her members as they journey toward the life that will never cease. The miracles of resurrection that the Church works are not spectacular like those of Elijah or those of Christ at Nain and Bethany, but they are utterly real, and the Church is constantly working them in anticipation of the last day.

Our Christianity is a religion of life. It supposes indeed a kind of death through asceticism and renunciation, but this death is only a means of liberation. Christian existence, in fact, develops in an atmosphere of profound and intense life. How often we find in someone who is an invalid or ill or dying the signs of a life far more intense than what we find in the healthy! It is this deeper life that is signified by baptism and the Eucharist (sacraments of the "living") as well as by the sacrament of the sick which looks to the life of both body and spirit. We Christians are being perpetually raised up to new life, and we don't seem to realize it! And yet the world should be able to see in us witnesses to a life constantly being poured into us by Christ, the Son of the living and life-giving God.

To Preach Your Son among the Gentiles (Gal 1:11-19)

This is not the first time, of course, that the Sunday readings have urged us to reflect on the missionary activity of the apostles. In today's passage Paul tells us that as an apostle the message he passes on is that of Jesus himself, the Good News that Jesus came to preach.

We are confronted here once more with the mystery of God's choice. Paul had done nothing that he should be chosen and sent to preach the mysteries of Christ. Quite the contrary! Yet in fact, he was chosen from his mother's womb, and later the Lord revealed his Son to him so that he might preach that Son to the Gentiles.

Paul received a call, as had all the prophets before him. This is something on which he lays great stress, as he does on the fact that he was fully an apostle, having been chosen directly by Christ himself. He saw the risen Christ, who entrusted him with the preaching of the Gospel. He visited Peter, indeed, but it was not from Peter that he received his appointment to the work of evangelization.

Meditation on this passage should be combined with meditation on the other texts in the Lectionary. It is a very relevant passage. Paul is unexpectedly called, God choosing him without him having been in any way prepared; he responds to the call. His mission is to preach the Gospel of Jesus Christ; he carries out his mission, always remaining in contact with the other apostles.

The task of the missionary of today is exactly the same as Paul's. It is for the sake of the Gospel alone that all, each according to one's own vocation, are sent out to the nations of the world. Our vocation is to be witnesses to the Gospel of Jesus Christ, and we must answer the call faithfully and to the best of our ability.

Eleventh Sunday: Sin Forgiven

Forgiveness and Love (Luke 7:36–8:3)

The story of the sinful woman who bathed Jesus' feet with her tears, dried them with her hair, covered them with kisses, and anointed them is one of the best known in the whole of Scripture. In our day, interpreters have endeavored to apply it, without qualification, as a proof of the primacy of "love" (an ambiguous word that needs to be used with more care).

The important thing for us here is the parable that Jesus speaks to his host when the latter doubts the prophetic powers of a man who does not seem to realize what kind of woman has approached him. It is a simple parable, and we shall not go over its details. The concluding application to the woman, however, may leave us a bit puzzled, but this depends on how the verse is translated. The point is that the woman is forgiven much because she has shown great love; one who shows little love is not thus forgiven. The woman's love has been shown in the way she approached Jesus. It is for that reason that he tells her, "Your sins are forgiven."

As usual when Jesus uses these words, those present ask: Who is this who even has power to forgive sins? The real problem is: How are they to see God in this man? Jesus gives them the answer when he says to the woman: "Your faith has saved you." She has come to realize that salvation is from God alone. She has the faith that every Christian must have.

Christ then continues on his way, preaching the kingdom of God. The fact that he forgives sins has brought home to many the presence of the kingdom.

The Lord Has Put away Your Sin (2 Sam 12:7-10, 13)

The story of David, in the first reading, prepares us for understanding the gospel of the day. What we should focus on in the reading from the Second Book of Samuel is not so much God's stern rebuke as David's immediate repentance. The story then has God's forgiveness follow just as immediately; no sooner has David admitted his sin than he is forgiven. The liturgy has shortened the passage somewhat by cutting out part of the divine reproaches; this is quite legitimate since the emphasis today is on God's mercy.

The two accounts in today's liturgy—from the Second Book of Samuel and from St. Luke's gospel—are fully relevant today since the Lord continues to act as he is shown acting in these stories. That is to say, where he finds repentance, he immediately forgives. The two readings provide two examples of this pattern.

Catholics who have difficulties today with the sacrament of penance may well find them resolved if they meditate on these two stories. The act of faith toward the Lord through the Church, his instrument and "sacrament," forgives sin, and the past is blotted out. The thing that has probably created the obstacle that some cannot overcome is too much human casuistry and a presentation of God as a difficult and irascible being. The sacrament of penance has come to be seen in too negative a light; it does not sufficiently radiate the paschal joy of reconciliation, and there is not enough sense of the life the Lord wants to give again to those who repent.

Reconciliation with God requires an act of faith and therefore an act of adoring, joyous worship. Communal penance celebrations may help to gradually restore the true meaning of the sacrament, provided they present the sacrament chiefly in a positive way, as the renewal of sinful humanity and the restoration of union with the Lord.

Christ Lives in Me (Gal 2:16, 19-21)

We find here once again the theme of justification by faith. Four times in a row St. Paul uses the verb "justify" (in vv. 16-17). Let us recall briefly what the term means for him. To the Jews, the justified person was the one whom God will accept on the day of judgment; in language more familiar to us, the "justified" person is the person who is "saved."

The Galatians must realize, says Paul, that they are justified not because of their practice of the (Jewish) law but because of their faith in Jesus Christ. No one becomes just by fulfilling the Mosaic law. Paul's thought is well expressed in a short sentence that we ought to keep in mind: "through the law [which put Christ to death] I died to the law, that I might live for God" (v. 19). In other words, it is because Christ went beyond the Mosaic law, coming to accomplish and perfect it by love, that the Jews put him to death. That death of Christ, accordingly, liberated Paul from the Mosaic law and justified him; he has therefore ceased to live under that law and lives instead for God. That which justifies is faith in the Christ who died and rose from the dead. If the practice of the law could justify, Christ's death would have been without purpose.

What are we to do, then? How should Christians live if they wish to be saved? Even in their human condition they must live by faith in the Son of God who gave himself for them. In their present life, they are to live as if nailed to Christ's cross; it is no longer they who live, for Christ lives in them.

That kind of life is not reserved for the mystics but is to be the life consequent upon baptism. If our spiritual life is not of that kind, it is really nonexistent, an appearance without reality.

Twelfth Sunday: The Suffering Messiah and Savior

Take Your Cross and Follow Christ (Luke 9:18-24)

Once again, Jesus makes known his messianic dignity. The crowds have not yet gotten a clear idea of Christ's person, but he wants the disciples to be really and fully convinced of his true identity. Jesus first asks the disciples who the crowd thinks he is. The apostles are aware of what the crowd thinks, and they tell Jesus. Then Jesus goes a step further: "But who do you say that I am?" Peter speaks immediately for the others, and his answer is clear and straightforward: "The Christ of God." At this point Jesus once again forbids the disciples to say anything of this to others.

We shall not repeat what we said earlier about the significance of the "messianic secret," especially since the point of the gospel pericope, as read in the light of the first reading, is that the Messiah must suffer in order to redeem humankind. It is on this prediction of the passion that we should dwell and on the consequences of the passion for every disciple of Christ. For all who will believe in the suffering Messiah and in the efficacy of his sufferings will have to share them with him. That is why Jesus here sets forth the basic program of every Christian life: Take up your cross daily; lose your life in order to save it.

St. Luke does not emphasize the messianic secret the way Mark does, but in this passage he does link it to the prediction of the passion. The crowd is not capable, despite Isaiah's prophecies, of accepting a suffering Messiah.

The evangelist emphasizes the Messiah's sufferings and the part they play in God's plan of salvation that was conceived before the world began: "The Son of Man must suffer greatly." Everything in Christ's life is part of the carrying out of God's plan. Luke is here closely attuned to John, whose whole gospel echoes the theme of the Father's will and its accomplishment by the Son.

But if the Messiah is to suffer a great deal, he is also to rise from the dead. Thus, it is the whole paschal mystery that Jesus predicts here. From this point on, the apostles know the journey that Jesus must take. Do they fully understand it at this first mention? It would be difficult to say with certainty; at least we can say that their reactions at the time of the passion, which presumably they believed would come, show them to have been inadequately prepared for the reality.

Peter's act of faith, spoken in the name of the other disciples, and Jesus' detailed prediction of the paschal mystery of his death and resurrection lead to the statement of the principles that must guide the Christian's life. Follow Christ, take up your cross daily; save your life and you will lose it, lose it and you will save it. Here we already have the foolishness of the cross of which Paul would later write.

They Shall Look on Him Whom They Have Pierced (Zech 12:10-11; 13:1)

St. John (19:37), in a passage used on the feast of the Sacred Heart (Year B), applies this passage from Zechariah to Christ. The words of the prophet are not crystal clear and apparently underwent several revisions. Whom did he have in mind when he spoke of the one who is pierced and who attracts the looks of others? An earlier passage had spoken of the messianic king as riding on an ass (9:9-10). In the present passage, this messianic king has been misunderstood and killed. But his sufferings and the sufferings of Jerusalem that put him to death will purify the city. We are reminded here of Isaiah's fourth song of the Suffering Servant (Isa 53).

This first reading is an invitation to emphasize, in the gospel, the sufferings of the Messiah and the efficacy of his purifying passion. But we must go a step beyond contemplative meditation and learn to share in the cross of him who was pierced for our sake.

Clothed in Christ (Gal 3:26-29)

The gospel sets down the basic plan for Christian life. In this second reading Paul reminds us of our baptism and of the fact that we share deeply in the life of Christ, so much so that we can be said to be clothed in Christ. So fully are we transformed into Christ that there is no longer slave and free person, male and female among us, for we are now all one in Christ Jesus. This is the main point of this passage from the Letter to the Galatians.

The fact that we have been united to Christ through baptism allows us to connect this reading with the other two of today's liturgy. Baptism is an act of faith in the suffering and rising Messiah. It is an act of faith that clothes us in Christ to the point where we are closely associated with all he did. His paschal mystery of death and resurrection becomes ours. Since we are clothed in Christ, we must accept our own daily cross in order to rise with him.

Baptism thus presents us with a whole program of life. Each Christian is baptized into the suffering Messiah. No wonder, then, that his sufferings take on their full meaning only when seen as a dying with Christ in order also to rise with him. If we truly believe in Christ the Messiah, then that is what we believe. Take this faith seriously and you have the answer to so many otherwise unintelligible things that happen.

Thirteenth Sunday: Follow without Delay

Do Not Look Back (Luke 9:51-62)

This passage has evidently been chosen in order to teach us what it means to "follow Jesus" and what demands the decision to follow him makes upon us. Even the first part of the reading, in which we see Jesus courageously going up to Jerusalem, is part of the lesson, since Jesus is going to Jerusalem for his passion; we are being told indirectly what "following him" ultimately entails.

The will to follow Jesus requires a blind self-surrender, without any security for the future. The Son of Man, we are told, had no place to lay his head. Following Jesus also means that everything takes second place to the preaching of the kingdom. Jesus is unyielding on this point: "Let the dead bury their dead. But you, go and proclaim the kingdom of God" (Luke 9:60). Following in Jesus' steps also means not looking back. Once we have abandoned everything, we must not think of the past but simply move on ahead; we must not try to evaluate what we have done or ask whether some other way might be better.

Leave Everything (1 Kgs 19:16b, 19-21)

The story of Elisha's call will help us to a better understanding of the gospel. Elisha is called while he is out plowing; the call comes in the midst of his daily work. The circumstances are significant, but we often find God calling people in this way in both the Old and the New Testaments. Moses (Exod 3:1), David (1 Sam 16:11), and many others were called while tending their flocks; Simon and Andrew while at their fishing (Mark 1:16); and Matthew while sitting in his tax office (Matt 9:9). The call is unyielding in its insistency. True enough, Elisha, though he immediately leaves his possessions, asks that he may say goodbye to his father and mother before following Elijah. But then he slaughters the oxen that were the means of his livelihood.

It would be a mistake to apply these texts solely to a religious vocation or a call to the priestly ministry. Doubtless there is need of frequently recalling the requirements of these particular vocations and the manner in which people should answer them. But it is also true that every Christian receives a call and must respond to it. For simple examples, we might think of the requests people make to be allowed to meet a given pastoral need. There can be no doubt, of course, that obligations to family come first; it would be neither just nor prudent to neglect them and perhaps destroy a necessary cell (the family) in the Church's life for the sake of what might seem more heroic but in this case would be illusory.

On the other hand, many Christians feel able to meet a need of the community with generosity and without having to be asked. Sometimes they will set their work aside for a time and deprive themselves in order to respond in the Lord's name to what is asked of them without looking back and with the sole intention of answering what

they rightly think of as a call from God. Holiness is not the prerogative of religious and priests.

Today's texts should make us review our attitudes. Perhaps we are
closing our ears to divine inspirations and accustoming ourselves to
waiting until we are good and ready.

Called to Freedom (Gal 5:1, 13-18)

St. Paul returns here once more to the problem of the law. Christ
has set us free. We might better say: Christ has freed us for freedom.
Such a way of putting it, modeled on Hebrew idiom, reinforces the
image and helps us grasp the reality more fully.

The law imposed on God's people represented a first step toward
their salvation. Its purpose was to educate, but it was also meant to
be observed, and we know that it was not. What the law in fact did,
therefore, was to make people realize their sinful state, to enslave
them rather than to free them from the guilt of sin. Fulfillment of the
external obligations of the law could not lead people to total freedom;
on the contrary, they found themselves more fettered than ever.

Christ came to free humanity completely. The promise of liberation
had been given long ago to Abraham, whose faith in God justified
him. We too find freedom through faith in the liberation that was
promised and given in Jesus Christ. Christ frees us from sin and from
all the external constraints of the law.

Such teaching would evidently offend converts from Judaism who
thought that while they must follow Christ, they must also still obey
the law of Moses. In their eyes, justification or salvation depended
on both of these obediences. Paul, however, tells them that justification is a gift freely given to all whom God wishes to save, even if they
are not members of the Jewish people. The only necessary condition
for salvation is faith.

The passage read here reflects the doctrinal and practical situation
that was causing a crisis among the Galatians. Paul bids them realize
that they have been freed; they should not put on themselves once
again the chains of their ancient bondage. The Gospel is a revelation
of freedom; we should not assign to the Gospel the characteristic
traits of the law and assimilate it to the law!

Fourteenth Sunday: Joy and Peace

Joy Springing from Mission (Luke 10:1-12, 17-20)

Today's reading is parallel to the passage from Matthew for the Eleventh Sunday in Year A (Matt 9:36–10:8). There are, however, some special details in Luke's account that merit our attention. In addition, the first reading of the day constitutes an invitation to read the gospel with a particular theme in mind: that of the peace and joy that is the lot of those who have carried out their mission of preaching the kingdom.

Jesus first chooses those he will send. The emphasis here is not so much on the individuals he chooses (for this, see the Eleventh Sunday, Year A) as on their missionary activity and especially on the joy it will bring them. (This is not to say, of course, that being chosen as a messenger who will proclaim the coming of Jesus is something inconsequential!) We see Jesus sending his newly chosen disciples ahead of him to the places he himself intends to visit. Their mission will chiefly be to announce his coming, to present him to the crowds, to open their hearts to faith, and to arouse in them a desire for his coming. The whole passage thus carried a special meaning for those who would be reading Luke's gospel, since in the early Church, the Church described for us in the Acts of the Apostles, disciples would still be chosen and sent (see Acts 1:24; 6:3-6; 13:2-3; etc.), and their mission would consist in announcing the Christ who would come at the end of time.

Jesus urges prayer to the Father that he would send laborers into the harvest, as we have already heard him urging his disciples in St. Matthew's gospel (13:39). Then he goes into detail concerning the missionary activity of those he is sending. The part the missionaries must play is not an easy one, for it is that of the sheep who is sent among wolves. Despite this opposition, which at times will lead people to reject them, they are to wish peace upon every house they seek to enter. How could it be otherwise, since they are coming in order to proclaim God's kingdom?

The peace of which Christ speaks is almost like a concrete, material entity: "If a peaceful person lives there, your peace will rest on him; but if not, it will return to you." This peace, which is a fruit of the Holy Spirit (according to Gal 5:22), is linked to the coming of God's kingdom. This peace is the only thing the missionaries are to bring with them. They are to expect food in exchange for the incomparable service they perform in bringing peace with them into people's homes. St. Paul tells us the very same thing (1 Cor 9:14; 1 Tim 5:18). The missionaries are then to stay awhile in the village and confirm their proclamation of the kingdom by curing the sick and saying (which amounts to the same thing): "The kingdom of God is at hand for you."

The missionaries who bring peace and the message of the kingdom are not always received. If they are refused, they are to give the prophetic sign of judgment on God's behalf. The Acts of the Apostles tells us that Paul and Barnabas used the same gesture at Antioch when they were rejected there: they shook the dust from their feet (Acts 13:51). God's judgment will be more severe on the towns that hear the message of the kingdom and reject it than it was on Sodom.

Today's pericope omits some verses of Luke and passes immediately to the return of the missionaries. They come back rejoicing and filled with youthful wonder that even the demons obeyed when expelled in the name of Jesus.

Jesus' response to their enthusiasm encourages the disciples and gives them further theological instruction concerning the efficacy of the mission they have carried out in Jesus' name. Their apostolic work in his name means that the end of the reign of Satan is at hand; Jesus even sees him fall like lightning from heaven, an apocalyptic vision of the end of time. Jesus has given them his own power to crush serpents and destroy the powers of evil. He now encourages them and gives them a new cause for joy by telling them that their names are written in heaven.

The Joy and Peace of the Messianic Age (Isa 66:10-14c)

The sorrowing are here urged to rejoice. For her infidelities, Jerusalem has been punished by exile, but the exile is now over and the exiles are gradually coming home; the city is coming to life again. The prophet expresses his joyous amazement at this in the verses just preceding today's pericope (v. 8). Peace is now returning to Jerusalem, like a river that the Lord is making flow in her direction. The prophet describes the joys this peace brings with it.

The joy that Isaiah speaks of is also described for us in psalms with which we are quite familiar; for example: "When the LORD brought back the exiles of Sion, / we thought we were dreaming. / Then was our mouth filled with laughter; / on our tongues, songs of joy. . . . /

What great deeds the Lord has worked for us! /Indeed, we were glad"
(Ps 126:1-3).

This Sunday conveys to us something of the vibrant emotions of
the early Church as she saw the slowly ripening fruits of her missionary activity in the name of the Lord Jesus. We can feel a touch of
her joy, of her awareness of the presence of the God whose kingdom
was spreading. Do we still feel any of that joy today? Has not our
enthusiasm diminished somewhat? The centuries have passed, it is
true, and yet history, despite its sometimes unedifying pages, surely
provides in the past and at the present time a magnificent vision that
should stir us to joy and fill us with peace!

We should all ask ourselves the same questions we put to the
Church as such. Is our missionary zeal sufficiently focused on the
proclamation of Christ's kingdom? Do we spread peace and joy to
others? Do those who come in touch with us sense that we are filled
with peace and joy because we are convinced that the kingdom is
among us and that we are experiencing it? These are important questions, and the answers are more important than any considerations
of missionary technique, for technique is of value only if we are
spreading peace and joy because the kingdom is at hand. They are
questions each of us must answer individually.

Bear in Your Body the Marks of Jesus (Gal 6:14-18)

The two verses preceding today's pericope recall the trouble caused
by the Jewish Christians. The latter wanted to make salvation dependent on belonging to the Jewish people and on circumcision. These
Jewish Christians wanted to "boast of your flesh" (Gal 6:13), that is,
they were still proud of belonging to a people they regarded as privileged and of observing the Mosaic law. In fact, however, they would
"compel you to have yourselves circumcised, only that they may not
be persecuted for the cross of Christ" (6:12). In other words, the Jewish
Christians regarded their membership in the Jewish people chiefly
as a means of protecting their lives and their peaceful existence.

Paul, on the other hand, wants his readers to be faithful to what
Christ has done. We now live a new life in a new world. It was the
sufferings of the crucified Christ that saved us; they are the mark of
our salvation and of our belonging to a new people. We should bear
them in our own bodies and make them our source of pride.

It is clear that Paul fears a return to the law. May we not fear the same for ourselves? In what sense is such a return possible for us? It is possible for us paradoxically to feel proud and secure because we are faithful to certain observances and because we receive the sacraments—as though the sacraments were chiefly meant for security instead of being a way of sharing in Christ's sufferings so that we may also reach the resurrection with him. The tendency to seek refuge in the letter of the law or in practice will be a trap for human beings until the end of time. We must be conscious of the danger and on guard against yielding to the tendency, lest we easily slip into a life based chiefly on practices and develop a kind of Christian pride of caste.

Fifteenth Sunday: The Law of Love

Who Is My Neighbor? (Luke 10:25-37)

St. Luke was a disciple of St. Paul. It is not surprising, therefore, that he has relatively little use for the letter of the law and is much more concerned about compassion and the spirit of the law. This is his frame of mind when he tells us the parable of the Good Samaritan.

The lawyer's question, "what must I do to inherit eternal life?" is typical in that it is wholly concerned with obligation and fulfillment of a law. But the lawyer does know the law, and his answer to Jesus' own question is perfect. Then, moved by a desire to justify himself, he asks a second question, and it shows that he has not gotten to the bottom of the problem of love and that his grasp of the law he has quoted is superficial. This is not a negligible point, since Christ has just told him, "do this and you will live"—that is, observe the law of love for God and neighbor, and you will have life therefrom. If the lawyer does not really understand the law he has quoted, he cannot fully observe it.

It is clear that Christ does not reject the Jewish tradition that the lawyer has just quoted to him from the books of Deuteronomy (6:5) and Leviticus (19:18). On the contrary, Christ tells us that the attainment of eternal life is bound up with the concrete fulfillment of the twofold commandment of love for God and neighbor.

The purpose of the parable is to shed light on what "neighbor" means. The priest and the Levite who pass by have no understanding of who their neighbor is. Jesus deliberately chooses a Samaritan, a person the Jews regard as a heretic, to illustrate the true concept of "neighbor."

Live by the Word of God (Deut 30:10-14)

Moses is concerned to show that the law is not something outside of humanity, remote, majestic, and as inaccessible as if it were stored up in heaven. On the contrary, the law is very near; it is even in a person's mouth and heart as a dynamic principle of life. It should never even be thought of as distinct from practice; that is, "law" by its nature is something to be put into concrete practice. The law is not beyond people's power or out of their reach, for it is within them. We should read here the earlier passage in which the commandment of love is enunciated (Deut 6:4-9); in this latter passage the law is presented to us as a source of life that slowly fills the person who puts the law into practice.

These passages from the book of Deuteronomy lead us over to the Gospel and its demands. Our age, like the book of Deuteronomy and the gospels, is hardly legalist-minded, but this does not mean that we have nothing to learn from these passages.

Christianity is characterized precisely by the dynamic practice of love for God and neighbor; indeed, such practice is the most direct proof we can give the world that our faith is living and powerful. Love must be in our mouths and in our hearts, and we must put it into practice.

Our age thinks it has discovered the reality of the "other," yet it is a time when ever more numerous rifts are dividing people. In the very groups that should be marked by the practice of genuine love, we find people devouring one another in the name of openness. Evidently, then, the lessons of this Sunday still have their point! The commandment of love is directly related to life, and true life is impossible if the commandment is not put into concrete practice in relation to each person. Many an ascetical effort, many an hour of prayer and contemplation are rendered ineffective for the Church's life because these words of God on love are not found in the mouth and the heart or, if they are, are dead words that do not influence people's lives. "This is how all will know that you are my disciples, if you have love for one another" (John 13:35). Do people know us as his disciples by this sign?

All Things Were Created through Christ and for Him (Col 1:15-20)

Verses 12-14 of this first chapter of the Letter to the Colossians are a prayer of thanksgiving for our translation into the kingdom of Christ, in whom we have redemption and the forgiveness of sins.

The pericope read today is a great hymn to the glory of Christ, who is the image of the invisible God, both as Creator and Redeemer. It is divided into three parts: the first gives praise to Christ as Creator of all things; the second gives thanks for the Redeemer, the Head of the Body that is the Church; the third honors him who has reconciled everything in himself.

Christ is the Creator. This action, however, is not to be isolated from another action of his: redemption. It is he who creates, and it is he who remakes creation so that it is better than it originally was. Christ is the image of the invisible God and the sacrament of our encounter with God. He is the firstborn of all creation; he has primacy in the created order because he is the incarnate God. Everything has been created through Christ, in Christ, and for Christ. If he is the firstborn of all creation, it is because he is above all other creatures and because he exists before them. Creation through Christ means that included in the creative plan is the incarnation that is to restore the created order.

Christ is also the Redeemer. Creation already contains within itself the second creation, because through his paschal mystery Christ creates a Body, the Church, of which he is the Head. The fact that the creative and redemptive roles of Christ are so closely united gives us a rounded idea of God's plan and helps us look at redemption, not as though it were an event apart, but as an internal force that shatters the old world in order to create it anew. It is one and the same Person who, as image of the Father and as Word made flesh, creates, re-creates, and forms a Body of which he is the Head. In fact, he re-creates the world as a single reality (John 17), which he organizes and of which he is the Head.

Christ has reconciled everything in himself, and he is the fullness of all. By the blood he shed on the cross he has reconciled everything on earth and in heaven. He humbled himself, "emptied" himself, and accepted poverty and self-stripping, especially in his passion (Phil 2:7), but now he is filled and is the source of life in the fullest possible sense of this last term. Because he dedicated himself to the Father's will and lowered himself beneath the angels, he has been exalted and has received the name that is above every name (Phil 2:9).

We are called to share the fullness that is in Christ; in fact, we are already in contact with that fullness because we are members of the Body whose head Christ is. We also have access to this fullness every time we receive a sacrament (for example, the sacrament of penance, which we do not think of often enough from this point of view) and especially when we celebrate the Eucharist, as on Sundays. The Christ who created all things continually re-creates us.

This is evidently a very active outlook on the life of Christ and the life of his members. It is an outlook that will spur us to action and to constant renewal. We must be willing to be re-created by Christ, in his Body the Church, as he wishes and in the way he wishes.

Sixteenth Sunday: God Visits Us

Receive Jesus in Your House (Luke 10:38-42)

Today's gospel contains several points of teaching. In particular, we could well find help here in solving the ever-current problem of activity and "contemplation." We should not let ourselves go overboard in this direction, however, since, as the first reading shows, the gospel passage was chosen chiefly for the idea of God's visit to us. The fact of that visit should be the focus of our attention. It is also important to see how and under what conditions we should receive God's visit.

The Lord's visit presupposes an attitude on the part of those he visits, and from this point of view today's passage is especially valuable. The evangelist does not tell us the name of the place Jesus visits, but he does tell us the names of the two women who are thus favored. This naming of names is unusual, for Luke does not normally give the names of the people who enter into dialogue with Jesus. Perhaps Luke had an intuition that this passage would be of permanent importance in the life of the Church, since it tells us how to receive Jesus. For that reason too the evangelist goes somewhat into detail.

There are two possible ways of receiving Jesus. One is symbolized by the attitude of Mary as she sits at the feet of Jesus. Is her attitude one of mere contemplative idleness? No, she listens actively to the Lord, and her sitting is the sitting of the disciple at the teacher's feet. Thus, the crowd sits down around Jesus and waits to be taught

(Matt 12:47; Luke 8:19-20); thus too, a man freed from demons sits at Jesus' feet (Luke 8:35). The other attitude is one of activity that is inspired by respectful love of the Lord. So respectful indeed is Martha that Luke lets us feel a certain anxiety in her behavior, as well as a zeal so sure of itself that she can call on the Lord to be witness to all she does, while her sister abandons her to do the work alone.

In his answer to Martha's complaint, Jesus gives his judgment on the two attitudes. It is less one-sided than people sometimes seem to think. For example, his answer in no way condemns the zeal of Martha, and it would be very subjective, to say the least, to see in his words a condemnation of zeal and apostolic activity in the Church! If we are to interpret the words properly, we must attend to the context in which Luke places them. It is easy to see that the evangelist wants to emphasize the hearing of the word and the attitude of a disciple. Receiving Christ requires, first and foremost, hearing him and having the soul of a disciple. But Jesus' response does not make a choice of one attitude against another; that is, Christians are not forced to choose between acting and contemplating. The point is rather that they must first of all listen and receive Christ with interior peace and simplicity. Any reproach of Martha is for her anxiety, not for her zealous activity in receiving Jesus.

Unfortunately, the text of Jesus' answer raises problems of literary criticism that have not been resolved. In the New American Bible, Revised Edition, Jesus says: "Martha, Martha, you are anxious and worried about many things. There is need of only one thing." This translation is possible because the original text is found in three different forms: "few things are needed"; "only one thing is needed"; and "few things are needed, even only one." This third text joins the first two into one; the reading is attested by important manuscripts, and many editions have adopted it.

The first option would seem to mean that Martha should not worry because only a few things are needed. Such a reading would render Jesus' remark completely trivial, and as a matter of fact there are few manuscript witnesses to this reading. The second and third readings really mean the same thing, namely, one thing is necessary. What is that one thing? In the context of the proclamation of the gospel, and given the attitude of Mary who listens to the Lord, the one thing needed is evidently God's word. Everything else is secondary when compared to this listening to God's word.

"The better part" that will not be taken from Mary does not mean her not being at the service of others; it means only her listening to the word of God. This is doubtless why the reading used to be used on the feast of the Assumption of the Blessed Virgin, who, beyond all others, listened to the word and kept it in her heart. We must repeat once again—for the point is important—that Jesus was reproaching Martha not for her service to others but only because she tended to overemphasize and give priority to what should be secondary in relation to listening to God's word.

God Comes and Fulfills His Promise (Gen 18:1-10a)

The story from Genesis is like a fairy tale that transports us into a world of Eastern warmth and hospitality. We could well be carried away by the story and led to imagine that it is intended to encourage the virtue of hospitality. The author of the narrative goes beyond any such intention, however, and treats the Lord's visit to Abraham as the patriarch sits at the door of his tent.

The story has its strange side. The Lord appears, but, in fact, three men are suddenly standing in front of Abraham. He greets them, but he addresses only one of them, and he uses both singular and plural pronouns in his invitation to them. Some fathers of the Church, such as Augustine and Ambrose, see in these three men the Trinity; others think one of the three is the Word, and they concentrate on him. Exegetically, of course, neither of these interpretations is justifiable, but the passage remains a literary conundrum.

In any case, the story depicts divine messengers or perhaps even God himself, manifesting himself in this triple form. The three ask Abraham: "Where is your wife Sarah?" and they promise him a son. Here God is fulfilling the promise he had made to Abraham if the latter would leave his homeland. Abraham had first received the Lord in the latter's word and promise ("I will make of you a great nation"; Gen 12:2) and had done so with faith. Such faith now brings the fulfillment of the promise.

The gospel, as we have seen, follows the same line of thought, since listening to the word is a way of receiving the Lord. This does not mean that the warm welcome Abraham gives his guests is useless. The point is rather that receiving God by accepting his word and promise is more basic and more important.

The responsorial psalm reverses the perspective and sings of God's hospitality as he receives us into his house. It also tells us the qualities required if one is to be God's guest. Between Psalm 15, which praises God's hospitality, and the reading, which tells us of Abraham's hospitality, there is a close connection. The two together describe the exchange thus set up between God and humans and amount to a new way of expressing the covenant that exists between them.

It seems to me inappropriate to compare the two readings (Genesis and Luke) in detail. The reader might point out contradictions; for example, Sarah, who bustles about to serve the guests, is rewarded, while Martha does the same and is reprimanded. But such criticisms would show that the reader has not understood the two passages. The real point in both is the priority that must be given to the reception of the Word and its heralds, and the fact that this reception is not primarily a matter of outward actions but of an attitude of listening.

The commentaries have too often seen in these texts an opposition between action and contemplation. Only an excessively anecdotal reading of the text could have created such a simplistic, moralizing opposition.

We must look more deeply than that and see a point that is important for us today. The point is that listening to the Lord is the primordial Christian activity. The welcome we give to him consists first and foremost in our receptive attitude of attentive faith. The first thing we have to do is understand what the Lord wants of us and, therefore, be alert to hear him. This first step is the basis for the whole of concrete Christian life. We can call this listening "contemplation" if we want. Certainly, if we want to hear Jesus, we must find a quiet place apart from the noise of the crowd; we must find the time to read the Scriptures; we must have the courage to avoid the discussions, the endless roundtables, sharings, and workshops, that are now fashionable so that we have the opportunity to listen to Jesus in silence. We can also hear him, however, in the midst of our work, in good spirits, or amid physical or moral suffering. The interior attitude of love is the decisive thing when it comes to hearing God.

The Mystery Hidden and Revealed (Col 1:24-28)

St. Paul requires us to accustom ourselves to an unfamiliar terminology. As we use the word today, a "mystery" is something hidden that we can neither see nor understand. We like to call religious realities "mysterious," but we tend to mean by speaking of, for example, the "mysteries of Christ" that there are aspects of Christ that we have trouble understanding, for example, the eucharistic presence. In the language of St. Paul and of later theology, however, "mystery" is just the opposite of the hidden and incomprehensible. It is a word applied to God's plan, which was indeed hidden through the ages but which has now been revealed in order that we might share in it. This "mystery" is Christ himself, present among us, our hope of glory.

St. Paul is a prisoner when he writes this letter, but his sufferings do not disturb his joy, since he puts up with these sufferings for the sake of the Church. His attitude is a "moral" one but also a good deal more. Christ's sufferings were undoubtedly efficacious and do not inherently need to be completed. But the Body of Christ is unfinished and is constantly being built. It is therefore the sufferings of Christ as experienced by his body that Paul shares through his own sufferings. The Church is always in the process of carrying out God's plan more fully. As a minister whom God has chosen, Paul is intimately involved in this constructive work that completes what was lacking in Christ's sufferings, that is, his unfinished Church. Paul's ministry on behalf of this construction is twofold: a ministry of suffering and a ministry of evangelization.

The mystery hidden through the ages and revealed in the person of Christ is now at work in the world and leading the world to its fullness and completion. The purpose of every apostolate is precisely to lead people to their full being in Christ—to lead them, that is, to an interior balance that will enable them to bear suffering in Christ so that the Church may grow.

Seventeenth Sunday: Ask and You Shall Receive

Learn to Pray (Luke 11:1-13)

St. Luke wishes to show us how Jesus prayed. He is not the only one, of course, to record Jesus' teaching on prayer. St. Matthew too tells us how Jesus saw the act of praying: "when you pray, go to your inner room, close the door, and pray to your Father in secret. And your Father who sees in secret will repay you" (Matt 6:6). Prayer in secret is effective. But Matthew also emphasizes the presence of Christ when people gather to pray together: "if two of you agree on earth about anything for which they are to pray, it shall be granted to them by my heavenly Father. For where two or three are gathered together in my name, there am I in the midst of them" (Matt 18:19-20).

St. John lays special emphasis on the efficacy of prayer "in the name of Jesus." "In my name" means "united to me": "If you remain in me, and my words remain in you, ask for whatever you want and it will be done for you" (15:7). If we ask in Jesus' name, our prayer will be answered: "whatever you ask in my name, I will do" (14:13); "so that whatever you ask the Father in my name he may give you" (15:16); "ask and you will receive" (16:24), provided we ask in the name of Jesus (16:23, 26).

Both Matthew and Luke show us Jesus teaching his disciples the Our Father. In St. Luke's account, Jesus' teaching is elicited by a request from the disciples themselves: "Lord, teach us to pray just as John taught his disciples." The disciples who followed a prophet wanted to learn of the prophet's own experience in prayer.

Luke, like Matthew, has preserved the prayer that Jesus offers as a model. We may be surprised, however, to realize that the two texts of the Our Father are not identical. This means that the evangelists thought it unnecessary to transcribe verbatim the model prayer offered by Jesus but only to capture its essential content.

Many of the fathers, of course, wrote commentaries on the Lord's Prayer. In addition, the ancient ritual for the catechumenate contained a "presentation" (*traditio*) of the Our Father to the catechumens; on this occasion a short commentary on the prayer was preached so that the catechumen might use the prayer intelligently.[1] In the Roman liturgy the Lord's Prayer was originally sung immediately before Communion. Pope St. Gregory the Great, however, shifted it to its present position immediately after the eucharistic prayer; he was astonished that we should use prayers composed by humans during the main part of the celebration, while postponing the Lord's own prayer to a much later point.[2]

The liturgy uses the version of the Lord's Prayer that St. Matthew supplies. Here are the texts of Matthew and Luke set side by side for comparison.

Matthew 6:9-13	Luke 11:2-4
Our Father in heaven,	Father,
hallowed be your name,	hallowed be your name,
your kingdom come,	your kingdom come.
your will be done, on earth as in heaven.	
Give us today our daily bread;	Give us each day our daily bread
and forgive us our debts, as we forgive our debtors;	and forgive us our sins for we ourselves forgive everyone in debt to us,
and do not subject us to the final test, but deliver us from the evil one.	and do not subject us to the final test.

In St. Matthew, the Our Father is followed by a commentary on the penultimate petition: "If you forgive others their transgressions, your heavenly Father will forgive you. But if you do not forgive others, neither will your Father forgive your transgressions" (6:14).

The structure of the Our Father is evidently similar to that of traditional Jewish prayers, with their exclamation of praise and their petitions, which are another form of praise. We have already analyzed this structure on several occasions.

Prayer to the "Father"

It would become customary in the Latin Church to address prayer to the Father, through Jesus Christ, in the Holy Spirit. Psalm 89 had long before expressed God's own wish that people should address him as "Father": "He will call out to me, 'You are my father'" (v. 27). Nonetheless, even though the Old Testament had a very true and loving idea of the fatherhood of God, both as Father of the nation he had brought into being and as Father of the individuals who made up the people, the Lord's Prayer is typically Christian. According to St. Paul, only the Spirit makes it possible for us, after our baptism, to address God as *Abba*, "dear Father" (see Gal 4:6; Rom 8:15); this is because in baptism the Spirit of Jesus, the Son, becomes our Spirit and enables us to address God as Jesus did.

St. Matthew's version of the prayer amplifies the address "Father" into "Our Father in heaven," whereas St. Luke is content with the simple name. That is how Jesus often addresses the Father in the gospels. Commenting on the Lord's Prayer, St. Ambrose writes, "You have changed from evil servant to good son. . . . Therefore, lift your eyes to the Father who begot you through the bath, the Father who redeemed you through the Son."[3] The commentary on the Our Father that accompanied the rite of the presentation of the prayer to the catechumens follows the same line of thought: "These are the words of a free person, and full of confidence. You are to live in such a way that you may indeed be children of God and brothers and sisters of Christ."

St. Luke seems to reflect better the original prayer as spoken by Jesus, inasmuch as, like Jesus, he addresses God simply as "Father," without the "our" and the "in heaven." The prayer is thus rendered more intimate. At the same time, however, it is surely less apt for a communal celebration.

HALLOWED BE YOUR NAME

"Name" in the Bible is a way of designating the very person. But what can it mean to say: "May you be hallowed [sanctified]"? St. Ambrose raises the question and gives an answer: "What does 'sanctified' mean? . . . It means 'May he be hallowed in us,' so that his holiness may reach us." The commentary on the presentation of the Our Father says: "We ask that his name be made holy in us, so that after being sanctified in his baptism, we may continue as we have begun."

How did St. Luke himself understand this holiness of the Father's name? In the *Magnificat*, the holiness of God is associated with his mercy and power: "The Mighty One has done great things for me, / and holy is his name. / His mercy is from age to age / to those who fear him. / He has shown might with his arm" (Luke 1:49-51). God is holy because he carries out the work of salvation on behalf of his people and because in so doing he manifests both mercy and power.

In the prophet Ezekiel, the Lord proclaims that despite the infidelities and profanations of which his people are guilty, "I will show the holiness of my great name, desecrated among the nations. . . . Then the nations shall know that I am the LORD—oracle of the Lord GOD— when through you I show my holiness before their very eyes" (36:23). This mighty and merciful action of God will be manifested when he puts a new heart and a new spirit into his people (Ezek 36:26).

Your Kingdom Come

The Lord's name is sanctified when he continues his mighty and merciful action in us and we respond to it. Such a response must be continued until the fullness of time when the kingdom of God comes. St. Ambrose writes, "The kingdom of God comes when you have obtained his grace. For he himself says: 'The kingdom of God is within you.'" Closely following Ambrose, the commentary at the presentation of the Lord's Prayer says: "But when does our God not reign, since his reign is unending? Therefore, when we say, 'Your kingdom come,' we are asking that our kingdom may come, the kingdom promised us by God and won for us by the blood and suffering of Christ."

According to these commentaries, then, the petition looks to the end of time. At the same time, however, the petition is also an exhortation to Christians who were contemporaries of Matthew and Luke, and to all of us as well, to manifest and promote God's rule in our lives.

Your Will Be Done

St. Luke omits this petition, which is, in fact, an explication of the preceding, inasmuch as the sanctification of God's name and the desire that his kingdom should come necessarily imply the doing of God's will. St. Ambrose sees in the accomplishment of God's will, however, the successful carrying out of the plan of salvation: "'Peace is bestowed on all things in heaven and on earth by the blood of Christ' (Col 1:20). Heaven has been sanctified, and the devil has been expelled. He is now on earth, along with the humans he deceived. 'Your will be done,' that is, let there be peace on earth as there is in heaven." The commentary in the ritual of presentation understands the doing of God's will as referring especially to us who dwell on Earth: "Your will be done in the sense that what you will in heaven, we who dwell on earth may accomplish in an irreproachable way."

Give Us Our Daily Bread

St. Matthew adds "today" and thus puts the emphasis on the present day; we ask for today's bread without being anxious for tomorrow's. St. Luke adds "each day," thus stressing rather the fact that the Father cares for his children day after day.

The petition is thus in a line with Jewish prayer, in which there was frequent petition for earthly food.[4] The prayer is, moreover, the prayer of one who is poor, and the thought of the poor must inevitably come to mind as we ask for "our daily bread." In addition, the fathers thought at this point of the Eucharist. St. Ambrose writes:

> He spoke of bread but called it *epiousios*, that is, "substantial." This bread is not the bread that enters the body but the bread of eternal life that strengthens the substance of our souls. That is why it is called, in Greek, *epiousios*. The Latin text calls it a "daily" bread, because the Greeks call "tomorrow" *ten epiousan hēmeran*. Thus, the Latin and Greek texts are both useful. The Greek, however, captures the two meanings in a single word, while the Latin expresses only the "daily" aspect. . . . Receive each day what is of profit to you for each day.

The commentary on the presentation says: "The 'bread' here is to be understood as spiritual bread. Our real bread is Christ, who said: 'I am the living bread who have come down from heaven.' We speak of it as 'daily' because we must always be asking to be preserved from sin so that we may be worthy of the heavenly food." It is clear that the spiritual and liturgical interpretation can differ from that reached by a straight exegesis of the text. The use of the Lord's Prayer in the eucharistic celebration has given it an undeniable eucharistic meaning.

FORGIVE US

St. Luke has us pray for the forgiveness of our sins, while St. Matthew speaks of the forgiveness or cancellation of debts. We may find it odd that Luke did not keep the image of a debt, since he is the one who has preserved for us the little parable about the creditor who forgave two debtors (Luke 7:41-42). In any case, we must note that in the Lord's Prayer Luke immediately goes on to say that we must forgive those indebted to us if we would ourselves be forgiven by God.

The measure of our forgiveness by God will be determined by the measure of our forgiveness of others. After explaining that Christ has cancelled our debts by shedding his blood, St. Ambrose continues: "Pay attention to what you are saying: 'As I forgive, so do you forgive me'! If you forgive, you make an agreement that you in turn will be forgiven. If you do not forgive, how can you expect God to forgive you?" The commentary on the presentation clarifies the petition by reference to other words of Jesus: "The sense of this petition is that we cannot win forgiveness of our sins unless we first forgive those who have offended us. As the Lord says in the gospel: 'if you do not forgive others, neither will your Father forgive your transgressions.'"

DO NOT SUBJECT US TO THE FINAL TEST

In St. Luke's version of the Lord's Prayer, these words are the final ones, while in St. Matthew's version this negative appeal is followed by a more positive one: "but deliver us from the evil one." St. Ambrose seems to have correctly grasped the meaning of this petition, and many modern commentators agree with him:

> He does not say: "Do not lead us into temptation," but, like an athlete, he wants a testing such as human nature can sustain; he wants each person to be delivered from evil, that is, from the enemy, from sin. But the Lord who has taken away your sins and forgiven your offenses has power also to guard and protect you against the snares of your adversary the devil. . . . Those who entrust themselves to God have no fear of the devil. For if God is for us, who is against us?

The liturgical commentary at the presentation of the Lord's Prayer says simply, "'And lead us not into temptation.' That is, do not let us be led into temptation by the Tempter, who is the source of all corruption."

After recording the Lord's model prayer for his readers, St. Luke continues his teaching on prayer by recording a parable that Jesus spoke to his disciples. It is the familiar parable of the importunate friend, and its main point is the unwearying constancy with which we must pray. The parable is easily applied to the one who prays, but especially to God who hears our prayer: "[A]sk and you will receive; seek and you will find; knock and the door will be opened to you. For every one who asks, receives." The parable is an exhortation to both confidence and perseverance in prayer. For if among us who are evil, a father cannot refuse his child anything, how much more will God be willing to answer our prayers!

This teaching on prayer would doubtless be somewhat dangerous if it did not follow upon the model prayer just given. A simplistic mind—and this kind of simplicity does exist, even among highly educated people when they deal with things religious—might think that we need only have this shameless persistence and unshakable faith, and we will obtain anything we want from God. The Lord's Prayer corrects such an impossible theology of prayer. It tells us that what we can obtain with certainty is the sanctification of God's name, the coming of his kingdom, and the doing of his will. We obtain forgiveness but only on certain conditions, whose fulfillment depends on us. If God, being a Father, gives us what we ask, he is not, however, forced to answer any and every petition whatsoever; prayer is not something that works mechanically. God hears our petitions only if they are in keeping with his will and if we do our best to carry out what he wants of us for our salvation.

Pray Tirelessly against All Hope (Gen 18:20-32)

Nothing could better show that prayer is a bold dialogue with God than this passage from the book of Genesis, in which we see Abraham speaking with the Lord and almost straining the limits of respect in an effort to catch God, as it were, in the snare of his own goodness and his own sense of justice. The whole dialogue should be read in its entirety, for in it we see the Lord being pushed to the extreme of mercy.

The style and manner of proceeding are truly Semitic. The appeal to God's honor and reputation for justice might seem to us highly disrespectful; as a matter of fact, however, it shows great confidence in God and demonstrates the "friendly" intimacy of God with Old Testament humanity. Abraham makes it clear that along with Moses, Samuel, and Jeremiah, he is one of the great spiritual leaders of all time, one of those whose spirit of trusting prayer is an example for every generation. In the psalms too we find God taken to task and "forced" to save his honor by hearing the prayers of his people: "Not for our sakes, Lord, but for your name's sake you must give us what we ask"!

The responsorial psalm, Psalm 138, praises God for being always attentive to our prayer: "On the day I cried, you answered me" (v. 3). He stretches out his hand to save us and exerts his power for us, "O Lord, your merciful love is eternal; / discard not the work of your hands" (v. 8).

Buried and Risen with Christ (Col 2:12-14)

It is a known fact that Christians used to think of the baptismal font as a tomb in which we are buried with Christ but also as a maternal womb that brings us to new birth. These symbols were connected with the very expressive rite of immersion. But the ritual that symbolized and effected this death and new life has power to do so only if the recipient has faith in the God who raised Jesus from the dead.

Sin and death, death and resurrection with Christ, faith and baptism—these are correlative terms of which Paul reminds us in his brief but pregnant statement. Because of the perspective he is adopting, he adds that forgiveness of sin means liberation from the law and its observances—law, sin, and death being connected, as he teaches in his Letter to the Romans (7:7-9). Here Paul uses an extremely expressive image: the law has been nailed to the cross.

Eighteenth Sunday: The Passing and the Abiding

Rich in God's Sight (Luke 12:13-21)

Today's gospel speaks to our instinctive tendencies and concerns, in order to put us on guard against them: "Take care to guard against all greed, for though one may be rich, one's life does not consist of possessions."

Following his usual catechetical approach, Jesus is not content with this abstract warning but brings it home to his hearers with the help of the parable of the rich man who piles up possessions against the future, driven by a concern that is familiar to every generation: "Now as for you, you have so many good things stored up for many years, rest, eat, drink, be merry!"

If, in Jesus' eyes, riches are suspect, the same is already true of the Old Testament. The latter undoubtedly does regard wealth as a sign of God's blessing. Thus the patriarchs were wealthy (Gen 13:2; 26:12; 30:43). Deuteronomy shows us God concerned for the prosperity of his people (Deut 8:7-10; 28:1-12). Abundance goes with uprightness of life (Ps 37:19).

At the same time, however, the Old Testament is also conscious of the dangers that accompany wealth; evidence of this attitude is especially to be found in the Wisdom literature. "Happy the rich person found without fault, / who does not turn aside after wealth" (Sir 31:8); "Let not . . . the rich man boast of his riches" (Jer 9:22); "the rich answer harshly" (Prov 18:23); "You whose [the city's] wealthy are full of violence" (Mic 6:12). Riches are unprofitable: "No man can . . . / pay a price to God for his life. / How high is the price of his soul!" (Ps 49:8-9); "the abundance of the rich allows them no sleep" (Eccl 5:11). When life draws to an end, riches prove useless: "The riches he swallowed he will vomit up" (Job 20:15); the rich man "is like the beasts that are destroyed" (Ps 49:13); "Wealth is useless on a day of wrath" (Prov 11:4); "People's riches serve as ransom for their lives" (Prov 13:8); "wealth does not last forever" (Prov 27:24).

Wealth is, then, a gift of God, but it must be handled carefully, and it never becomes an unqualified good or the most important of blessings. Wisdom must be preferred to it (1 Kgs 3:11; Job 28:15-19; Wis 7:8-11; Prov 2:4; 3:15; 8:11). Moreover, it is difficult to remain faithful in time of prosperity, for an easy life tends to blunt the heart's sensitivity (Deut 31:20; Ps 73:4-9). In the book of Isaiah we even find riches being cursed: "Ah! Those who join house to house, who connect field to field" (5:8). The prophet here anticipates the "woe to you who are rich" of the gospel (Luke 6:24).

Jesus adopts the same perspective in the parable of today's gospel: wealth may not be intrinsically evil, but it does make it difficult to lead a life centered on the reign of God.

Leaving One's Possessions to an Unknown (Eccl 1:2; 2:21-23)

The text might lead us to think that we are to be uninterested in work or progress: "All things are vanity!" But that would be to mistake the author's thought. He is really preaching a balance: work should not become the main concern of our life; our attention should be focused primarily on God. The real need, therefore, is to give work its proper meaning. This meaning does not clearly emerge, however, from this highly realistic book of the Old Testament.

The Sermon on the Mount gives us Christ's thinking on wealth. The sermon must be completed, however, by the Lord's teaching on the precious pearl (Matt 13:45), on the obligation of serving only one master (Matt 6:24), on the difficulty of following Jesus along the way of perfection (Matt 19:21), and on the necessity of renouncing all of one's possessions in order to be a disciple of Jesus (Luke 14:33).[5]

There is a danger that riches may cause us to close our hearts. The responsorial psalm (Ps 95) puts us on guard against this danger: "O that today you would listen to his voice! Harden not your hearts" (v. 7-8).

Seek the Things That Are Above (Col 3:1-5, 9-11)

The balanced moral outlook on life should result from what people have become in virtue of baptism. Raised up with Christ, they must seek the things that are above. This quest is the very meaning of life. Christians are new people and are constantly being remade anew by the Creator in his own image so that they may attain true knowledge.

Christians must put to death in themselves the vices Paul lists in verses 5-8 (vv. 6-8 are omitted from today's reading), where the emphasis is on the appetite for pleasure and the worship of idols. But he does so for the sake of the true knowledge that leads him to a share of God's glory, his goal being to appear someday with Christ in glory. That we should seek the things above is not only a moral precept promulgated by Paul but also a consequence of our new being. We belong now to the heavenly kingdom and must therefore rid ourselves of the preoccupations and ways of acting proper to the old, unreconstructed self.

Nineteenth Sunday: Be Ready to Receive God's Glory

Be Ready (Luke 12:32-48)

In this passage from St. Luke's gospel, Jesus describes the attitude of expectation that should characterize his disciples in every generation. The little flock waits amid difficulty, conflict, and the sameness of every day. It knows, however, that the Father has been pleased to bestow the kingdom on it. For that reason, an attitude of expectant waiting is quite logical, and Jesus wishes to clarify this attitude through four examples that will foster understanding.

In St. Luke's view, the four parables tell the Christians whom he is evangelizing what kind of interior outlook they should have. Each of the parables in turn brings out the nature of Christian expectation: the image of the treasure in heaven, the image of the servants who are awaiting their master's return, the image of the burglar who comes unexpectedly, and the image of the faithful and the unfaithful stewards.

These parables are still relevant to us individually and to the Church of our day. They bid us be expectant and ready. We are to set our hearts on heavenly treasure, not because earthly things are evil, but because we rightly judge that the treasures of heaven are inexhaustible, permanent, and in every way good.

We are to be as servants awaiting their master. Those who listened to Jesus were all doubtless awaiting the reign of God; their vision of that kingdom was not always a purified one but was frequently colored by political views. St. Luke's readers, however, like the Church of our day and like each of us, thought in terms of an encounter with God, now and at the end of time. Consequently, we are able to look beyond the meaning that Jesus' words had for many in his original audience to the meaning Jesus actually intended. This is to say that we, like Luke, look for the coming of Christ at the end of time as described by both Matthew (10:23; 24:44) and Luke himself (18:8).

These parables, which illustrate the duty of expectant waiting, doubtless lend themselves to legitimate moralizing. At the same time, however, we should not allow ourselves to forget the deeper vision they offer us of the very nature of the Christian as one who has been reborn from above. The spiritual nature of the Christian is made both to wait for and to move toward an encounter with God. If one's soul is always pointed toward this encounter, one cannot be taken by surprise. The treasure of Christians is in heaven; they have received from the Lord natural and spiritual talents to be used for the advancement of the world and the good of others, and they are the faithful stewards of these talents. How, then, could the Lord take them by surprise, like a burglar coming unexpectedly?

Readiness is not a kind of accessory quality, either for the Church or for the individual. Rather, it is something inherent in the nature of both the Church and the individual. Only forgetfulness of what they really are could allow Christians to be surprised by the coming of Christ. If they follow their true nature, they will want that coming, look for it, await it, and regard it as a blessing.

Called to Glory (Wis 18:6-9)

This passage, with its high literary quality, shows God's people awaiting the glory of God. The night of deliverance, of which we are told in the book of Exodus (chap. 12), had been known in advance by the patriarchs, because God had promised it to them. Abraham especially, as we know, had received the promises from Yahweh and had responded to them with faith (Gen 15; etc.). The fulfillment of the promises necessarily implied both the destruction of the wicked and the salvation of the just; divine judgment was typified by the crossing of the Red Sea and by the Deluge before it; on these occasions God struck down his people's enemies and brought his chosen ones to glory.

It was this kind of expectation based on faith that Jewish families celebrated at the Passover. The people of God must go on celebrating the Passover in the solidarity of a people that is forming itself and striving toward completion, sharing both the good and the bad. The Passover, which commemorated God's encounter with his people in the process of forming them, ended with a song of praise (the Hallel, Pss 113–18 and 136).

"Our soul is waiting for the LORD. / He is our help and our shield. . . . / May your merciful love be upon us, / as we hope in you, O LORD" (Ps 33:20, 22). These words are from the responsorial psalm and bring out the deeper meaning both of the Old Testament reading and of the entire celebration. Abraham joyfully accepted the promise, but he received it amid darkness, and faith alone enabled him to overcome that darkness.

So too, it was during the night that the people of God were liberated and formed into a new people under the covenant. That covenant was to be transformed into the final, eternal covenant by the sacrifice of Jesus, which was made present and operative both beforehand at the Supper and later in the eucharistic celebration of the Church. Catholics are invited to unite themselves to this Sacrifice whereby the Lord renews and rebuilds the world. Each is called, during the night of faith, to stand ready for the final encounter unto which God calls.

This invitation and summons is most important. Everything else must take second place when it comes to having one's lamp lit and trimmed, to being a faithful steward, to being always alert and watchful by the light of faith. That is the lesson of today's celebration. The whole existence of the Church is a long, seemingly endless watch in which, century after century, she awaits her encounter with the Lord. She is ever alert and ready, confident as she is of the glory in store for her. Christ has promised that glory; more than that, he enables his Church to perceive the sign of it in the eucharistic sacrifice.

Look for the City of God (Heb 11:1-2, 8-19)

By a happy chance, today's second reading fits in with the theme of the other two. It begins with a lapidary definition: "Faith is the realization of what is hoped for and evidence of things not seen." Given the relationship between this pericope and today's gospel, it is clear that we are being reminded chiefly of the element of expectation that is inherent in faith.

Abraham sets out without knowing his destination; faith makes him sure that something and some One lie ahead. In his eyes, the true values are those that the Lord has pointed out to him. He looks, therefore, for the city that has genuine foundations, the city of which God is architect and builder. Many of those who have been chosen by God have died without seeing the promise fulfilled, but they have glimpsed it from afar, and they insist that they have been but strangers and exiles upon the earth. They have been seeking a homeland— heaven—and yearning for a better land than the one they left. But a time of expectation is also a time of trial. Abraham had to offer Isaac in sacrifice; he stood ready even for this, because he believed that God can give life to the dead. That is why Abraham was capable of sacrificing his only son, the one from whom the promised posterity was to spring. His son was spared, and the posterity came.

When linked with the gospel, this passage from the Letter to the Hebrews is very relevant to each of us. We await the Lord; that is why we endeavor to bear in mind that we are indeed only pilgrims. On our journey we advance in faith toward the Lord. But belief is true knowledge, and we know therefore that we already possess the beginning of eternal life: "this is eternal life, that they should know you, the only true God, and the one whom you sent, Jesus Christ" (John 17:3).

Twentieth Sunday: Signs to Be Contradicted

Violence for the Sake of the Kingdom (Luke 12:49-53)

It frequently happens that the words of Jesus that an evangelist records without at all inventing them reflect the author's concerns as head of a church; in this he acts under the inspiration of the Holy Spirit. Today's gospel pericope offers an interesting example of this kind of conjunction. On the one hand, Jesus depicts himself as having come to establish the kingdom; this requires a purification that he must undergo and that he is anxious to undergo. On the other hand, Luke expresses the concrete concern of a young community that finds itself amid a hostile world that cannot understand it.

Jesus has been sent "to set the earth on fire," and he tells us that he is anxious indeed for the fire to be kindled. What does he mean by describing his mission in this way? We cannot suppose that Christ's role is really to cause division. We should interpret his words, therefore, as referring to the last days and to the eschatological events that are to purify the world. In the Old Testament, fire has several symbolic references: the fire of judgment that condemns the wicked (Gen 19:24; Amos 1:4, 7, 10, 14); the fire of the last days (Isa 66:15-16; Ezek 38:22; etc.); and the fire that purifies (Isa 1:25; Zech 13:9). Fire has, in our passage from Luke, its third symbolic meaning and leads over to Jesus' words about the baptism for which he longs.

"Baptism" is used here in its Semitic sense of a purification; Jesus is looking forward to his suffering. Each of those who believe in him and desire to follow him must be single-minded; they must make their choice. It is possible that in this passage Luke is thinking of concrete situations in his Church. In any case, he does not hesitate to set aside an image of Christ that he himself has often presented: that of the prophet who brings peace (Luke 1:79; 2:14; 7:50; etc.), in accordance with the way the Old Testament prophets had depicted the Messiah (cf. Isa 9:5-6; 11:6-9; etc.). Here, instead, Luke portrays Jesus as one who brings fire.

One of the Alleluia chants for use before the gospel brings out well the practical lesson this particular passage contains: "I am the way, the truth, and the life, says the Lord; no one comes to the Father, except through me." The baptism with which Jesus must be baptized and which he impatiently awaits is a baptism each of us must accept. But following Christ in his purifying passion requires a choice that often involves opposition. The coming of Christ is thus a proclamation of peace but also of violence. That is the paradoxical position of the Church and her members. We can see it already in the story of St. Stephen the deacon. He proclaimed the peace of Christ, but in doing so he could not help suffering the violence caused by division and persecution. Christianity is neither diplomacy nor the study of an equitable religious environment.

The Prophet, a Person of Discord (Jer 38:4-6, 8-10)

Today's reading refers to events in such a way that we can assign them a precise date. Jerusalem is under siege by Nebuchadnezzar (beginning of 588 to July 587). Jeremiah is already in prison, accused of demoralizing the remaining combatants and the population at large. He seems to be seeking not the happiness but the misfortune of the people. Of what exactly is he accused? The verses preceding today's selection tell us: Jeremiah has been prophesying that the city will be taken and that those who surrender to the Chaldeans will save their lives; the city will be delivered into the hands of the king of Babylon.

It is not easy for us to understand the prophet's attitude, and we may be tempted to regard him as a traitor to his country. We must, however, interpret the facts differently. The Lord is using the Chaldeans to punish his people; consequently, those who had been merely Gentiles have now become the Lord's servants. According to the Lord's words, Jeremiah must take the side of those who are now the enemies of the Israelite king but God's servants, since the city has proved unfaithful. The prophet cannot but proclaim what the Lord bids him say. Israel, of course, cannot understand this turn of events: How can the Lord be even imagined as having any people but Israel for his own?

Given this state of affairs, it was inevitable that Jeremiah should be destined for martyrdom. The Lord did save him from death, and the prophet lived on. Yet his life as a whole was a long martyrdom, for he was compelled to pronounce God's judgments and to follow his orders faithfully. He was always to be seemingly the cause of discord.

Psalm 40 uses language quite close to that which describes Jeremiah's fate and suffering: "[The LORD] drew me from the deadly pit, / from the miry clay. / He set my feet upon a rock, / made my footsteps firm" (v. 3).

Hostility from Sinners (Heb 12:1-4)

By chance, the theme of this New Testament reading fits in with the theme of the day. The Letter to the Hebrews tells us the meaning of the trials and sufferings a Christian endures, the meaning of the violence to which we must all submit in some degree.

Jesus is both the origin and goal of our faith; it is toward him that we advance through trials. The first opposition we meet in our following of Christ is the sins that bind us. We are thus faced with a choice. Jesus had to face the hostility of sinners; he endured the humiliation of the cross, but he is now seated at God's side and rules with him. This fact should encourage us. At the same time, however, the letter gives us a warning: we have not yet resisted to the point of shedding our blood in the struggle against sin. A violent course is thus set before us.

The readings of this Sunday may well be an attack on our usual ways of thinking, for they do not present Christian life as a life of sweet and easy peace and a facile observance of the commandment of love. Instead, they tell us that violence marks the climate proper to an authentic Christianity.

This should make us stop and think. The ideal we have to offer to today's world does not rest on a kind of resignation in the face of God's demands. Neither do we propose an earthly happiness and a human peace to be won by religious practice, no matter how exemplary. We have only one thing to offer: the cross of Christ, which we must take up uncompromisingly. This means we must be a sign of contradiction in the eyes of others. Is that the image of Christianity we present? The point is not that we are to have closed minds and to refuse to understand others. The point is rather that, while opening ourselves to the world and seeking to understand varied human situations, Christians cannot compromise with the world's demands but must speak to the world the language of God, even though we suffer for it.

Twenty-First Sunday: The Whole World at the Feast in the Kingdom

The Last Will Be First (Luke 13:22-30)

This Sunday seems to be placed under the sign of universalism, like the Twentieth Sunday in Year A. Today's gospel once again requires of us a liturgical interpretation that departs somewhat from a strictly exegetical interpretation. If we were to read the gospel pericope without regard to its context in the celebration (a context determined by the first reading), we would be likely to emphasize the parable of the narrow door and to focus our reflection on the difficulties of and requirements for entry into the kingdom. Such an emphasis and focus are, of course, quite legitimate, but they do not take into account the context provided by the liturgy itself.

The liturgy does not deny that it is difficult to enter the kingdom. In keeping with the first reading, however, the fact that some have not faced up to the difficulty and are therefore unable to enter the kingdom, and that they knock at the door but find themselves refused admission, leads to an emphasis on the last two sentences of the pericope: "And people will come from the east and the west and from the north and the south and will recline at table in the kingdom of God. For behold, some are last who will be first, and some are first who will be last." Some of the last (that is, the Gentiles) will be saved, while some of the first (that is, the Jews) will be rejected.

The question asked by a Jew, "Lord, will only a few people be saved?" (a question often asked today), receives no direct answer. Instead, Jesus encourages his hearers to merit their salvation so that they will not be replaced by non-Jews. The Lord is saying that salvation belongs not to a race but to those who accept Christ.

Gather All Nations (Isa 66:18-21)

God wants to bring together people of every nation and tongue. The author of today's first reading gives symbolic expression to this totality that God desires and to which he will show his glory. Even Moses had not been able to look fully on the Lord's glory but had been given only a glimpse of it (Exod 33:18-23); now, however, all the nations will see it. In the midst of this immense assembly a sign will be set up, a banner telling everyone that this is the gathering of those who are given the vision of God's glory. In the verses following today's passage, the assembly is spoken of as utterly new: "the new heavens and the new earth" (Isa 66:22).

God will send messengers forth from Jerusalem to take charge of the distant nations that have not seen his glory. Some from these nations will in turn act as God's servants, messengers sent out to be a light for the nations (see Isa 49:6). Their purpose will be to proclaim God's glory.

The response will be the journey of the nations to Jerusalem. Using every possible means of transportation, they will come to the holy mountain, these foreigners and these Jews from the Diaspora. All will offer a sacrifice in clean vessels. The climax of this universalist vision resides in the statement that the Lord will even draw some of his priests and Levites from among the foreigners. In the first reading of the Twentieth Sunday, Year A, we read that all will offer sacrifice in the "house of prayer for all peoples" (Isa 56:7; cf. Matt 15:21-28; Mark 11:17).

How can we avoid seeing in these texts an image of the Church, which Vatican Council II speaks of as "a sign lifted up among the nations" (in an allusion to Isa 11:12) and "a sign under which the scattered children of God may be gathered together" (cf. John 11:52)?[6]

The vision of the prophet is to be found again in Revelation: an immense throng from every nation, race, people, and tongue, all standing before the throne and the Lamb (Rev 7:9). The Church of our day must live by this vision; it is this vision that explains her missionary activity. She is a sign of Christ, who, being "lifted up from the earth," draws to himself God's scattered children.

To Correct Is a Sign of Love (Heb 12:5-7, 11-13)

This passage offers encouragement to Christians in times of trial, for it bids them stop looking at trials as a form of persecution by God and to look upon them rather as signs of God's special love for them. When the Lord loves someone, he teaches them what they should learn; he corrects all those he acknowledges as his sons and daughters.

The Christians to whom these words are directed have already suffered a great deal and now find themselves being tested once again (Heb 10:32-34). We ourselves, or others whom we love, may be in a similar situation. The author of the Letter to the Hebrews here offers us consolation that does not rest on empty words. The point, of course, is not that we should close our eyes and pretend the suffering is not real or that we should convince ourselves it is not as bad as we thought. On the contrary, we are to look on trials and sufferings realistically and see them for what they are, for only then will we be able to pass a correct value judgment on them. That is why the author bids us meditate on the sufferings of Jesus—these sufferings brought Jesus to his glory!

When those being tested react with bitterness, they close in on themselves and cease to understand; they think life has become absurd. What such people should really be doing is remembering the strengthening words here addressed to the person who suffers as a son or daughter of God. Trials are not punishments; such a view is inconsistent with God's mercy and certainly does not apply to those who have abandoned themselves body and soul to the Lord. We should rather look at trials as preparation for the glory that awaits us. There is no reason, then, to be discouraged; rather, we should regard trials as means of attaining a more perfect union with God, who is proving his love for us through these very trials.

Initially, then, trials may sadden us, but if we reflect on what they really mean and if we reap the fruit that God intends from them, we experience a profound peace and joy that permeate our soul and our whole life. For when trials are accepted and offered to God, they always prove healing to the soul, a doctrine Paul confirms with citations from the prophet Isaiah (35:3) and the book of Proverbs (4:26).

Twenty-Second Sunday: Humble Yourself, and You Will Be Exalted

The One Who Exalts Oneself Will Be Humbled (Luke 14:1, 7-14)

The gospel pericope gives two pieces of advice. One is for those who are guests at a banquet, the other for the host. In today's eucharistic celebration, we should attend more to the first piece of advice, for it fits in with the Old Testament reading from the book of Sirach.

Let us begin, however, with the advice to the host. This will enable us better to link the advice to the guests with the Old Testament reading. Hosts, we are told, should be disinterested; that is, they should not invite people in order to win invitations in return. Consequently, they will invite not their relatives and friends but the poor, the lame, and the blind. These were unfortunates who were excluded from the temple. At the end of this piece of advice and of the pericope as a whole, Jesus gives an eschatological dimension to the banquet of which he is speaking: "you will be repaid at the resurrection of the righteous."

We may turn now to the first piece of advice, the one given to the guests and the one on which today's celebration focuses our attention. The occasion is a dinner to which Jesus has been invited at the house of a Pharisee. Such invitations to him were not infrequent. He uses them as an opportunity for dialogue, for teaching, and for the manifestation of his concern for the Pharisees, who, like others, are called to enter God's kingdom and find salvation therein. On this occasion the meal would have been a special one, since it took place on the Sabbath, when banquets were more lavish than usual. The other guests are teachers of the law and Pharisees, the host being one of the leaders. As at every worldly gathering, the guests seek to put themselves forward; conscious as they are of their rank and concerned for their reputation, they are skillful in maneuvering themselves into the places of honor.

The key to the whole pericope is at the end of the advice to the guests: "everyone who exalts himself will be humbled, but the one who humbles himself will be exalted." But before we reflect on this statement of Jesus, let us look at the teaching contained in the Old Testament reading.

Humble Yourself and Find Favor with God (Sir 3:17-18, 20, 28-29)

The advice given in this passage shows a realistic evaluation of life in the world. At the same time, the author is not concerned solely with mundane shrewdness, for we also read as a motive, "you will find favor with God." This shows that the humility recommended is to be taken not simply as a recommendation of worldly prudence but as part of the proper conduct of a just person before God. "There is One who exalts and humbles" (Sir 7:11); "the eye of the LORD looks favorably upon [broken-down drifters], / shaking them free of the stinking mire" (Sir 11:12).

The theme of humility occurs frequently in the Old Testament. Sometimes we even find it treated in a manner that reminds us of the New Testament. Thus a humble person acknowledges that he or she is a sinner (Isa 6:5); the person who is lowly will receive God's favor (Prov 3:34) and exaltation (1 Sam 2:7). Israel learned humility through hard experience, and the psalms show a deep awareness of the fact, for they emphasize the prayer of the humble and poor. The latter, above all others, know how to praise the Lord (Pss 22:25-27; 34:7; 69:3). The Old Testament also provides many exemplars of humility, for example, the Servant whom Isaiah describes (53:4-10) and the Messiah who is expected to come as a humble king (Zech 9:9). Pride, on the other hand, as today's text tells us, is a condition that cannot be healed, for wickedness has taken root in the proud.

When, therefore, Jesus speaks of humbling oneself, his hearers know what he means. They had long ago heard Ben Sirach say, "Humble yourself the more, the greater you are." The attitude of the truly wise is to listen humbly.

The responsorial psalm (Ps 68) bids us meditate on the prayer proper to the poor and provides an occasion for praising the God of the lowly and the poor:

> Father of orphans, defender of widows:
> such is God in his holy place.
> God gives the desolate a home to dwell in;
> he leads the prisoners forth into prosperity. . . .
> In your goodness, O God, you provided for the poor. (vv. 6-7, 10)

For us Christians, humility has acquired a new and priceless dimension ever since Jesus exemplified this virtue in his life. At the same time, however, the key sentence of today's reading—"everyone who exalts himself will be humbled, but the one who humbles himself will be exalted"—does not seem to be spoken in view of Christ's own abasement in his passion. The sentence refers rather to the humility proper to the wise and, indeed, to anyone who sees reality as it is.

Any lessons from Jesus' statement must be carefully drawn, for an extremist interpretation would make it either unacceptable or psychologically dangerous. For one thing, humility does not suppose that one is indifferent to one's situation or work or human progress. There is a kind of "pride" that is salutary and necessary for the human advancement that God wills. Inability to accept responsibility, inferiority complexes, indecisiveness, fearfulness—these are not humility.

On the other hand, Jesus does condemn any quest of power for its own sake, any harsh domination of others, any self-satisfaction that is unconcerned about others. Between these two extremes lies humility, and it takes an ongoing effort to determine just what humility requires in the modern world. One thing that can be said is that we must search out the applications of humility, not in the light of a purely human prudence, but in respect for our own circumstances as willed by God and in respect for others as well.

The Church today is increasingly aware that authority is for service. This is one necessary form of humility. Authority in the Church is always intended for service and ministry. But while the service meant is limitless, it does not justify the intrusion of a vulgar democracy that is not humility. Humility requires precisely that we each keep our proper place. Concern for others will then help us to find these proper places and to readjust them, for they are always difficult to maintain and must be the object of a continual, honest examination of conscience.

You Have Approached Jesus, Mediator of a New Covenant
(Heb 12:18-19, 22-24a)

A comparison is here being made between the manner in which the former people of God was established and the manner in which the new has now been established. At Mount Sinai, the Israelites were confronted with material realities and signs, terrifying ones in fact, since the children of Israel asked that they might not have to go on listening to this fearful voice and these fearful words.

The new covenant is established in an entirely different sort of encounter that brings with it none of those ancient manifestations. The baptized "have approached Mount Zion and the city of the living God, the heavenly Jerusalem, and . . . the assembly of the firstborn enrolled in heaven." Without the ancient external, fearful manifestations of divinity, believers have approached the Lord, the community of the baptized, the Church—all those who have become one through one baptism in one and the same Spirit and whose names are written in heaven. They are the "firstborn," because they all share closely in the life of Jesus Christ, who is the firstborn of all creation. Christians have drawn near to God himself, the Judge of all, and have entered into an intimate sharing with him. He remains the Judge who knows human hearts, yet they have not feared to approach him. They have also been united to the spirits of the just, that is, to their dead who are now enjoying the future life and are just in God's sight.

In short, the entire Church, earthly and heavenly, was present, and to it the baptized and all Christians have come. But it is above all Jesus, Mediator of the new covenant, whom they have approached. It is because he is their Mediator that they have dared cross the distance separating the human condition from the glory in which the Lord dwells. Now that they have been transformed through baptism into the Father, Son, and Spirit, they can live in intimate union with the Trinity. Such is the situation of the Christian as a member of the new people of God.

Twenty-Third Sunday: Be Free, and Understand the Lord

Renounce Your Possessions and Become a Disciple (Luke 14:25-33)

At first reading or hearing, this passage may give an impression of disorder and incoherence. The specialists therefore attempt to distinguish between the words of Jesus himself and others that are spoken by the editor, St. Luke. Thus the two short parables are certainly in Jesus' manner, even though Luke is the only evangelist to report them.

On the other hand, verses 26-27, on the denial of loved ones and the duty of carrying the cross, are also to be read in St. Matthew (10:38; 16:24) and St. Mark (8:34); Luke, moreover, has already recorded the words of Jesus on carrying one's cross (9:23). Even so, the words do seem to stem from Jesus himself, even if Luke is combining statements here. Luke seems to have drawn up the entire passage as an instruction for his Christians. It was extremely important that they not cherish illusions but grasp the real demands of Christian life.

The disciple is, first of all, a person who is detached from everything; such detachment is the first condition required for being a disciple. A detachment that is sought in order to be without ties and to be able to follow Jesus characterizes, or should characterize, every Christian. Since this detachment is so important, the necessity for it is expressed here in language that our psychological sensibilities find harsh and even somewhat aggressive.

We must not take the word "hate" in its narrowly literal sense. Jesus is speaking of a value judgment and a freedom from ties that have nothing in common with a refusal of charity or with self-centeredness. He is demanding an unconditional love of himself that gives priority to everything that concerns him and makes everyone and everything else secondary. He is asking for a preferential love that entails the leaving behind of all else. Legitimate human relationships are a love subordinate to love for Jesus.

At the same time, however, Jesus is also asking for something that is unqualified, not for a "more or less" or a "for the most part." It is this radical and uncompromising demand that St. Luke is trying to bring out; that is why he lists the objects of our affection that must take second place if there is a conflict. He includes in the list even one's own life, one's very self. In our civilization, which is still somewhat Christian, the obligation of separating oneself even from one's family rarely arises, but it was a frequent occurrence for the Christians of Luke's day who met with opposition from their own kin when they embraced Christianity and put aside Jewish or Gentile practices.

Jesus even demands that one be ready to surrender life itself. "Carrying the cross" has come to mean for us, often exclusively, a voluntary acceptance and submission to the worries of life and to great trials when they come. In the time of Jesus, however, "carrying the cross" meant the surrender of self even to the point of accepting death. The disciples were used to seeing the torment of crucifixion imposed on criminals, who were forced to carry the instrument of their torture and death to the place of execution. For these disciples, then, the words of Jesus must have revealed a full depth of meaning after their Master's passion.

"Following Jesus" and "carrying the cross" thus became two ways of expressing the same radical requirement of self-giving, even to the point of death. Disciples are not called to carry just any cross or to follow just any person; they are called to follow Jesus and to carry Jesus' cross.

One may not, therefore, lightly decide to follow Jesus. In fact, Jesus himself here offers two little parables that are intended to stir the listener to adequate reflection before deciding to follow Jesus. The Christian of today, like the disciple of Jesus' time, must not be led astray by an idealistic or romantic vision of Christian life. Christianity is not a philosophy but a life to be lived. There can be no compromise; one must walk in Christ's steps unconditionally, not for a moment or a day, but for a lifetime.

Wisdom Enables Us to Understand God's Will (Wis 9:13-18b)

If in reading this passage we did not keep the gospel pericope in mind, we might well feel fearful and discouraged. In fact, the passage reveals its deeper meaning precisely because of its liturgical context.

As we read, we may well be disconcerted at first. How, indeed, is knowledge of God's decrees to be gained, and who has power to understand them? We have trouble enough understanding what lies directly before us; how, then, are we to discover what is stored up in heaven? Only wisdom and the Spirit can reveal God's will to us. Without their intervention we must live in uncertainty and walk hopelessly in the darkness. It is of our need of wisdom that we sing in the responsorial psalm (Ps 90): "Then teach us to number our days, / that we may gain wisdom of heart" (v. 12).

In this reading, however, one sentence links the passage with the thought of the gospel: "the corruptible body burdens the soul / and the earthen shelter weighs down the mind that has many concerns." The words point to the need of unconditional self-denial and a radical quest for liberation. If we are to know and follow God's will, we must abandon the "earthen shelter" of our body and our self-will.

The lesson of this Sunday is an important one, for it presents the charter of Christian life and shows the radical demands that Christianity makes. One may not live the Christian life unthinkingly; the life of a disciple is something that must be taken very seriously.

Onesimus Is to Be Treated as a Brother, Not as a Slave
(Phlm 9b-10, 12-17)

Philemon is the specific addressee of this letter, yet it is meant for others as well—in fact, for the whole community. Its authors, or at least those who sent it, are Paul and Timothy. Onesimus, a slave, has run away and is therefore liable to harsh punishment. Paul becomes his advocate, and in his plea he is not afraid to appeal to sentiment: An old man, now a prisoner for Christ, asks a favor for a child to whom he, while in prison, has given the life of Christ. Paul had instructed and baptized this slave, and the two are now very close.

The modern reader may feel disappointed at the way Paul acted. Why did he not keep the slave with him instead of sending him back? But that would have been to put pressure on the owner, and Paul was unwilling to do this. He wanted the master to be free in dealing with his slave in a Christian manner. So too, it was not for a very long time that the Church spoke out against slavery; in the interim she respected the social conditions of each age. It is hard for us to accept her silence, and yet our criticism of her for it would be unjust. The Church evidently attempted to better the lot of slaves, especially if they were baptized; she sought at least to improve relations between masters and slaves.

The decisive argument is kept for the last: if Philemon considers Paul his partner, that is, if he understands them to be united in the Christian community, then let him receive Onesimus as though he were receiving Paul himself.

Twenty-Fourth Sunday: The Lord's Forgiveness

Joy in Heaven for a Sinner's Conversion (Luke 15:1-32)

The parable of the prodigal son is thoroughly familiar to us and has, in fact, already been proclaimed on the Fourth Sunday of Lent

(Year C).[7] Today's proclamation, however, has a different emphasis. In Lent the focus of attention was the conversion of the prodigal son and his desire to be reconciled; this emphasis was due to the fact that Lent has the paschal mystery and the renewal of baptismal conversion for its goal. In today's gospel it is instead God's forgiveness on which we are urged to meditate.

The story gives us a glimpse of the constant concern of the father for the son who has left him. He catches sight of his son when the latter is still far off; the father had evidently been hoping for the day when the son would return and, thus hoping, had often looked into the distance and thought of his son. To this earthly father we may compare God, who does not forget the sinner but waits with unwearying patience.

When the father sees his son in the distance, he is seized with pity. How often God too reacts thus—with pity! He is a God of forgiveness. The book of Exodus (a passage of which is today's first reading) speaks of the Lord as "a God gracious and merciful, slow to anger and abounding in love and fidelity," and to his God Moses will pray: "come along in our company. This is indeed a stiff-necked people; yet pardon our wickedness and sins, and claim us as your own" (Exod 34:6-9).

The father does not suppress his compassion for his son; rather, it is he who takes the initiative and goes out to meet him: "his father . . . ran to his son, embraced him and kissed him." Thus does God take the initiative at the very beginning of a conversion. We see Jesus acting in the same way whenever he finds repentance and the desire for conversion. Zacchaeus, for example, wants to see Jesus; Jesus, discovering this first movement to a new way of life, takes the initiative and invites himself into Zacchaeus's house (Luke 19:1-10); he asserts that he is following a principle: "the Son of Man has come to seek and to save what was lost."

The intentions of the returning son are not entirely selfless. His return home is not motivated solely by a sense of his own ingratitude and lack of love for his father. The parable shows that there is still a certain self-centeredness in the son's attitude: "How many of my father's hired workers have more than enough food to eat, but here am I, dying from hunger." Here, as with Zacchaeus, we do not find in the very beginning an utterly pure intention or an authentic sorrow at having done evil. The sinner must first be drawn by the desire to escape the suffering his own actions have brought. In God's eyes this beginning holds great promise, however; that is why the father runs out to meet his son.

The prodigal son expresses his regret, but the father seems so overwhelmed by joy that he hardly notices what the son says. "Quickly bring the finest robe and put it on him; put a ring on his finger and sandals on his feet. Take the fattened calf and slaughter it. Then let us celebrate with a feast." The father has forgotten the past. No resentment shows in his behavior; his only feeling is joy, because "this son of mine was dead, and has come to life again; he was lost, and has been found."

Not everyone understands God's forgiveness. It may be that Luke took advantage of this parable of Jesus to insist that the Christian community must accept those who have sinned but still live in the Church. Jesus himself encountered people who rejected sinners and regarded them as rejected by God as well. The purpose of his parable is to make these people understand what God's attitude really is.

The reaction of the elder son was the reaction of some of Jesus' contemporaries and some of Luke's disciples, and it is the reaction of some Christians today. The elder son regards himself as a faithful servant, and he is indeed such. He also feels injured by his father's reception of his erring brother. He, after all, has always been faithful, yet he has never been given a banquet! But this fellow who left home and squandered his possessions is now received with honors and with a joy never shown toward the faithful servant. The elder brother is scandalized, and so are many Christians today. At least in their imagination and feelings, they find it hard to accept that a person who led a dissolute life should be welcomed by God after death no less than a person who has spent a whole life in God's service. These people have a mercenary concept of Christian life and of God's justice; it leaves little room for love.

It is this attitude that Jesus seeks to correct. He is strongly opposed to any religious attitude that is based on a kind of contractual agreement between God and people, according to which each party is bound to give such and such. No, love must come first and be the basis for all else. The father does not value less the elder son who has always been faithful; on the contrary, he reminds him that "you are here with me always; everything I have is yours." But the father is not unjust toward the elder son when he chooses to pardon and restore life to the younger son who had been dead.

The Lord Relents and Does Not Punish His Sinful People
(*Exod 32:7-11, 13-14*)

The people of God have gone astray and worshiped the golden calf. How unforgivable such a sin seems when we realize that it occurred only shortly after the promulgation of the Ten Commandments!

Moses' prayer for forgiveness on behalf of the people is the focal point of the passage. It is a bold plea based on three solid arguments. The first is that God will be destroying his own people. This people is indeed his, for he brought it out of Egypt by the power of his arm and hand. It would therefore be contradictory for the Lord to destroy a people he has saved by such spectacular means.

Second, since the Lord liberated his people in such a spectacular way and since this people glorifies him far beyond other nations, it would be a dishonor for him to destroy it, the very people that is peculiarly his own. In other words, God's own honor is at stake. If he destroys Israel, what will be left of humankind's respect and fear of his power? This is really blackmail, yet Moses does not hesitate to use such an argument in his prayer, for faith sets no limits to boldness.

The third and strongest argument is the appeal to God's own fidelity. The people may be unfaithful, but God cannot be unfaithful. He promised the patriarchs that he would give them a great posterity. He must be faithful to his promise.

In response, the Lord decides not to punish as he had intended. Thus, despite the enormity of a sin, it is always possible to win God's forgiveness. Forgiveness is always his most basic will.

Christ Came to Save Sinners (*1 Tim 1:12-17*)

St. Paul lets us know here his own experience: he had been a sinner, and yet God chose him as a minister; God chose to trust him. Paul's case interested the entire Church. The other apostles had been chosen by the earthly Jesus and had lived with him; now Paul, who persecuted the others, saw himself overwhelmed by grace and chosen to be Christ's servant no less than the other apostles. Paul's case might indeed be a stumbling block for some!

Paul reminds us that conversion in Christ Jesus is always possible through faith and love. More than that, he believes that his sins and his conversion are part of a providential plan: because Jesus came to save sinners like Paul, "for that reason I was mercifully treated, so that in me, as the foremost, Christ Jesus might display all his patience as an example for those who would come to believe in him for everlasting life."

Paul thus regards himself as the first of sinners but also as the foremost witness to the long-suffering patience of God. The main point he wants to make is that "Christ Jesus came into the world to save sinners." St. Luke shows us Christ expressing the same sentiment: "I have not come to call the righteous to repentance, but sinners" (Luke 5:32), and again, "the Son of Man has come to seek and to save what was lost" (Luke 19:10).

The readings of this Sunday are of great value, for they undercut all forms of rigorism. They do this, not by encouraging indulgence or an easygoing attitude toward human sin, but by exalting the forgiveness God shows to those who believe and to whom, despite their sins, he sometimes gives very special graces. We must not condemn others,[8] since God forgives and does not withhold his grace once he sees a person repenting. Thus, any pride that the "just" and observant individual might feel collapses in the face of the forgiveness God bestows so freely.

Twenty-Fifth Sunday: Mammon—Money

The Service of God and Money Are Incompatible (Luke 16:1-13)

The first part of this passage of the gospel is so shocking to us that preachers allow themselves to pass over it and go immediately to the second part. It would be a shame, however, for the Sunday congregation never to experience this shock.

The case of the dishonest steward, whom Christ praises and offers as a model, is certainly repugnant to us at first glance. And yet every Christian is aware that Jesus cannot be praising dishonesty! We admit, therefore, that we must be missing the point of what is being said, but we would have preferred to hear from Jesus an outright condemnation of the steward. That would have been the right thing, we feel, and we would not be disturbed by the passage. Perhaps too we could then have felt our own superiority to this contemptible fellow!

The actual extent of the steward's fraudulent dealings does not matter. What interests us is that he is an able fellow and goes about his wrongdoing in an intelligent way: he makes his creditors his accomplices so that they will have to take him in when the times become hard. Some interpreters think that Jesus was using a real case, not in order to condemn dishonesty (there would be no point to that, since Jesus would evidently be against dishonesty), but to turn it into a springboard for some new teaching of his own. One thing is sure: despite efforts of interpreters to prove the contrary, Jesus is clearly defending the dishonest steward and even praising him. How are we to understand this?

Jesus seems to be anticipating and defending himself against any accusation of complicity by his statement that "the children of this world are more prudent in dealing with their own generation than are the children of light." The children of this world are clever and quick to make decisions when it comes to business, whereas the children of light, whose goal is the kingdom, are often so slow and lacking in cleverness when it comes to the means of finding the kingdom. If people can show themselves so able in the pursuit of perishable blessings, why is it that we are so halfhearted in seeking the kingdom?

Thus, Jesus is not by any means praising the dishonest actions of the steward. He praises only the steward's shrewdness and regrets that such shrewdness should always be found in those who live for the present world and not in those who seek the kingdom but often seem so clumsy in their ways.

One means of entry into the kingdom is to be generous and make friends in the eternal dwellings so that they may intercede for us at our death. Jesus is here encouraging us to generosity and almsgiving. Use money in order to give generously and you will have intercessors in heaven when the time comes for you to die.

Jesus takes advantage of the parable to point out the true meaning of money. A person cannot serve two masters, namely, God and mammon, or money. There are people who come close to this kind of idolatry every day. If we possess money, it is given to us not so that we should become attached to it as though it were something of unqualified value but so that we might share it. To cling to money is to show that we have not really understood God and the absolute values he embodies. We are bidden, therefore, to use money but also to be detached from it; this we will do to the extent that we are shrewd in our seeking of the kingdom.

Greed of the Merchants (Amos 8:4-7)

Amos here refers to trade that involves the falsification of weights and measures; it is another kind of fraudulent dealing. He is writing against the civilization of his day, and his protests are the same as we might make in our own day. The prophet, however, is protesting in the name of the Lord, who bids him speak. His contemporaries are observing the moons and the Sabbath, but they make use of the time to conspire and think up ways of getting greater profits. For a pair of sandals, they can buy or sell a poor individual who cannot pay personal debts.

The connection between this text and the gospel is rather tenuous, but both do preach the need of detachment from money.

We would misinterpret the gospel passage if we took it to be approving dishonesty; as a matter of fact, Jesus praises only a shrewdness that he would like to see the children of light display in their quest of the kingdom and urges them to be detached from money for the sake of the same kingdom. Similarly, we would misinterpret the Old Testament reading if we saw in it an attack on all trade and on every economic system and the well-being it makes possible. What the prophet is, in fact, assailing is an attachment to money that makes a person closed to the needs of the poor and willing even to impoverish them further. Such an attitude is in full contradiction to the attitude of the Lord; it turns money into an idol and makes it impossible for a person to serve the Lord, who reacts by saying, "Never will I forget a thing they have done!"

The responsorial psalm (Ps 113) sings of the way in which God shows his concern for the poor: "From the dust he lifts up the lowly, / from the ash heap he raises the poor, / to set them in the company of princes, / yes, with the princes of his people" (vv. 7-8).

Pray That Everyone May Be Saved (1 Tim 2:1-8)

We are urged here to pray for everyone so that all may be saved. Such prayer is efficacious, but its efficacy derives from Christ Jesus, who gave himself as a ransom for all. The apostle's role is to bring this gift to others. The Christian community is meant to be a community of prayer, and Paul asks that in every place Christians should pray, "lifting up holy hands, without anger or argument." This is to say that their intention must be upright; they do not pray to draw down wrath from heaven on their enemies or to further their personal ambition.

What we have here is the source of, or at least a witness to, the "universal prayer" now offered in the liturgy after the homily or Creed. These intercessions found a place in the liturgy at a very early date. In his *First Apology* (addressed to Emperor Antoninus Pius in AD 150), St. Justin mentions that the intercessions come at the end of the celebration of the word (chap. 67). In today's passage from the First Letter to Timothy, we already find a simple list or litany of persons and intentions to be prayed for. It is the kind of litany we find again and again through the centuries and in our own liturgies today: "for everyone, for kings and for all in authority, that we may lead a quiet and tranquil life in all devotion and dignity." Even the pattern is unchanged through time: "Let us pray: for . . . , that. . . ."

Paul is here urging us to frequent prayer that is not limited to the time of liturgy. We are to be really preoccupied with the salvation of everyone, for whom we share responsibility with Christ.

Twenty-Sixth Sunday: The False Security of the Rich

Final Lot of the Rich and the Poor (Luke 16:19-31)

The parable of Lazarus and the rich man is familiar to all. Egyptian and Jewish literature of the past had contained rather similar stories, to which the commentaries on this passage call attention.

The personages of the parable represent two classic types who are contrasted in the Old Testament writings: the rich man and the poor man. The basic aim of the parable is to show a reversal of situations; in the next life the rich man is in torment and can see Lazarus at rest in the bosom of Abraham. Lazarus reclines at Abraham's side at a banquet while the rich man is tormented by thirst. The general conditions of life in the next world are not a concern of the parable, however; the description simply brings out the new and radically changed circumstances of each of the two main personages.

What we have here is an old theme: the rich man condemned and the poor man exalted in a reversal of situations that is frequently depicted or asserted in the Old Testament. The New Testament took over this theme, as we have had occasion to note in speaking of the beatitudes.[9]

The state of those in the next life is definitively and irrevocably determined, and a great abyss separates the blessed from the others, so much so that no communication between them is possible. The rich man, who is now so unhappy, can only pray that his friends on earth may be warned and give thought to changing their ways.

With this thought we come to the real point of the parable, as far as its useful lesson goes. The rich man's request misses the point: Abraham replies, "They have Moses and the prophets. Let them listen to them. . . . If they will not listen to Moses and the prophets, neither will they be persuaded if someone should rise from the dead."

Two important points are being made in this parable: the necessity of listening and hearing and the necessity of conversion. Listening and hearing is doubtless easier for the humble and the poor, since they are not tangled up by wealth and its many consequences (pride, for example). The parable has directly in mind the leaders of the Pharisees and tells them that they must indeed listen to and heed Moses and the prophets.

But the parable also reflects the larger problem Jesus faced: The Jews did not listen or did not hear because they were hindered by their sense of security and their pride. What more can be done for them? If they did not listen to Moses and the prophets, why would they heed a dead person who came back to warn them? This is a first lesson of the parable, and it is a harsh and unsentimental one.

The other important point of the parable is the need of conversion, a need that the gospels are constantly inculcating. Conversion is urgent, because judgment is close at hand. Many passages teach the necessity of conversion (Luke 3:3; 10:13; 11:32; 13:3, 5; 24:47), and the Acts of the Apostles shows that it was the most frequent theme of the sermons preached by the apostles (Acts 2:38; 3:19; 5:31; 11:18; 14:15; 17:30; 26:18). St. Luke evidently regarded the theme as of the utmost importance for Israel.

A Corrupt Civilization (Amos 6:1a, 4-7)

The prophet Amos is vigorous in his criticism of the life of his day. He is unsparing of the rich and, more generally, of the whole society of the time. It was a society bent on enjoying every luxury and indulging in every debauchery, and yet it felt not the slightest tremor of unease about itself. Amos's description could readily be applied to some societies of our own time! The life that people were living had little to do with reality; the people living it were utterly unconcerned about Israel's real situation. They were living at the expense of society generally and especially of the poor; the faith and law of Israel meant nothing. Where was the covenant in their lives?

The prophet certainly intends to condemn not improved living conditions but only abuses and the gulf between the lives of the rich and the poor, with the former profiting by the toil of the latter while leaving them in utter destitution. Amos addresses his criticism chiefly to those who live such a life of injustice while outwardly professing the religion of Israel.

We do not have a detailed knowledge of social conditions in Israel at this time, but the text itself makes clear the situation of those the prophet is criticizing. The prophet himself feels like an outcast, for the lives of the rich and powerful are utterly alien to the covenant. They are people who are officially the beneficiaries of the covenant, yet they are living like the Gentiles. The situation is a scandal, and those who have caused it will be made an example: they will be the first to go into exile; the society of revelers will cease to exist.

The reading does not relate one's excesses to one's state in the next life, but it does predict chastisement in the present life. Will the prediction cause its addressees to stop and reflect? Will it be an effective sign to all?

Keep the Lord's Commandments until He Returns (1 Tim 6:11-16)

Today's second reading can be linked with the other two; the fortuitous connection of themes enriches the teaching of this Sunday. As in the gospel pericope and the reading from the prophet, we are told in this passage from the First Letter to Timothy that we must concentrate our attention and energies on faith and love; we must be especially vigilant in regard to faith and willing to struggle in its behalf; we must keep the last day before our minds.

First of all, then, we must try to be just and devout, looking sincerely for God. In St. Paul's view, being just and devout has nothing to do with outward appearances but means that we live by faith and love and that we are gentle and steadfast. The list of spiritual qualities here yields a picture opposite of that which Amos draws of the society of his day and that which Luke gives us of the rich man during his life on earth.

Second, we must fight for the faith. This is indeed the chief activity of us all during the period before the last day. We have been called to eternal life, and we attain it by living the faith we have professed before many witnesses. We must also keep the commandments, for faith alone does not save but must lead to good works. We must show ourselves to be upright and irreproachable, until the time when the Lord Jesus Christ will manifest himself. The whole of our life is a preparation for the last day.

Finally, the last day is the all-important moment. On that day the Lord of lords, the King of kings, who dwells in inaccessible light and whom no one can see, will cause Christ to manifest himself.

A short doxology ends the reading and turns it into a liturgical hymn of praise that asserts the power and glory of him who gives all life its authentic meaning.

Today's readings are very pertinent to our situation. We too must keep before our minds the coming parousia; we must know how to assign all things their true value; we must be firm in the faith and live by the faith. Such is the Christian ideal. We cannot deny that too often we look for security and think we have found it in an illusory well-being that only hides approaching catastrophe. But we are made for life in the world to come. We must not think of that future life as requiring a discouraging loss of transient values! Rather, we must be persuaded that in that future state we will be forever fixed in good or evil, depending on how well and fervently we have sought God in faith during our earthly lives.

Twenty-Seventh Sunday: The Dynamism of Faith

The Power of Faith (Luke 17:5-10)

Today's gospel seems to contain two unconnected themes: an answer to a plea and a parable. If we look more closely, however, there is indeed a connection between the two.

The answer to a plea of the disciples has to do with faith and all that faith can accomplish when it is strong. The parable shows this same effectiveness as flowing from a gift of God. The apostles receive faith as a gift; the effectiveness of this faith is not rooted in them and their merits but, like faith itself, a precious gift given to them by God.

The plea of the disciples is a touching one, but it is also limited in its scope: they know that they believe, and they ask Christ that they may believe more fully and strongly. If we are to understand what it is they are requesting, we must read the passage in its proper context. At this point Jesus is not teaching the crowd but conversing with the disciples; this tells us immediately that the subject is serious and important.

In St. Mark's gospel, Jesus' teaching on faith is introduced by the incident of the fig tree that he had cursed and that the disciples find dried up the next day. Christ then speaks to them of a faith that can move mountains (Mark 11:23).

In St. Matthew, Jesus' teaching on faith is given in reply to a question from the disciples who have been unable to expel a demon (Matt 17:19-20). Later on in the First Gospel, the same teaching on faith and its power is given again in the context of the dried-up fig tree (Matt 21:21). In view of these contexts, we may ask whether the apostles' request for a greater faith was not prompted by a desire to perform miracles.

In St. Luke's gospel, however, there is no hint of any such desire on the part of the apostles. To understand today's passage, therefore, we must broaden our perspective a bit and ask how Luke thinks of faith, both in the Acts of the Apostles and in his gospel.

In the Acts of the Apostles, St. Luke connects faith with the acceptance of God's word. "Many . . . came to believe" or "were becoming obedient to the faith"—this is the kind of expression we find Luke using when people hear and accept the word as preached by the apostles (Acts 4:4; 6:7; 13:12; 14:1; 17:12, 34; 21:20; etc.). In the gospel there is not the same constant linking of faith with the hearing of the word, but it does come up in, for example, the parable of the sower (Luke 8:12-13). The gospel also emphasizes believing in the person of Jesus, that is, abandoning everything for him and following him (Luke 9:59, 61).

All in all, then, we must not link the apostles' request for a deeper faith solely with a desire to perform miracles. They are also asking for a deeper faith so that they may better understand God's word and follow Jesus more perfectly.

The fact that the apostles do ask for a deeper faith is important for Luke's catechesis. Faith is a gift; it must be requested. It is God who "opened the door of faith to the Gentiles" (Acts 14:27). Elsewhere we see Jesus praying to the Father that Peter's faith may not fail (Luke 22:32).

In today's passage, Jesus does not answer by saying that he will give them what they ask; instead, he shows them what they could do if they did have a stronger faith.

Faith is always a gift and so is its effectiveness. The parable that Jesus uses at this point is a simple one: servants have no right to recognition because of what they do, since they belong to the master. Similarly, the apostles are servants, and if they accomplish great things, it is only because the Lord gives them the power to do so; he is not obliged to be grateful to them, because if they accomplish anything, it is by his power.

The Just One Who Is Righteous because of Faith Shall Live
(Hab 1:2-3; 2:2-4)

When we turn to the reading from the prophet, we find ourselves in a world of destruction, violence, strife, contention, and greed. It is a depressing world. The prophet complains that the Lord seems to be deaf to his cries; he asks how long he must endure this trial. According to the beliefs and customs of the time, to write a text on some lasting materials was in some measure to make what was written come true; the writing was a power-filled materialization of the word. God's answer is comforting to the prophet, but he still counsels patience. Finally the oracle and vision do come: "the just one, because of his faith, shall live." The one who is patient and persevering will win out.

It must be admitted that the choice of this text to accompany today's gospel was not a very good one. It is not at all clear that it adds anything to the gospel or that it helps us understand the gospel better. There is no point, therefore, in commenting on it during the liturgy. The prophet is counseling perseverance and a faith that can be translated as "life-giving fidelity." In the gospel, on the other hand, we are dealing with the faith that finds expression in confidence, self-giving, and the following of the Lord. There is no reason for trying to link the two kinds of "faith."

The gospel provides us with an opportunity to reflect on the faith that motivates and guides us and that we should be trying to rouse in others. St. Luke bids us realize that our faith is a gift and that everything we can accomplish is possible only because of God-given power in us. All that we see the Church doing in carrying out her mission is a gift of God; those who cooperate in that mission are servants and are simply doing their duty.

At the same time, however, we must not push such considerations to extremes. After all, Luke also speaks elsewhere of the reward the Lord will give those who have worked for him. Those who have suffered for him (Luke 6:23), those who are unselfish for his sake or abandon everything to follow him (Luke 14:14; 18:30) will all have their reward. As the responsorial psalm (Ps 95) puts it, "he is our God, we are the people he shepherds, the sheep in his hands."

Bear the Hardship That the Gospel Entails (2 Tim 1:6-8, 13-14)

Today's reading is a very beautiful passage from a letter the Apostle Paul wrote to a disciple on whom he himself had laid ordaining hands. The gift of God that Timothy received on that occasion must constantly be revived, for it is meant to be an active gift that will serve the entire Church. Timothy must not be timid or ashamed about bearing witness to the Lord but accept the suffering involved in preaching the Gospel.

It is a moving experience for us to read those lines and realize that the later ritual of ordination was, in its essence, already in use in Paul's day: imposition of hands, action of the Holy Spirit, the gift of God. It may even be that the kind of exhortation we find Paul delivering here to Timothy reflected a liturgical use. The person ordained received, we are told, a charism meant for the service and welfare of the Church. The charism is a spirit of courage, love, and prudence. Having received it, one must carry on the ministry and preach the Gospel fearlessly. Timothy is certainly prepared for such a ministry. He has been entrusted with the truth he is to teach; he must defend that treasure and faithfully pass it on.

This passage cannot be but a stimulus to those who received the gift of the Spirit in ordination. It will also help all Christians understand better the ministry of their bishops and priests and spur them on to aid their bishops and priests by their attitudes, service, and prayers.

Paul is here giving us a sacramental vision of the way in which the Church constantly receives its structure anew. In each generation the ministry requires self-surrender, renunciation, courage, suffering, and fidelity to the deposit of faith. That deposit must be studied, better understood, and made more explicit. It must never be betrayed, nor may personal ideas ever be substituted for it.

Twenty-Eighth Sunday: Gratitude to God

They Have Not Returned to Thank God (Luke 17:11-19)

The cry of the lepers to Jesus is a moving expression of faith, as the two names or titles—"Jesus" and "Master"—that they apply to Jesus make clear. In the form known as the Jesus Prayer ("Lord Jesus Christ, Son of God, have mercy on me, a sinner"), the cry of the lepers is now frequently used by Eastern monks and also by the faithful of those Churches. Its constant repetition forms a rosary of prayer. This kind of prayer is very biblical and is found frequently in the psalms (see, for example, Pss 31 and 51).

Jesus does not immediately respond to the lepers' plea with a startling cure. Instead, he sends them to the priests, thus testing their faith still further. But as they go their way to the priests, they are cured. The evangelist does not describe the miracle directly, for that is not his purpose. His concern is with the importance of faith and of gratitude. But what he is emphasizing most is that a right faith and true gratitude can be found even in a non-Jew. The pericope ends with a sorrowful remark by Jesus: "Has none but this foreigner returned to give thanks to God?" The others were cured, but it does not follow that they were therefore saved. It is only to this Samaritan that the Lord says, "Stand up and go; your faith has saved you."

Naaman Returns to Glorify God (2 Kgs 5:14-17)

In the gospel the cure follows upon faith; in the episode concerning Naaman, the cure leads to faith. The story as read in today's liturgy begins with the moment of the miracle. We know, however, that Naaman was initially angered by Elisha's order to go and bathe in the Jordan. Naaman had expected that the cure of someone like himself would be accomplished in a more ceremonious way. He does not really believe that he will be cured by bathing in the Jordan, but he yields to the pleas of his servants and obeys the prophet. Of course, he is cured. He returns to thank Elisha and offers him a gift, which is refused. Then Naaman makes his profession of faith. His cure and his gratitude have brought him the great gift of faith.

Christians are saved by faith, which is a gift; it does not matter whether they are Jew or Gentile by descent. That is the point St. Luke wants to make, along with the value of the gratitude that Jesus received only from a foreigner. Today's liturgy shows the same faith and the same sense of gratitude at work in another foreigner, Naaman. Faith and salvation are always gifts; we cannot merit them, no matter who we are. Unfortunately, we often forget to be grateful and to show it.

We Have Died with Christ and Shall Live with Him (2 Tim 2:8-13)

Timothy has been urged to recall and revive in himself the grace given him through the imposition of hands. That grace had been a gift of courage in proclaiming the Good News and preaching sound doctrine. Paul himself is in chains like a criminal, but the Word of God cannot be chained, and Paul must carry on his mission to bring that Word to others. He endures everything for that Word and for the elect, those whom God has chosen as recipients of salvation and eternal glory through Jesus Christ.

This part of Paul's exhortation ends with a paschal hymn that may have been used in the liturgy of Christian initiation: "This saying is trustworthy: / If we have died with him / we shall also live with him; / if we persevere / we shall also reign with him. / But if we deny him / he will deny us. / If we are unfaithful / he remains faithful, / for he cannot deny himself."

Exegetes have often called attention to the fact that Paul likes to make up verbs that include the preposition "with" (in Greek, the "with," or *syn*, is prefixed to the verb), as a way of bringing home our close union with Christ. This union implies that we must suffer with Christ but also that we will be glorified with him. Thus Paul speaks of us as suffering with Christ (Rom 8:17; 1 Cor 12:26); being crucified with him (Rom 6:8; Gal 2:20); being buried with him (Rom 6:4; Col 2:12); rising with him (Eph 2:6; Col 2:12; 3:1); coming alive with him (Eph 2:5; Col 2:13); being made like him (Phil 3:10); being glorified with him (Rom 8:17); and being seated with him in heaven (Eph 2:6).

In the paschal hymn in today's pericope, we find the same effort to emphasize our close union with Christ: we die with him (see also 2 Cor 7:13); we live with him (Rom 6:8); we reign with him (1 Cor 4:8). This union is why Paul sees Christian suffering as such a splendid thing.

Twenty-Ninth Sunday: The Prayer of Faith

Pray Unwearyingly and with Faith (Luke 18:1-8)

Today's parable hardly needs explanation, but, though simple, it contains important lessons. If a judge, however lazy and neglectful of his duty, finally does justice to a poor woman simply so that she will leave him in peace, how much more surely will the heavenly Father hear the patient and persevering prayer of his chosen ones? If we read this parable with the attitudes of Jesus in mind, we may think that Jesus' attention is focused on the judge in the story. St. Luke, however, who is concerned for the needs of his flock, seems more interested in the widow and her perseverance in prayer, since she is a model for Christians.

The final verse of the passage turns our attention to the second coming. Will Jesus still find faith when he comes again? The point is that faith is connected with perseverance in prayer. Perhaps St. Luke is alluding to the difficulties and persecutions amid which the first Christians were living. Prayer was necessary if they were to remain faithful and await the coming of the Lord as people confident that their petitions were being heard.

The Power of Moses' Intercession (Exod 17:8-13)

The Amalekites and the Israelites were locked in battle. As long as Moses kept his hands raised, his prayer for the Israelites was heard. His hands grew weary and fell, but his perseverance was such that he had others support his arms, and he remained in this intercessory posture until sunset, and the Israelites were finally triumphant.

Moses' example of perseverance is important and encouraging. Care must be taken, however, not to interpret it in too mechanical a manner, that is, as though the physical raising of Moses' arms was the decisive factor.

To the Old Testament passage we might join the words of Jesus at the end of the gospel pericope, where he says that faith can move mountains.

Continuous prayer inspired by faith and accompanied by submission to God's will has always been the ideal of the Church. Christians have always attempted, though in different ways, to "pray without ceasing." The liturgy today urges us to reflect on the fervor with which we pray and the methods we use.

Be Inspired by the Wisdom of Scripture and Proclaim the Word
(2 Tim 3:14–4:2)

St. Paul continues to give wise and valuable advice to the disciple he had ordained. Timothy must respect the oral tradition he has received from his teachers, for the guide of the Christian is not Scripture alone but Scripture as read in the Church and by the Church. He must also, however, continue to make himself familiar with the inspired writings themselves, for the teaching of an apostle must be based first and foremost on Scripture.

With this as his background, Timothy must devote himself to preaching the Word. The task is an urgent one. Paul is insistent, and we can see how utterly serious he is. He charges Timothy, by the Christ who is to come again, to preach the Word and to do so in season and out of season. He must rebuke evildoers and encourage all but always with patience and always trying to instruct.

Thirtieth Sunday: The Prayer of the Humble

The Tax Collector Is Justified by His Humble Prayer (Luke 18:9-14)

It is considered good form to condemn the Pharisee and to be gracious to the tax collector for his attitude. But this facile approach may well be pharisaical itself. It is easy to acknowledge oneself a sinner without really believing what one says; there is a humility that is in fact a form of pride and that remains an idea in the mind without ever becoming a conviction of the heart.

It is our impression that Luke has deliberately reported this parable in order to provoke reactions from his Christians, especially from those among them who were tempted to live secure in their own sense of uprightness. Those to whom St. Luke is addressing this parable of Jesus might best be compared to those practicing parishioners who are quite sure of themselves and convinced of their fine observance. It is to such people as these that Jesus' words are addressed elsewhere in the Third Gospel: "You justify yourselves in the sight of others, but God knows your hearts; for what is of human esteem is an abomination in the sight of God" (16:15). At the same time, we must not be too hard on all of the Pharisees, for among them there must have been truly just ones who really obeyed the law. The real problem with the Pharisees generally was their self-sufficiency and pride.

There is no point in giving a description here of the divergent attitudes of the two extremes, the Pharisee and the tax collector. The conclusion alone is of interest to us: the tax collector went home "justified." The word is important. The just ones are those who are "justified" by God; they receive God's favor, not because they are already just, but because in their humility they believe that God can be merciful to them and forgive their sins. The deeds of individuals, even if these deeds be not all evil, could never be such as to merit forgiveness; only the sacrifice of the incarnate Son has that power. Because of that sacrifice, the Spirit bestows forgiveness on those who believe, and they return home justified.

The Prayer of the Humble Pierces the Clouds (Sir 35:12-14, 16-18)

The most important part of this passage is the verse that describes the conditions of prayer. "The one who serves God willingly is heard; his prayer reaches the heavens." God thus makes no distinctions among them; that is, he does not hear only the rich or those who have an official ministry of prayer and belong to a priestly caste. People may offer him the finest gifts, but what brings from him a benevolent answer to prayer is the absence of formalism and an attitude of generous service. The person praying may be a widow or an orphan, the kind of people so often subjected to injustice. No matter—the Lord hears them, as he hears anyone whose prayer shows a readiness to serve him wholeheartedly.

All this amounts to saying that prayer must be prayer in Spirit and truth. If we take the time to read the whole of this chapter 35 in the book of Sirach, this impression is strengthened. The writer is speaking of the kind of sacrifice that God finds pleasing. There must be operative in one's life profound attitudes toward God that express the interior sacrifice and without which the sacrifice is unauthentic and ineffective. The writer becomes more concrete and explains, through the use of images, that the substance of our sacrifices must be our very selves, our inner dispositions, the uprightness of our life.

We may note once again that the liturgy does not hesitate to modify the strictly exegetical sense of a text by introducing and emphasizing a spiritual sense. On this Sunday the spiritual emphasis is on the idea that God alone is the true Judge and that he alone justifies people, that is, makes them just, if they present themselves before him with a selfless faith.

Anyone with even an elementary understanding of the Scriptures will know that the situations of the widow and orphan in Sirach are real, concrete situations, whereas the humility of the tax collector is a spiritual and moral attitude. In themselves, therefore, the two texts deal with two different types of situations. Nonetheless, the liturgy, while aware that the two situations cannot be really paralleled, uses the passage from Sirach to reinforce the central idea of the gospel pericope and the lessons we are intended to draw from it.

"Pharisaism" is not dead and doubtless never will be until the second coming of Christ. Moreover, we must be humble enough to recognize that none of us are wholly free of its taint. It is difficult, even in prayer, not to feel secure; the reception of the sacraments may even serve to confirm us unconsciously in a way of life that is not in conformity with God's will. People are not always fully conscious that they pay lip service to an ideal but live rather differently.

One lesson we must take with us is that our prayer is ineffective at times because it is not integrated into our lives or because we lack, for example, a real sympathy for others or because other factors are at work that it would behoove us to search out. We are weak human beings, and God knows it, but while recognizing the fact, we must also try to change our ways.

Receive the Reward of a Winner (2 Tim 4:6-8, 16-18)

St. Paul has come to the end of his earthly life. He is a prisoner, condemned to death, and he may be called to execution at any moment. He therefore looks back over his life and sums it up for us, for he is ready to leave it. He has fought the good fight; he has been faithful. Now he looks forward to his reward from him whose coming he has always longed for.

During the trials and interrogations he underwent, Paul was always supported by the Lord, even though all others had abandoned him. How can this same Lord fail to strengthen him when he departs for the kingdom? He has a pledge of this: his own fidelity and the Lord's. If the Lord was with him in all he has suffered, the Lord will certainly be with him as he enters the kingdom.

Paul's confidence is encouraging to all who want to be faithful and to live their faith as members of the Church. Their fidelity is a pledge that Christ will be at their side to help them into his kingdom.

Thirty-First Sunday: The Compassion of a Loving God

The Son of Man Has Come to Seek out and Save What Was Lost
(Luke 19:1-10)

Today's story from the gospel is one of the most moving in the entire New Testament. It has many facets and conveys many lessons, but its proclamation in the context of the first reading turns our attention in a specific direction. The central point today is not the coming of Jesus into the house of Zacchaeus, as it is when this passage is read at the dedication of a church. Our attention should be focused rather on the salvation Jesus brings, and especially on the divine search for the sinner and God's unwearied patience as he waits to transform the sinner as soon as the latter shows a willingness to be converted.

Zacchaeus is short and finds it difficult to see Jesus as he passes by. Zacchaeus's conscious motive is probably simple curiosity, yet hidden within that is a secret desire to meet Jesus and enter a new kind of life. He feels, and is, cut off from his fellow citizens, since he works for the Romans and has grown rich in the process. He seems to feel a certain disgust with himself, and this surely plays a part in his desire to see this Jesus of whom he has heard so much.

Zacchaeus's motives, such as they are, are enough for Jesus, and the latter now takes control of the situation. God has patiently waited for Zacchaeus; Zacchaeus has taken a first step; the Lord now reaches out to him—to the scandal of the bystanders: "He has gone to stay at the house of a sinner"!

Zacchaeus's conversion is somewhat spectacular. He gives half of his goods to the poor, and if he has defrauded anyone, he makes fourfold restitution. Jesus makes the situation clear: despite what Zacchaeus has done in the past, he too is a descendant of Abraham. Jesus has brought him to salvation because "the Son of Man has come to seek and to save what was lost" (an idea that is a favorite of St. Luke; see 15:6, 9, 24, 32).

There is no point in dwelling here on other facets of this story, since the liturgical context points us in a very particular and limited direction.

The Lengthy Patience of God, Who Urges People to Conversion
(Wis 11:22–12:2)

The Lord can do all things. Therefore he takes pity on people and overlooks their sins so that they may repent and be converted.

God has created everything that exists. How, then, could he possibly hate the sinner? Nothing could perdure in being, after all, if God did not will it to exist; he is Creator and Master of life and loves all living things.

The passage contains a fine theology of God's "anxiety" for the creature, his creature, who has rejected him. This anxiety is the source of all God's efforts through history to create anew what sin has destroyed.

Above all, the text emphasizes the lengthy and unwearying patience of God, who does not abandon fallen sinners but little by little corrects them and brings them back. The Lord does not act in a brutal manner; he respects his creatures, even when they are faithless. This divine respect for the creature is something that modern people find very attractive. God respects even the person who has been unfaithful to him; he does not punish brutally. In fact, God's first reaction is not to punish at all but to convert. He warns people and reminds them of their sinful state. He wants them to turn away from evil and believe in him. Does not a conversion originate in a great faith in a God who has created all things and who can and will do everything to bring them back to him?

In today's readings the Church is telling her children of God's marvelous pedagogy and the ideal she herself seeks to follow. We may think that in the passage from his gospel, St. Luke, mindful of the fact that his Christians are not yet free from all sin, wishes to teach them that sin should be seen in the perspective of God's mercy rather than exclusively of his justice. The New Testament sees sin as an offense against Christ, but its primary reaction, when the thought of sin occurs, is to think immediately of Jesus' mercy and forgiveness.

The responsorial psalm (Ps 145) reminds us that "The LORD is kind and full of compassion, / slow to anger, abounding in mercy. . . ./ The LORD supports all who fall, / and raises up all who are bowed down" (vv. 8, 14).

In these passages, the Scriptures are not encouraging either the Church or us individually to be indulgent toward sin. They are simply telling us the attitude we should have: Our first reaction to the sinner and to sin should not be either despair or a determination to punish but a desire for conversion. We are to wait patiently for sinners, take the occasion to reproach them gently, speak to them of God's mercy, teach them faith in the power of God, who through his Holy Spirit can lead all back to the right path.

The formula of absolution in the rite of penance emphasizes this mercy of God: "God, the Father of mercies, through the death and resurrection of his Son has reconciled the world to himself."

The Lord Jesus, Glorified in Us (2 Thess 1:11–2:2)

The hopes and wishes that fill the Apostle's heart will be fulfilled at the coming of Christ. Will the Thessalonians be judged worthy of the call God gave them? Paul prays that they will. They have been called to faith, and this faith must be an active faith; that is, they must do all the good in their power. But none of that can be accomplished without the help of God. It will indeed be accomplished, and Christ will be glorified in them.

This is a theme to which, despite the Second Vatican Council, we are not yet accustomed: that the Church, as a living community, is a sign of the glory of God, a sign of Christ present in the world. It is the responsibility of the Church and of each of her members to see that she is indeed such a sign.

If their fidelity hastens the coming of Christ, the Thessalonians should not on that account grow fearful or listen to false prophecies. St. Paul denies writing any letter to the effect that the Day of the Lord has come. Some people in their religion will always be looking for the extraordinary or the frightening or for new revelations. St. Paul is against this approach to Christianity. The mark of the Christian is not extraordinary deeds of any kind but a life that bears witness to Christ's presence in the world.

Thirty-Second Sunday: The God of Life

All Receive Life from God in the World to Come (Luke 20:27-38)

All peoples in every age have been keenly aware of the problem of life's meaning and of what happens after death. Our contemporaries may not make their own the naïve (and insidious) questions of the Sadducees, but they are nonetheless often quite preoccupied with the next life. Now, as in Jesus' time, these are questions people have at heart. In the apostolic period, after Jesus' departure, the evangelists must have met with similar kinds of questions; St. Paul's letters reflect them at times, and the Acts of the Apostles reminds us that the Sadducees did not accept the idea of a resurrection from the dead, although this had become regular teaching in Judaism (Acts 23:8; Dan 7:13, 27; 12:2).

In today's gospel pericope the Sadducees think they have gotten Jesus into a corner and will be able to make fun of him. They ask what they regard as a tricky question to which he can give no satisfactory answer: If a woman successively married seven brothers, whose wife will she be after the resurrection?

Jesus does not attempt to describe the kind of life lived by those who will rise from the dead. All that can be said is that, while remaining themselves, they will also be different and that sexual life as we know it on earth will have no place in the next life, because our bodies will be transformed.

What Jesus chooses to emphasize is the fact of the resurrection. His answer may strike us as weak, but this is very likely because we do not have the same kind of biblical sensibility that the contemporaries of Jesus or of the evangelists had. In any case, it seems Jesus might have chosen more persuasive proofs from Scripture.

All the Synoptic Gospels report this incident, probably because all three evangelists had been asked questions about the next life and felt obliged to pass on to their communities the replies of Jesus and his teaching on the subject. St. Matthew and St. Mark emphasize that the answer is to be found in the Scriptures: "You are misled because you do not know the scriptures or the power of God" (Matt 22:29; Mark 12:24). If God is not a God who gives life, and if Abraham, Isaac, and Jacob are forever dead, then what can it mean to say we have entered into a covenant with the God of the living?

All three evangelists quote Jesus as saying, "he is not God of the dead but of the living." Luke, however, adds a further explanation: "for to him all are alive." Others translate "to him" as "through him" or "because of him" or "thanks to him." This second set of alternative translations makes better sense of what immediately precedes: God is a God of the living and therefore gives life. Yet this interpretation is far from being evident, and not all scholars accept it.

The overall argument is nonetheless cogent: If the patriarchs lived for God but are now forever dead, then their life was a great mistake and the covenant is meaningless.

Raised up for Eternal Life (2 Macc 7:1-2, 9-14)

Jesus might well have used this text from the book of Maccabees as a proof of the resurrection and a justification of Jewish belief in it. As the fourth of the seven brothers was about to die, he gave clear expression to his belief: "It is my choice to die at the hands of men with the hope God gives of being raised up by him; but for you, there will be no resurrection to life." Several of the other brothers likewise express their belief: "the King of the world will raise us up to live again forever"; "It was from Heaven that I received these [limbs]; for the sake of his laws I disdain them; from him I hope to receive them again."

The responsorial psalm (Ps 17) expresses the same confidence: "As for me, in justice I shall behold your face; / when I awake I shall be filled with the vision of your presence" (v. 15).

The Church knows that the risen Christ is only the first of those to be raised from the dead. She knows, too, that the Holy Spirit transforms men and women into new creatures and adopted sons and daughters, and therefore she is sure of the resurrection. Christ died to give us life—not a passing life but a life that lasts forever. The letters of St. Paul makes it clear that the Church held to these beliefs from the very beginning. God's love for people and the love of the redeemed for him in return make the resurrection sure, even though we cannot now penetrate the mystery and know anything of the life to be lived by those who rise to eternal happiness.

The Lord Is Faithful; He Strengthens Us and Protects Us from Evil (2 Thess 2:16–3:5)

St. Paul is again offering the Thessalonians a message of hope. The life of Christians may be one of struggles and difficulties, but God loves them and gives them consolation and joyous hope as well as strength to do good and proclaim the Gospel.

The Christian must pray that the Gospel may be spread and God's Word heard everywhere. The spread of the Gospel will bring persecution from nonbelievers, but God is faithful; he protects his messengers from evil and gives them courage and strength. We must therefore persevere on our journey.

This passage is short but bracing and can be of great help in our everyday routine and when we are tempted to get bogged down and grow discouraged. The certainty of God's love for us and of the help he gives us will raise us up and keep us from dwelling too long on the big and little afflictions of life.

Thirty-Third Sunday: The Day of the Lord

Persevere through Suffering so as to Obtain Life on the Day of the Lord (Luke 21:5-19)

The thirteenth chapter of St. Mark's gospel reports the same discourse but gives it a somewhat different context. Jesus is emerging from the temple, and one of his disciples calls his attention to the splendid building Herod had constructed. Jesus then predicts that of this building that was to defy time, not a stone will be left upon a stone. A group of four disciples then accompanies Jesus to Mount Olivet, where he speaks to them alone.

In St. Luke's account, Jesus is in the temple, and the whole crowd is listening to him.

In the other two evangelists' accounts, the destruction of the temple has connections with the end of the world. The question of the date and the preliminary signs has to do only with the destruction of the temple. In both Luke and Mark, however, the discourse of Jesus is not limited to the destruction of the temple but also covers the catastrophe at the end of the world and the glorious coming of the Son of Man. St. Luke seems to be clearly dissociating the destruction of the temple, in AD 70, from the events at the end of time and from the glorious coming of the Son of Man; the destruction of the temple is not one of the signs that the end is at hand.

In this discourse Jesus first tells of the events to come; then he gives instructions on how Christians are to react. He tells them they must be wary on two counts. They must not let themselves be led astray: "many will come in my name, saying, 'I am he,' and 'The time has come.' Do not follow them!" Second, they must remember that wars and tumults are not the signs of the end and have no connection with the final events. St. Mark regards such wars and tumults as the beginning of the sufferings that will come (13:8).

Jesus then describes the various catastrophes: struggles of nation against nation, earthquakes, great and terrifying signs in the heavens. The precise description of these events is irrelevant. The important thing is that when they occur, Christians will know that their salvation is at hand.

Prior to these events, Christians will be subjected to persecution. St. Luke is here bent on instructing his community, which must live in the time between their liberation through baptism and the return of Christ. During this period the Gospel must be preached, but it is precisely this that will lead to persecution. The disciples must not be afraid. Jesus himself will give them a wisdom and words that their enemies cannot withstand. Yet the situation will be an extremely difficult one, for even the members of a disciple's own family will betray him, and Christians will be universally hated because of Jesus' name. Even the hairs of their head are numbered, however, and no evil can touch them. Those who persevere will be saved.

Jesus here exhorts his disciples, and all who hear him, to perseverance. In St. Luke's view, persecutions are not a sign that the end is near. They are part of the normal Christian condition, for the Christian is constantly bearing witness amid a perverse world. Each Christian must therefore cultivate patience and perseverance. A firm faith, the acceptance of God's word, fidelity to God's word despite persecution—these make up the Christian attitude.

The Day of the Lord, a Blazing Oven for the Wicked, a Sun of Justice for the Good (Mal 3:19-20a)

This text is situated in a time of great discouragement for Israel. The exiles have been back home for fifty years, and the temple has been rebuilt, yet there is great disillusionment. The returning exiles had not been very well received: their possessions had been taken by others; they were isolated and poor; there was little concern for them. The city was insufficiently fortified and often subject to raids. All this had serious repercussions on the religious life of the people. They were disillusioned, and their faith was weak; fidelity to the covenant was endangered. The disillusionment is summed up in words that Malachi quotes a little before today's pericope: "It is useless to serve God" (3:14).

Malachi now endeavors to revive the people's spirit by telling them that the Day of the Lord is coming. First, the wrath of God will be unleashed against the wicked and the arrogant. They will burn up like straw, and there will be neither root nor branch left of them. Straw, brush, trees—these are comparisons other prophets had already used (for example, Nah 1:10; Amos 2:9; Isa 5:24).

Fire symbolizes the chastising wrath of God. Thus in the book of Deuteronomy, the Lord says that the fire of his anger has been lit (32:22), and in the book of Job we read that on the wicked "God shall send . . . the fury of his [burning] wrath" (20:23). In Jeremiah, fire as a symbol of divine vengeance occurs a number of times: "Or else my anger will break out like fire" (4:4; 21:12); "For fire has broken out from my anger, / it is kindled against you" (15:14; 17:4). Ezekiel makes use of the same image: "I will blast you with the fire of my anger and smelt you with it" (22:21); "with my fiery wrath I have consumed them" (22:31).

The image of the tree is also used by other authors. In the book of Job, "may wickedness be broken like a tree" (24:20). In the book of Jeremiah, God's wrath is poured out on the trees (7:20). In the Gospel of St. Matthew, John the Baptist says that "the ax lies at the root of the trees" (3:10).

The second phase of the Lord's coming will be the appearance of "the sun of justice," the rays of which bring healing. The Israelites, especially during their exile, were familiar with cults of the sun, but that is not a comparison Malachi is using here. In this passage the sun symbolizes the powerful intervention of the Lord in defense of the poor and the oppressed.

Are today's readings meaningless for today's Christians? Will they regard them as poetry from another time? Yet it is the Lord himself who speaks in these passages. Has he nothing to say? Does he not wish to be heard? Does he intend the passages to be simply museum pieces? That is impossible. We must therefore attempt briefly to see how the teaching in these passages certainly applies to us today.

Some Christians are habitually disillusioned and therefore close to abandoning all zeal and discipline. In what way are they disillusioned? Often they expect of their faith and religious practice what it is not meant to give: earthly happiness. Christianity makes no promise of earthly happiness.

Faith and fidelity do not guarantee happiness in this world. On the contrary, faith and fidelity often lead to persecution and misunderstanding, even between members of the same family. Some forms of disillusionment are thus due to an incorrect understanding of Christianity. For these people, the vision of the Day of the Lord can be salutary, reminding them that the Christian religion exists only for the sake of that last day and makes no sense except in its light.

Disillusionment may have other causes. For some, it is the lack of spiritual depth in many areas of the Church. They see laxity, infidelity, weak faith, moral weakness, and, everywhere uncertainty. Even in religious orders hitherto fervently dedicated to the expectation of the Lord's coming, they find a betrayal of purpose. In all this, however, disillusionment is nonetheless an insidious temptation. Its causes may be objectively there, but the clear vision of our destiny in God makes illegitimate any kind of morose disillusionment; on the contrary, it should, as in Malachi, rouse our courage and make us vigilant.

More serious still is the danger in which many live who make no efforts to come to grips with the problems of their own life or the life of the parish to which they belong. Without realizing it, these people live lives of carefree conformity; the world will never persecute them, because their religious lives attract no attention of any kind and have no impact on their environment. To these Catholics, who do not feel in any way at odds with their world, today's readings should be a summons to profitable reflection.

Nothing worthwhile is acquired without suffering. If a parish community and its members experience no suffering in their effort to lead a religious life, they may well be simply tepid. They have lost the sense of their mission in the world; they have become closed in on themselves or are content to work solely for the advancement of human values but have no interest in spiritual values. These communities and individuals are living off their capital and gradually using it up; when the time comes for mobilizing every resource in order to proclaim the primacy of God's kingdom, such people may have nothing left.

These readings, then, urge upon us a valuable confrontation with our final destiny. They urge upon the Church and upon all her members a confrontation with the ultimate meaning of life itself.

Earn Your Own Bread (2 Thess 3:7-12)

This passage suggests that some of the Thessalonians had developed a distorted attitude. A somewhat perverse "contemplation" of the Day of the Lord had led them to abandon all work and to spend their time talking about the parousia, imagining its conditions, and calculating the time of its occurrence.

St. Paul is critical of this state of affairs. He reminds his readers that he has worked for his livelihood, even at a time when his ministry gave him a right to support from others. He takes the occasion to emphasize that a Christian is one who works. Anyone who can work and will not is not to be fed by others. This is not simply a piece of advice—it is an order.

It is always possible, even today, to get an unbalanced view of what a life lived for God means. There have been periods when the practice of the "contemplative life" was thought to be a claim to support from others when it came to material needs. Such an attitude is impossible in our day (other deformations remain possible!), and we should doubtless regard it as a divine favor that in our day everyone must work for a living while trying to achieve a correct balance between prayer and work in life.

Our Lord Jesus Christ, King of the Universe: A Crucified King

Jesus Crucified, Remember Me When You Come as King (Luke 23:35-43)

"Gospel" means "good news," the news of salvation. Today's gospel makes this point for us when it says: "Jesus, remember me when you come into your kingdom," and when Jesus replies: "Amen, I say to you, today you will be with me in Paradise." Here is the proclamation of salvation through the cross and a promise made by a crucified King.

This King is conqueror of death; of this, Jesus' answer leaves no doubt. His words are not a vague promise but the statement of one who is truly in command. The Good Thief drew from Christ an answer that will give hope to all generations until the end of time: the hope that death is the door to Paradise and that "to be with Christ" is indeed the goal to which all Christian life is leading and the reality that lies beyond death.

David, Anointed as Shepherd and King of Israel (2 Sam 5:1-3)

There were numerous symbols and prefigurations of this crucified King. David, for example, is such a prefiguration and type, for he receives royal anointing as shepherd-king.

We must dwell for a moment on the special character of a king in Israel. He was not a king such as the Gentiles had. The people of Israel were God's people and belonged to him alone, so that the king's role could only be to direct and lead the people for the time they were entrusted to him. The king was thus meant to be a manifestation on earth of God's presence and power. If the king wins a victory, it is God who really wins it (2 Sam 5:17-25; 8:1-14; 19:10).

At the same time, his function is a sacred one, for he is the anointed of the Lord. God manifests his presence to his people through the person of the king; through him too God manifests his sovereignty, power, and glory (Pss 72:8; 110:1). The king is thus a sign of God, but since he remains also a weak human being, he often experiences opposition, although this never goes to the extreme of denying any and every royal power. The person of the individual king is open to criticism, but the kingship itself is an indispensable condition of Israel's life and a guarantee that God is always present to his people.

In these circumstances, it is quite to be expected that Israelite literature, and especially the psalms, should paint an idealized picture of the king. He becomes a symbol of hope, and at times the hope is precisely for a truly just king who will lead Israel. It is along these lines that we are to understand Jeremiah when he sees rising out of the family of David a virtuous branch who will reign as true king and save his people (Jer 23:5-6). Ezekiel too has a vision of a future king who will be a true shepherd and gather together the scattered nations (Ezek 34:23; 37:22).

The hour of salvation is gradually drawing near, and when Jesus comes on the scene, a few people will realize that the hour is now at hand. The prophets, especially Isaiah, will depict the coming king as a servant who humbles himself and gives his life in order to establish his kingdom (Isa 53).

In the Kingdom of the Beloved Son (Col 1:12-20)

In this passage St. Paul describes the unfolding of Christian life in relation to the history of salvation. In God's plan, first came the Son, the image of the invisible God and the firstborn of all creation. By the shedding of his blood he reestablished the primacy that had been his at the beginning of creation. Now all things find their total fulfillment in him.

Christians take their place in this plan of reconstruction, and their lives unfold in accordance with that same plan. We shall enter into the kingdom the Son has founded by restoring creation to its rightful state and by reconciling all things in himself and through himself, making peace through the blood of his cross.

This part of Paul's Letter to the Colossians is a hymn to the glory of God. By our baptism we have been incorporated into Christ the King, who is Head of his Church; we have thereby become a holy nation and a royal people.

Today's first reading directed our attention to the awaited messianic king; the gospel shows us how the crucified Jesus by his cross brings the history of salvation to its goal. The second reading is a hymn of praise to all that Christ, King of the universe, has done to establish the kingdom of which we are now a part. We are all thus being urged to live a life under a King, as part of a kingly people, but under a King whose kingdom is not of this world.[10]

Notes

2. The Lord's Day: A Theology of Sunday

1. CL 102. All citations of documents from the Second Vatican Council are taken from *Vatican Council II: The Conciliar and Post Conciliar Documents*, ed. Austin Flannery, vol. 1 (Northport, NY: Costello, 1998).

2. CL 106.

3. Let Us Give Thanks to the Father on the Lord's Day

1. "Anaphora" means "offering" and is the word used in the Eastern Churches for the eucharistic prayer in which Christ and the Church make offering to the Father in prayers of thanksgiving.

2. *Sermo* 27.2 (*SC* 22bis: 152–54).

3. See vol. 2, Holy Thursday: The Exodus meal.

4. St. Ambrose, *De sacramentis* 4.14–21 (*SC* 25bis:108–14).

5. Chap. 4; text in Paul F. Bradshaw, Maxwell E. Johnson, and L. Edward Phillips, *The Apostolic Tradition: A Commentary*, ed. Harold W. Attridge, Hermeneia (Minneapolis: Fortress Press, 2002), 37–41.

6. *De sacramentis* 4.15 (*SC* 25bis:108).

7. Ibid., 4.14–17 (*SC* 25bis:108–10).

8. *De mysteriis* 52 (*SC* 25bis:186).

9. *De sacramentis* 4.14 (*SC* 25bis:108–10); emphasis added.

10. Ibid., v. 21 (*SC* 25bis:114). Trans. Annotator; see *At the Supper of the Lamb: A Pastoral and Theological Commentary on the Mass* (Chicago: Liturgy Training Publications, 2011), p. 69.

11. Text in M. Férotin, ed., *Le Liber ordinum en usage dans l'Eglise Wisogothique et Mozarabe d'Espagne du cinquième au onzième siècle,* Monumenta Ecclesiae Liturgica 5 (Paris, 1904), col. 322; *idem,* ed., *Le Liber mozarabicus sacramentorum et les manuscrits arabes,* Monumenta Ecclesiae Liturgica 6 (Paris, 1912), no. 1440. Trans. Annotator.

12. *Le Sacramentaire Grégorien* I:88-89. Trans. Annotator.

13. *De sacramentis* 4.27 (*SC* 25bis:116). Trans. Annotator.

14. *Liber mozarabicus sacramentorum,* no. 627; *Liber ordinum,* col. 625. Trans. Annotator.

15. Text in Hänggi-Pahl, *op. cit.,* 131.

4. Liturgical Theology of the Presidential Prayers: God's Love for Humanity, Humanity's Love for God

1. See *Notitiae* 7 (1971), 35–42, 74–77, 94–95, 134–36, 276–80, 409–10.

Year A

1. Jean Paul Sartre saw this and brought it out in his book *Existentialism and Humanism,* trans. P. Mairet (London, 1948).

2. St. Ephrem, *Commentarium in Diatessaron* 1.18–19 (*SC* 121:52–53), in *The Liturgy of the Hours according to the Roman Rite*, vol. 3 (New York: Catholic Book Publishing, 1975), 199.

3. Isabelle Rivière, *Sur le devoir d'imprévoyance: Petit traité d'économie pratique* (repr. Paris, 1946).

4. St. Gregory the Great, *Moralia in Job* 1.36 (PL 75:543–44), in *The Liturgy of the Hours*, 261.

Year B

1. See Vatican Council II, Dogmatic Constitution on the Church 4 and 7.

2. See chapters 23, 24, 26, 27, 28, 30, and 44 of the Rule of St. Benedict.

3. See above pp. 8–16.

4. See vol. 2, The Fourth Sunday of Easter, for the theme of the Good Shepherd.

5. See, e.g., J. Daniélou, *The Bible and the Liturgy* (Notre Dame, IN, 1956), 177–90.

6. *Catecheses mystagogicae* 4.7 (*PG* 33:1101, 1104; *SC* 126:140–42).

7. *De sacramentis* 5.12–13 (*SC* 25bis:124–26).

8. *In Christi Ascensionem* (*PG* 46:692).

9. *Explanatio in Psalmum* 22 (*PG* 69:840).

10. St. Cyprian, *Epist.* 63.5 (*CSEL* 3:703).

11. Origen, *In Canticum Conticorum* 3, on Song 2:4 (*PG* 13:154–55).

12. St. Ambrose, *De Cain et Abel* 1.5.19 (*CSEL* 32/1:356).

13. Council of Trent, Sess. 24 (Nov. 11, 1563), in H. Denzinger and A. Schönmetzer, eds., *Enchiridion symbolorum*, 32nd ed. (Freiburg, 1963), no. 1799.

14. See vol. 1, pp. 91–92, "Characteristics of Our Messianic Age."

15. See vol. 2, Good Friday.

16. See vol. 2, Good Friday: A Great Priest over the House of God.

17. Ibid.

18. In the Christian reading of Scripture during the liturgy, there are three reasons for not using the name "Yahweh": (1) the word was never pronounced by the Jews; "Lord" is therefore preferable in English; (2) we read the Old Testament as Christians; on this score, too, "Yahweh" is unsuitable; (3) the avoidance of "Yahweh" is especially to be urged in the psalms. In these, we should at times see Christ and the Church praying to the Father; at times, the Church praying to Christ. Particularly in this second situation is the name "Yahweh" unsuitable. [In 2008, the Congregation for Divine Worship and the Discipline of the Sacraments excluded the use of the name "Yahweh" in liturgical songs and prayers (Prot. N. 213/08/L). —Ann.]

19. Chap. 21; text in Paul F. Bradshaw, Maxwell E. Johnson, and L. Edward Phillips, *The Apostolic Tradition: A Commentary*, ed. Harold W. Attridge, Hermeneia (Minneapolis: Fortress Press, 2002), 112–24.

20. See J.-P. Audet, *La Didachè: Instructions des apôtres* (Paris, 1958).

Year C

1. The text of this commentary is translated in vol. 2.

2. *Epistula ad Joannem Syracusensem*, in Gregory the Great, *Registrum Epistularum* 9.26, ed. Paul Ewald and Ludo Moritz Hartmann, 2 vols., Monumenta Germaniae historica inde ab anno Christi quingentesimo usque ad annum millesimum et quingentesmum (München: Monumenta Germaniae Historica, 1992), 2:59–60.

3. *De sacramentis* 5.19 (*SC* 25bis:128–30). The following quotations from St. Ambrose on the Our Father are from *De sacramentis* 5. 20–30 (SC 25bis:130–36).

4. See vol. 2, Holy Thursday: The Exodus meal.

5. See the commentary on these passages in the various years of the cycle.

6. CL 2.

7. See vol. 2, Year C, Fourth Sunday of Lent, Gospel.

8. See this Sunday, Year A, pp. 141–42.

9. See Sixth Sunday, Year C, pp. 309ff.

10. On this point, see the conclusions drawn from the readings for Our Lord Jesus Christ, King of the Universe, Year A, p. 395.

Bibliography

Nocent chose not to include a bibliography, partly because the Lectionary was so new and comments on various sets of readings were readily available. Since then, the commentaries have grown in number, and this list is supplied for the sake of the reader.

America. "The Word." Weekly. http://americamagazine.org/sections/word.

The Anchor Bible Commentaries. New York: Doubleday.

At Home with the Word: Sunday Scriptures and Reflections. Chicago: Liturgy Training Publications. Annual.

Bergant, Dianne, with Richard Fragomeni. *Preaching the New Lectionary.* Three volumes. Collegeville: Liturgical Press, Year A, 2001; Year B, 1999; Year C, 2000.

Bergant, Dianne, and Robert Karris, general editors. *The Collegeville Bible Commentary.* Collegeville: Liturgical Press, 1992.

Birmingham, Mary. *Word and Worship Workbook: For Ministry in Initiation for Year A, Preaching, Religious Education and Formation.* Mahwah, NJ: Paulist Press, 1999. *Year B,* 2000. *Year C,* 1998.

Bonneau, Normand. *The Sunday Lectionary: Ritual Word, Paschal Shape.* Collegeville, MN: Liturgical Press, 1998.

Bradshaw, Paul F., and Maxwell E. Johnson. *The Eucharistic Liturgies: Their Evolution and Interpretation.* Collegeville, MN: Liturgical Press, Pueblo, 2012.

Bradshaw, Paul, Maxwell E. Johnson, and L. Edward Phillips. *The* Apostolic Tradition: *A Commentary.* Hermeneia. Edited by Harold W. Attridge. Minneapolis: Augsburg Fortress, 2002.

Catechumenate: A Journal of Christian Initiation. "Sunday Word." Chicago: Liturgy Training Publications, 6 issues annually.

Celebrating the Lectionary. Chicago: Liturgy Training Publications. Annual.

Celebration: An Ecumenical Worship Resource. Monthly resource from *National Catholic Reporter* in Kansas City, MO.

The Center for Liturgy at Saint Louis University. www.liturgy.slu.edu.

The Collegeville Pastoral Dictionary of Biblical Theology. Edited by Carroll Stuhlmueller. Collegeville, MN: Liturgical Press, 1996.

Connections: The Newsletter of Ideas, Resources and Information for Homilists and Preachers. Monthly. Londonderry, NH: Connections/Media Works.

Connell, Martin. *Guide to the Revised Lectionary*. Basics of Ministry Series. Chicago: Liturgy Training Publications, 1998.

Days of the Lord: The Liturgical Year. Seven volumes. Collegeville, MN: Liturgical Press, 1991–94.

Donahue, John R. *Hearing the Word of God: Reflections on the Sunday Readings*. Three volumes. Collegeville, MN: Liturgical Press, Year A, 2004; Year B, 2002; Year C, 2003.

Dunning, James B. *Echoing God's Word: Formation for Catechists and Homilists in a Catechumenal Church*. Arlington, VA: The North American Forum on the Catechumenate, 1993.

Faley, Roland. *Footprints on the Mountain: Preaching and Teaching the Sunday Readings*. Mahwah, NJ: Paulist Press, 1994.

Foundations in Faith Catechist Manual Catechumenate. Kathy Brown, Bob Duggan, Carol Gura, Rita Ferrone, Gael Gensler, Maureen Kelly, Steve Lanza, Donna Steffen. Three volumes. Allen: Resources for Christian Living, Year A, 1998; Year B, 1999; Year C, 1997.

Fuller, Reginald H., and Daniel Westberg. *Preaching the Lectionary: The Word of God for the Church Today*. 3rd edition. Collegeville, MN: Liturgical Press, 2006.

Galipeau, Jerry. *Apprenticed to Christ: Activities for Practicing the Catholic Way of Life*. Franklin Park, IL: World Library Publications, 2007.

————. *We Send You Forth: Dismissals for the RCIA*. Franklin Park, IL: World Library Publications, 2005.

Handbook for Proclaimers of the Word. New York: Catholic Book Publishing Co. Annual.

Harper's Bible Dictionary. Edited by Paul J. Achtemeier. New York: HarperCollins, 1985.

Henderson, Frank J. *Remembering the Women*. Chicago: Liturgy Training Publications, 1990.

Homily Helps for Sundays. Cincinnati: St. Anthony Messenger Press. Monthly.

Johnson, Maxwell E., ed. *Issues in Eucharistic Praying in East and West: Essays in Liturgical and Theological Analysis*. Collegeville, MN: Liturgical Press, Pueblo, 2010.

Johnson, Maxwell E. *Worship: Rites, Feasts, and Reflections*. Portland, OR: Pastoral Press, 2004.

Just, Felix. *The Lectionary: A Treasure for Liturgy and Prayer*. Audio-CD program. Now You Know Media, 2010.

Kavanaugh, John. *The Word Embodied* (Year A). *The Word Encountered* (Year B). *The Word Engaged* (Year C). Maryknoll, NY: Orbis Books.

Keifer, Ralph A. *To Hear and Proclaim: Introduction to the Lectionary for Mass with Commentary for Musicians and Priests*. Washington, DC: National Association of Pastoral Musicians, 1983.

Leon-Dufour, Xavier. *Dictionary of Biblical Theology.* New York: Seabury Press, 1973. Paperback, 1995.

Living the Word: Scripture Reflections and Commentaries for Sundays and Holy Days. Franklin Park, IL: World Library Publications. Annual.

National Conference of Catholic Bishops, Committee on Priestly Life and Ministry. *Fulfilled in Your Hearing: The Homily in the Sunday Assembly.* Washington, DC: United States Catholic Conference, 1992.

Pilch, John J. *The Cultural World of the Apostles: The Second Reading, Sunday by Sunday.* Three volumes. Collegeville, MN: Liturgical Press, Year A, 2001; Year B, 2002; Year C, 2003.

————. *The Cultural World of Jesus: Sunday by Sunday.* Three volumes. Collegeville, MN: Liturgical Press, Year A, 1995; Year B, 1996; Year C, 1997.

————. *The Cultural World of the Prophets: The First Reading and the Responsorial Psalm, Sunday by Sunday.* Three volumes. Collegeville, MN: Liturgical Press, Year A, 2004; Year B, 2003; Year C, 2003.

————. *The Triduum and Easter Sunday: Breaking Open the Scriptures.* Collegeville, MN: Liturgical Press, 2000.

Ralph, Margaret Nutting. *Breaking Open the Lectionary: Lectionary Readings in their Biblical Context for RCIA, Faith Sharing Groups, and Lectors.* New York: Paulist Press, Cycle B, 2005; Cycle C, 2006; Cycle A, 2007.

Siciliano, Jude. *Preacher Exchange.* Sisters of St. Dominic of Amityville, NY. www.preacherexchange.org.

Sacra Pagina. Daniel J. Harrington, series ed. Collegeville, MN: Liturgical Press.

Sánchez, Patricia Datchuck. *The Word We Celebrate: Commentary on the Sunday Lectionary, Years A, B, and C.* Kansas City: Sheed & Ward, 1989.

Sloyan, Gerard S. *A Commentary on the New Lectionary.* New York: Paulist Press, 1975.

Sunday by Sunday: Lectionary-Based Reflection for Adults. Edited by Joan Mitchell. St. Paul: Sunday by Sunday, seven units yearly.

Talley, Thomas J. *The Origins of the Liturgical Year.* New York: Pueblo Publishing Company, 1986.

Turner, Paul, et al. *Foundations for Preaching and Teaching: Scripture Backgrounds.* Chicago: Liturgy Training Publications. Annual.

United States Conference of Catholic Bishops. *Preaching the Mystery of Faith: The Sunday Homily.* Washington, DC: United States Conference of Catholic Bishops, 2012.

The Word among Us. Ijamsville, MD: The Word Among Us, twelve issues annually.

Workbook for Lectors and Gospel Readers. And/or: *Manual para Proclamadores de la Palabra.* Chicago: Liturgy Training Publications. Annuals.